Commonly Used Hand Signals

Okay

Stay there

Come here

Going down

Going up

Go that way

Which way?

Watch me

Level off

Ears won't clear

Cold

Something's wrong

Get with your buddy

Hold hands

Danger

Low on air

Scuba Diving & Snorkeling For Dummies®

Dive Buddy Check

Good dive buddies, like good waffles, stick together. Do the following procedure and equipment checks together.

Procedure check

Before you enter the water, make sure that you and your buddy have discussed a few of the following ground rules:

- Establish entry and exit points and techniques.
- Choose a course to follow.
- Agree on a maximum time and depth limit.
- Establish and review communication procedures.
- Establish an agreed-upon air pressure for returning to the surface.
- Discuss the technique that you'll use to stay together.
- Agree on what to do if you're separated.
- Discuss what to do if an emergency arises.

Equipment check

After you're suited up for the dive, check your buddy's equipment and have your buddy check you, too. (See Chapter 2 for the lowdown on equipment.)

1. **Check the BC.** The BC must be snugly adjusted, with all releases firmly secured. Also check to see that the BC — including the low-pressure inflator and the oral inflator — operates properly.

2. **Check the weight belt.** The weight belt should have a right-hand release, and be free and clear of other equipment and straps for easy, fast, one-hand removal.

3. **Check all releases.** You should be familiar with the operation and location of all of the releases on your buddy's equipment.

4. **Check the air supply.** Check that the air is turned on, the tank pressure is somewhere near 3,000 psi (pounds per square inch), and the regulator is functioning. Make sure the hoses aren't tangled or trapped by straps. Know where the alternate air source is and how it's used.

5. **Give the final okay.** After completing Steps 1 through 4, give an overall inspection, looking for dangling straps and missing equipment.

Praise for Scuba Diving & Snorkeling For Dummies

"Since my father threw me overboard at the age of seven, I've been exposed to the magnificence of the underwater world. *Scuba Diving & Snorkeling For Dummies* provides a comprehensive guide to the basics of diving skills and proper techniques — and it's not only useful, but entertaining, as well. Like the many books in the *...For Dummies* series, it inspires and instructs. I give it a top recommendation for anyone who's intrigued by our oceans' environments."

— Jean-Michel Cousteau

"*Scuba Diving & Snorkeling For Dummies* continues the tradition of these informative yet not 'impressed-with-themselves' guides to various sports and activities. John Newman knows when it's time to tell it straight and when it's time to let the humor shine through — something he's quite adept at. I recommend this book to anyone interested in taking up diving — and I recommend you read it *before* starting the scuba diving certification process. You'll be surprised how much easier the process will be. And if you're already a diver and still can't figure out the difference between Boyle's, Henry's, and Dalton's gas laws, I suggest you read Newman's version. This is a well-done treatise on the art and sport of scuba diving (and snorkeling) that doesn't bore, condescend, or mystify. No secret handshakes or eyebrow-raised buzzwords to dazzle you; just solid info with some fun thrown in."

— Gary P. Joyce, Editor, *Sport Diver* Magazine

"My everyday life is about taking experienced divers to exotic reefs where we film hungry sharks, giant whales, and tiny seahorses. But when I'm ashore and people demand to know why on earth we do the stuff we do, I'm at a loss for words. The thrill of diving is both too simple and too complex to explain easily. John Newman's *Scuba Diving & Snorkeling For Dummies* lays out the magic and the mechanics of diving in terms that even my mom will understand! From now on, when someone asks, 'Aren't you afraid of sharks?' or 'Don't you get claustrophobic down there?', I'll just hand them one of John's books."

— Rob Barrel, Owner/Operator, S/S NAI'A Fiji Islands

SCUBA DIVING & SNORKELING FOR DUMMIES®

**Text and illustrations
by John Newman**

WILEY

Wiley Publishing, Inc.

Scuba Diving & Snorkeling For Dummies®

Published by
Wiley Publishing, Inc.
909 Third Avenue
New York, NY 10022
www.wiley.com

Copyright © 1999 by Wiley Publishing, Inc., Indianapolis, Indiana

Published by Wiley Publishing, Inc., Indianapolis, Indiana

Published simultaneously in Canada

For general information on our other products and services or to obtain technical support, please contact our Customer Care Department within the U.S. at 800-762-2974, outside the U.S. at 317-572-3993, or fax 317-572-4002.

Wiley also publishes its books in a variety of electronic formats. Some content that appears in print may not be available in electronic books.

Library of Congress Cataloging-in-Publication Data:

Library of Congress Control Number: 99-63112
ISBN: 0-7645-5151-5

Manufactured in the United States of America
10 9 8 7
1B/RS/QT/QT/IN

About the Author

John Newman was born in Indiana, but before he was five years old his family moved to coastal California and he discovered the ocean. By high school, he was boating, surfing, and drawing cartoons when he should have been studying, but somehow he managed to slip past the admissions officers at the University of California at Santa Cruz, where he attended classes and continued his relationship with the Pacific. He paid his way through school by working as a freelance commercial illustrator.

John lived briefly in Hawaii where he did T-shirt designs and continued to play in the water, but returned to California to continue his education. By the time he entered graduate school at San Jose State University, he had become an accomplished kayaker, waveskier, and diver, and had also developed a love of literature and writing. By the time he completed graduate school, he'd won five separate Phelan Awards for his works of short fiction. After he left the university, he went to work as the Editor and Art Director for the newly launched *Paddlesports* magazine, but the publication folded within a few years. John moved on to *Oceansports* magazine, and stayed on when the publication was reorganized as *Dive Travel* magazine, assuming the role of Editor and Art Director of that publication. He stayed at *Dive Travel* for 12 years, until that publication was purchased by World Publications, and combined with *Sport Diver* magazine. Today, he serves as West Coast Field Editor for *Sport Diver,* and pursues a freelance career.

Dedication

To my mother, who showed me the meaning of endurance.

Author's Acknowledgments

Writing this book was a lot of work, but it was also a lot of fun and the main reason it was fun was Tere Drenth, the project editor, who, as near as I can tell, must be the best one in the world. I believe she could make cleaning out the grease trap in a burger joint seem like fun, and make it seem interesting, too.

I also want to thank Stacy Collins, who gave me the opportunity to write this thing in the first place, worked hard to put this whole package together, and put up with all my embarrassing foolishness and half-baked scheming in New Orleans.

Thanks for Susan Wilmink, former publisher of the great (although now defunct) dive magazine, *Dive Travel,* who helped me cook up this entire book idea.

Gratitude to my friends Amos Nachoum, Stuart Westmorland, and Michelle Westmorland, who provided many of the photos for this book. Big thanks for Matt and Lucy Harris, who not only provided many more of the photos, but bought the Hurricanes.

Special thanks to Karen for putting up with me and providing the kind of nourishment it takes to make it through every day on planet earth, and to my dive and surf buddy Joe Hartley, for his friendship, thorough technical review, and words of encouragement. I miss you out here, dude.

Thanks to the folks at PADI for their help and for the scuba-training photos, to the staff at Dacor, and to everybody else who helped make this thing happen and whose name I can't remember right now. I apologize for leaving you out. Please keep in mind that it's not because you weren't essential to this book, but because I'm becoming forgetful.

Publisher's Acknowledgments

We're proud of this book; please send us your comments through our online registration form located at www.dummies.com/register.

Some of the people who helped bring this book to market include the following:

Acquisitions and Editorial

Project Editor: Tere Drenth

Acquisitions Editor: Stacy S. Collins

General Reviewer: Joe Hartley

Media Development Editor: Marita Ellixson

Associate Permissions Editor:
Carmen Krikorian

Media Development Manager:
Heather Heath Dismore

Editorial Directors: Mary C. Corder;
Kristin A. Cocks

Editorial Coordinator: Maureen F. Kelly

Production

Project Coordinator: Cindy L. Phipps

Layout and Graphics: Thomas R. Emrick,
Angela F. Hunckler, Barry Offringa,
Anna Rohrer, Brent Savage,
Jacque Schneider, Janet Seib,
Brian Torwelle, Dan Whetstine

Proofreaders: Laura L. Bowman,
Melissa D. Buddendeck, Nancy Price,
Marianne Santy, Rebecca Senninger,
Janet M. Withers

Indexer: Ty Koontz

Special Help
Ingrid Llewellyn, Leslie Schuette,
Suzanne Thomas, Michelle Vukas

Publishing and Editorial for Consumer Dummies

Diane Graves Steele, Vice President and Publisher, Consumer Dummies

Joyce Pepple, Acquisitions Director, Consumer Dummies

Kristin A. Cocks, Product Development Director, Consumer Dummies

Michael Spring, Vice President and Publisher, Travel

Brice Gosnell, Publishing Director, Travel

Suzanne Jannetta, Editorial Director, Travel

Publishing for Technology Dummies

Richard Swadley, Vice President and Executive Group Publisher

Andy Cummings, Vice President and Publisher

Composition Services

Gerry Fahey, Vice President of Production Services

Debbie Stailey, Director of Composition Services

Contents at a Glance

Foreword ....*xxi*

Introduction *1*

Part I: Water, Water, Everywhere! **7**
Chapter 1: The Lure of the Sea 9
Chapter 2: Gearing Up 29
Chapter 3: Breathing Lessons 59

Part II: Making a Splash **73**
Chapter 4: Not Wet Yet..75
Chapter 5: Getting Down 89
Chapter 6: Physics and Physiology 107
Chapter 7: Feelin' All Right 121

Part III: Under the Sea **143**
Chapter 8: Ocean Reveries 145
Chapter 9: What's Down There? 167

Part IV: The Wet Set..**209**
Chapter 10: The Dive Traveler 211
Chapter 11: Where in the Watery World? 229
Chapter 12: Keeping Up 249

Part V: The Part of Tens....................................**257**
Chapter 13: Ten Great Snorkeling Adventures 259
Chapter 14: Ten Rules of Safe Diving 277
Chapter 15: Ten Great Dive Destinations 281
Chapter 16: Ten Ways You Can Help to Save the Reefs 301
Appendix 305

Index...**313**

License Agreements..**327**

Installation Instructions **331**

Cartoons at a Glance

By Rich Tennant

page 209

page 257

page 73

page 7

page 143

Fax: 978-546-7747
E-mail: richtennant@the5thwave.com
World Wide Web: www.the5thwave.com

Table of Contents

Foreword...xxi

Introduction 1
    About This Book...1
    Conventions Used in This Book 2
    What You're Not to Read 2
    Foolish Assumptions 3
    How This Book Is Organized...3
        Part I: Water, Water, Everywhere! 3
        Part II: Making a Splash..3
        Part III: Under the Sea 4
        Part IV: The Wet Set...4
        Part V: The Part of Tens...4
        Appendix 5
        Color photo section 5
    Icons Used in This Book...5
    Where to Go from Here...6

Part I: Water, Water, Everywhere! 7

Chapter 1: The Lure of the Sea 9
    Snorkeling, Free Diving, and Scuba Diving...........................10
    Thanks, but No Tanks 10
        The mask 11
        The snorkel 12
        The fins 12
        Setting up..13
        Location, location, location 15
        In your face...16
        Clearing your mask 17
        Clearing your snorkel...19
        Getting your kicks 20
        The real deal 20
    Free Diving 21
        The slant dive 21
        The pike dive..22
        Equalizing your ears 24
        Too cool 25
        Weighty matters...25
        In-vest-ments..25
    Advanced Free Diving...26
    Beyond Free Diving — Scuba...26

Chapter 2: Gearing Up 29
The Basics 29
Diving mask 30
Snorkel 32
Fins 34
Other Stuff That You Need 36
Exposure suit 36
Additional protection 40
Tank 42
Regulator 45
Alternate air source 47
Buoyancy control device 48
Weights 50
Gauges 50
Computer 51
Dive watch 53
Optional Gear 53
What You Don't Need 57
General Maintenance and Repairs 57

Chapter 3: Breathing Lessons 59
Are You Ready? 59
Certifiable 60
School days 61
Upward and onward 62
Basic Safety 63
Under pressure 63
The right stuff 64
Your buddy 65
The best laid plans 66
Know your limits 66
Hands off 66
Ascend slowly 66
Emergency Procedures 67
Equipment failure 67
Octopus to the rescue 67
Emergency ascent 68
Buddy, can you spare some air? 68
Make Mine Nitro 69
Cocktails at 100 feet 69
(Don't) get bent 70
Dive tables 71
Computers 72

Part II: Making a Splash..................................**73**

Chapter 4: Not Wet Yet **75**

Pre-Dive 75
Boat diving 77
Shore diving 79
Setting up your gear 81
Suiting up 85
Dealing with dive anxiety 88

Chapter 5: Getting Down **89**

Making Your Entry 89
Boat dive entries 90
Shore dive entries...91
Down There..92
Going down 92
Form and buoyancy control...........................93
Sign language 94
Air consumption...94
Underwater navigation 96
Your dive profile 98
Coming up 100
Post-Dive 101
Getting out..102
Maintaining your gear 103

Chapter 6: Physics and Physiology **107**

The Wonder of Water...107
Why it matters 107
Meet your density 108
Hot stuff 108
What you see ain't always what you get 110
Sound advice...111
It's a Gas 113
What is air?..113
All I need is the air that I breathe................114
Laying down the law 115

Chapter 7: Feelin' All Right **121**

Seasickness 121
Problems from Heat and Sun.................................123
Sunburn 123
Dehydration 123
Heat exhaustion and heat stroke................124

Sinus and Ear Problems...125
    Complications from colds, allergies, and sinusitis......................125
    Ear infections 125
    Exostosis 126
Respiratory Problems 127
    Complications from smoking 127
    Complications from asthma 128
Barotrauma 129
    Pulmonary barotrauma 129
    Ear squeeze 130
    Sinus squeeze...131
    Abdominal squeeze 133
    Mask squeeze 133
Nitrogen Absorption and Elimination..133
    Decompression sickness 133
    Recompression 136
    Narcosis 136
Hypothermia 138
Drowning 139
Emergencies..140
    The ABCs 140
    CPR (cardiopulmonary resuscitation)....................................141

Part III: Under the Sea *143*

Chapter 8: Ocean Reveries **145**
The World Ocean..145
    The Pacific...146
    The Atlantic...148
    The Caribbean 150
    The Mediterranean..151
    The Indian Ocean 152
    The Red Sea...153
Wind on the Water 154
    A current affair..155
    Waves 156
    Surf 158
    Rip currents...159
Tides 160
    Tidal waves 161
    Tidal currents...161
Recipe for Blue Water 163
    Hydrologic cycle..163
    Visibility 164
    Temperature...165
    Thermoclines 165

Chapter 9: What's Down There? 167

The Coral Reef 167
    The reef community 171
    Divers and the reef 174
The Reef Ecosystem 176
    Aquatic plants 176
    Invertebrates 177
    Fish 183
    Reptiles 185
    Mammals 190
Dangerous Marine Creatures 194
    Things that sting 195
    Things that are poisonous 197
    Things that bite 201
Special Underwater Environments 206
    Kelp forest 206
    Wrecks 206
    Artificial reefs 207
    Cenotes 207
    Freshwater 208

Part IV: The Wet Set *209*

Chapter 10: The Dive Traveler 211

Running Hot and Cold 211
    Hot stuff 212
    Cool stuff 213
By Land or by Sea 215
    Liveaboards 215
    Resort-based 217
Choosing a Liveaboard 219
    Size matters 219
    Numbers matter 219
    Ownership matters 220
    Liveaboard checklist 220
Choosing a Dive Resort 221
    The accommodations 222
    The diving 222
    Dive resort checklist 223
What Kind of Diving? 223
    Reef dives 224
    Drift dives 224
    Wall dives 225
    Night dives 225
    Kelp dives 226
    Wreck dives 226
    Shark dives 227

Chapter 11: Where in the Watery World? 229

Another Topside Attraction...229
Around the World in 68 Paragraphs 230
  The Red Sea...230
  East Africa..231
  The Seychelles 231
  The Maldives 232
  Thailand...232
  Malaysia...233
  Indonesia 234
  The Philippines 234
  Australia 235
  Papua New Guinea..236
  Micronesia 236
  Fiji...237
  Polynesia 238
  Hawaii..239
  The Galapagos Islands 239
  Central America..240
  The Caribbean Islands 241
Cautions 242
  You can't get there from here 242
  Immunizations 242
Pack It Up 243
  Dress for success...244
  Other stuff 244
Staying Healthy..245
  Eat right 245
  Drink right 246
  Take cover 247
  Don't get bugged 247
Disabled Divers 247
Traveling with Nondivers..248

Chapter 12: Keeping Up 249

Without Luggage 249
  Gettin' up there..250
  Refreshments 250
  Shape up 250
Ever Onward 251
  Photography and video 251
  Enriched air...252
  Professional and technical diving 253
Eco-Diving 255

Part V: The Part of Tens *257*

Chapter 13: Ten Great Snorkeling Adventures *259*
Spotted Dolphins — Little Bahama Banks 259
Manatees — Crystal River, Florida.................................261
Stingray City — Grand Cayman 263
Molokini — Maui, Hawaii 264
Humpback Whales — SilverBank and Tonga...........................266
Bunaken Island — Indonesia 267
Sperm Whales — the Azores 269
Jellyfish Lake — Palau 270
Whale Sharks — Western Australia 272
Lizard Island — Queensland, Australia 274

Chapter 14: Ten Rules of Safe Diving *277*
Get Proper Training 277
Use Proper Equipment 278
Never Hold Your Breath While Scuba Diving.........................278
Don't Dive Alone...278
Plan Your Dive 279
Don't Be Afraid to Cancel a Dive 279
Don't Be Afraid to Abort a Dive 279
Do the Deepest Part of Your Dive First...........................280
Don't Touch Anything...280
Ascend Slowly..280

Chapter 15: Ten Great Dive Destinations *281*
Blue Corner — Palau..281
Chuuk Lagoon — Chuuk...283
Palancar Reef — Cozumel 285
Galapagos Islands — Ecuador 287
Bunaken Island — Indonesia 288
Great Barrier Reef — Queensland, Australia 290
Papua New Guinea 292
Great White Wall — Fiji...295
The Maldives 296
The Red Sea — Southern Sinai 298

Chapter 16: Ten Ways You Can Help to Save the Reefs *301*
Ask Questions..301
Secure Your Equipment 302
Never Stand on the Reef..302
Control Your Buoyancy 302
Don't Kick Up Sand 303

Don't Touch Marine Creatures 303
Don't Feed Marine Creatures 303
Leave the Area Cleaner Than You Found It 303
Purchase Only Certified Tropical Fish..304
Get Involved..304

Appendix **305**
Diver's Checklist..305
Additional Tour Operators...306
Environmental Organizations 307
Certification Agencies and Organizations..309
Magazines and Book Publishers...311

Index..*313*

License Agreements..................................*327*

Installation Instructions............................*331*

Foreword

· ·

*A*ll right, I know what you're thinking: What does an actor from *Baywatch* possibly know about scuba diving? All that Hollywood underwater stuff is done with stunt doubles and smoke and mirrors in a special-effects tank, right? How can being filmed underwater with a bunch of full-figured, beautiful women give a guy the expertise to write a foreword to a scuba diving and snorkeling book? I admit that I'm not the world-renowned marine biologist, Dr. Sylvia Earl, that my diving experiences aren't quite as noble as hers, and that the diving we do on *Baywatch* may not be considered difficult work by most people's standards, but you may be surprised how many times we're out in the middle of the ocean in deep water with less-than-perfect conditions.

I am writing this foreword because diving has allowed me to stay in touch with something that I have truly loved since I was a 10-year-old boy. I grew up spending my summers in Catalina Island, free diving in water with 100-foot visibility. Now, 30 years later, as a father, I get to relive that wide-eyed amazement through my children's eyes, as we swim down through a kelp forest and see a bright-orange garibaldi for the first time. There is a wonderful world beneath the surface — an area of mostly unspoiled beauty and a place that's quiet and private (which can be tough to find these days in most of our recreational endeavors).

The book you're about to read was designed for diving Dummies, but you can find many bits of information that even an experienced diver can benefit from. Whatever your level of ability, take advantage of the vast experience of the author, John Newman. If you're a novice, this books gives you the information to make your first time in the water safe and enjoyable. If you're an old salt, remember that you don't have to tell anyone where you picked up your depth of knowledge and wisdom!

Dive safely and have fun!

Michael Newman

Baywatch's Real Lifeguard

Introduction

● ●

*H*uman beings have long entertained the fantasy of visiting other worlds, and with a great deal of effort and expense, society has placed a few people on the moon and brought them back — along with a few gray rocks. A remarkable accomplishment, perhaps, but anyone who has donned snorkeling or diving gear knows that you can find a better way.

With minimal equipment and training, you can glide over an alien world of stunning beauty and complexity that's as fascinating as anything you're likely to find beyond the tug of earth's gravity — and you won't need a 12-story booster rocket to get there. What you do need is the right equipment, the right training, and probably a plane ticket to some exotic port city (unless you're fortunate enough to live near one already). These items are your passport to one of the most diverse and spectacular environments known — the oceans of planet earth.

It may be a while before human beings are gliding over the canals of Mars or meditating on the beauty and wisdom of the inhabitants of Alpha Centauri 3, but in the shallow, sunlit waters of the tropical oceans, you can find a whole universe of lurking, mottled, shimmering, secret life. And after you master the skills of snorkeling and scuba diving and are a regular visitor to the underwater world, you come back with a lot more than gray rocks.

About This Book

Perhaps you've seen the *National Geographic* specials that feature the undersea world of Jacques Cousteau. Or, you may have watched Philippe and Falco gliding around down there with the sharks, eels, and giant mantas and thought to yourself, "Hey, that looks pretty cool. I'd like to try that someday." Or maybe you went on vacation on a cruise ship in the Caribbean, and all of the other passengers who went on dives came back grinning and jabbering about all the great stuff they saw.

You'd like to try it, but you have a few questions first. So, you bought this book. Smart.

This book familiarizes you with the equipment, from mask and fins to regulator and buoyancy compensator to dive computers and gear bags. If you don't have any idea what I'm talking about, don't worry, you find out in Chapter 2. This book also gives you a basic understanding of diving physics, an idea of what you can expect to see underwater, and information on how to get certified.

For a trained diver, scuba diving is a safe recreational activity. Statistically, the accident rate is well below that of skiing or mountain biking, but because it takes place underwater, the consequences can be more severe. A safe diver requires good training and sound, sober judgment. Don't assume that, having read this book, you're ready to borrow your cousin's equipment and give it a try at the local lake or seashore. This book isn't a training manual, and you're not ready to dive until you've been taught to do so by a certified instructor (see Chapter 3).

Conventions Used in This Book

Diving takes place all over the world. In fact, in my opinion, the best diving is in tropical countries in the Pacific and the Caribbean. Most of these countries use the meters and Celsius (from the metric system), but I have chosen to use feet and Fahrenheit throughout the book. There are several reasons for this. First, if you're American, you'll most likely get certified in the United States. When you do, you will be dealing with feet and degrees Fahrenheit. Second, most tropical dive operations book so many Americans they usually express everything in both. Lastly, it's the system that I'm most comfortable with!

Information about underwater creatures mentioned along the way can generally be found in Chapter 9 and the physics of water in Chapter 6. The index can also help you locate specific topics.

A list of certifying agencies, environmental organizations, and so on — many of which I mention throughout the book — can be found in the Appendix.

What You're Not to Read

You don't need to be completely versed in the physics of water and gases to know how to dive. It's interesting stuff (to me anyway), but if it bores you, you can skip it and still be a safe and competent diver. Lots of experienced divers start scratching their necks and rolling their eyes when this kind of technical discussion starts. Chapter 6 has a lot of this stuff, so feel free to avoid that chapter — in fact, you can skip any of the Technical Stuff icons (covered in the "Icons Used in This Book" section, later in this Introduction) throughout this book.

Foolish Assumptions

I assume that you're looking at this book because you're interested in snorkeling or in becoming a certified scuba diver. If you can breathe through your mouth, you can snorkel. Scuba diving, however, is a little more restrictive — legitimate certifying agencies won't certify you for the following reasons:

✔ **Age:** You must be at least 12 years old.

✔ **General health problems:** You won't be able to obtain certification (without a doctor's approval) if you suffer from heart disease, epilepsy, diabetes requiring insulin therapy, or disabling mental illness.

✔ **Respiratory health problems:** This includes severe sinus problems, severe ear problems, severe asthma, or any other serious respiratory problems.

People who don't know how to swim can and do snorkel and dive, but I don't recommend it. If you don't know how to swim, take lessons before beginning to snorkel or scuba dive. (You can evaluate your swimming skills in Chapter 3.)

How This Book Is Organized

I've organized this book into the following five parts.

Part I: Water, Water, Everywhere!

In this part, you can evaluate your swimming skills and find out whether you fit the profile of a modern diver. You can also discover how you can get a low-cost sample of the sport before investing in a certification program and equipment. This part also gets you in the water, understanding the basics of snorkeling and scuba diving. I walk you through a typical scuba certification program from check-in to C-card, and discuss all of the ways that you can get certified. Finally, I look at the essential gear and help you save money by avoiding the esoteric, high-tech, neon-paneled offerings — you do have a titanium regulator, don't you?

Part II: Making a Splash

Three-quarters of the earth's surface is covered with water, and you're ready to explore it. In this part, you find out what an actual scuba dive is all about — how to pick a site, set up your equipment, get in the water, get down, and get back up again. (You also find out how to become a better diver and deal with any anxieties that you may have.)

This part also gives you the basics of the physics and chemistry of water and air. You don't have to know this stuff to enjoy snorkeling and scuba, but it does explain a lot of things and, besides, it's interesting! This part also helps you understand the problems inherent to an air-breathing, terrestrial mammal in a submarine realm, and looks at how you can avoid diving-related health problems that may arise.

Part III: Under the Sea

In this part, I take a close look at what's below that shimmering, ever-changing surface — surf, tides, currents, thermoclines, visibility problems — they all affect your diving. You don't usually dive just to float around in blue water; instead, you dive to see the stuff that's down there.

This part also shows you what you can expect to see when you're cruising over a coral reef, a shipwreck, or a kelp forest. This is also where the stuff about sharks and other potentially dangerous creatures is.

Part IV: The Wet Set

Suppose you're ready to go diving, but aren't sure where. Temperate or tropical? Liveaboard or resort? How do you choose the right one for you? What do I pack on a dive vacation? Should I bring my teenage daughter? And what's a drift dive, anyway? What about volcanoes and political uprisings? Never fear — just read this part. It answers all of your dive traveling questions.

Even after you become an open-water diver, you're not necessarily finished with your scuba education. In fact, nearly half of the certified divers go on to earn an advanced certification, take up underwater photography, or pursue some other diving specialty. So, in this part, I take a look at some of the options that lie beyond the basic C-card. Perhaps you, too, want to come back with an album full of pictures, dive deep on a mixture of exotic gases, or slither through the confines of an underwater cave. Maybe you just want to keep your scuba skills up to snuff between trips to exotic locations. This part shows you how.

Part V: The Part of Tens

In this part, you find out about my favorite diving sites — for both snorkeling and scuba diving. I've experienced so many great dives and snorkeling sites around the world that I could've made these chapters twice as long and still not covered them all. I'm sure I'll get an argument from passionate devotees of other places, but these are my choices and I'm sticking with them! One thing is sure, you can't go wrong with any of the choices that I give you.

I also give you ten ideas for making you safer underwater, and ten ways that you can help preserve the world's reefs.

Appendix

No matter how enthusiastic you are about the underwater world, you can't stay there all the time. It's a shame, I know, but you can take solace in all of the organizations and publications that cater to divers during the periods in which they must remain topside. The Appendix provides you with great lists of them.

Color photo section

It isn't easy to communicate the beauty and magic of the underwater world — that's why we put a section of color photos smack in the middle of this book. But even these pictures, taken by some of the world's top underwater photographers, only give you a hint of the look and feel of diving, snorkeling, and some of the creatures that make their home in the sea. The real magic is waiting for you out there, after you have that snorkel or regulator between your teeth.

Icons Used in This Book

As a diver, you get used to using and reading signs — divers have a whole vocabulary of sign language. So, just to get some practice, I cook up a few signs — called *icons* — for this book. Here's what they look like and what they mean:

Every specialized human activity has its own jargon, and diving is no exception. Every time I introduce one of these techno-terms, I give you the heads up with this icon.

This icon highlights ways to save time, trouble, money — maybe all three — that may not be perfectly obvious at first glance.

Pay attention to this icon — it helps you steer clear of situations, practices, and some creatures that can be hazardous. This icon can save you a lot of grief.

In my view, you should train to be a responsible diver as well as a safe diver, right from the beginning. This icon indicates some ways that you can preserve and protect the underwater environment.

This icon highlights information that's you don't necessarily have to know to dive safely, but that you may find interesting anyway. This is the stuff that tells you *why*, as well as *how*.

Where to Go from Here

This book is arranged so that you can get in the water as quickly as possible, so all of the pre-dive information is covered in Part I. After you're out snorkeling or scuba diving, you can come back and read about the biological makeup of the reef in Part III, the techno-physics stuff in Chapter 6, or the information about dive traveling in Part IV. Of course, just because it's laid out this way, doesn't mean you have to read it this way. Jump in anywhere you want. After you read the section on sharks in Chapter 9, start back at the beginning or go to Part V about the best dives in the world, and then come back and read the section about sharks again — sorry, though, they're not really as scary as they are in the movies.

Part I
Water, Water, Everywhere!

IT WASN'T LONG BEFORE BILL AND IRWIN DECIDED TO TRY DIVING AS A WAY TO PASS THE TIME.

©RICHTENNANT

In this part . . .

You don't need a drawer full of swimming medals to figure out how to scuba dive or snorkel. So, what exactly do you need to know to snorkel or dive successfuly? This part is where you find out.

This part also goes over the basics of snorkeling, all of the gear that you need to either snorkel or scuba dive, and what you have to do to get certified to scuba.

Chapter 1

The Lure of the Sea

In This Chapter

▶ Evaluating your water skills

▶ Discovering the ins and outs of snorkeling

▶ Understanding free diving

▶ Getting to know scuba diving

Snorkeling and scuba diving are pretty easy — what could be hard about floating around? However, before you dive, you should know how to swim, but you don't have to be able to knife through the water like an Olympic athlete. A basic, flopping-around kind of crawl is all that's required.

Lots of nondivers labor under the illusion that diving is some kind of hairball, gonzo sport that's practiced by the kind of barnacle-backed mariners who shrug off the loss of a limb and perform their own root canals with a rusty fishhook. Nothing could be further from the truth. In fact, diving isn't really even a sport. It's more of a pastime or activity. Under most conditions, it isn't much more strenuous than taking a walk around the block, and it isn't even as dangerous as driving your car to the convenience store for a quart of milk.

That is not to suggest that diving is entirely without risk. Diving is a visit to another world, one that's different than the one you're occupying right now, and one that could be dangerous — or even fatal — should you have a lapse in judgment and fail to respect its natural laws. But the same thing is true when you're zooming over a stretch of asphalt in a car — and statistically, driving is more dangerous than diving.

The undersea realm is another world, but it still functions according to specific, predictable physical laws. These laws are not esoteric or overly complex, and understanding them not only allows you to function in the watery world, it also relieves a lot of the fears you may have about being underwater.

Snorkeling, Free Diving, and Scuba Diving

The world of diving is divided into two distinct, but similar activities: snorkeling and scuba diving. As a *snorkeler,* you wear a diving mask — a watertight airspace in front of the eyes with a window through which you can observe the underwater world. You float face down on the surface, breathing through a plastic tube — called a *snorkel* — that extends along the side of your head and above the water, and propel yourself forward by kicking a pair of fins attached to your feet. To *free dive,* you fill your lungs with air and dive below the surface holding that single breath, exploring the underwater world until you're compelled to return to the surface for more air.

Most people get started snorkeling on a vacation to Hawaii or the Caribbean — in clear tropical, bath-warm lagoons, under the rattling fronds of a coconut palm and beyond a dazzling white sand beach. They rent the gear and wade out in the sparkling, clear water. They bend over and have a look around. Before long, they're splashing all over the lagoon. Snorkeling doesn't take a lot of training and is a good way to explore whether you enjoy diving sports before plunking down the bucks necessary for scuba lessons and equipment.

There is a natural progression between snorkeling and scuba, and most scuba divers come to the sport by way of snorkeling. *Scuba* is an acronym for Self-Contained Underwater Breathing Apparatus. As a scuba diver, you wear the same mask and fins as if you were snorkeler, but take along a bottle of compressed air; a few simple mechanical devices that facilitate breathing from the bottle; a vest that can be inflated with air or purged to adjust your buoyancy; and gauges to monitor air supply, how long you've been underwater, your depth, and so on. As a scuba diver, you can stay down a lot longer than you can on one breath, but to scuba dive you must first become certified (see Chapter 3).

Thanks, but No Tanks

If you already have a mask, a snorkel, and a pair of fins, you're ready to go snorkeling. If you don't have a mask, fins, and snorkel yet, flip to Chapter 2 to find out how to shop for them, and then go buy a set. These three pieces of equipment come in a wide range of prices, but keep in mind that fit and comfort are critical. If your mask doesn't fit right, it will constantly leak — this is one of the most annoying situations in diving and can spoil an otherwise perfect dive. Fins that pinch or rub raw spots on your feet can cut your fun short just as quickly.

Spend whatever is necessary to get the right equipment for you, but keep in mind that spending more doesn't always ensure better results — sometimes the cheaper equipment fits better! The key is to take your time and shop around until you have the best fit you can find.

Most scuba certifying agencies (listed in the Appendix) also offer snorkeling classes, available through your local dive shop. Snorkeling isn't anything that you can't figure out how to do on your own, but taking classes shortens the learning curve and boosts your confidence, especially if you're not comfortable in the water.

The mask

The human eye is designed to see only in air and doesn't work as well in direct contact with water. If you've ever been swimming in a pool, you've probably noticed that things look really blurry when you open your eyes underwater. A mask, shown in Figure 1-1, creates an airspace in front of your eyes so that you can see clearly underwater. It's also designed to keep water out of your nose, to allow you to clear water that may leak into the mask, and to let you to equalize pressure inside the mask. Flip to Chapter 2 for more on shopping for a diving mask.

Figure 1-1:
A mask keeps water out of your nose and eyes.

When you dive, water pressure outside the mask increases as you descend, pushing the mask against your face. The deeper you go, the greater the pressure. This is known as *mask squeeze* (more about mask squeeze in Chapter 7). In order to equalize the pressure inside the mask and eliminate mask squeeze, you must be able to breathe air into the mask through your nose. Although few snorkelers dive deep enough to experience serious mask squeeze, it is a significant phenomenon for scuba divers. Whatever style of mask you decide on, make sure it is one that encloses the nose. Swimming goggles don't enclose your nose, so they can't be cleared or equalized underwater — do not use them for snorkeling or scuba diving.

The snorkel

Picture this: Pursued by hostile enemies, you make it to the river. Growing along the bank is a stand of hollow reeds. Thinking fast (as always), you snap a reed off, break off a foot-long section, hold one end in your mouth and submerge quietly — breathing through the hollow reed until the enemy passes. Almost. Unfortunately, you are unable to control your buoyancy. You float to the top and are spotted immediately and captured. (To avoid this situation in the future, flip to Chapter 5 to find out more about buoyancy control.)

Your reed is essentially a *snorkel* — a hollow tube that allows you to breathe while most of your head is underwater. Of course, the modern snorkel, shown in Figure 1-2, exhibits a lot of improvements over the hollow reed, including modern materials, wrap-around design, comfortable mouthpiece, maybe even a purge valve and a splash guard. Every year, you can find a new and improved snorkel, which is amazing for a device that's so simple. Like the diving mask, the most important thing about a snorkel is that it is comfortable — oh yeah, and that it is color-coordinated. Check out Chapter 2 for more about how to shop for a snorkel.

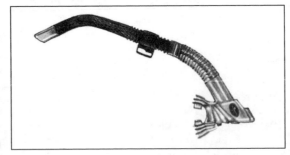

Figure 1-2: A snorkel allows you to breathe in shallow water.

The fins

Fins propel you forward in the water. Two types of fins, both shown in Figure 1-3, are used in snorkeling and diving: full-foot and adjustable.

- ✔ *Full-foot fins* enclose the heel like a pair of shoes, and are normally the preferred fin for snorkeling. Because they are more flexible than adjustable fins, full-foot fins are easy to use and are efficient while swimming on the surface.

- ✔ *Adjustable fins* are more commonly used in scuba diving. They feature an open heel with an adjustable strap. These are the fins of choice in cold water, because you need to wear a bootie (see Chapter 2) to protect your feet from exposure, but many scuba divers favor adjustable fins in warm water as well. Because they're adjustable, they can be worn with or without booties, although most aren't very comfortable without. Generally, they have a more rigid *blade* (the flat part that pushes against the water) than the full-foot fin and provide more forward thrust, but they require more effort to use and don't perform as well when swimming on the surface.

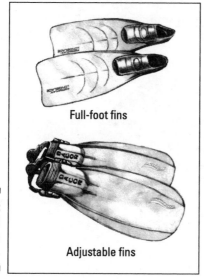

Full-foot fins

Adjustable fins

Figure 1-3:
Full-foot and adjustable fins.

With the exception of the difference between a heel strap and an enclosed heel, modern fin design and materials have blurred the distinctions between the two types of fins. You can find a pretty flexible adjustable fin these days, or conversely, a fairly rigid full-foot fin. Personally, because I usually only dive in warm water, I like to snorkel and free dive as well as scuba dive, and I only want to pack one pair of fins when I travel — I use a medium-rigid, full-foot fin for everything. If you want to snorkel only in warm water, stick with the full foot. If you think you may like to try scuba, or that you need to wear booties, consider getting adjustable fins.

The most important consideration when purchasing fins is comfort. Remember: The most expensive fins aren't necessarily the most comfortable. Consult Chapter 2 for more about how to shop for fins.

Setting up

Suppose you have your mask, fins, and snorkel, and they're a perfect fit. Now, in the privacy of your living room or hotel room, it's time to try them all on together. Go ahead. If someone comes to the door, I'm sure he'll understand perfectly.

The first order of business is to attach the snorkel to the mask (as shown in Figure 1-4). (If the last time you snorkeled was years ago, you may remember attaching your snorkel with two rubber rings connected by a rubber strip — called a *figure-eight snorkel keeper*. Today, just about every manufacturer of snorkel gear has its own proprietary *clip* that works just as well as the old figure-eight.) Here's how to proceed:

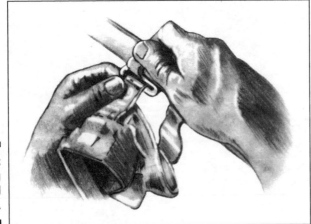

Figure 1-4:
Attaching
the snorkel
to the mask.

1. **Open the package.**

   The clip that's near the middle of the tube is called the *snorkel keeper*. If you don't have one, take your snorkel down to the nearest dive shop and ask them for a figure-eight or whatever kind of snorkel keeper they have. Make sure that it fits. It shouldn't cost more than a little pocket change.

2. **Clip the snorkel to the strap on your mask.**

   The snorkel can go on either side of your mask, but scuba divers normally clip it to the left side. This is because the air supply for scuba always comes over the right shoulder — if the snorkel is attached to the right side of the mask, it gets in the way when scuba diving. If you think that you may get involved in scuba one day, get in the habit of wearing your snorkel on the left side of the mask. If you think you'll stick with snorkeling, put it on whichever side you prefer.

   Silicone masks and snorkels are usually covered with a waxy protective coating that you need to scrub off before you use them. If you don't treat your mask with some kind of solution before every dive it will fog up and you won't be able to see all the great stuff that you went snorkeling to see (don't worry, I show you how to defog your mask in the "In your face" section, later in this chapter). The coating on your new mask interferes with the mask defogging solutions you may use, and sometimes makes the straps slip out of adjustment. To scrub off the coating, get a little gob of toothpaste on the end of your finger and rub it all around for a few minutes. Scrub the lens of the mask on both sides. A word of caution: Some new masks have a defogging coating applied at the factory, so don't scrub the lens if the manufacturer advises against it. When you're through scrubbing, rinse the toothpaste off and put the mask aside.

3. Try on the fins.

If you're using adjustable fins, put the booties on first. With some fins, you have a left foot and right foot; with others it doesn't matter. After your figure out which kind you have, slip your foot into the appropriate pocket and secure the strap around the back of your heel. Then, adjust the strap so that your foot is held firmly in place, but not pinched.

If you have full-foot fins, fold the heel down so that it's inside out. Slip your foot into the pocket, and then pull the heel cup up. Your fins should be snug, but shouldn't chafe or pinch.

4. Put on the mask.

Loosen the straps of the mask and hold the mask in the palm of one hand, facing down. Put your other hand through the strap so that the strap lies against the back of that hand with your fingers pointing toward your chest. Fit the mask in position on your face and bring the other hand over the top of your head palm down until the strap is on the back of your head and most of your hair is still rooted in your head. Hold onto the strap with your free hand and release the other hand. Voilà!

Adjust the straps until the mask is snug, but not too tight. You're going to have to readjust it after you get in the water, so don't worry about it too much now.

5. Put the snorkel in your mouth.

Slide the snorkel up or down the snorkel keeper until the snorkel rests comfortably along side your head. The end of the snorkel should be behind your head. Comfy? Can you breath easily and freely through the snorkel? Good. If not, try some more adjustments. If that doesn't work, take your snorkel back to the store and get one that fits better.

As soon as your mask, snorkel, and fins are in place, the phone will ring in the other room. Never mind — let the machine get it. You're ready to get in the water.

Location, location, location

The first few times that you snorkel, you're familiarizing yourself with a whole new world of sensations. To keep distractions to a minimum and to ensure your safety, make your first snorkeling forays in a pool or somewhere with pool-like conditions — calm, clear water with no current, good visibility, and a shallow bottom. If you decide to try it somewhere other than a pool, scout the location beforehand. Make sure that you have safe exit and entry places and no boat traffic, wave action, or submerged objects such as rocks, coral, or discarded rubbish. Also make sure there aren't (and haven't been) any fishermen around. Fishermen are famous for littering the bottom with hooks and tangles of fishing line — encounters with these charming little artifacts can be really unpleasant, especially on your first time out.

In your face

Here's how to handle your first venture into water:

1. **Sit on the edge in the shallow end or on the stairs of a pool (or on the beach area of a lake or other body of water) and put your fins on.**

   Keep your mask at hand, but don't lay it face down on the pool deck or you'll risk scratching the lens.

2. **Pick up your mask and wade out a little into the pool until the water level should be just below your waist.**

   If you're going in a lake or other body of water, slowly walk backward into the water — watching where you're going over your shoulder. If you're with a companion, hold onto each other for more stability.

3. **Take your mask in the palm of your hand and spit on the inside of the glass — you heard me, spit on the glass!**

   This may sound a little strange, but you must show your mask who's boss right from the start! There's nothing worse than an uppity mask. Also, spit makes an effective defogging solution — without some kind of defogging solution your mask will fog up within a few minutes and obscure your vision.

   If you're too delicate to spit in your mask, you can use a few drops of a commercially prepared defogging solution — you can get one at any dive shop — but how much fun can you really have without a spit-in-your-mask attitude? Besides, now you have that little bottle of defogger to deal with.

4. **After you have a good loogie or some kind of defogging solution on the inside lens of your mask, rub it all over the glass with the tip of your finger then rinse it with a little seawater or pool water.**

5. **Put the mask on.**

6. **Put the snorkel in your mouth.**

7. **Breathing through your snorkel, bend slightly at the waist and squat down until your face is in the water.**

You may want to keep one hand on the end of the snorkel so that you can be sure it's not underwater. Enjoy your first view of the underwater world from the *squatting position*. You may notice that everything is magnified — because of the way light behaves underwater objects appear about 25 percent bigger. You can find a more detailed description of this phenomenon in Chapter 6.

At this point you may discover that your mask is leaking water. If so, you may need to tighten or loosen the strap — sometimes a mask that's too tight can leak as badly as one that isn't snug enough. If neither tightening or loosening seems to help, try a light coating of lip moisturizer on the skirt. The *skirt* is the little flap of silicone rubber that goes around the perimeter of the mask and makes contact with your face.

Almost no mask is completely watertight. Nearly every diver has to figure out how to cope with a little seepage, so don't be overly concerned. On the other hand, your mask shouldn't be constantly letting in water. If it is, take it back to the dive shop and exchange it for one that fits better. For instructions on clearing water from your mask, see the next section, "Clearing your mask."

8. **Extend one hand to the bottom and stretch your legs out behind you so that you're floating, face down, on the surface with one hand touching the bottom.**

This is the *floating posture*. Relax and float for a few minutes. Look around. Breath slowly. You may notice that, as you inhale, your body floats a little higher in the water and when you exhale, a little lower — when your lungs are filled with air you have more buoyancy, when you empty them, less.

9. **Kick your feet a little, and you're snorkeling!**

Go ahead, give it a try. Pretty cool, huh?

Clearing your mask

To understand how to clear your mask, do the following:

1. **Flood your mask with water.**

You can flood by pulling it gently away from you face until the mask is about half full of water. Don't panic, just keep breathing calmly through your snorkel.

2. **Tip your head back slightly and hold the top of the mask gently against your forehead with one hand, as shown in Figure 1-5.**

3. Take a deep breath through your snorkel and exhale gently through your nose.

Notice how the air you exhale bubbles up in the mask forcing the water out the bottom. Nifty, huh?

Figure 1-5:
Clearing
your mask.

4. After you clear your mask, get it snug on your face again and continue breathing normally through the snorkel.

If this doesn't work, stand up, empty the water out, and start again. If it still doesn't work, check to make sure that the skirt of the mask isn't twisted or folded in some way and make sure you don't have any hair (or anything else) between your skin and the silicone skirt of the mask.

Be sure to practice clearing your mask while in the floating posture. While floating face-down and looking directly at the bottom of the body of water, you can't clear it successfully. Instead, tilt your head back so that you're looking up and try your clearing procedure again. Now kick a little and try it a few times while you're moving forward. As long as the air you blow into your mask is escaping from the lowest point of the mask, you can clear the water.

Try this alternate technique: While swimming forward, hold the mask against the left side of your face. Now, turn your head over your left shoulder and breathe into your mask through your nose. Again, as long as the air is escaping from the lowest point of your mask, it works.

Diving with a 'stache

If you're a man with a mustache, you may find it difficult to get a good seal on the bottom edge of your mask. I've heard lots of suggestions for dealing with this situation — like smearing your mustache with gobs of petroleum jelly. Ugh. In the end, you have to decide whether to shave the thing off or live with the extra seepage. Rest assured, if you keep the cookie broom, you'll quickly become an expert at clearing your mask. Practice the procedure until you're comfortable with it.

Clearing your snorkel

Your snorkel allows you to view the underwater world from the water's surface, without raising your head every few minutes to take a breath. However, when you see something down there that piques your curiosity and you want to go down for a closer look, your snorkel fills with water. Even if you never dive below the surface, eventually a wave submerges your snorkel or water splashes into it, so you have to know how to clear it.

You clear your snorkel with a sharp, forceful exhalation that blows the water out. To practice, try the following:

1. **Get into the squatting position — face underwater, breathing through your snorkel.**

2. **Take a deep breath, hold it, and squat down until your snorkel is completely submerged.**

3. **Rise to your original position and blow a sharp blast of air through your snorkel.**

   Try not to exhale all your air, just enough to clear the snorkel. Try inhaling — slowly and cautiously. If the snorkel still has water in it, exhale sharply again.

   Don't suck a huge gulp of air through your snorkel when you first surface. Inhale slowly until you're sure the airway is clear. This may be difficult at first, but with a little practice, it becomes second nature.

When you free dive, you can use another method for clearing your snorkel: At the end of your dive, just before you reach the surface, tilt your head back so that the end of your snorkel is pointing down, and exhale slowly into your mouthpiece. The air you exhale into the snorkel forces most of the water out, just as it does when you clear your mask. When you reach the surface, a small puff of air clears the remaining water. This technique requires a little more practice, but after you master it, clearing your snorkel is virtually effortless.

Getting your kicks

The same *flutter kick* used in freestyle swimming is used for snorkeling. The difference, of course, is that you're getting a lot more forward motion for your efforts, because you have fins on. Everybody kicks a little bit differently, just as everybody runs a little bit differently — there isn't really a wrong way. Keep your arms at your sides so that you're beautifully streamlined (you can also clasp them in front of or behind you, for a change of pace), keep your knees fairly straight, and kick your feet up and down in a scissors motion and go — see Figure 1-6. Let your body find its own style.

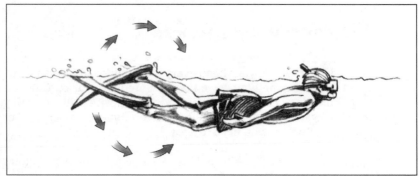

Figure 1-6:
Flutter-
kicking.

Try not to let your fins come out of the water. All of your forward momentum comes from the fin blades pushing against the water. When they're pushing against air, you're not going anywhere, and you're wasting your energy.

The real deal

After you're able to clear your mask and snorkel and have a good flutter kick to move you around, you're ready to begin exploring the underwater world. Your first few times out, look for conditions similar to those in which you practiced clearing your mask and snorkel — calm water; good visibility; and no current, wave action, or boats. In addition, you want a place where you can observe lots of marine life. Small bays and coves, the side of a point of land that's protected from the wind, a protected lagoon, or a lake can all make a good first snorkeling location. If you're at a resort, the folks in the dive shop or experienced locals can usually direct you to an appropriate place. Consult Chapters 8 and 9 to better understand some of the features of the ocean and the coral reef — this information can help you select a spot.

One of the cardinal rules of diving and snorkeling is never go alone — that way, you always have at least one person to help if the other gets into trouble. Of course, two divers with poor water skills aren't much safer than one, and they may take risks that they wouldn't take alone. Even one competent snorkeler isn't any help if that person is the one who gets into trouble, and he may inspire the less-experienced diver to take risks that he isn't prepared for. Obviously, the best situation is to snorkel only with other divers who are competent in the water, but you may not even be able to gauge the skills of your companions before you leave the beach or the boat. Snorkeling is certainly more fun when you share it with someone, but ultimately, you should consider yourself your own best lifeguard — know your limitations and don't exceed them. Some experienced snorkelers enjoy going solo and relying strictly on their own expertise and judgment. Don't. If you want to send me letters and e-mail arguing your philosophy of self-determination, that's fine, but until you become an expert, snorkel in a group or at least with a friend.

After you find an appropriate spot, try a few shallow dives to get some practice clearing your snorkel and swimming underwater among the coral heads and clouds of colorful tropical fish. After that, you're snorkeling for real. Congratulations.

Free Diving

Eventually, your developing snorkel skills allow you to investigate the mysteries of deeper waters. As you cruise along on the surface, you may find that you want to investigate some of the things you see below more closely. To do that, you need to *free dive* — get down to the bottom and back up again on a single breath of air, as the original (pre-scuba) divers did.

The first thing you discover when you begin to free dive is just how much natural buoyancy your body has — especially holding a full breath. You may find it somewhat challenging to even get below the surface at first. One way you can decrease your buoyancy is to inhale less deeply, but this shortens the time that you can stay down. Another solution is to carry dive weights, but that's a more advanced technique — the use of weights is covered in the "Weighty matters" section, later in this chapter.

The following sections show you how to dive down among the corals, the fish, and the eels, and how to enjoy yourself when you're down there.

The slant dive

The slant dive is probably the easiest dive to execute and in fact, it's probably what you've been doing if you've been free diving at all. The *slant dive* is executed by doing the following (see Figure 1-7):

1. **Swim forward on the surface, take a breath, and then suddenly duck your head below the surface.**

The water pressure on your back, caused by your forward momentum, pushes you down. As long as you keep your body angled to the surface and continue kicking, you descend. The more you duck your head, the steeper the angle of your descent.

2. **When you're ready to ascend, arch your back so that you're looking at the surface and continue kicking.**

   This reverses the pressure of the water so that it's pushing on your chest and lifting you to the surface.

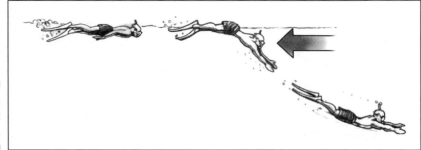

Figure 1-7:
The slant
dive.

The slant dive is fairly easy to execute, but it takes a good deal of effort, because it requires that you continue kicking the entire time. A more efficient dive, but one that's a bit more difficult to learn, is the pike dive, discussed in the following section.

The pike dive

The *pike dive,* shown in Figure 1-8, requires less energy to execute because you needn't be kicking to perform it. It also takes you deeper faster and requires no forward momentum — although you may find it easier, on your first attempts, to do the pike dive while swimming forward.

The pike dive takes you much deeper more quickly than the slant dive. Before you attempt, it you must master the technique of equalizing the pressure in your ears, discussed in the following section, "Equalizing your ears."

To make a pike dive, do the following:

1. **Take a breath and bend at your waist until the upper part of your body is as perpendicular to the surface of the water as possible.**

2. **Extend your arms above your head and straighten your legs above you.**

3. **As the weight of your legs pushes you below the surface, use your hands to help your descent (one stroke should do it).**

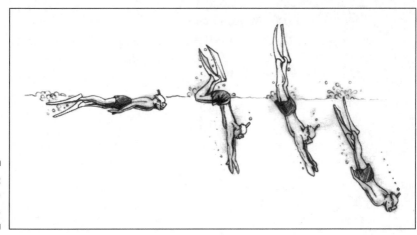

Figure 1-8:
The pike
dive.

4. **After your fins are below the surface, kick as you would on the surface and you descend easily on a nearly vertical line.**

At this point, you need to equalize your ears. See the following section, "Equalizing your ears," for instructions. After you're well-practiced at equalizing your ears, you can dive as deep and for as long as you're capable.

Head for the surface as soon as you feel the urge to breathe. You can't stay down very long at first, but your performance improves as you become move relaxed and more efficient in the water. Don't push it and try to stay down "just a little longer" — this can put you at risk for hypoxia and shallow-water blackout, both of which come from insufficient oxygen (see the "Hyped on hyperventilation" sidebar, later in this chapter, for more on these problems).

5. **When you're ready to surface, look up to the surface and use your flutter kick to ascend.**

Your mask may restrict your field of vision, but you can compensate for this by turning in a 360-degree circle as you ascend. Watch out for boats, overhangs, other divers, or anything that can obstruct your ascent or provide an undesirable rendezvous. As a precaution, extend one arm over your head — kind of an aquatic bumper.

As you ascend, the pressure on the outside of your ear decreases, but the increased pressure of the middle ear vents easily — you shouldn't need to take any action to equalize on the ascent.

Be sure to rest for a few minutes between dives until your breathing and heart rate return to normal. Remember, diving isn't about how many trips to the bottom you can log in an hour. It's about relaxing and maximizing your resources.

Equalizing your ears

If you've ever gone up in an airplane or driven over a mountain pass, you may have noticed your ears "popping." This is the result of pressure on your eardrums equalizing suddenly.

At sea level, a pressure of 14.7 pounds per square inch (psi) is pressing down on your body, including your eardrums. You don't notice it because, just like your mother always told you, there's an empty space between your ears — two of them in fact, called the *middle ear*. Air pressure in the middle ear at sea level is also 14.7 psi. Equal pressure is pushing in and out on the eardrum. When you go up in a plane or up on a mountain, the pressure pushing on the outside of your eardrum decreases and you begin to notice the difference, usually by experiencing some slight discomfort. A small passage called the *Eustachian tube* connects the middle ear with the back of the mouth. When the higher pressure of the inner ear is released by means of the Eustachian tube, the ears seem to "pop" and, once again, the pressure is equal on both sides of the eardrum. When you descend, you encounter the opposite situation — pressure outside the ear increases.

This "popping" occurs when you dive, too, but because water is so much heavier than air, you don't have to go down very deep (less than 3 feet) before you begin to notice the effects of the increase in pressure. If you should continue to descend without equalizing the pressure on your eardrum, you experience sharp pain in the ears and risk permanent injury (see Chapter 7 for more on avoiding this and other types of injury). Fortunately, you can easily correct this situation in one of two following ways. (Be sure to extend your jaw forward as far as you can — without losing your snorkel — as you perform either of these techniques.)

  ✔ **As you descend, pinch your nose closed and swallow.** This causes the throat muscles to compress air in the middle ear and equalizes the pressure. Perform this technique constantly as you descend. Don't wait to feel discomfort or pain in your ears. If the pressure difference becomes too great, you have more difficulty equalizing your ears.

  ✔ **Blow gently against your pinched nose.** This also compresses air in the middle ear.

Occasionally, some people have difficulty equalizing their ears. If this sounds like you, don't give up — persistence and practice of the techniques makes a lot of difference.

Colds, allergies, and sinus problems make the situation worse — don't dive if you are suffering with any of these conditions. If you can't equalize the pressure in your ears for any reason, discontinue the dive.

Too cool

You can be quite comfortable with an air temperature of 70° because air doesn't conduct heat very well. Water, on the other hand, is a good conductor and in 70° water, you may become chilled very quickly. If you spend any amount of time in the water, even in the warm water of the tropics, you may want to invest in a *wetsuit* (a full-body suit that you wear underwater). Wetsuits are made from a material called *neoprene* that protects you from the cold by trapping a layer of water inside the suit that's warmed by your body. Because the neoprene is full of air bubbles (air being a good insulator), very little heat escapes. Wetsuits come in a wide variety of thicknesses and styles (see Chapter 2 for more about wetsuits).

Weighty matters

Diving weights come in a variety of sizes and shapes. Weights are used to compensate for the extra buoyancy of a wetsuit or other gear. How much weight you need to carry depends on what kind of (and how thick) a wetsuit you wear. You have to experiment a little to get the right buoyancy, but do your experiments in a pool or some other shallow water, where you have no danger of being carried to the bottom in an uncontrolled descent and where you can retrieve the weights if you have to drop them.

Weights are worn on a weight belt — there are several different kinds of these as well, but they all have one feature in common: a quick release buckle. Every dive shop rents weights, and there're usually very cheap, so divers almost never travel with them. The dive shop should be able to help you determine how much weight you need or least give you a place to start. Tell them what you plan to do, show them your wetsuit, and ask them how much weight they think you need.

When you're snorkeling, put your weight belt on last, after all of your other equipment. Make sure that nothing interferes with it dropping away if you need to release it. Try releasing it a few times before you get in the water. Remember, you're just testing the buckle, you don't need to actually let it hit the floor.

In-vest-ments

If you're using weights, you may want to use an inflatable snorkeling vest. Even some snorkelers who don't use weights appreciate the added sense of security they get from a vest. Essentially, a snorkeling vest is an airtight bag that goes over your head and secures with a strap behind your back. It is inflated by blowing air into it through a valve on the front. The air can be dumped through a purge valve when you want to dive. Usually a snorkeling vest has a CO_2 cartridge attached for emergency inflation, but CO_2 cartridges don't hold up well under repeated exposure to salt water and they're not very dependable.

Advanced Free Diving

Advanced free diving is about extending your dives. You may be perfectly happy snorkeling and making occasional shallow free dives. Many people are, but if you're the type who wants to go deeper and stay longer, you need to master a few additional techniques and be advised of a few additional risks.

- ✔ **To go deeper, you only need to be able to equalize your ears quickly.** You do this with practice, practice, practice.

- ✔ **Get regular, vigorous exercise.** Unless you get regular vigorous aerobic exercise, your use of oxygen is probably inefficient and your dive times are not what they can be — how deep you can go and how long you can stay both depend on how long you have to get down and back up. To extend your dive times, adopt a program of vigorous, regular aerobic exercise. Yoga and several forms of breath control meditation have also proven to be quite effective.

- ✔ **Try hyperventilating.** *Hyperventilation* (taking a series of deep breaths in rapid succession) can also prove effective in extending dive times, but should be used with caution because it can result in potentially deadly shallow-water blackout. See the "Hyped on hyperventilation" sidebar for more information.

Beyond Free Diving — Scuba

If you're irresistibly drawn to the aquatic mysteries that lie beyond the range of a single breath, investigate scuba diving. If you think you'd like to try scuba, but aren't entirely sure, consider experimenting with a resort course. A *resort course* is an introduction to scuba diving, usually offered by the dive shop that's associated with a resort.

Say you're spending a week at a resort, and you notice a dive shop down on the beach, and, sure enough, they offer an introductory scuba course. Typically, this course is inexpensive, because they want to bring you into the fold. You sign up and you're at the dive shop the next morning. Here's how a course usually goes:

1. **The instructor gives you a brief orientation to scuba diving.**

2. **The instructor sizes you up for some gear from the shop's rental department.**

3. **You try the stuff out in a pool or in a shallow lagoon in front of the resort under the ever-attentive eye of the instructor.**

4. **The instructor takes you on a closely supervised, fairly shallow dive on the nearby reef.**

Hyped on hyperventilation

The sensation of needing to breathe is triggered by the buildup of carbon dioxide in the body, not by the depletion of oxygen. When you're deprived of oxygen, you go unconscious, but as long as the levels of carbon dioxide in your body remain low, you don't experience the need to breathe.

When you take a several deep breaths in rapid succession, or *hyperventilate,* you can easily hold the last one a little longer than you normally could. That's because you've eliminated much of the carbon dioxide in your body — no carbon dioxide, no urge to breathe. This can be an effective technique in extending your dive times, if used cautiously.

Problems arise when the diver hyperventilates excessively before a dive, which eliminates most of the carbon dioxide from the body. During the dive, carbon dioxide doesn't accumulate fast enough to stimulate the diver with the need to breathe. The diver continues to consume oxygen until he or she reaches a state of insufficient oxygen, or *hypoxia,* and still the diver may feel no need to breathe. The increased pressure of the air in the lungs underwater allows the body to continue consuming oxygen at levels that would render him unconscious on the surface. When the diver finally ascends, the pressure of the air in the lungs drops, oxygen becomes instantly unavailable and the diver suddenly blacks out (called *shallow-water blackout*).

If you intend to use hyperventilation to extend your dives, you should keep it to a total three deep breaths — maximum — before your dive. More than that, and you're putting yourself at risk for shallow-water blackout.

This only happens after you're feeling comfortable in your new surroundings and with breathing compressed air through a mouthpiece.

5. **You come back, you rinse the gear, and they entice you to take the open water course.**

    You're not a certified diver, but you've had your first real experience with the world of scuba and usually under the best of circumstances — in the clear warm waters of the tropics with lots of personal attention from an experienced diver. If you had fun and you'd like to become a scuba diver, your next step is to earn an open water certification, covered in Chapter 3.

Successfully completing an open water course earns you a *C-card* (certification card) — with that, you can rent tanks, weights, and other equipment all over the world. (Chapter 3 tells you how.)

Chapter 2

Gearing Up

● ●

In This Chapter

▶ Getting the gear you need

▶ Renting gear versus purchasing it

▶ Maintaining and repairing your gear

● ●

*E*quipment makes diving possible. Like most adventure sports, to fully outfit yourself presently costs more than $1,000 — that's a lot of money, but keep in mind that your purchases are a one-time expense: The equipment should last you ten years or more. If you're planning to travel and dive, you don't need to buy tanks and weights — they're too bulky and heavy to carry as airline baggage, and are almost always available at your destination. If you plan to dive most often in your home waters, you may find it more cost-effective to buy tanks and weights.

If you take up scuba after you've been snorkeling, you can use your same mask and snorkel, and probably the same fins, depending on what kind you buy and what kind of diving you plan to do.

Diving is an equipment wonk's paradise — there's lots of stuff to buy and lots of maintenance to do on it afterward. In addition to all of the stuff you need, you can buy optional equipment to facilitate your fun and allow for diving specialties, like underwater photography and video. This chapter covers all of that.

The Basics

Chapter 1 covers the three basic pieces of equipment — mask, snorkel, and fins — in detail. This section gives you tips on purchasing these basic pieces of equipment, and provides some details on the options that are available.

Diving mask

Your eyes are meant to see through the medium of air, not water. When you open your eyes underwater, things look all blurry, and if it's salt water, it probably stings like heck, too. You need a mask. A mask creates an airspace in front of your eyes and a window through which you can have a clear view into the underwater world.

After you create an airspace in front of your eyes that allows you to see clearly, you must be able to equalize the pressure in that airspace as you descend into water and the water pressure increases. This is accomplished by blowing additional air into the mask through your nose — that's why a diving mask, shown in Figure 2-1, must enclose the nose. Failure to equalize the mask results in *mask squeeze* (see Chapter 7 for more on this condition) — not a dangerous condition, but not a pleasant one either.

Figure 2-1:
The diving mask must enclose the nose so you can equalize the pressure in the airspace.

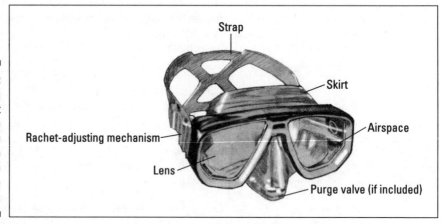

Strap

Skirt

Rachet-adjusting mechanism

Airspace

Lens

Purge valve (if included)

Diving masks are made by setting a lens, or lenses, in a plastic frame surrounded by a silicone rubber *skirt* that seals around the eyes and nose, with a silicone strap that goes around the back of the head and holds the mask to the face. They come in a wide variety of colors and styles. Which mask you select is, for the most part, a matter of personal preference, but you must get a good fit. In diving, there are few things more annoying than having to clear your mask every few seconds. You may want the ultra low-volume wraparound model, but if it doesn't fit you, it's going to leak and you're not going to be a very happy diver. If you have to choose between style and fit, choose fit.

In general, you want a mask with a low volume of airspace. The less airspace inside your mask, the easier the mask is to equalize and clear. A low-volume mask is closer to your eyes, too, so it allows a wider field of vision.

Selecting a mask

Fit is the most important criteria in selecting a mask, so how do you buy a mask that fits? It's pretty easy actually. Here's how:

1. **Move the strap.**

   Fold the strap out of the way so that it's in front of the lens.

2. **Hold the mask against your face.**

   Settle the mask so that the skirt rests comfortably around your eyes and under your nose.

3. **Inhale through your nose.**

   The vacuum created in the mask should hold it against your face when you take your hand away, even when you shake your head. If it doesn't stay tight against your face, try another mask.

You may find more than one that fits. If you do, compare some of the other features.

Discovering additional mask options

Some of the following features are standard on most masks; a few modern masks have them all. First and foremost is a good fit; after that, select the one that has the most features you want.

- ✔ **Tempered glass:** Tempered glass crumbles into little glass pellets when it breaks, rather than into wicked shards. This is an advantage for anything around your eyes. Tempered glass also resists scratches better than regular glass, so it's standard on most masks today.

- ✔ **Double skirt:** An inner skirt is also pretty standard on masks. Double-skirt masks are more comfortable and keep water out better. Normally, the inner skirt parallels the outside skirt all the way around, except under the nose — the bottom of the mask. This allows the mask to be more easily cleared.

- ✔ **Purge valve:** Some masks come with this small one-way valve, usually right under the nose, that allows water to be cleared without breaking the seal of the skirt. Theoretically, you should be able to clear your mask without using your hands, but hey, you have to have something to do with your hands! Most divers concede that a purge valve doesn't really make a lot of difference.

- ✔ **Fog-free coating:** I haven't tried this option, but it sounds like a good idea, depending on how much maintenance the coating requires and how sensitive the coating is to damage.

Snorkel

A snorkel, shown in Figure 2-2, is a hollow tube that allows you to breathe air while your head is mostly submerged. The tube extends from a mouthpiece that's gripped between the teeth, contours around and behind the head, and extends above the water's surface while the diver floats or swims face-down. It is secured to the strap on the mask by a clip or band.

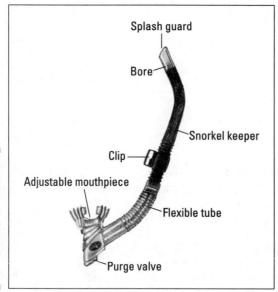

Splash guard

Bore

Snorkel keeper

Clip

Adjustable mouthpiece

Flexible tube

Purge valve

Figure 2-2:
The snorkel allows you to breathe while your head is mostly submerged.

There are primarily two factors that affect the performance of a snorkel — the length and the diameter of the *bore* (the tube on the snorkel).

✔ **Bore length:** A long bore ensures a high and dry intake opening, but it increases the dead air space. (*Dead air* is the stuff that you exhaled with your last breath that is still hanging around in your snorkel.) A long bore is also harder to clear water from, because there's more water in there. A short bore is better, but if it's too short, the opening may be submerged by surface waves. (If that happens, Chapter 1 shows you how to clear your snorkel.)

✔ **Bore diameter:** A larger bore diameter is better because it reduces breathing resistance. If the bore diameter is too large, however, it can't be cleared, because exhaled air will bubble up in the bore and not blow the water out. Most of today's snorkels have evolved to the optimum bore length and diameter.

Snorkels also come in two different designs:

- ✔ **Contoured:** The contoured model features a rigid tube that contours around the head.

- ✔ **Drop-away:** The drop-away model — generally preferred by scuba divers — features a tube that's flexible in the bottom contour and drops out of the way when the diver is using a scuba regulator.

Selecting a snorkel

The second most important thing about a snorkel, after the ease of breathing, is how comfortable it is in your mouth. There's only one way to find that out, but then, you don't want to go around sticking every snorkel in the store in your mouth, and the management would probably prefer that you didn't, as well. Fortunately, there is a very low incidence of snorkel discomfort — in the past 20 years I've had only one that I couldn't live with. If you get one that's uncomfortable, you won't be able to get to the store to buy a new one fast enough!

Snorkels feature a lot of options and are well-designed for comfort, so unlike shopping for a mask, select one with all of the options that you want, and then check the fit.

The bottom line, however, is the same — don't sacrifice fit for options, color, or any other lesser considerations. When you're in the water, fit and function are all that matter.

Discovering additional snorkel options

It's amazing how many features the manufacturers have managed to come up with on such a simple device. Some of them are really ingenious, some of them are pointless. You be the judge:

- ✔ **Adjustable mouthpiece:** Some snorkels allow you to adjust the angle of the mouthpiece that comes off the main tube.

- ✔ **Purge valve:** These snorkels have a one-way valve beneath the mouthpiece that allows for easier clearing. The majority of snorkels sold have purge valves.

- ✔ **Flexible tube:** This determines whether a snorkel has a drop-away design. The bottom contour of the snorkel tube is made of ribbed silicone. This allows the mouthpiece to "drop away" when not in use. If you think you may scuba dive in addition to snorkeling, this is the preferred feature.

- ✔ **Snorkel keeper:** This is the little gizmo that secures your snorkel to the strap of the mask. Every manufacturer has its own proprietary clip or keeper of some kind. Just make sure it can be adjusted up and down the tube.

✔ **Colors:** Whoopee! Go crazy. You have the whole rainbow at your fingertips. Most manufacturers make their masks and snorkels in matching-color sets.

✔ **Splash guard:** This device is attached to the top end of the snorkel to minimize water splashing into the tube. Every manufacturer seems to have its own proprietary design — some work better than others. A snorkel works pretty well without one, too.

Fins

Fins, shown in Figure 2-3, are designed to convert your kicking energy into forward thrust as efficiently as possible. There are two kinds of fins in the world of diving:

✔ **Adjustable fins:** These fins have an open heel and an adjustable strap to keep the foot in place. Most adjustable fins are larger and stiffer than full-foot fins. They provide the additional forward thrust necessary for diving in current and surge. In cold water, where exposure protection (including wearing booties) is necessary, adjustable fins are the fins of choice. Adjustable fins are heavier and more expensive than full-foot fins, and can't be worn comfortably without booties (covered in the "Booties" section, later in this chapter).

Most adjustable fins today come equipped with a Fastex-type buckle for quick release and fastening, and a ratchet-adjusting mechanism for easy, one-tug adjustment. Normally, the strap swivels at the point it connects to the fin, making it easier to take off and put on the fin.

✔ **Full-foot fins:** These fins enclose the heel like a pair of shoes. The full-foot fin is the preferred fin for snorkeling, and is popular among scuba divers who dive only in warm water destinations. Full-foot fins are generally more flexible than adjustable fins. That's why they work better for surface swimming — they don't break the surface as often as a more rigid fin. More contact with the water means more forward thrust.

Full-foot fins also don't require booties. Booties are made of *neoprene,* the same stuff as a wetsuit. They create a little extra buoyancy, which you have to compensate for with additional weight. Some divers feel that full-foot fins make their feet float up, making it harder to submerge — some wear ankle weights, in addition to the regular weights, to counteract this problem. If you like full-foot fins and plan to use them scuba diving, you want some that are more rigid than the typical snorkeling fins. Many divers who dive *and* snorkel, and who dive in warm *and* cold water, own both.

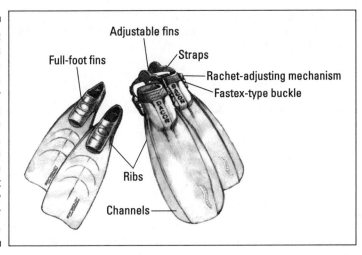

Figure 2-3:
Full-foot fins
provide
more
flexibility for
swimming
on the
surface.
Adjustable
fins provide
more thrust
and allow
you to wear
booties.

Most fins are made of several different materials. The foot pocket and strap are made of neoprene or a similar material, while the blades of the fins are made from more rigid thermoplastics. Fins are subject to a lot of hydrodynamic theorizing and variations in blade design — all trying to squeeze that extra bit of efficiency out of the kicking stroke. Some are well-accepted and have settled in as standards in the industry; others are highly speculative and unproved.

Some of the more better-accepted design features include:

- ✔ **Ribs:** Nearly all fins have vertical ribs to reinforce the blade and give it stability in the power stroke. Ribs keep the fin from moving side to side as it moves up and down.

- ✔ **Channels:** Channels work by forming a U-shape in the blade during the up and down strokes. This captures and moves more water, creating more forward thrust.

- ✔ **Vents:** Vented fins are supposed to reduce resistance to fin movement while maintaining efficiency.

When selecting fins, the first thing you must decide is whether you want full-foot or adjustable fins, or both. If you intend to buy full-foot fins, you need only zoom off to your favorite dive shop, strip off your shoes and socks, and try on the available merchandise until you find the pair you want. They should be snug (but not tight and pinching) and comfortable (but not loose and wiggling around) on your foot.

If you're opting for the adjustable fins, you first need a pair of booties (see the "Booties" section, later in this chapter). After you have a pair of booties, take them with you to the dive shop of your choice and start trying on fins. You're looking for the same kind of fit that you want with full-foot fins. In addition, test the strap adjustment mechanism to make sure that it's easy to operate. Keep in mind that you may have to adjust it underwater, perhaps while wearing gloves (if you plan to dive in cold water).

Other Stuff That You Need

After outfitting yourself with a mask, snorkel, and fins, you may require additional equipment, which is described in this section.

Exposure suit

Water is a far better conductor of heat than air. When the air temperature is 70° most human beings feel comfortable, but in 70° water the same person becomes chilled in a very short time. Water conducts heat away from the body more than 20 times as efficiently as air. That's why divers wear exposure suits — even in warm tropical waters. Sensitivity to cold varies among individuals, and from day to day with a given person, but nearly every diver, after prolonged and repeated submersion, gets chilled and therefore requires some kind of exposure suit. An exposure suit, shown in Figure 2-4, also provides protection from scrapes and stings. Ideally, a diver touches nothing underwater, but diving takes place in the real world, not the ideal world.

Figure 2-4:
An exposure suit provides warmth and protection from scratches and stings.

Exposure suits come in three varieties: dive skins, wetsuits, and dry suits. The one you choose depends on how much thermal protection you need.

Dive skin

Dive skins are made from lycra — a very elastic kind of nylon fabric. They come in a whole rainbow of colors, in both men's and women's sizes. They are form-fitting, usually zip up the front, and have stirrups to keep the legs from riding up. A dive skin does a good job of protecting the diver from stings and abrasions, but because water saturates the suit and circulates freely over the body, it offers very little thermal protection. A dive skin is used exclusively in warm, tropical waters, and is sometimes worn under a wetsuit. Some dive skins have a synthetic fleece lining that adds a little thermal protection.

Wetsuit

Most divers use wetsuits for exposure protection. Wetsuits are made from *closed-cell neoprene*. Closed-cell means the neoprene is full of separate little gas bubbles. This gives neoprene good insulating properties, and is one of the ways that a wetsuit keeps you warm. Wetsuits allow a layer of water to leak in next to your skin — don't worry, that's what it's supposed to do. The gas bubbles in a wetsuit compress with water pressure at depth, so it loses some of its insulating properties, but it still keeps you warm because the layer of trapped water is heated by your body. As long as this water remains in place, very little energy is required to keep yourself warm.

Wetsuits come in a variety of thicknesses, ranging from about 2mm for warm water to 7mm for the cold water. Wetsuits are usually lined with a nylon fabric for greater durability and to make them easier to put on and take off. They also come in just about every style configuration you can imagine, so you should be able to find something to suit your needs, whatever they may be. Here are a few:

- **Shorty:** Shorty suits are for diving in warm, tropical waters. Shorties are usually made from 2mm or 3mm neoprene. They are one-piece suits usually with short sleeves and legs, but some have long sleeves. Shorties are best in water that's 80° or warmer. They are usually sufficient for thermal protection, but still leave your arms and legs exposed to possible scratches and stings.

- **Full suit:** Full wetsuits are usually one piece, and zip up the front or the back. They come in the full spectrum of thicknesses — thinner for warmer water; thicker for colder. They provide complete protection from scratches and stings, and offer more thermal protection than a shorty. Depending on the thickness, full suits can be used down to about 70° water temperature.

✔ **Two-piece suit:** Two-piece suits are usually made from thicker neoprene (5mm to 7mm) and are intended for cold water. A two-piece suit normally consists of *farmer johns* (something like a snug, neoprene, bib overall) and a jacket. (Sometimes the jacket extends to midthigh like a shorty and can be worn alone as a shorty in warm water.) A two-piece suit doubles thermal protection in the critical torso area, and along with a hood, booties, and gloves (covered in the "Additional protection" section, later in this chapter), is generally effective in water down to 50°. Below that, most divers require the protection of a dry suit.

Dry suit

Dry suits are for diving in cold water, and they only come in one style: full length arms and legs. The differences in dry suits are in the materials from which they are made, the placement of the zippers, and so on.

Dry suits maintain warmth by surrounding the diver with a layer of warm air trapped in the garments worn under the dry suit. Air in the suit is compressed as the diver descends, but pressure can be equalized by inflation from a low-pressure hose connected to the divers air supply. Of course, as the diver ascends, air added to the suit expands and must be vented. All dry suits have a deflation valve to vent expanding air. They are usually made from neoprene, crushed neoprene, or some kind of lightweight fabric impregnated with a waterproof material (like vulcanized rubber). Dry suits seal at the neck and the wrists with collar and cuffs made of neoprene or latex rubber. Dry suit booties are usually part of the suit.

Dry suits are made possible by technology developed in the space program — a special water-tight (and air-tight) zipper. These zippers are usually positioned across the shoulders or the chest, but manufacturers are always looking for a new place to put the zipper to help reduce zipper stress. A terrible thing, zipper stress.

Today's dry suits are manufactured from one of three waterproof materials:

✔ **Coated fabric:** Fabric suits have no insulating value of their own. They rely on the insulating properties of the undergarments. Generally, they offer more freedom of movement than the heavier neoprene suits.

✔ **Neoprene:** Neoprene dry suits, like wetsuits, have some insulating value of their own, so you can wear lighter-weight undergarments and they retain some insulating properties, even if they flood.

✔ **Crushed neoprene:** These suits are a lot tougher than neoprene suits, but like the coated fabric suits, they have few insulating properties of their own. They are more comfortable and flexible than coated fabric, but they require the same kind of warm undergarments. They are bulkier and heavier than coated fabric.

In really cold water (50° and below) dry suits are the only way to go. They come with a few drawbacks, however.

✔ **Maintenance:** The biggest problem with dry suits is that they can be a maintenance hassle. They have to be cleaned, dried, lubricated, stored, and cared for after each and every dive. Fail in your duties and your expensive suit may die a moldy, early death. Of course, a dry suit is no problem at all if you can afford a valet.

✔ **Expense:** If you can afford a valet, you can afford a dry suit. If not, well, maybe you'd better check the piggy bank. Dry suits are the most expensive kind of exposure suit on the market. Expect to drop a good-sized chunk of change. Oh yeah — you'll also have to buy bigger fins to go over those built-in booties, too. Still, if you're serious about cold water diving, it's a good investment.

✔ **Bulkiness:** Not exactly the perfect traveling companion. One of these suits just about gags your dive bag — never mind the all the other junk. Dry suits also require you to wear more weight than other kinds of suits, to offset the added buoyancy.

✔ **Training:** You need to learn how to use the dry suit. Essentially, you have to know how to vent the expanding air when you ascend to keep from doing an uncontrolled butt-first ascent and pop up next to the boat like Bobo the balloon boy.

If you plan to dive intensively in cold-water environments, and you can put up the extra cash and deal with the extra hassles, you'll definitely be more comfortable underwater in a dry suit. If all of this seems too daunting, get a wetsuit.

Selecting an exposure suit

The first decision you have to make is what kind of suit you're going to buy: a dive skin, a wetsuit, or a dry suit. What kind of suit you buy depends on how much thermal protection you need. That seems like a pretty straightforward call, but whether you're going to feel cold at a particular time and temperature depends on many complex, interrelated factors. The average water temperature in the places that you plan to do most of your diving is important, but water temperature may drop quickly as you descend. How much energy you expend before and during your dive makes a difference in how warm you feel, how long you stay down, the weather on the boat ride out, the air temperature, your personal tolerance to cold, and so on. All you can do is make your best guess. Most divers get a wetsuit of some kind because it can be used in a broad range of temperatures and is fairly low-maintenance.

✔ **Dive skin:** If you've never put your toe in anything under 80°, and you're more concerned about scrapes and sunburn than cold, a dive skin is probably all you need. If you opt for the dive skin, it's as simple as finding the one you want in your size. If you've been buying your own clothes for a while now, you shouldn't need much help. Dive skins are meant to fit snug on the body and people hate the way they look in one.

✓ **Wetsuit:** For a wetsuit, the procedure isn't much different. You have to decide whether you want a shorty, a full suit, or a two-piece suit, and how thick you want it to be. This is a judgment you should make depending on where you expect to dive: tropical or cold water. If you have to compromise, you're better off with a thicker suit than a thinner one. You may want to buy both a dive skin and a wetsuit.

✓ **Dry suit:** Buying a dry suit is somewhat more involved. Because the dry suit relies on airspace for warmth, fit is important. A dry suit shouldn't be snug like a dive skin or a wetsuit, because this leaves no room for the insulating airspace. It should be loose, but it shouldn't be baggy. The dry suit dealer will help you get a good fit. He'd better, for that price!

Additional protection

Your head loses body heat faster than any other part of your body. That's not a very good thing because, in most people, this is where the brain is located and most physiologists agree that the brain is a fairly important organ. In cold water, your head needs thermal protection. Hands and feet can stand more exposure, but they don't have much in the way of insulating body fat (compared to the rest of the body); in cold water, they need protection as well. If your hands aren't working very well, you may have trouble performing with them and that could compromise your safety. Not to worry: Those ever-resourceful dive equipment manufacturers have addressed all of these problems, as you notice in the following sections.

Hoods

Hoods made for dry suits are usually made from thick neoprene wetsuit material. This type of hood, shown in Figure 2-5, is worn over the dry suit neck seal, and ends at the neck. Hoods that are meant to be worn with wetsuits usually have an attached bib that is worn inside the jacket and over the farmer johns in a two-piece suit, or inside a one-piece. Some hoods feature an attached sleeveless vest. These offer good additional thermal protection under a one-piece suit.

Lycra hoods offer additional protection for your sensitive noodle in warm water. The material used in a lycra hood is usually heavier than the stuff used in a dive skin, while the bib is made of the lighter stuff so that it tucks neatly into the top of your dive skin or wetsuit.

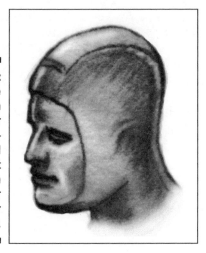

Figure 2-5:
Hoods are
essential in
cold water
diving —
your head
loses heat
faster than
any other
part of your
body.

Gloves

If you've ever tried to perform any kind of task requiring manual dexterity when your hands are icing up, you know why gloves are important. Some divers like to wear lightweight, noninsulated gloves even in warm water. I'm not a big fan of this practice. I feel that it encourages divers to handle things that they shouldn't. Diving with bare hands in the tropics serves as a subtle reminder to keep your hands to yourself.

In cold water, you need neoprene gloves like those in Figure 2-6. Even the best of these compromise your manual dexterity to some degree. Gloves generally come in three varieties:

- ✔ **Light, noninsulated:** These are made from synthetic materials that resist deterioration. Usually the palm is synthetic leather. You don't get much thermal protection in these, but these gloves offer protection from scrapes, cuts, and stings that can be avoided by keeping your hands to yourself underwater. They're also great for kayaking and surfing.

- ✔ **Neoprene gloves:** These gloves offer good thermal protection and protection from scrapes, cuts, and stings (which you don't have to worry about if you keep your hands off things underwater). Neoprene gloves feel clunky, but they keep the thermal rigor mortis from setting in.

- ✔ **Neoprene mittens:** These are made of thicker neoprene, with separate appendages for the thumb, index finger, and the remaining three fingers. When it's really cold, go with the three-finger neoprene mittens. A pair of these severely limit your guitar-playing. For a variety of reasons, though, the popularity of underwater guitar has been waning since the '60s.

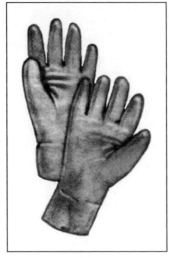

Did I mention you should keep your hands off the marine life? If I didn't, consider it mentioned.

Booties

Booties keep your feet warm and protect them from chafing when you wear adjustable fins. They protect your feet when you're wading out to make a shore dive (see Chapter 5), and they also look really stylish.

Standard features on neoprene booties, shown in Figure 2-7, include molded soles and zippers up the side for ease of entry. Shopping for booties is easy — get the thickness you want and find a pair that fits. Because they're made of squishy soft neoprene, the fit isn't as critical as it is with a pair of shoes.

Tank

The tank, or air cylinder, supplies the air you breathe while underwater on scuba, as well as air for buoyancy control. All scuba tanks have a simple on/off valve that usually incorporates a burst disk to guard against overfilling, and a standardized o-ring valve that attaches to the first-stage regulator (covered in the "Regulator" section, later in this chapter). If you plan to do all of your diving on vacation in a exotic, tropical destination, you probably don't need to buy a tank — tanks are bulky and difficult to transport. Because the o-ring valve has become pretty well standardized, you can find a rental tank that's compatible with your gear at any dive shop. If you live within driving distance of great diving and you plan to do most of your diving close to home, you may find it worth your while to invest in a tank of your own, rather than rent.

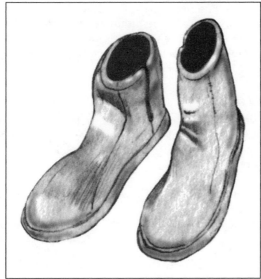

Figure 2-7:
Booties
keep your
little
tootsies
snug and
protect
them from
chafing
when you
wear
adjustable
fins.

Tank materials

For recreational diving, tanks are made from either steel or aluminum.

- **Steel tanks:** These tanks are hard and resist damage better than aluminum. They are also heavier than aluminum tanks, and allow the diver to use less weight (see the "Weights" section, later in this chapter). The drawback to steel tanks is that they require more maintenance to prevent rust and corrosion.

- **Aluminum tanks:** These tanks also corrode with exposure to the elements, but exposure forms a coating of aluminum oxide of the surface that inhibits further corrosion. Because of their low maintenance, aluminum tanks are common as rentals in dive shops.

Steel tanks are usually galvanized (and sometimes painted) to prevent corrosion. Aluminum tanks don't really need to be coated, but they frequently are for cosmetic reasons.

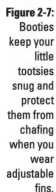

Most tanks have a plastic boot around the bottom to prevent damage and help them stand upright. These are frequently flattened around the rim to help keep the tank from rolling when it's laid on its side.

Tank size

Rental tanks are generally uniform in size and shape, but if you're shopping for your own, you can find them in a wide variety of sizes and shapes from short and squat to tall and thin. The most important measurement in a scuba tank, however, is its *holding capacity*. Capacity is measured by how much air it will hold at working pressure — 80 cubic feet is most common for aluminum tanks, that's why they are commonly referred to as *eighties*. One hundred cubic-foot tanks are popular with divers seeking more *bottom time;* that is, diving deeper. Multiple tanks used to be popular and some divers still prefer this kind of setup to a single, larger tank.

Tank inspection and testing

Scuba tanks should be inspected every year and pressure-tested hydrostatically every five years. Take your tanks to a retail dive shop that's certified to do tank inspections and testing. Only a certified technician can perform inspections and tests on scuba tanks.

- ✔ **Inspection:** Inspection consists of the technician removing the valve and looking inside the tank, with the aid of a special light, for signs of corrosion. He also examines the valve. If the tank passes the inspection, the inspector reassembles it and affixes a sticker telling where and when the tank was inspected. Responsible dive shops won't refill a tank that doesn't have a current sticker.

- ✔ **Hydrostatic testing:** Every five years, the tank needs to be hydrostatically tested. This procedure tests the integrity of the metal by measuring the expansion of the tank with water pressure. This is a test that can only be performed by a certified technician. A tank that doesn't pass a hydrostatic test (or doesn't have an up-to-date sticker) shouldn't be refilled.

Tank codes

Stamped on the shoulder of every scuba tank is a mysterious string of letters and numbers. Not many people give it much thought, because almost every kind of product has some kind of indecipherable serial number or code on it. If you're going to own a tank, though, you may be curious.

- ✔ The code stamped on your scuba tank is in two or three rows. The first marking is several letters, such as DOT or CTC. This designates the governmental agency responsible for regulating the manufacture, sale, and use of the tank. (*DOT* means Department of Transportation; *CTC* is Canadian Transportation Commission.)

- ✔ The second series of characters designates whether the tank is steel or aluminum — 3A and 3AA designate steel tanks; 3AL is aluminum.

- ✔ The third series of characters tells you the maximum pressure to which the tank can be filled in pounds-per-square-inch (psi). In common aluminum tanks, it's about 3,000 psi.

- ✔ In the second, third, and maybe even fourth rows, the information may be presented in all kinds of different orders, but in there someplace will be the serial number of the tank, the manufacturer's identification, and the date that the first hydrostatic test was performed on the tank.

Tank care and maintenance

Damage to the exterior of the tank, such as denting, can weaken the tank structurally. Aluminum tanks are softer than steel tanks and consequently more vulnerable to this kind of damage. The tank valve, usually made from brass, is also susceptible to impact damage and should always be protected. If your tank sustains damage of this kind, have it tested before using it.

Inside a pressurized tank, rust and corrosion occur much more rapidly than outside — that's why it's crucial that moisture be kept out of the cylinder. The compressors used to fill scuba tanks filter and remove moisture from the air before it is pumped into the tank. Make sure that any compressor used to fill your tank has adequate filtering and moisture-removal capability.

When you're not using your tank, keep a couple hundred pounds of pressure in it. Don't store the tank empty completely — moisture can migrate into an empty tank when the valve is open. When you remove the first-stage regulator (covered in the following section) after every dive, partially open the tank valve for a few seconds to blow out any water droplets that may have collected in the valve.

Regulator

It doesn't do you a lot of good to have 80 cubic feet of compressed air on your back unless you can breathe it. The pressure of the air you breathe has to be the same as the pressure surrounding you, otherwise known as the *ambient pressure*. When you're underwater, you're at increased ambient pressure and the air you breathe must be delivered at the same pressure — that's the job of the regulator. A scuba *regulator* is a *demand valve;* that is, it provides air when you inhale and closes when you exhale. This allows for much more economical use of air than you could expect from a free-flowing air supply. Scuba divers generally use *open-circuit scuba* — the diver inhales the air from the regulator and exhales through the regulator into the water. When the diver uses up most of the air in the tank, he must return to the surface for a fresh supply.

Modern regulators consist of two stages: the first-stage regulator and the second-stage regulator. I know it sounds confusing, as if there are actually two regulators, but the first-stage regulator and the second-stage regulator *together* make up *the* regulator. Don't ask me. I would have called it something else.

✔ **First-stage regulator:** The first-stage regulator attaches to the on/off valve on the tank. Pressurized air from the tank feeds directly into the first stage of the regulator. Some of this air is sent directly to the pressure gauge or the dive computer by way of the high pressure hose. The first-stage regulator then senses the surrounding water pressure, adjusts the remaining airflow to match it, then sends it to the second-stage regulator and the other low-pressure hoses.

✔ **Second-stage regulator:** The second-stage regulator is the at the end of the low-pressure hose and delivers air on demand through the mouthpiece (see Figure 2-8). Second-stage regulators come in a variety of styles, but they all function in essentially the same way: When you inhale, the drop in pressure in the mouthpiece depresses a diaphragm in the second-stage regulator that triggers a valve releasing air from the low-pressure hose into the mouthpiece. Voilà! Air — sweet life-giving air! When you exhale, the pressure is equalized in the mouthpiece and the valve closes.

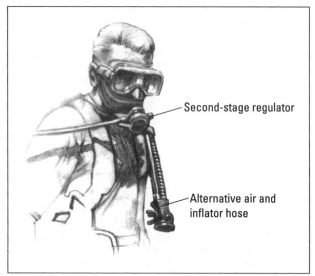

Figure 2-8: Combining the alternate air source with the BC inflator helps cut down on the number of dangling hoses.

Second-stage regulator

Alternative air and inflator hose

Ports in the mouthpiece direct the exhaust into the water — usually out the sides, keeping the bubbles from rising directly in front of your face. A purge valve on the front of the mouthpiece depresses the diaphragm mechanically, allowing you to clear the mouthpiece with the touch of a button, should you need to. Some second-stage regulators allow you to adjust the ease with which the valve opens — a handy feature on your backup that keeps it from leaking air accidentally.

Whether a regulator has a piston or diaphragm sensor or is made from brass or titanium doesn't make a lot of difference to you. You want the thing to deliver air when you need it. You want it to be easy to breathe through, provide a dependable air supply, and be easy and cheap to fix (should repairs be required). Fortunately, regulators are simple devices that are manufactured to a high standard. It's really pretty hard to go wrong, but ask around before you buy — the experiences of other divers are a good resource in evaluating all kinds of equipment. Try out some regulators in the store for comfort and breathing ease.

The most important consideration in buying a regulator is the availability of parts, and how quickly and easily you can get it serviced. Buy your regulator from a reliable shop with a good reputation for service.

Alternate air source

Every certified diver receives training in the use of an alternate air source, and it's considered standard equipment for every diver to carry one. An alternate air source can be used as backup to your primary second-stage regulator in the unlikely event that it malfunctions. Far more likely, though, is the possibility that your alternate air source is used by another diver who runs out of air (or you may have to use another diver's alternate air source, if you run out). The alternate air source allows you to make a normal ascent. Of the four types in the following bullet list, the vast majority of divers use one of the first two because both draw from your scuba tank. The final two types require you to carry a second, smaller tank.

- ✔ **The octopus:** Most often, the alternate air source is an additional second-stage regulator connected to your first-stage regulator by a low-pressure hose exactly as your primary air supply. This additional second-stage regulator is known as the *octopus*. It normally has a slightly longer hose than the primary second-stage regulator, and is used in the same way.

- ✔ **Alternate air and inflator:** This device (refer to Figure 2-8) combines the buoyancy control device inflator (see the following "Buoyancy control device" section) with an additional second-stage regulator, using the same low-pressure hose for both. Consolidating the alternate air source with the inflator hose helps cut down on all the hoses and dangling stuff.

- ✔ **Pony bottles:** A *pony bottle* is a separate, smaller, scuba tank carried along with the main air supply. A pony bottle has its own first- and second-stage regulator, so it's an entirely independent air supply, unlike the octopus or alternate air and inflator, which both draw from the main scuba tank. Pony bottles usually contain between 12 and 20 cubic feet — enough to make a safe ascent, including a safety stop. They are most popular with deep divers, wreck divers, and others who stands more chance of using up their own air.

- ✔ **Ascent bottle:** An *ascent bottle* is like a small pony bottle, but the regulator is built into the valve on top of the tank. The ascent bottle doesn't contain a lot of air, but it's enough to get you to the surface. This little bottle is usually attached to the buoyancy control device (see the following section) and can be passed between divers.

Buoyancy control device

The *buoyancy control device (BCD)* or *buoyancy compensator (BC)*, shown in Figure 2-9, is mandatory equipment for a scuba diver. It serves as a backpack to carry the air cylinder, provides flotation at the surface, and adjusts buoyancy underwater. The BC is the one piece of scuba gear that's subject to the most tinkering and reinvention with brand new features you simply can't do without, but underneath it all, it's a simple bladder that can be filled with, or purged of, air. Even with all the differences in styling and extra gimmicks, they all share a few features:

Figure 2-9:
Your BC and regulator are the heart of your diving equipment. Your regulator allows you to breathe underwater, and your BC lets you adjust your buoyancy.

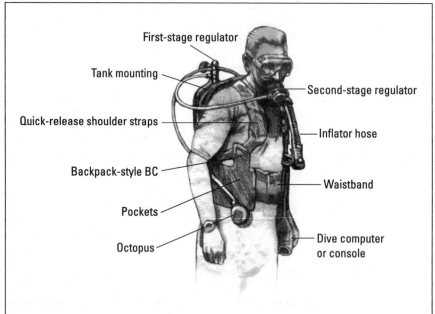

First-stage regulator

Tank mounting

Quick-release shoulder straps

Backpack-style BC

Pockets

Octopus

Second-stage regulator

Inflator hose

Waistband

Dive computer or console

- ✔ **Air bladder:** An internal air cell, usually a single or double bladder on the back, on either side of the tank, or wrapping around under the arms. It's made from tough, durable urethane plastic.

- ✔ **Inflator hose:** An inflator hose attached at the left shoulder allows the diver to inflate the BC manually by depressing a button and blowing into the mouthpiece, or by means of a low-pressure hose connected to the diver's first-stage regulator by depressing a separate button. On some BCs, the power-inflator low-pressure hose is also equipped with a alternate air source. (See the "Alternate air source" section, earlier in this chapter.)

- ✔ **Pressure release valve:** The pressure release valve pr◯ from rupturing if it overfills with air. Usually the press◯ integrated with the dump valve (see the following bu◯ mally placed where the inflator hose attaches to the ᴮᴄ◯ shoulder).

- ✔ **Dump valve:** The dump valve vents air from the bladder of the BC. Most commonly, it is located at the left shoulder where the inflator hose connects to the BC and is integrated with the pressure release valve. Many BCs have an additional dump valve at the bottom, at the right hip. This arrangement allows the diver to vent air in the upright position from the shoulder, or inverted from the hip valve.

- ✔ **Tank mounting:** All modern BCs incorporate a tank mounting — usually a rigid, backpack-type design built into the BC. The tank is held in place by a heavy nylon web strap with a locking buckle. This allows the BC to secure almost any size and shape tank.

- ✔ **Waistband:** The front of the BC jacket is normally closed by an adjustable Velcro cummerbund or an adjustable strap with a Fastex-type buckle.

In addition to the standard features, a typical BC comes with one or more optional features, as well:

- ✔ **Integrated weights:** Many BCs feature special pockets for holding weights that allow you to drop the weights easily in an emergency situation. These systems allow you to dispense with awkward, and often uncomfortable, weight belts.

- ✔ **Pockets:** Some BCs feature pockets with quick-draining mesh bottoms for carrying a slate, dive table, safety sausage, or other loose items. (See the "Optional Gear" section, near the end of this chapter.)

- ✔ **Accessory rings:** These let you clip additional stuff to your BC, such as lights, tools, reflectors, fuzzy dice, and so forth. They're usually located on the front where they are easy to reach, and made from stainless steel so that they don't corrode.

- ✔ **Hose retainers:** These are little plastic clips and Velcro tabs that allow you to secure all those dangling hoses. That way, you know exactly where to find them and aren't dragging them across the reef.

- ✔ **Quick-release shoulder straps:** Fastex-type buckles on the shoulder straps make the BC easier to get in and out of, whether you're in or out of the water.

Manufacturers are always coming up with new features on their BCs. Maybe unlimited air and jetpack propulsion units aren't too far in the future.

Weights

Divers wear weights to compensate for their natural buoyancy and the buoyancy of their wetsuit and other gear. Unless they're integrated into the BC, weights are worn on a belt. There are a couple of different kinds of belts and weights:

- ✔ The most common is a nylon web belt with a plastic, quick-release buckle and rectangular lead block weights. The individual weights are slotted so that the belt can be threaded through them and is fastened around the hips below the BC. This kind of weight belt is simple and cheap. If you travel to your dive destinations and don't want to carry weights, this is the kind of weight belt you most commonly encounter. If you have a BC with an integrated weight system, it is normally designed to accommodate the rectangular block weights used on this type of weight belt and several other kinds as well.

- ✔ Some divers find the standard weight belt uncomfortable, and find adding or removing weight (a pretty common practice) time-consuming. Instead, you can use a belt with pockets that takes block weights or pre-measured bags of lead shot, or a belt that takes only the bags of lead shot. These types of belts are softer and more comfortable than the block weights and the pockets, are usually sealed with a Velcro closure, and are quick and easy to access.

In addition to rectangular blocks, lead weights also come as cylinders with rounded ends — these are known as bullet weights. Bullet weights are threaded through a slot in the center. Both bullet and block weights are sometimes coated with a heavy duty vinyl. Lead is a soft metal and is easily damaged.

Gauges

To dive safely there is certain information you need to have. You need to know how much air remains in your tank at any given time, your current depth, the maximum depth you reach during your dive, and how long you've been under. (A dive computer, covered in the following section, provides all of this information, calculates your nitrogen absorption, and provides a lot more information that may not be crucial, but is certainly nice to have.) A standard instrument console and a good dive watch will provide all the information you need for a particular dive, but you will be required to calculate your own nitrogen absorption. A standard instrument console, shown in Figure 2-10, consists of the following:

- ✔ **Pressure gauge:** It is essential that you know how much air you have left at all times. When your remaining air gets down around 500 psi, it's time to end the dive and start back to the surface. When you reach the halfway mark between your starting pressure and 500 psi, you know it's time to start back to the boat or shore.

✔ **Depth gauge:** Exceeding the depth limits for recreational diving can take you outside the guidelines for no-decompression diving and put you at risk for decompression sickness and nitrogen narcosis (see Chapter 7). A depth gauge keeps you informed of your present depth. You should monitor it continuously during your dive.

✔ **Compass:** You're probably already familiar with a magnetic compass. A common compass usually has a circular rotating *bezel* (divided into 360 degrees) and a free-floating magnetic needle, suspended in some kind of liquid, that points to magnetic north. Dive compasses work exactly the same way as the terrestrial variety.

Figure 2-10:
A typical dive console includes a compass, depth gauge, and pressure gauge.

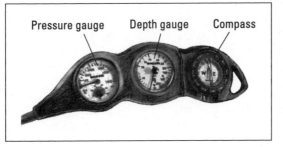

Pressure gauge   Depth gauge   Compass

Computer

Dive computers have virtually revolutionized scuba diving. In addition to showing your remaining air pressure and present depth, a dive computer (shown in Figure 2-11) provides some or all of the following information:

✔ Maximum depth reached during the dive

✔ Water temperature

✔ Elapsed bottom time

✔ Time remaining based on rate of air consumption

✔ Rate of ascent and required safety stops

✔ Cylinder pressure at the beginning and end of the dive

✔ Temperature at maximum depth

✔ Date and time

Probably the single feature that has made dive computers so popular, however, is their capacity to calculate nitrogen absorption and provide divers with accurate, ongoing information on the following:

✔ Decompression time required (if any)

✔ Required surface interval before diving again

✔ Projected depths and times for subsequent dives

✔ Surface time required before flying

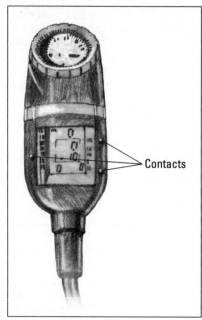

Contacts

Figure 2-11:
Dive computers provide all of the information you need on your dive, including your nitrogen absorption.

Because computer calculations are ongoing and based on the record of your actual diving, they allow more bottom time than more conservative estimates.

Most dive computers are activated on contact with water, but don't register the event as a dive unless the computer exceeds a given depth — usually about 5 feet. All computer calculations are based on the fitness of the average diver. Most computers are capable of making adjustments, but no computer can tell whether you're anxious, tired, or battling a current — no computer can monitor the actual physiological condition of an individual diver.

Computers are a tremendous tool for divers, but they aren't infallible. Don't become completely dependent on the computer. Dive computers are reliable, but they have been known to conk out. Dive with a back-up pressure gauge, depth gauge, and a watch (see the following section).

The dive computer records data from your dive every 60 seconds or so and stores it for later retrieval. That way, you can wait until you get home to fill in your logbook. Many computers allow you to download the data directly to your home computer, as well.

Dive watch

A dive watch is the same basic instrument you probably have attached to your wrist right now. They come in both analog and digital varieties. The important difference in a dive watch, of course, is that it is waterproof and pressure rated down to a certain number of feet (depending on how much you spend). An analog dive watch also has a rotating bezel divided into 60 minutes. Align the 0 mark with your minute hand at the beginning of your dive to keep track of the elapsed time. A digital watch often has a stopwatch, alarm, and lots of other stuff, but it can be hard to read in the dim underwater light.

Optional Gear

In addition to all the stuff you need, there's lots of stuff that's nice to have and makes diving safer, more fun, or just gives you more opportunities to dispose of that annoying disposable income.

✔ **Dive light:** A dive light is mandatory equipment on a night dive, a cavern dive, or a wreck dive; in fact, you may want to have two. They are handy on just about any dive to see the true colors of objects underwater, and to peek into dark cracks and crevices where some of the reef's most fascinating inhabitants may be hiding out.

Dive lights come in a whole array of sizes and shapes. If you plan to do any night diving, you probably want a large primary light and a smaller back-up unit. For day use only, the smaller back-up-sized unit is probably sufficient, but nothing lights up those hidden underwater colors like one of those mondo lanterns. Of course, they can't be clipped to your BC or dangled from your wrist the way a more modest light can.

✔ **Knife:** A dive knife is one of those marginal items. You could make thousands of dives without one and never miss it, but if you ever get tangled in some fishing line or a discarded net, it's absolutely essential. Maybe you don't need one, but at least one member of your party of divers should carry a knife, like the one in Figure 2-12.

Knives are also handy for taking rough measurements and especially for tapping on your tank to attract the attention of other divers underwater. Dive knives come in a wide variety of styles, but they are usually all made from stainless steel. In addition to a cutting edge, look for a dive knife that has an edged notch for cutting line and a second, serrated edge for sawing. Most dive knives come with a sheath that has two rubber straps and a quick-release locking mechanism. A dive knife can be worn on any limb, but most often is worn on the inside of the calf for easy access and to avoid entanglement.

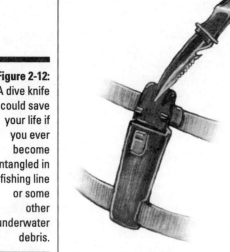

✔ **Safety sausage:** You may never need it, but it's a good idea to carry a safety sausage. A *safety sausage* is a bright-orange plastic tube, about 4 feet long, that rolls up and stashes in the pocket of your BC until you need it. Its function is to make you more visible at the surface. A diver at the surface can be difficult to see, especially in choppy surface conditions. At the surface, you inflate the safety sausage and hold on to one end to create a highly visible pylon at the surface that announces your location.

✔ **Slate:** Every diver should know basic hand signals (see Chapter 5), but at some point, hand signals may be inadequate to the task. Your dive buddy may be waving his arms around and making all manner of esoteric gestures and the only thing you're really sure of is that he has no future as a mime. With a slate, he can share his thoughts with written language. A slate is usually about 5 x 7 inches and comes with a pencil for writing underwater. It's a great way for you and your dive buddy to share an experience near a reef and your feelings about dialectical materialism at the same time.

✔ **Logbook:** Your logbook is a record of your dives. A certification card substantiates your certification, but a dive guide or dive shop really has no way of gauging your level of experience from a *C-card* (certification card) alone. Some operators may want to see both your C-card and your logbook before they will provide services. Logbooks may be accepted as proof of experience for advanced scuba training and they just make good reading on a rainy night — go back and relive those fond underwater memories that would otherwise have been forgotten.

Every major certification agency prints a logbook. Just fill in the blanks. In addition to the traditional written logbook, a number of companies sell logbook software that allows you to download data directly from your dive computer to your home computer, make additional comments, and print the record. Cool.

✔ **Dive bag:** Dive bags provide a place for you to consolidate all the considerable pile of dive stuff you accumulate, and a way to haul it from place to place. They come in all kinds of configurations, but they usually have a single, large main compartment and several smaller pockets, including two long ones for your fins (see Figure 2-13). Dive bags are constructed of heavy nylon fabric (which won't rot when it gets wet) and nylon zippers (which won't corrode and freeze up when they, inevitably, are pickled in ocean brine). Some have wheels, a retractable handle, backpack straps, and a zip-off pocket for your regulator and computer — you can get just about any options you want.

Another handy dive bag is made entirely, or mostly, of nylon mesh and is known as a *dunk bag*. These things are great for hauling around all your dripping gear after a dive, but before you've had the opportunity to rinse and dry it.

✔ **Scooter:** A scooter is essentially a propeller enclosed in a streamlined waterproof housing. Some have a variable speed control, some are simply on/off, but they all shut off when the diver releases the handle.

Figure 2-13:
Your dive bag allows you to consolidate your gear and get to your diving destination with ease.

With a scooter, you can cover a lot more terrain with a lot less effort, but they also make getting into trouble pretty effortless as well. It's all too easy to be zooming all over the reef and completely lose track of your dive buddy, the direction of the boat and everything else — oops, when was the last time you checked your air? Oh man, is that all that's left?

It's no fun to have your scooter conk out a half-mile from the boat either, and face a long swim back dragging a dead scooter, or have it conk out anywhere and discover you don't have enough air to get back.

Scooters can take you down, and back up again, a lot faster than you could normally make the trip. Going down isn't a problem, as long as you are able to equalize quickly; coming up is a different matter — several kinds of injuries and other problems are associated with too fast an ascent. If you do use a scooter, make it a rule never to use one to ascend.

✓ **Comlink:** There are lots of different underwater communication systems available these days. If simple hand gestures or a slate don't seem to be enough, you can check out one of these systems, but it's probably more than you need. A *comlink*, or communication system, comes in a range of prices, although none is really cheap. They range from high-end stuff, with fully enclosed mask/regulator, to a simple microphone that can be used with an ordinary mask.

Renting versus purchasing

Almost every beach resort has snorkel gear for rent, but sooner or later, most divers — whether free divers or scuba — want their own mask, fins, and snorkel. There's nothing wrong with rental gear, but sometimes you have a hard time getting a good fit from a rental setup. Owning your own ensures a good fit, and the same fit, every time.

Likewise, most scuba divers get used to the buoyancy and controls of their own BC, the fit of their own wetsuit, the readout on their own computer and so forth, and the more comfortable you are, the better the dive you're likely to have. On the other hand, it's hard to justify the expense if you dive so infrequently that your own gear is no more familiar to you than rental stuff. So, think of how often you plan to use the stuff. If you want to go on vacation to exotic destinations all over the world and dive until your

middle name is nitrogen, you better have your own gear.

Don't expect the rentals — except for tanks and weights — to be up to snuff on every island under the tropical sun. Wherever you go, the quality of the air in the tanks is almost always very good, and an 8-pound weight weighs exactly 8 pounds. So, if you're going to travel to dive, don't bother buying tanks and weights. Often, your dive destination will require a connecting flight from the international airport on a smaller plane that monitors overweight baggage very closely, so you'd pay a small fortune in additional fees. Most airlines won't allow a pressurized cylinder on the plane and require that your cylinders travel with the valve completely open — a really bad practice for scuba cylinders, because this allows moisture to enter the cylinder and hasten the end of its useful life.

What You Don't Need

You do need scuba training and certification by a qualified agency (see Chapter 3 and the Appendix), basic equipment, good sense, and good judgment. You don't need all the latest high-tech proprietary gadgets. If you really want a titanium regulator, ergonomic fins, and a tri-color, neon Lamotex wetsuit (don't look for it — there's no such thing as Lamotex), that's fine, but ordinary diving equipment works nicely and is a lot cheaper.

General Maintenance and Repairs

Diving equipment, like everything else in the universe, is composed of restless molecules that long to continue their journey through the chaos of protean forms crowding the world. Few things in the world hurry them along their way as effectively as seawater. Nothing can arrest the process of deterioration that affects dive gear, but in can be slowed with proper maintenance and repairs.

Rinse your gear thoroughly in freshwater as soon as possible after every dive. Saltwater can make pretty short work of just about anything. Dive gear is made from the most resistant materials, of course, but that doesn't mean they're immune. After you've rinsed your stuff, dry it and store it in a dry place away from sunlight — UV radiation isn't gear-friendly.

Dive equipment is extraordinarily rugged and reliable, but every now and then, something goes wrong. Fortunately, dive gear is also quite simple and some of the simplest repairs — like replacing an o-ring — you can probably do yourself. More complex operations should be left to the experts. Take equipment back to the dive shop where you got it, or contact the manufacturer. When you're at 80 feet, you don't want to find out that you're not as handy with a screwdriver as you thought!

Chapter 3

Breathing Lessons

● ●

In This Chapter

▶ Obtaining scuba certification

▶ Pursuing advanced certification

▶ Diving safely

▶ Monitoring nitrogen

● ●

*A*s a scuba diver, your time underwater isn't restricted to what is possible on a single breath of air — you can use compressed air. While breathing from a bottle of compressed air carried on your back, you can dive as deep as 130 feet and stay underwater until your diminishing air supply forces you to return to the surface (exactly how long that takes depends on how deep you go and how quickly you, as an individual, use air). This astonishing luxury of breathing underwater allows you to explore the underwater world in ways you may never have imagined.

To become a scuba diver, you need to complete a course sponsored by one of the many certifying agencies that currently train scuba divers (see the Appendix for a complete list). When you successfully complete the course, you're issued a *certification card* (also called a *C-card*) that allows you to rent scuba gear, get tanks filled, plan and engage in recreational open-water dives, and participate in guided dives in exotic places — in other words, a certification card is quite literally your passport to underwater adventure.

Are You Ready?

Most certifying agencies require that you be at least 12 years old to become a certified diver. Certifying agencies will undoubtedly decline to certify you if you suffer from heart disease; severe respiratory, ear, or sinus problems; epilepsy; diabetes requiring insulin therapy; disabling mental illness; or severe asthma. For some of these conditions, a doctor may provide a waiver, but you should evaluate the risk carefully before you pursue such a course.

Scuba diving can be physically demanding, especially in less-than-ideal conditions. A grossly out-of-shape diver can get in trouble in a hurry underwater, and represents a danger to others, as well as himself. You don't have to be a conditioned athlete to dive, but you shouldn't be a dedicated sofa tuber, either. If you get some kind regular aerobic exercise, you're probably fit enough to dive.

Most certifying agencies require that you meet a standard similar to the following one before they can certify you. These criteria will also serve as a good fitness test if you have a pool available.

- ✔ Swim 200 yards (approximately four lengths of an Olympic-size pool).
- ✔ Submerge your head and open your eyes underwater.
- ✔ Stay afloat for 10 minutes without snorkeling gear or outside assistance.
- ✔ Swim underwater for 15 yards without gear and without pushing off the side of the pool.

Certifiable

There are devotees and detractors for each and every certifying agency — many divers who have certifications from more than one. This is the kind of thing that people love to argue and debate endlessly, but the object of becoming certified is to learn how to scuba dive safely and competently, not necessarily to become a member of a club. I'm certified by PADI, so I'm more familiar with its program than with the others, but all of the agencies do a pretty good job.

If you dive long enough, you hear old-timers complaining about how the agencies are only concerned with making money, how divers were so much better trained in the old days, and so on. Baloney. Even if it were true, it wouldn't make any difference because you have to make use of the training that's available now. Today's training is as good (or better) than it ever was — that's because it's essentially the same. If you want to be well-trained, be a good student: Pay attention and make sure that you understand everything the instructor is trying to teach you before you move on to the next subject. And ignore the curmudgeons.

Which certifying agency you choose may come down to which one the dive shop nearest your house subscribes to — that's as good a criterion as any. If you want to shop around, contact those in the Appendix, ask them to send you their materials, and talk to one of their representatives. Go with the one that best meets your specific needs.

School days

No matter which agency you sign up with, your basic scuba training generally takes a three-pronged approach: academic training, pool or confined water training, and open water training. *Confined water* is usually a pool, but it could be a protected, shallow lagoon or similar body of water. *Open water* is the ocean, a lake, a quarry, or any similar body of water. Your diver education goes something like this:

✓ **Academic:** In a classroom, you study the information presented by your instructor — subjects like the effects of the underwater environment on the human body, use of the equipment, emergency procedures, communications, navigation, and so on. You're tested on the knowledge you accumulate — through a written test — as you go. If you did pretty well on it, you move on to the next subject. If you don't get it yet, you get extra training on your area of weakness, and then try it again.

If you're one of those people who hated school, barely scraped by in math and science, and live in perpetual fear you may one day be required to do basic arithmetic, relax. Learning to dive is not quantum physics or even high school algebra. Rest assured, the dive shop will be more than willing to take all the time you need, and give you the kind of personal attention you never got at your old elementary school.

Another option is to study with interactive CD-ROM or video — at home, on your own schedule — and then schedule meetings with your instructor at your mutual convenience. This has the advantage of fitting into your busy schedule. If you choose to train this way, you can still usually do your pool sessions with a group, or you can schedule private pool sessions. All of the major agencies offer this option.

✓ **Pool or confined water training:** All of the lessons from the classroom are reinforced with practical demonstrations and hands-on learning in the pool or in confined water. After you master one skill, you move on to the next. Pool sessions are usually scheduled for a group (see the color photo section of this book for an example), but you can schedule private ones if you're willing to pay extra.

✓ **Open water training:** After you go through the entire list of skills, and the instructor deems you ready, you demonstrate your skills in open water. Usually, open water training is held for a few hours on weeknights over the course of a couple weeks, or on a couple of intensive weekends. Your open water dives can be done with a group or privately, although scheduling private lessons with your instructor costs more.

You can also get a referral letter to do your open water dives at the vacation destination of your choice. That's a pretty good option if you live somewhere where open water diving conditions are less than optimum, or if you're planning a vacation. Do your classroom and pool work at home, and then head for some exotic tropical destination to get your open water dives and your C-card — an especially attractive option in the winter. While your neighbors shovel snow and dry their mittens, you float around in the bath-warm waters of Cozumel, Hawaii, or the Bahamas blowing bubbles and come home as a certified diver. If you choose to pursue this option, PADI training has some advantage over the other agencies — 90,000 instructors at 4,000 resorts in 175 countries and territories worldwide — that's a lot more than everybody else.

✔ **C-card:** After your instructor passes you in open water, you are issued your C-card and membership in the community of divers.

Upward and onward

If you decide to get further training (see the "Continuing on" sidebar in this chapter), you proceed according to the plan of the particular agency in which you become certified. I'm most familiar with PADI, so I use its terminology here. They're all a little different, and they all call it something slightly different, but they're all very similar in substance. The progression goes something like this:

✔ **Scuba Diver:** This is the basic certification course that you need to become a scuba diver. You study the principles involved in diving, how to set up and use the equipment, and how to dive safely. You get this certification by completing a portion of the Open Water Diver course — essentially it allows you to dive under supervision. If you want to go to vacation destinations and dive, you want at least a Scuba Diver certification.

✔ **Open Water Diver:** This is the full entry-level certification. It allows you to dive without supervision (but with your buddy), get air filled, and plan and conduct your own dives.

Continuing on

All of the certifying agencies issue an entry-level certification card, but they don't stop there. In fact, they all have enough advanced and specialty courses to keep you busy for years. How far you want to go with it is up to you, of course. You can discover many useful and wondrous things and be a better diver for it, but if all you ever plan to do is dive on the local reef or at your vacation destination, all you *need* is an entry-level certification.

Advanced courses (covered more thoroughly in Chapter 12) are helpful — some of them are

necessary if you want to pursue a special interest like cave or wreck diving — but there's no substitute for the knowledge you acquire by logging a lot of dives and sharing experiences with the people you meet on dive boats. You won't meet many out there who aren't friendly and generous about sharing their experience and wisdom. Because they're doing something they like, and because they're usually on vacation, they're almost always in a good mood. In fact, most divers are usually eager to share, and for free. What a deal!

✔ **Advanced Open Water Diver:** All of the agencies call it something different, but the key word here is "advanced." In this course, you take your basic knowledge a little further. You generally complete a night dive, a deep dive, or a drift dive (see Chapter 10 for more about the different kinds of dives), a wreck dive, some underwater photography or videography, and demonstrate some other advanced diving skills. Prerequisite: Open Water Diver.

✔ **Specialty:** In this course, you select some particular focus from the agencies list, and get special training in the skills, procedures, techniques, and hazards associated with it. You can become specialized as a night diver, drift diver, underwater photographer, enriched air diver (more about enriched air in Chapter 12), wreck diver, and so on. Open Water certification is a prerequisite to all; some, like wreck diving, also require Advanced Open Water as a prerequisite. Check with your agency for specific requirements.

✔ **Rescue Diver:** A Rescue Diver certification teaches you things that you won't pick up on your own. This course teaches you to deal with other divers in distress, administer first aid, find a missing diver, and so on. This is a really worthwhile course to take, and one that's required if you plan to become an instructor or take some other kind of leadership role. Prerequisite: Open Water, CPR (cardiopulmonary resuscitation).

✔ **Master Diver:** This is generally the highest ranking that you can achieve as a recreational diver. As a Master Diver, you've reached the official apex of recreational diving nomenclature. From there, you enter into the ranks of aspiring instructors. As a candidate for instructor certification, you go through another schedule of courses. (If you want to go on to become an instructor, inquire with your certification agency.) Prerequisites: Advanced, Rescue, Specialty (varies).

Basic Safety

Your basic scuba certification covers all of the basic safety procedures and practices that you need to be a safe diver. Be sure to go over this information before you get in the water — every time that you go diving, particularly if you haven't been diving for six months or more. A much more complete briefing, as well as some valuable practice, is provided in your certification course, but the following sections familiarize you with some of the most important safety issues.

Under pressure

Air spaces in, and around, your body are compressed by the dramatic increase in pressure underwater, and must be equalized. Just as in free diving, the most noticeable air spaces are your ears and your mask.

Equalizing them is done in the same way as it is in free diving (see Chapter 1 for a brief discussion of free diving).

The largest air space in your body is, of course, your lungs. When you free dive, you hold your breath to descend. The increasing pressure compresses your lungs, but because the lungs are quite flexible and designed to compress and expand, you don't experience any discomfort. When you ascend, the lungs return to their original volume, minus whatever air you've consumed during your dive. No problem.

Things are different when you breathe compressed air from a scuba tank. The regulator on your scuba tank delivers air at the same pressure as the surrounding water. If it delivered air at surface pressure, you wouldn't be able to draw a breath underwater because of the water pressure compressing your lungs. When you're 33 feet underwater, you're under twice the pressure you are at the surface, and the regulator on your scuba tank is delivering air to you at twice the pressure as on the surface. You experience no difficulty breathing. No problem.

If you take a breath of compressed air 33 feet underwater, however, and then hold it and ascend to the surface, the air in your lungs (no longer confined by increased pressure) expands to occupy twice the space it occupied at 33 feet — potentially a big problem. That's why the number one, most important rule of scuba diving safety is simply this: Never hold your breath while scuba diving.

As long as you breathe continuously as you ascend, the expanding air vents easily and safely. Should you hold your breath and block your airway, you risk serious injury from the overexpansion of the compressed air — possibly even the rupture of your lungs.

Keep your airway open and allow the expanding air to vent as you ascend. By making an "ah" sound as you ascend and exhaling a slight, steady stream of bubbles, you can ensure that you vent the expanding air. It's possible to make an emergency ascent of this kind, but it's unlikely that you'll ever need to do this in an emergency.

The right stuff

Your scuba equipment is what allows you to make your extended visits to the underwater realm. Your safety and the quality of your underwater experience depend on it — make sure your equipment is functional and in good repair.

Scuba equipment is simple in design and function, and is generally manufactured to a high standard. Failures are rare, but you should inspect your gear carefully before you use it, especially if you haven't used it for a while. Test your equipment underwater, if possible, before you depart on an overseas vacation. All of your plans could be foiled by the lack of an inexpensive part that may not be available at your destination.

Your buddy

The buddy system is the basic scuba diving fail-safe. Whenever you make a dive, you're teamed with another diver who stays close to you at all times. That diver is your buddy, and you assist each other putting on and checking out your equipment before the dive, monitoring depth and remaining air, and helping each other with any kind of problem or emergency that may arise during the dive. It's nice if your buddy is a friend that you already know and trust, but buddying up on dive boats is a great way to make new friends, too.

If possible, your buddy's interests and experience should be more or less equivalent to your own. If your interest is in seeing a spectacular reef and your buddy wants to spend his entire bottom time getting the perfect photo of a stationary purple leaf fish, one of you is going to be a pretty unhappy diver — or possibly wander off. Underwater, you should never let your dive buddy out of your sight. (See Chapter 5 for information on communicating with your dive buddy underwater.)

Even though your buddy is there to provide assistance, be careful not to dive in situations or conditions that you're not prepared to deal with, and then take it for granted that your buddy will save you. Assumptions can be dangerous underwater. A friend of mine who is a dive instructor took a group of beginning divers on a dive in the channel islands off Southern California. He was buddied with one of the beginners, but responsible for leading the dive and looking after the entire group. His inexperienced buddy, assigning responsibility for the dive to him, immediately swam off exploring on her own. He signaled for the group to wait where they were and swam off after her, but she had already disappeared into the dense growth of the kelp forest. He was forced to abort the dive and institute missing diver procedures. She was found none the worse for the experience, but the other divers weren't very happy about having to abort their dive, and this annoying incident could easily have become a full-fledged disaster had she become tangled in the kelp without any assistance. You're diving to see the wonders of the underwater world, but don't get so caught up in the spectacle that you forget about your buddy.

A dive buddy is important underwater, of course, but the most critical function of a dive buddy comes back on the boat after the dive — when you spit out your regulator and rip off your mask and shriek: "Man, did you see that gigantic eagle ray?" Your dive buddy's duty is to shout: "Holy moly, that thing was as big as an aircraft carrier!"

Without a dive buddy, it could be depressingly quiet.

The best laid plans

Good planning can avoid a whole raft of trouble. You and your buddy should agree on some limits on time and depth before you go, and allow for a margin of safety. Make sure that you're both familiar with and agree on emergency procedures, and that you both review the hand signals (see Chapter 5 for the lowdown on hand signals). Make sure you're familiar with the dive site — be aware of the conditions and possible hazards before you get in the water. If you're not familiar with the area, make sure you have an experienced guide. Always be prepared to deal with emergencies that may arise.

Know your limits

Don't be afraid to cancel a dive if the weather or the conditions at the site are unfavorable. Diving in bad conditions is more struggle than fun and if an emergency should arise, you'll be that much less prepared to deal with it. It's not unusual to feel a little anxiety before you get in the water (see Chapter 4 for more information on dealing with dive anxiety). It goes away as you gain experience and begin to fill your log book with memories of fun and excitement. Don't let this kind of anxiety keep you from diving, but don't be reckless either. Go at your own pace. Have fun. If you feel that the dive is more than you're prepared to deal with, don't do it.

Likewise, don't hesitate to abort a dive if you feel really uncomfortable. If you begin a dive and don't feel up to it for any reason, you and your buddy should return to the boat or the shore.

Hands off

Don't touch anything that's really beautiful or really ugly — it's probably venomous (the most common venomous creatures can be found in Chapter 9). In fact, try not to touch anything at all. Many marine creatures are extremely delicate. They may not hurt you, but you could be seriously compromising their survival by touching or feeding them. Keep your hands to yourself (which is also an excellent way to practice good buoyancy control). See Chapter 16 for more ways to preserve the underwater environment.

Ascend slowly

When you're ready to end a dive, do the following:

1. **Signal your buddy and begin the ascent together.**

2. **Begin your ascent when you still have sufficient air remaining in your tank. (Never wait until your air supply is exhausted.)**

Go slowly. Check your watch and depth gauge or dive computer and ascend no faster than one foot per second. Make sure you take at least 10 seconds to ascend 10 feet. It's a lot slower than you think.

Breathe continuously as you ascend. Never hold your breath.

3. **Extend one hand over your head, look up at the surface and slowly rotate 360 degrees as you ascend.**

   Looking up and rotating as you ascend allows you to see everything above and behind you. Watch out for boats or any other overhead obstruction.

4. **Whenever possible, make a safety stop when you reach 15 feet.**

   A *safety stop* allows you a little extra time to eliminate nitrogen from your body, further decreasing your risk of decompression sickness (see Chapter 7). To do this, stop, hang in the water column, practice your buoyancy control, and check out conditions on the surface. Wait three minutes at 15 feet before you surface.

Emergency Procedures

If an emergency situation arises, you must do your best to remain calm and not panic. Panicking prevents you from thinking coherently and causes you to use your air faster. You can deal with most situations effectively if you remain calm, determine the problem, and deal with it as you've been trained to do. The most common problems are covered in the following sections.

Equipment failure

Equipment failure is very uncommon. Scuba equipment is simple in design and is manufactured to very high standards. Nevertheless, it can happen. Obviously the chief concern for a scuba diver is the loss of air supply. Scuba equipment is designed so that if it fails it provides continuous airflow rather than no airflow at all. Normally, this is sufficient for the diver to get to the surface. If the air supply does quit, you must go immediately to your alternate air source (see Chapter 2). You must also immediately get your buddy's attention. Swim toward your buddy and bang on your tank at the same time.

Octopus to the rescue

These days, every diver carries an alternate air source— a regulator that can be used as a backup for the primary, or to come to the aid of another diver. This alternate air source is known as the *octopus* (see Chapter 2 for more information). If your primary regulator fails, it's likely that your octopus still works. It can be tested by pushing the *purge button* — this also clears the mouthpiece and prepares it for use. The octopus is used in exactly the same way as your primary regulator. Insert the octopus mouthpiece and make a normal ascent. If both your primary regulator and octopus fail, you must use your buddy's octopus.

If you need to breathe from your buddy's octopus, get his attention and indicate that you're out of air by drawing a finger across your throat — the cutthroat gesture — so that your buddy recognizes the problem. If you don't have the time to make this gesture, simply take his octopus, clear it, and breathe as you normally would. Hold onto him as both of you immediately make a normal ascent. If, for some incomprehensibly bizarre reason, all three of these air supplies should fail, you must make an emergency ascent or ascend while buddy breathing (see the "Buddy, can you spare some air?" section, later in this chapter) on the same air supply.

Emergency ascent

If you somehow become separated from your buddy and your air supply fails, or if your equipment becomes hopelessly tangled in something on the bottom, you must make an emergency swimming ascent. PADI advocates an emergency swimming ascent over buddy breathing (covered in the next section), because buddy breathing is more complicated, requires the cooperation of your buddy, and calls for a lot of practice. PADI teaches the emergency swimming ascent in its certification course. To make an emergency ascent, release and drop your weight belt, kick off the bottom (if you're near it), and swim to the surface making an "ah" sound and exhaling continuously as you ascend. Then manually inflate your BC when you reach the surface.

Buddy, can you spare some air?

Suppose your air supply fails, and, uh oh, your buddy's octopus isn't working either. You now have the option of making an emergency swimming ascent, or sharing your buddy's primary regulator — a procedure known as *buddy breathing*.

Buddy breathing can be difficult if you've never practiced it, but essentially, the procedure goes like this: If you've tried your buddy's octopus, you should already have your buddy's attention, and he is probably aware of the nature of the problem. Point to your buddy's primary air supply. He will take a breath and hand it to you. Take his regulator in your right hand and grab his right shoulder strap with your left hand (it's the one on your left side) — he will grasp your right shoulder strap as well. Take several breaths and hand the regulator back to him as you both start for the surface. This is called buddy breathing. (See the color photo section, near the middle of this book, for an example of this technique.)

It sounds pretty scary for two divers to be relying on the same air supply, but it's surprisingly easy after you get the hang of it. You even develop a kind of rhythm very quickly. The problem is, because you only use this procedure in an emergency, you're not likely to get enough practice with it to develop a level of comfort. If you're forced to resort to buddy breathing, remember that when you aren't breathing from his regulator, blow a thin stream of bubbles and make the sound "ah." This ensures an open airway and allows you to vent expanding compressed air as your surface.

Make Mine Nitro

The air you're breathing as you read this book is a mixture of gases. Most of it, about 79 percent, is nitrogen. Nitrogen isn't a problem at the surface, but underwater, it's another story. Nitrogen in air dissolves in your blood the same way that oxygen does. While oxygen is pretty important to your body's metabolic processes, nitrogen isn't — it plays no part in the processes of your body, not at the surface anyway.

Walking around every day, your body is saturated with nitrogen, which means it has as much nitrogen dissolved in it as it can hold at surface pressure. But if you increase the pressure on your body (like you do when you're underwater), it can hold more. In fact, the greater the pressure, the more dissolved nitrogen it can hold (see Chapter 6). If your body stays at greater pressure long enough, it eventually reaches saturation again and can't dissolve any more nitrogen. If you increase the pressure once more, more nitrogen can be dissolved and your body takes on more until it again reaches saturation for that particular pressure. For all practical purposes, you can never reach a state of nitrogen saturation underwater — it takes about 12 hours and I don't know anybody that can stay underwater that long on a tank of air.

The deeper you go, the greater the difference between the nitrogen dissolved in your tissues and the amount of dissolved nitrogen that your body can hold — so, the deeper you go, the faster you absorb nitrogen. The longer your stay underwater at increased pressure, the more time you have to absorb nitrogen into your tissues — the longer you stay, the more nitrogen you absorb.

Cocktails at 100 feet

"So what?" I hear you asking. "Nitrogen is inert, right? What's the big deal?" Well, it turns out there are two significant problems related to the increased absorption of nitrogen under pressure. The first one is *nitrogen narcosis,* also known as *rapture of the deep* or *getting narked.* (For the second, see the following section.) The theory is that nitrogen that's dissolved in the tissues interferes with the transmission of nerve impulses, and creates an anesthetic effect.

Typically a diver gets narked at 100 feet or below. The effects vary from individual to individual, depending on their physical state and environmental factors. Most divers don't notice any effect above 70 feet. Most divers notice some effect at 100 feet. Nearly all divers notice the effects at 150 feet.

The effect is similar to drinking alcohol — slowed thinking and reaction time, a feeling of well-being and euphoria, carelessness for personal safety, and so on. Bad enough at the Christmas party; very dangerous underwater. Unlike alcohol, nitrogen narcosis occurs as soon as you reach a depth that will trigger it, and goes away as soon as you ascend to shallower water. Although nitrogen narcosis causes no lasting damage and the effects quickly subside, the danger lies in compromising the diver's ability to reason and to make the sound judgments required to complete a safe dive and deal with an emergency.

If you should begin to feel the effects of nitrogen narcosis during a dive, ascend to shallower water immediately.

(Don't) get bent

All that nitrogen dissolved in your tissues at depth may not bring on nitrogen narcosis, but it can still cause problems. As you ascend at the end of your dive, the pressure on your body decreases. At decreased pressure, the body tissues that have absorbed additional nitrogen now contain more than they can hold — they are supersaturated. Nitrogen begins reversing its migration, dissolves out of the tissues, and is eliminated by the body — a process known as *off-gassing*. However, if the rate of ascent causes nitrogen to dissolve out of the tissues faster than the body can eliminate it, it creates bubbles of nitrogen in the tissues. These bubbles result in *decompression sickness (DCS)*, also known as *the bends*.

DCS symptoms, covered in greater detail in Chapter 7, can vary a great deal depending on the size and location of the bubbles in the body. Recent research, in fact, seems to suggest that some bubbles are present after every dive — as long as they're tiny and few, they are carried to the lungs and safely eliminated. When many bubbles combine to form large bubbles, and when the bubbles are many and large, DCS is the result. The effects of DCS can range from annoying to deadly.

DCS most commonly manifests in one of the following ways:

- The skin may look blotchy and burn or itch. This type of DCS normally disappears after a couple of hours.
- Sharp pain may occur in large joints like the elbow.
- Limb paralysis, vertigo, unsteady gait, headache, and blurred vision may occur. DCS can effect the spinal column, the brain, or both. Spinal column symptoms usually start with back pain that may radiate around the trunk, and numbness and tingling in the legs.

This is a partial list of symptoms — the most common ones. DCS can manifest itself in a wide and puzzling variety of ways — there isn't room to list them all here, but they will occur from a few minutes to 48 hours after surfacing — usually within six hours. If you suspect you may have DCS after a dive, don't hesitate: Get treatment immediately.

The treatment for DCS is immediate recompression in a chamber designed for that purpose, and breathing 100 percent oxygen. The affected diver is then slowly decompressed at a rate that allows the body to off-gas the additional nitrogen. Although DCS is a serious condition, it is hardly ever fatal with proper treatment, and it can be avoided by observing the safe time and depth limits established in dive tables (covered in the following section).

Dive tables

The body can safely deal with some of the excess nitrogen that builds up as a result of diving. *Dive tables* have been established to estimate the amount of nitrogen that you accumulate, and keep it within safe levels. Individual physiology varies so greatly that no table can guarantee that you will never get the bends, but if you stay within the suggested limitations and dive conservatively, you shouldn't have any problems.

Nearly every certification agency publishes a dive table — becoming completely familiar with its use in planning your dives is an important part of your training.

Because more nitrogen can be absorbed — and absorbed faster — at greater depths, you should always do the deepest part of your dive first. This keeps nitrogen absorption on any particular dive to a minimum. Limit your first dives to 60 feet or less. When you become more experienced, you can venture deeper, but even then you should keep it within 100 feet — 130 feet maximum. If you do plan to go deeper — 100 feet or below — stay no more than a few minutes and surface slowly, allowing your body to off-gas the accumulated nitrogen. A safety stop is important after a deep dive, so make sure you have enough air left to make one (see the "Ascend slowly" section, earlier in this chapter).

The problem of nitrogen absorption isn't limited to a single dive. It takes several hours after surfacing to off-gas all of the nitrogen that you may have accumulated on a single dive. If you plan to dive again within six hours of your last dive, you must take into consideration the nitrogen that you absorbed on the first dive.

Dive tables are designed so that your diving is no-decompression diving. *Decompression diving* involves making prolonged stops during your ascent to allow for the off-gassing of accumulated nitrogen. Recreational divers should never plan decompression dives.

Computers

Dive computers have almost completely taken over the task of tracking nitrogen accumulation. Computers greatly simplify the task, but if you use one you should still be familiar with the use of tables — computers are not infallible.

Most electronic dive computers are activated when submerged. They continuously calculate nitrogen levels based on a theoretical tissue absorption model or on a mathematical model of the appropriate dive table. Computers display a warning when the no-decompression limit is approached, and display decompression time limits. Because computers continuously monitor time spent at various depths, they generally allow more time underwater than more conservative table calculations do. Most divers consider computers a substantial improvement over calculating from tables, but most divers don't like to balance their checkbooks either.

Part II
Making a Splash

In this part . . .

In this part, I show you what's involved in an actual dive, whether it's from a boat or from shore: From setting up you equipment to breaking it down, and everything in between. I tell you how and why the water, air, and your body behave as they do when you're scuba diving. I also describe the most common kinds of illness, injuries, and complications that affect divers, and how you can avoid running into these problems yourself. And if things do go wrong, I tell you what to do about that, too.

Chapter 4

Not Wet Yet

In This Chapter

▶ Understanding boat dives and shore dives

▶ Assembling your gear

▶ Suiting up for your dive

▶ Managing dive anxiety

Suppose you've finally left that coach-class nightmare behind, checked into the hotel, and you're ready to get wet. So, where do you go from here?

Most often, the answer is to go down to the local dive operator to rent some tanks and weights, and arrange to go on the morning dive boat for a ride to whatever site they plan to visit. Dive shops in most of the world operate to a pretty high standard. Even in countries where abysmal poverty is everywhere, the dive operators always seem to have pure air in their tanks and decent equipment. Very rarely, you come across the fly-by-night entrepreneur filling questionable tanks with a homemade compressor; if that's all you can find, better you should go sightseeing.

Your fellow divers are a valuable resource — don't hesitate to use them. Most are more than happy to fill you in on their opinions about who runs the best operation, what's the best local dive, and so on. Of course, if you book a package trip, it's all taken care of ahead of time. (See Chapter 10 for more information on choosing a dive travel location.)

Pre-Dive

You can dive two ways: from the shore and from the boat. *Shore diving* means — not surprisingly — diving from shore, and involves hauling your equipment to the beach (probably in your car or in a rental), suiting up, and entering the water right there. *Boat diving,* in a curious twist, means riding on a boat out to the dive site somewhere offshore, suiting up, and entering the water from the boat. Weird, huh? Shore diving is usually cheaper than boat diving because you don't have to pay for the boat.

If you're planning to dive someplace that you can drive to on your own, you're probably, although not necessarily, going to be shore diving. If you plan to go on a packaged trip, you're probably going to be boat diving. Whichever type of diving you choose, you need diving equipment (check out Chapter 2 for the story about gear) and if you're scuba diving (as opposed to snorkeling), you need to be certified (see Chapter 3). If you're traveling — especially flying — to a dive destination, you may want to rent gear when you get there, but I prefer to take my own, with the exception of tanks and weights. The tanks and weights available in most places around the world are perfectly adequate and taking your own with you on the plane is a very large pain in the neck. (Keep in mind, though, that owning your own can save you money if you dive a lot locally.) If you're using your own tanks and weights, you need to get your tank filled at the dive shop. If you don't have your own tanks and weights, you need to rent some.

Rental tanks are usually 80-cubic-foot aluminum cylinders, although sometimes you find steel tanks. Steel tanks are heavier than aluminum, so if you're using a steel tank, you can usually use fewer weights. Both kind of tanks operate the same way. Aside from the weight, the material they're made from makes no difference. (Occasionally, you find the odd 100-cubic-foot cylinder in there. If you're a heavy breather, you can get more underwater time from a 100, but they are uncommon in rental gear.) Rent a tank for each dive that you plan to make. Rental tanks almost always look beat up and scuffed, but they are inspected regularly and work just fine.

How much weight you require, on the other hand, is a very individual thing. You may get some idea when you go through your certification training, but you may have been certified back in your chilly home waters in a 7mm wetsuit and so much weight that you could barely stagger around, and now you're doing your first tropical dive in just a dive skin and a smile? Hmm.

Perform this exercise before you go diving to determine how much weight you need:

1. **Go down to a beach or pool with the equipment that you plan to use on your dives.**

   You need water that's over your head, so you don't want a beach with a half-mile hike out to 6-foot water. Don't scoff, there are many such places in the tropics. Obviously, a wading pool is no help either, but you can use a swimming pool.

2. **Put on your gear, including weights.**

   Begin with weight equaling 10 percent of your body weight, if you're wearing a full, cold-water wetsuit. For example, if you weigh 200 pounds, use 20 pounds of weight to start. In warm water, if you're using a shorty or a dive skin, you can start with half as much, or 5 percent of your body weight.

Most rental weights are the old rectangular block style. Ordinarily, you thread them onto a nylon web belt, but you can also use them with most BCs (buoyancy compensators — see Chapter 2) that feature integrated weight systems. If you have to use a belt, get one that goes around your waist, with your wetsuit on, plus about 8 inches to spare.

3. Get in the water.

You need to be in water over your head — wade or snorkel out until you are. If you're in freshwater, remember that you need a little more weight than you do in the ocean. (You have more buoyancy in saltwater than you do in freshwater.)

4. Hang in the water.

Use your scuba tank. Hanging vertically in the water, as motionless as possible, take a normal breath. The water level should be right in the middle of your mask when your lungs are filled, and you should start to sink a little as you exhale.

5. Adjust your weight.

If your mask is completely underwater when your lungs are filled, you need to lose some of the weight. If your mask is completely out of the water, add a little.

Boat diving

More often than not, the best dive sites are only accessible by boat — the ride may take a few minutes or over an hour. In most places, local operators run dive boats out to the best sites. You can charter your own boat, of course, but you can usually save money by booking with a local operator, and you also get the added value of their knowledge of the site. It is possible for you and your buddy to book your own boat and dive the site without the group. For more experienced divers, this is a viable option, but I don't recommend it for beginners. If you choose this option, follow the same kind of planning that you would for a shore dive, explained in the "Shore diving" section, later in this chapter, and make sure the boat operator is experienced with taking divers.

The local operator's boat usually goes out for a morning dive (one or two tanks) and returns for lunch or brings a box lunch to be eaten on board or at a nearby beach before doing a second dive in the afternoon. Bring warm clothes for these day-long excursions. Weather can be extremely variable at sea, especially in the tropics. You may be surprised how cold you can get, even in the warm, humid tropical climate, when you're soaked to the skin from a sudden downpour with the wind blowing on you the whole ride.

Some boats provide storage in which you can stash your dive gear, but even so, make sure that you mark your gear with your name or initials — other people on the boat may have exactly the same fins, BC, or mask that you have. Things tend to get mixed up after a dive when everybody's shedding their equipment and groping for towels.

If you're prone to seasickness (see Chapter 7 for more information), take preventative medication before you get on the boat. It won't do you any good to take it after you're out there chumming the snappers. Stay in the middle of the boat during the trip, where the rolling and pitching is minimized, and try to keep your eyes focused on the horizon.

Normally, you can use the time it takes to get to the site to set up your gear, but if it's a short ride, you may need to set up before you get on the boat.

Boat talk

Here are a few nautical terms so that you don't sound like a total landlubber.

✔ **Bow:** The front end of the boat — the pointy end. When you go to the bow, you are going *forward*. When somebody spots dolphins off the bow, for example, the dolphins are out in front of the boat.

✔ **Stern:** The back end of the boat. When you go to the back end of the boat to put on your snorkeling gear so you can get in the water with the dolphins, you are going toward the stern, or going *aft*.

✔ **Starboard:** The right side of the boat when you're facing the bow.

✔ **Port:** The left side of the boat when you're facing the bow.

✔ **The head:** The toilet.

✔ **The bridge:** Where the controls for the boat are.

✔ **The galley:** Where the food is.

✔ **Windward:** The side of the boat that the wind is coming from.

✔ **Leeward:** Opposite windward — the side you hang over when you're seasick, if you value your clothes and your diving companions at all.

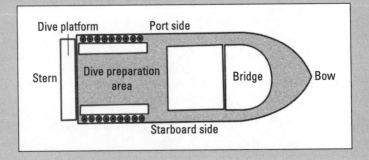

After you arrive at the site, the dive guide or the captain evaluates the conditions and decides whether everything looks good to proceed — don't get in the water until you get the okay. Even if the weather is perfect and everything looks good to you, the captain may notice adverse conditions, such as strong current, that you're not aware of.

Just before you get in the water, the guide gives a briefing of the site, explaining the underwater terrain, telling you where you can expect to see the resident marine life, and outlining the *dive plan* — the course you will follow, how deep you'll go, and so on. Frequently, these briefings are accompanied by illustrations on a chalkboard. For example: "We'll descend to the top of the reef at 40 feet, go over the edge of the wall, and continue down to 70 feet. There are some overhangs here, covered with beautiful purple and pink soft corals. From there, we'll proceed west along the wall. Right next to this giant barrel sponge there's a big green moray living in the reef — I'll see if I can coax him out," and so on. After the briefing is completed, the guide gives instructions on how to enter the water, and it's time to suit up.

The dive plan is a well-researched routine that ensures that you stay safe and that you get the best dive possible for your money. Don't give the guide a lot of grief or make unreasonable demands. If you're an experienced diver, you and your buddy can plan and dive your own dives. If not, stick with the plan that you're presented and earn your stripes.

Shore diving

You and your buddy can charter your own boat and plan your own boat dives, but booking a planned dived with a local operator is usually a lot easier and more cost-effective. Shore diving, however, is a different matter. While local dive operators offer guided shore dives, you may find it cheaper and just as much fun to plan your own. Keep in mind that even a simple shallow dive takes more work and planning on your part than a guided dive does. Some people find this kind of challenge more rewarding — self-reliance is a bonus in diving! Even so, try to make your first few dives with a more experienced buddy.

Planning the dive

Planning your own dive begins by deciding where you want to go and who is going to be your buddy. Many couples enjoy diving together and that certainly makes finding a buddy on a vacation trip easier, but if your partner isn't a diver and you still want to plan your own dives while on vacation, try asking around at the dive shop. You'll have to rent your tanks and weights there anyway (or at least get your own tank filled). If you're planning a local dive and you don't have a buddy, you should be able to locate one through the local dive shop or dive club.

Choosing the appropriate site is somewhat dependent on your objective. Books and magazines can be helpful, as are Chapters 10, 11, 13, and 15 of this book, but the local dive shop is also a good resource. Consult with it about what kind of diving you want to do — the dive shop should be able to help you select the appropriate site and determine the best time of day with the most favorable currents and visibility. Don't forget to take into consideration how far the dive site is from parking — even in the tropics, you have a lot of equipment to carry down to the shore and back again. When determining a primary site, try to decide on an alternative site as well, just in case you can't dive your first choice.

After you select a site and a time, discuss the selection with your buddy and figure out how you're both going to get there with your equipment, what time to meet if you're not going together, and what procedures you plan to follow in the event of an emergency.

Making preparations

The night before you plan to leave for a morning dive, or the morning before an afternoon outing, do the following:

- ✔ **Share your dive plan with somebody who's not going with you.** Just like you would if you were going on a backpacking trip into the wilderness, before you venture into the watery wilderness, share your dive plan with somebody who's not going. Include the time that you expect to return and what procedures they should follow if you don't show up at the appointed time.

- ✔ **Check your equipment.** Gather all of your equipment together in one place and check it to make sure that it's in good shape and functioning correctly.

- ✔ **Check the weather report.** Obviously, you don't want to be trying to dive in the teeth of Hurricane Gertrude or some other atmospheric event, but try to get a report on sea conditions, as well. Sometimes storms that are thousands of miles away can kick up a monster swell — maybe you want to leave your dive gear at home and take your 10-foot pintail down to the beach instead, dude.

- ✔ **Load your stuff.** Make sure you load up so that the things you need first are the last things packed and therefore, the first things unpacked. That way you don't have to spread everything out in the parking lot and keep explaining to all the people who stop that it really isn't a yard sale. Don't forget the stuff that you'll want when you're not in the water, like sunglasses, drinking water, sunscreen, lunch, and so on.

Evaluations

When you and your buddy arrive at the dive site, you want to evaluate the conditions before you suit up or start trudging all your gear down to the beach.

✔ **Sea conditions.** If the surf is large, the currents strong, or if for any other reason you don't feel confident about attempting your dive under current conditions, consider your secondary dive site. If that one looks bad too, abort the dive. Every diver has to abort a dive from time to time.

✔ **Set a course.** With your dive buddy, decide on an entry point, a course to follow, and a place to exit the water.

✔ **Set limits.** Set limits as to how deep to go, and do that part of your dive first. Set a maximum time limit and air supply limit. Agree on a procedure to follow when the first person reaches the minimum air supply limit.

✔ **Review the hand signals.** Briefly go over all the hand signals (covered in Chapter 5) that you think you may need on the dive — you'll have an easier time reviewing this when you can still talk to each other.

✔ **Agree to a plan of action in the event that you get separated.** Something to be avoided, of course, but sometimes these things happen. Like the Boy Scouts, be prepared. Review your emergency procedures (see Chapter 7). Know ahead of time the quickest way to summon help.

Diving the plan

Stick with your dive plan — your agreed-upon course, depth limits, and so on. Communication is always more difficult underwater, but everything is simplified when both you and your buddy have an objective and a reasonable framework of expectations. You're bound to get your share of the unexpected when you're diving; having a plan to deal with all the contingencies that you can anticipate helps make sure all of the surprises are adventures, rather than ordeals.

Setting up your gear

The procedure for setting up your equipment is the same on a boat and on shore, but on shore you must take additional care to make sure no dirt or sand get in valves or contaminate airways. Pay close attention to what you're doing — it's pretty important that your equipment functions correctly. Here's a reminder of what your certification class teaches:

1. **Secure the tank on the BC.**

   Your BC has one or two straps on the back that secure the tank to the BC with a cam buckle. Slide the tank into the strap loops from the top, as shown in Figure 4-1. Make sure the valve opening is facing toward the BC. The valve should be about even with the top of the BC; if it's too high it can keep knocking you in the back of the head — very annoying. Adjust the strap(s), and secure the tank in the BC with the buckle. The straps are adjustable, so that you can use different size and shape tanks with the same BC. Because of the variation in buckles and straps, you have to figure out how yours works, but they are usually pretty straightforward.

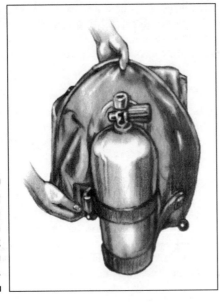

Figure 4-1:
Slide the
tank into the
backpack
strap on
the BC.

2. **Check to see that the tank is secure.**

   Lift the BC and tank a few inches off the ground by the shoulder straps and shake it a little. If the tank slips or comes loose, the straps aren't tight enough. Release the buckle, tighten the straps, and secure the buckle again. Now try it. Nice and snug? Good.

3. **Attach the first-stage regulator to the tank.**

   The first time I go diving after a lay-off of six months or more, I spend a few minutes trying to figure out how the darned regulator goes on the tank. With all the swivels, hoses, and stuff, it's like a three-dimensional puzzle. If you're not very good at these abstract spatial relationships either, don't get flustered — Figure 4-2 and the following steps show you how.

   • **Examine the o-ring on the tank.** The tank valve is probably covered with a plastic cap or tape, so take that off and examine the o-ring in the valve: It should be clean and smooth. If it isn't, it needs to be replaced.

   • **Open the tank valve a smidge.** Just for a second, and just long enough to blow out any dirt or water that may be in the valve.

   • **Take the cap off the first-stage regulator.** Unscrew the knob on the regulator and take out the dust cap. Usually, they have a retainer string so that they just dangle from the yoke when they're not in place.

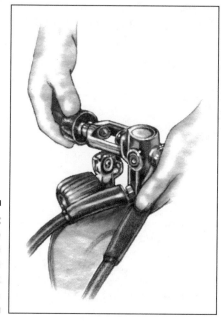

Figure 4-2:
Attach the
first-stage
regulator to
the tank
valve.

- **Attach the first-stage regulator.** Fit the opening on the first stage to the tank valve. The body of the first-stage regulator and the yoke make a right angle. When you screw the yoke to the tank valve, the body of the first-stage regulator can be pointing either up or down — it doesn't really matter, but the first-stage regulator is more streamlined and less likely to snag on something or hit you in the back of the head when it's pointing down. Whichever way you put it on, make sure the second-stage regulator (and the octopus regulator if you are using one as your alternate air supply) is on the right side of the BC, and the inflator hose and console are on the left. After everything is the way you want it, tighten the screw on the yoke to secure the first-stage regulator. Make it finger-tight, but don't over-tighten the screw — you could damage the o-ring.

4. Attach the inflator hose.

The inflator hose is the one that comes off the same side of the first-stage regulator as the console and isn't connected to anything — yet. At the end of the hose is a ring. Pull the ring back and push the end of the hose onto the inflator valve on the BC, as shown in Figure 4-3. When the hose is on there as far as you can push it, release the ring and the hose is locked in place. Normally, there are a couple clips to secure the hose to the inflator.

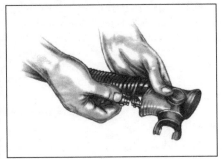

5. Turn on the air.

Hold the console in your left hand with the valve pointing away from you. With your right hand, slowly open the valve on the tank. Listen for leaks where the first-stage regulator attaches to the tank. If you have a leak, turn off the air, remove the first-stage, and check the o-ring again. If there are no leaks, open the valve up all the way, and then turn it back half a turn. Check the air pressure gauge to find out how much air is in the tank. If you have an integrated air computer (one that's connected to your tank with a high pressure hose), wet the contacts: This activates the computer and gives you a readout.

6. Test the second-stage regulator.

Press the purge button on the front of the second-stage regulator just for a second — the air should flow freely and stop when you release the button. Exhale through the mouthpiece to make sure that the exhaust port isn't blocked. Take a few breaths through the second-stage regulator to make sure the air is flowing freely and easily. If you encounter any problems during the test, the regulator has to be serviced before you can use it.

7. Lay the scuba unit aside.

Literally — don't leave it standing up. The tank can easily be knocked over or fall over, especially on a pitching boat, resulting in ruptured hoses or a damaged regulator. Place the tank on the deck or on a drop cloth on the ground, with the BC upper-most. Place the second-stage regulator and the octopus on top of the BC (if it's on the ground), to keep dirt and sand out of the mouthpiece and airways. If you have a long boat ride to the dive site, turn the air off during the trip.

8. Set up your weight belt.

If you have an integrated weight system in your BC, use it. If you're making a warm-water dive, that may be all the weight you need. If you don't have the integrated weight BC, or if you need more weight than you can carry in your BC, you need a weight belt.

The most common dive weights are rectangular blocks of lead, but you sometimes see the rounded cylindrical type, known as *bullet weights.* You need to use a retainer on the belt to keep bullet weights in place. Otherwise, they may slide around on your belt, making buoyancy control difficult. A retainer can be used on regular block weights also, but it's easier to simply thread the weight through one side of the weight, put a twist in the belt before you thread it through the other side — it keeps the weights in place just as effectively as a retainer and it's one less piece of gear to deal with.

There are two schools of thought on the placement of the weights: Space them evenly on the belt or put them all as close to the buckle as possible. Putting them all as close to the buckle as possible keeps the weight at the lowest point of your body when you're swimming through the water in the horizontal position (as you'll be doing, hopefully). Theoretically, this makes buoyancy control easier. Sounds good, as long as it doesn't interfere with the buckle release. I've tried it both ways and I'm unimpressed with the difference.

9. Adjust your mask, snorkel, and fins.

If you haven't done so already, refer to Chapter 1 to see how to set up your snorkel, mask, and fins.

Suiting up

After you arrive at the dive site and you've been briefed by the guide or gone over the dive plan with your buddy, it's time to get suited up. Put your gear on in a predetermined order — it's really difficult to get your wetsuit on if you've already got your BC on. The order of installation should go something like this:

1. Put on your exposure suit.

Doesn't matter if it's a dive skin; wetsuit; or polyester, bell-bottom, lime-green, neon disco-Elvis jumpsuit. A thick, cold-water wetsuit can be kind of a pain to get into sometimes, but it's infinitely preferable to diving in cold water without it. Don't forget the hood, booties, and whatever extras you require (see Chapter 2).

2. Put on the BC.

The easiest way is to have your buddy hold the tank while you slip into the BC like a coat. Make sure none of the straps are twisted or any of the hoses caught under the straps. Adjust the straps until the tank rests comfortably and the BC is snug. After the straps are fastened and adjusted, have your buddy release the tank and see how it feels. Tilt your head back to make sure the first-stage regulator won't be hitting you in the back of the head. Help your buddy with her BC.

3. Put on your weight belt.

Your weight belt has to be clear of your other equipment in case you need to ditch it in an emergency. Holding the buckle in your left hand, put the belt around your waist and fasten it so that it can be released with your right hand. You want the belt to release with your right hand, because most BCs release with the left hand. If you're in an emergency situation in low light or poor visibility and you have to ditch your weight belt, you don't want to get the two releases confused and undo your BC by mistake. This way, you know that the right hand release is your weight belt and nothing else. Sometimes, on a pitching boat, it's easier to buckle the belt loosely, step into it, and pull it up to your waist to tighten it.

4. Put on your mask and snorkel.

See the instructions in Chapter 1 for putting on your mask and snorkel. When you have your mask on, avoid wearing it up on your forehead. It's easy to lose your mask this way and in some places, it's considered a sign of a diver in distress.

5. Put on your fins.

Fins are the last thing you put on because walking around with fins on is difficult and can be dangerous. Put them on just before you get in the water. If there's a dive platform on the boat (see the "Boat talk" sidebar earlier in this chapter), you can often put them on while sitting on the platform. If not, or if you're shore diving, steady yourself with one hand on your buddy's shoulder. Put your fins on one at a time, and return the favor for your buddy.

6. Make a final review.

Before you get in the water, inspect your buddy's equipment to see that everything is in order and have her do the same for you. It feels pretty dorky to jump in the water without your mask or your weight belt, or with your inflator hose unconnected. Believe me, it happens.

- **Check the BC.** Make sure the hoses are all connected and not under any straps, that the straps are all fastened, and that the fit is snug.

- **Check the weight belt.** Make sure that the weight belt has right-hand release and is clear of the other equipment.

- **Check all of the releases.** Be familiar with the releases on all your buddy's equipment in case you have to do it for her.

- **Check the air supply.** Make sure the air supply is turned on, the pressure gauge is working, and the tank is full. Familiarize yourself with the location of her alternate air supply.

- **Give the okay.** If everything is in order and looks good, give your buddy the okay. After you've both inspected each others' equipment, you're ready to dive!

Greatest fears

What are most beginning divers afraid of? The list usually goes something like this:

- **I'll drown.** As long as you can breathe, you won't drown. Your regulator is a simple and sturdy piece of equipment, and all respected brands are manufactured to a high standard. If they do fail, they're designed to provide more air than you need, rather than less. In addition to your primary air source, you have a back-up, and a dive buddy who also has a primary and a back-up. The odds of all of these systems failing at one time are very minute. Most low-air emergencies are the result of failing to pay attention to the pressure gauge. Even then, your air flow doesn't suddenly cut off, but gradually diminishes — you find yourself having to suck harder for the air — which should be enough to alert you to the fact that you need to get back to the surface.

- **I'll be attacked by sharks.** There are 350 different species of sharks, only about 30 of those are known to have attacked humans. Most of those species are rarely seen by divers on an ordinary reef dive, and even when they are seen, they rarely show any interest in divers. Sharks have attacked divers, but you're twice as likely to die from a bee sting as you're from a shark attack. Of the shark attacks that have occurred, less than a third were attacks on divers and many of those cases involved spear fishing. Most experienced divers exhibit little fear of sharks, and in fact, shark-feeding dives are a popular activity offered by many dive operators (see Chapter 10). Leave the marine animals alone, and in all likelihood they'll do the same to you. If they can, most animals flee when they see human beings coming, whether on land or in the sea. Considering the kind of treatment that they've received at the hands of humans, you have to respect their wisdom.

- **I'll get the bends.** The bends, or decompression sickness (covered in Chapter 7), is caused by dissolved nitrogen building up in your body under pressure, and then forming gas bubbles when you ascend too quickly and the pressure suddenly releases. Divers usually get bent because they ignore the profiles recommended by dive tables (see Chapter 3) or computers. Even divers who do get bent are almost always successfully treated in a recompression chamber. If you follow safe diving practices, there is very little likelihood you will get the bends.

- **I'll be laughed at.** Everybody who dives, or does anything for that matter, is a beginner at first. There's nothing ridiculous about being inexperienced. Be honest about your level of inexperience and ask for help and advice — people can be amazingly generous and kind if you give them the opportunity. If you run into somebody who's not nice, you don't want to dive with him anyway — he has problems that don't have anything to do with you, and that's exactly how you should keep it. Don't take yourself so seriously that you can't afford to see yourself as a little bit ridiculous. Put in the time to build up your experience and in less time than you think, you'll be offering advice to some grateful rookie.

- **I'll be abducted by aliens:** There is not a single reported incidence of a diver ever being abducted by aliens — not while underwater anyway. Look to the skies!

Dealing with dive anxiety

Beginning divers are normally somewhat anxious — even fearful — before making a dive. Fear is not necessarily a bad thing: It makes you more alert and cautious, and heightened awareness is a useful thing when you're diving. Unfortunately, fear can also makes you overreact and exaggerate potential threats.

Statistically, diving is very safe — last year there was only one fatality for every 250,000 dives. A large percentage of those fatalities had contributing factors, such as heart disease, and many more were the result of divers failing to observe safe diving practices.

As you build experience, your anxiety is replaced by confidence, but you should never become complacent and reckless or lose your respect for the ocean. Use good judgment. Don't get yourself into situations that you can't handle, but at the same time don't let your fears spiral out of proportion. If you don't know whether you can handle a particular situation, ask the dive master or guide. Explain that you're a novice and that you're a little nervous. If possible, buddy-up with her or with some other very experienced diver.

Chapter 5

Getting Down

. . . .

In This Chapter

▶ Entering the water — gracefully

▶ Managing your time underwater

▶ Getting out of the water

▶ Maintaining your equipment

. . . .

*O*kay, you're all set up and ready to hit the water — this is where the fun really starts. But, of course, it's a lot more fun if you're not wasting your air and your energy and you feel as if you're in control rather than struggling the whole time. This chapter is full of pointers that can help make your first dives easier.

Making Your Entry

You can use several different kinds of entries for different diving situations, and this section explains those entries. Keep the following tips in mind, though, whichever entry you choose:

✔ **Strive to make as little splash and do as little thrashing around as possible.** This way, you save energy, save air, and minimize the possibility of knocking things loose.

✔ **Always hold your mask on as you enter the water.** It's the piece of equipment most likely to come loose.

✔ **Make sure the area is clear before you enter.**

✔ **Wait until both you and your buddy are ready to go.**

Boat dive entries

When you arrive at the dive site and you're suited up and ready, don't just jump in the water. Wait for the dive guide or one of the crew to give you the okay, and show you where to enter. The guide may need to determine current or other local conditions first, so be patient. On most dive boats you'll do the giant stride entry (see Figure 5-1), but if the boat has a dive platform or low sides you might use the seated entry or back roll entry (also shown in Figure 5-1).

Figure 5-1:
Entry dives.

The giant stride entry   The back roll entry

- ✔ **Giant stride entry:** Inflate your BC (see Chapter 2 for more on BCs and other equipment) slightly to give yourself a little positive buoyancy (you'll float on the surface). Hold your mask and regulator firmly in place with one hand. With the other hand, hold your console, octopus, or any other dangling stuff to your body. When you get the okay, check the water below you, and step out into space. Keep your legs spread until you hit the water, and then bring them together in a single kick. After you're floating on the surface, give the okay sign. At this point, you can usually switch to your snorkel. Join your buddy or swim out of the way to wait for him to enter the water.

- ✔ **Back roll entry:** If the sides of the boat are low, you can use the back roll entry. Sit on the edge of the boat with your back to the sea. Fill your BC about half full. Hold your regulator and mask in place with one hand and collect any dangling stuff with the other. Make sure the area behind you is clear, and then fall backward. Keep your knees up to make sure you don't scrape your legs against the boat. After you're in the water, floating on the surface, give the okay, switch to your snorkel, and wait for (or join) your buddy.

✔ **Seated entry:** You can use the seated entry if you're using a dive platform or any flat surface that's only a few inches above the water — if you can sit on the edge and dangle your feet in the water, you can use a seated entry. Fill your BC about half full. With your feet dangling in the water, twist at the waist so you can put both hands on the edge of the platform on one side of your body. Turn to face the platform as you lower yourself into the water. Give the okay. Switch to snorkel and join (or wait for) your buddy.

Shore dive entries

After you're suited up, make your shore entry by wading out (with your buddy) until you're deep enough to swim. Then, use your snorkel to swim to the site where you want to begin the dive.

In calm water

If the water is calm, you may prefer to carry your fins until you're about chest deep, and then put them on. If you have to keep them on, walk backward, looking over your shoulder, and hold onto your buddy to steady yourself. Shuffle your feet to scare away creatures that may be hiding in the sand and to keep from tripping over submerged obstacles. As soon as the water is deep enough, use your snorkel and swim to the site.

In breaking surf

A shore entry in large surf require special training and lots of experience — even a small wave can knock you down and give you a good beating. If you expect to wade out in surf that's larger than knee-high, you should get special training. Small waves can be negotiated by staying alert and working with the force of the waves (more about waves and surf in Chapter 8) — wade out through the surf just as you would in a calm-water shore dive, but use your regulator. That way, if you're knocked down by an oncoming wave, you won't suck water. Stay calm and hold onto your mask. As the wave approaches, squat a little, and lean into the wave as it hits you. Waves generally come in sets of three to five. It may be wise to let the set pass before you resume your progress. As soon as the water is deep enough, submerge and swim along the bottom until you're clear of the area where the waves are breaking.

Down There

Before you begin your descent, check your watch (see Chapter 2 for information on watches). Align the zero on the bezel to the minute hand so you can keep track of the elapsed time of your dive. Also, take a look at your compass (see the "Underwater navigation" section, later in this chapter), and make note of the direction of land, the boat, your picnic lunch, Hollywood, or any notable landmarks in order to establish some orientation.

Going down

When you're ready, give your buddy the signal to descend. If he returns it, switch to your regulator from your snorkel, take a normal breath, and as you exhale, purge the air from your BC by pulling on the inflator hose or by holding the end of the hose over your head and pushing the manual inflation button.

The inflator hose has a stainless steel cable inside that runs from the end to the exhaust valve at the left shoulder. When you pull on the end of the hose, the internal cable opens the exhaust valve and vents air from your BC. If you hold the hose over your head and depress the manual inflator button, air is vented through the hose.

Follow these tips as you descend into the water:

- **Descend feet first so that you can keep your fins underneath you if you need to ascend.** If you're properly weighted, you should sink slowly as you exhale and dump the air from your BC. If you don't sink, check to make sure the air is venting from your BC. If your dump valve is working okay, most likely you're taking shallow breaths and holding a lot of air in your lungs. That's pretty common for beginning divers who are feeling slightly anxious. Stop yourself and concentrate on taking regular, even breaths. Now try it again. If you're still not sinking, you need more weight.

- **Begin equalizing your ears immediately as you descend, and equalize continually as you go.** Read about equalizing your ears in Chapter 1. If you have trouble equalizing, signal your buddy and stop the descent. Go back up a few feet until the discomfort in your ears goes away, and then begin your descent, again equalizing as you go. If your ears won't clear after a couple of attempts, abort the dive.

> ✔ **If possible, try to use an anchor line or some other reference during your decent.** Try to adjust your buoyancy so that you don't crash down on the sea floor sending up a cloud of billowing sediment. Stay in contact with your buddy throughout the descent.

Form and buoyancy control

When your form and buoyancy control are good, you use less energy, less air, and feel more relaxed and in control.

Good form means nothing more than swimming in the most natural and efficient way possible. Everyone's body has its individual mechanics. There's no perfect form, but you should strive to be as streamlined as you can be in the water — water is much more dense than air and consequently, the drag it creates is much greater.

Keep the following in mind to maintain good diving form:

> ✔ Keep your arms at your sides as you swim to aid streamlining — some divers clasp their hands in front as an alternative posture.

> ✔ Your body should be as horizontal as possible to reduce resistance.

> ✔ In general, your movements should be as easy and graceful as you can make them.

Buoyancy control may seem difficult at first, but with a little practice it becomes second nature. Because buoyancy changes with depth, you must adjust your buoyancy continually throughout your dive. The following tips may help:

> ✔ _Neutral buoyancy_ (not too much, not too little) at the surface is negative buoyancy on the bottom — at depth you have to add a little air to your BC to regain neutral buoyancy.

> ✔ Conversely, as you ascend, the air in your BC expands and increases your buoyancy and must be vented to prevent you from ascending too rapidly.

> ✔ When you add air to your BC, the changes may take a few seconds to take effect. To further complicate the picture, your buoyancy changes as you inhale and exhale.

> ✔ Add air to your BC with the power-inflator button on your inflator hose, or manually by exhaling into the manual inflator mouthpiece with the button depressed. The former method is easy and quick, and doesn't

involve taking your regulator out of your mouth; the latter has the advantage of conserving your precious air supply, but is more difficult, especially when fine-tuning your buoyancy.

When you add air to your BC to increase your buoyancy, add it in short bursts, a little at a time. Be patient. Wait a few seconds for the changes to take effect. You don't want to overinflate your BC — that only causes more buoyancy problems and wastes your air. In time, you'll develop a feeling for just how much air to add.

✔ As you ascend, be prepared to dump air from the exhaust valve. If you don't, you may find yourself floating away from the bottom in an uncontrolled ascent. If this happens, swim toward the bottom and vent air from the purge valve on the bottom of your BC. If that fails, spread eagle to slow your ascent, and purge the air from the shoulder valve with the inflator hose as you would in a normal descent.

Sign language

It isn't easy to talk with a regulator in your mouth, and even if you could, the sound of your voice wouldn't transfer well between the air (where it's produced by your vocal chords) to water (where your buddy's ears can hear it). That's why divers rely on a set of hand signals to communicate the most common basic messages underwater.

Of course, first you have to get your buddy's attention. A common practice is to rap on your tank with the handle of your dive knife or some other hard object. After you have your buddy's attention, you can use one or more of the recognized hand signals, shown in Figure 5-2, to communicate your message. Or, you can make up your own signals — be prepared for the befuddled looks, though, and try not to spit your regulator out laughing.

If your message is more complex than you can get across signing, you may want to carry an underwater slate (see Chapter 2). There are many different styles available in most dive stores and they normally fit nicely in the pocket of your BC.

Air consumption

Oxygen is necessary to your metabolic processes. Equally important is the elimination of carbon dioxide, a by-product of the process. Both of these functions are taken care of by inhaling and exhaling. The air that you inhale

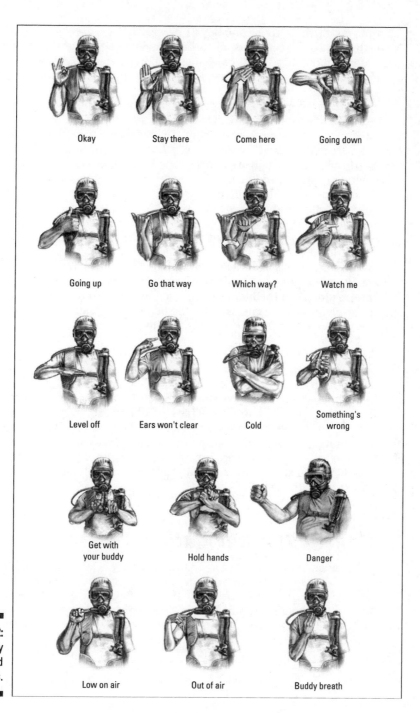

Figure 5-2: Commonly used hand signals.

from your tank is approximately 21 percent oxygen and 78 percent nitrogen, with only a miniscule trace of carbon dioxide. The air you exhale into the water is about 16 percent oxygen and 6 percent carbon dioxide — you use up some oxygen and eliminate some carbon dioxide with every breath.

The rate of the metabolic process and the consumption of air varies somewhat from person to person. Everybody uses air at a different rate, but the difference is relatively insignificant. The main reason divers use air quickly is *hyperventilation,* which means breathing more than you really need to. Nearly all beginning divers hyperventilate to some degree — it's a natural reaction to stress, and every new and unfamiliar situation is, to some degree, stressful. The more comfortable you become underwater, the lower your air consumption.

Normally, hyperventilation isn't really a problem. In extreme cases, a hyperventilating diver not only uses up his air quickly, he can actually induce symptoms such as light-headedness, a tingling sensation in the extremities, and even fainting. These symptoms are caused by a radical dip in level of carbon dioxide in the blood brought about by hyperventilation. Sometimes these symptoms are mistaken for the bends (see Chapter 7), which compounds the stress that the diver is feeling.

Most of the time, however, the only noticeable symptom of hyperventilation is the rapid consumption of air. A mildly hyperventilating diver may not even be conscious of it until he looks at his pressure gauge. Generally, a hyperventilating diver takes rapid, shallow breaths in the top of the chest; deep, sighing breaths; or both. This kind of breathing not only uses up air rapidly, but makes buoyancy control more difficult. As a beginning diver, you can reduce your air consumption by being aware of your breathing: Make an effort to take slow, moderate breaths. If you can focus on and control your breathing, you should notice an improvement in your air consumption almost immediately.

Underwater navigation

Even under the best of circumstances, visibility is somewhat limited underwater. Because of a lack of truly distinctive landmarks, you can easily become disoriented and lose your sense of direction. The best way to tell where you came from and where you're going is with a compass. Get in the habit of referring to your compass on every dive, even if you have a guide — know where you're going and how to get back.

You can plan some elaborate navigation with the aid of a compass, but for that you should take an advanced navigation course. Finding your way from point A to point B and back again, however, can be accomplished with a little basic navigation.

First familiarize yourself with the features — and jargon of the compass:

- **Compass needle:** The *compass needle* is the line that moves around when you turn the compass. The compass needle is a free-floating pointer that always indicates magnetic north. In most dive compass, the compass needle is suspended in a liquid and sealed in a watertight case.

- **Lubber line:** The *lubber line* is fixed line on the compass that indicates your direction of travel. It's either on the face of the compass or right along the side next to it. This is the line that always points wherever you point it.

  If your compass is part of your console, hold it in front of you, keeping the lubber line pointed in your direction of travel. If you don't swim directly along the lubber line, your navigation will be off.

- **Bezel:** The *bezel* is the ring around the face of the compass that you can rotate. It has a bunch of little lines etched on it that rotate with the bezel called *headings,* and two or three that can be lined up over the compass needle, called *index markers.*

- **Index markers:** When you line up the index markers on the rotating bezel with the magnetic compass needle (which always points north), the lubber line (your direction of travel) will indicate how far off of north, in degrees, is your direction of travel.

- **Headings:** The bezel is a rotating circular ring around the face of the compass, divided into 360 equal parts. These are the degrees of the compass and a numerical reference called *headings.* They tell you how far off of magnetic north your direction of travel (the lubber line) is when you line up the index markers with the compass needle.

Make sure that you hold the compass so that the compass needle is free to rotate. If you have a wrist-mounted compass, hold the arm without the compass straight out in front of you. Grasp that arm just above the elbow with the compass arm and you'll be looking right down on the compass.

With the compass needle pointing to magnetic north, line up the index markers on the bezel with the compass needle. If you swim in the direction of the lubber line and keep the compass needle within the index markers, you can be confident that your course is true. If the needle begins to wander, you're off course.

To return to your starting point, simply reverse your course 180°. If the bezel has an index marker on the opposite side, line up the north-pointing compass needle with it. If not, turn the bezel until the index marker is 180° of your original heading or is aligned with the south-pointing end of the compass needle. Now, turn until the north-pointing needle is aligned with the index markers and swim in the direction of the lubber line to your original position.

Your dive profile

The longer you breathe from a scuba tank at depth, the more nitrogen is absorbed into the tissues of your body. The deeper you go, the more nitrogen your tissues will hold before they become saturated (unable to hold more), because your body tissue can hold more nitrogen when under greater pressure. All of this nitrogen is absorbed into the body in accordance with Henry's Law (see Chapter 6 for the full explanation).

Seventy-eight percent of the air you're breathing right now is nitrogen. Under ordinary circumstances, it won't hurt you. The problem with nitrogen arises with increased pressure, such as you experience when diving. When this happens, your body becomes *super-saturated* — it contains more nitrogen than it can hold. When you're super-saturated, you have to get rid of some of that nitrogen.

If you go up to the top of a tall building, drive up a mountain, or fly in a plane, your tissues are super-saturated and begin eliminating nitrogen. You don't experience any problems because the difference is relatively slight and your body is capable of dealing with excess nitrogen — up to a point. When that point is exceeded, you develop *decompression sickness* (DCS), also known as *the bends.* Because water is so much more dense than air, the pressure changes that you experience when diving are far more dramatic, and the likelihood of developing DCS far greater — dive tables and computers were developed to keep that from happening. If you stay within the limits of the dive table or the dive computer, you can safely surface at any time during your dive without stopping and waiting for excess nitrogen to be eliminated from your body, and still avoid DCS. This is known as *no-decompression* diving.

During your certification training, you receive a *dive table* — a chart that indicates the maximum time permissible at different depths to avoid decompression. Dive tables have evolved over time to provide a guideline for the average diver, but because recreational divers are diverse and react differently to decompression, no dive table can ever be considered 100 percent safe for everybody, all of the time. In general, however, dive tables are designed to be fairly conservative, and few divers ever *get bent* (get the bends) when using them as a guide.

A *dive profile* is a graphic representation of your dive — the horizontal axis represents the time you spend underwater, and the vertical axis represents your depth at any moment during the dive (see Figure 5-3). Suppose, for example, you dive to 60 feet and cruise along a drop-off and after a few minute you see a turtle above you at about 50 feet, so you go up to take a look and cruise along there for a while until you see this incredible sponge back down at 60 that you had to check out, and so on. Safe diver that you are, you know to complete the deepest part of your dive first, so you ascend slowly throughout the course of your dive, but you can't help having lots of little ups and downs along the way. You surface after 45 minutes.

This kind of dive is pretty typical of what most divers do and is known as a *multilevel dive*. Most dive tables, however, have no way of tracking a multi-level dive. Dive tables typically assume that you went to 60 feet and stayed there until you came up, or dived what is known as a *square profile*. This assumption makes dive tables more conservative than dive computers.

Figure 5-3: Most dive tables assume a square dive profile (AB), most dives are actually multilevel dives (CD).

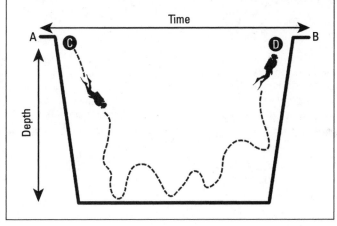

Dive computers are capable of keeping track of depth and time. They record this information every second or so, and monitor your nitrogen uptake and elimination based on a theoretical model. A computer can easily keep track of multilevel diving and give you a more accurate picture of your dive profile, but like tables, they calculate your nitrogen absorption based on what is safe for the average diver and, like tables, no computer can be considered 100 percent safe for everybody, all of the time. The computer doesn't know the particulars of your body, or the subtleties of the conditions in which you're diving. Undoubtedly, there will one day be a computer that knows all — your age, weight, percentage of body fat, level of conditioning — and may even be able to monitor the level of nitrogen dissolved in your individual tissues and the rate of elimination. For now, you have to use tables or a computer to monitor your nitrogen and stay within the limits of no-decompression diving.

Reacting to stress

As you encounter situations underwater, you're required to make decisions. Some decisions can lead to a stressful situation: Where the heck is my dive buddy going in such a hurry? Should I follow him? Why is my mask filling with blood? Is it safe to pet this shark? I wonder what's in that cave? That eel looks just like my grandmother! What were those symptoms of narcosis again?

A stressful situation is one in which you are anxious and fearful about the outcome. Your heart rate increases, you begin to hyperventilate, and you may feel as if things are out of control. Good judgment goes a long way toward avoiding stress underwater, but even the most cautious divers can encounter a stressful situation — becoming tangled in fishing line for example — the outcome of such a situation often depends on how you react to stress.

A panicked diver makes desperate, and often inappropriate, responses to stressful situations that may makes things worse. To minimize the possibility of making inappropriate responses remember the following steps:

1. **Stop.**

   Don't react without thinking through the situation. Stop before you act.

2. **Breathe.**

   Control your breathing while you reason through the problem. Take slow deep breaths.

3. **Think.**

   Remember your training. Decide on the best possible plan of action you can under the circumstances, keeping in mind what you know about diving physics and physiology (see Chapter 6).

4. **Act.**

   When you decide on a plan, act on it swiftly and decisively.

A stressful situation can happen to any diver, at any time. A diver who is prepared for the eventuality with these four steps generally fares better, though, than one who reacts by panicking.

Coming up

Sooner or later, every dive must come to an end and you must return to the surface. On a typical recreational dive, that time has arrived when either you or your buddy reaches the point where you still have enough air left for a safe ascent, usually about 500 psi of remaining air. As a safe diver, you have stayed within your dive profile (see the "Your dive profile" section, earlier in this chapter) and done the deepest part of your dive first, so all you need to ascend is the following:

1. **Signal your buddy.**

   Make sure that he acknowledges the sign before you begin your ascent.

2. **Check the time and your gauges.**

   Note the time as you begin your ascent. Also note your remaining air pressure and your depth.

3. Be ready to purge your BC.

Grasp the inflator hose of your BC to prepare to vent some air as you ascend. Air introduced into your BC at depth expands as you ascend, increasing your buoyancy. Vent air from your BC as needed to keep your ascent under control.

4. Extend one hand over your head.

A diving mask restricts your vision somewhat, so this keeps you from surfacing under some unseen obstacle and cracking your head in the bargain.

5. Look to the surface.

Keep your eyes open for boats, floating debris, or anything else above you. Rotate in a slow spiral as you ascend.

6. Ascend slowly.

Rise at no more than one foot per second or ten feet every ten seconds. It's slower than it sounds. Be deliberate, there's no need to hurry. Watch your depth gauge and your watch, and never ascend faster than your bubbles.

7. Make a safety stop.

If possible, make a *safety stop* — stop your ascent 15 feet below the surface and wait for three minutes. Because all of your diving is no-decompression diving, you can make a direct ascent to the surface at any time. If possible, though, always make a safety stop, because it helps you to eliminate excess nitrogen and allows you to adjust your buoyancy before making your final ascent. It also gives you a chance to take a last look around and meditate on the wonders you've have seen in quiet. It's a good time to practice fine-tuning your buoyancy control.

The deeper you go and the longer you stay down, the more nitrogen you accumulate, so, if possible, always make a safety stop if you dive to more than 100 feet, or if you're near the limits of the dive table. A safety stop is a good idea on any dive, but you may want to forego it if you're low on air, have been summoned back to the boat, are assisting another diver, or have some similar circumstance. As long as you stay within the no-decompression limits of the dive tables or the computer, the safety stop isn't absolutely necessary — it is always a good idea, though, to help your body eliminate nitrogen.

Post-Dive

After you're back on the surface, fully inflate your BC so that you float easily, and then rest and switch to your snorkel. All that remains is getting out of the water and taking care of your equipment so that it's ready for your next dive.

Getting out

If you're making a boat dive, you're faced with the task of getting back on the boat with your equipment. Every dive boat has an established procedure that's usually explained during the dive briefing before you enter the water. Normally, at least one member of the crew is assigned to help divers get out of the water. Most of the time, getting back on board is no problem, but in rough seas, with the boat pitching heavily, it can be a challenge.

The shore is always steady, of course, but getting through breaking surf can be a challenge, too. The "Surf exits" section may help.

Boat exits

After you're on the surface with your BC inflated, signal the crew of the boat you're okay and switch to your snorkel. If you surface and the boat isn't in sight, don't panic. Inflate your safety sausage (see Chapter 2), relax, and hold your position. The boat may have had an emergency to deal with or may simply have slipped anchor. Most liveaboard boats are equipped with global positioning system (GPS) and even on smaller boats the crew is aware of your general position and know where to look for you. If the shore is within sight, begin swimming slowly in that direction.

Most often, you can expect the boat to come to you, but if there are other divers boarding and you're fairly close, you can swim to the boat. Don't crowd around the boarding ladder if other divers are exiting the water. Wait your turn at a slight distance. A diver climbing the ladder may fall or lose a piece of equipment that could hit you.

When your turn comes to exit, do the following:

1. **Hand up any cameras or unattached equipment first.**

2. **On some boats, particularly if there is no boarding ladder, you're expected to hand up your weight belt and BC first.**

   Hand them up in that order — weight belt first — you don't want to lose the floatation provided by your BC before you get rid of the weight belt.

3. **After a crew member takes your weight belt, slip out of your BC.**

   Turn it so that the tank is between the side of the boat and the BC and the tank valve is upright.

4. **After the crew-person lifts it aboard, pull yourself up on the *gunwhale* of the boat (the top edge of the side) while kicking hard with your fins to propel yourself out of the water.**

   If there's a boarding ladder, you may find it easier to simply hand up your fins and climb the ladder wearing your gear. Wait until you have a hold on the ladder before you take off your fins — if you're pushed away by current, you may have a difficult time swimming back without your fins.

If you do elect to climb the ladder while wearing your gear, be sure to keep your regulator in your mouth. If you slip and fall back in the water, you still have an air source in position, and if the boat engine is emitting exhaust toward the rear of the boat, you're still breathing clean air.

After you're on deck remove your equipment. If you're planning another dive, you can switch your regulator to a fresh tank. If not, break it down and put it away. Things can get mixed up, lost, broken, and even become hazards on a deck cluttered with dive gear. Sometimes divers are just overcome with joy and start running around the deck in wild circles. You don't want them tripping over your stuff.

Surf exits

Before you attempt a surf exit, surface outside the *impact zone* — the area where waves are breaking — and evaluate the conditions. Surf, like all conditions in the ocean, is dynamic and can change quickly: It can be larger by the time you finish your dive than it was when you began. Just as you do when making a surf entry (see the "Shore dive entries" section, earlier in this chapter), use your regulator when making a surf exit so you need to save a little extra air at the end of your dive.

If the surf is fairly small, wait for a lull between sets and swim directly to shore as quickly as possible, staying with your buddy. Exiting in large surf takes special training, but if the waves aren't too big, you can still make it by swimming in, hugging the bottom, and crawling out on your hands and knees. When you reach shallow water, you may encounter strong out-rushing current — swimming against it can be tiring, and the hands and knees approach saves a lot of energy.

Maintaining your gear

Your dive equipment represents a respectable investment and when you're underwater, your life literally depends on it. You want it to work right and to last for a while. With the proper care, it will. The following sections show you how.

Breaking it down

Whether you're planning to switch to a fresh tank for another dive or you're done for the day, you should first remove your regulator from your used tank. Do the following:

1. **Turn off the air at the tank valve by turning it clockwise.**

2. **When the valve is closed, push the purge button on the front of your second-stage regulator: You can hear the air escape as the pressure is relieved.**

   If the sound doesn't stop after a second or two, the valve isn't closed.

3. **After the pressure is relieved, you can remove the first-stage regulator by unscrewing the yoke.**

   Don't let any water get into the high pressure inlet on the first-stage regulator.

4. **Clean and dry the dust cap and screw it in place.**

5. **Disconnect the air inflator hose and separate the regulator from the BC.**

Rinsing

The main purpose in rinsing your gear is to remove sea salt before it crystallizes. Salt corrodes metal. In addition, salt expands as it crystallizes — the crystals can be very sharp and when they form inside the weave of your BC, they can weaken the fabric and age it prematurely. It isn't absolutely necessary to rinse your gear if you're diving in fresh water, but a rinse in chlorinated tap water helps get rid of lingering micro-nasties that may develop odors or mold, so it's always a good idea.

Be sure to rinse your equipment as follows:

- All of your equipment should be thoroughly rinsed after every use. Ordinary fresh water does the job very effectively.

- Soak your gear in a *dunk tank* (any large container such as a plastic garbage can, filled with fresh water) for a short while, and then rinse it with a hose. If your gear has dried out completely before you are able to rinse it, let it soak overnight. Be sure to rinse your mask, snorkel, and fins.

- When you rinse, don't aim a stream of water from the hose at any of the valves or gauges. Rinse your BC and exposure suit thoroughly.

- Drain your BC by holding it upside down with the inflator hose at the lowest point, and then depressing the manual inflator button.

   It isn't unusual for the BC bladder (see Chapter 2) to have taken in some salt water during your dive. Let it drain and rinse out the bladder with fresh water.

- With the dust cap firmly in place, you can rinse the regulator. Some dive shops offer a mild antiseptic solution in which to dunk your second-stage regulator and octopus in order to prevent the growth of mold, mildew, and alien brain-eating space spores.

Drying

Air-dry your equipment somewhere where it can drip and where it has good air circulation. Packing gear away in a gear bag while it's still damp encourages the growth of mildew and that most unique and pungent of diving aromas, called *suit stink*. Make sure that your neoprene items dry someplace that's out of direct sunlight — UV radiation hastens the breakdown of neoprene. Hang your exposure suit on a broad, plastic hanger in a shady place. Don't use wire hangers — they'll rust, stain the suit, and stretch the shoulders out of shape.

Storing

After your stuff is rinsed and dried, you can stash it away. As long as your dive bag is dry and free of salt inside, it should be fine in there. Storage is best in a dry, dark place. You may want to hang your exposure suit in a closet. If so, use a broad-shouldered plastic hanger so that it doesn't stretch out of shape.

Chapter 6

Physics and Physiology

. . . .

In This Chapter

▶ Understanding the physics of the underwater world

▶ Seeing and hearing underwater

▶ Breathing underwater

. . . .

As that shop-worn axiom would have it: Knowledge is power. You don't absolutely have to know all of the physics and physiology to figure out how to dive, but like chicken soup, it can't hurt, and it just may bubble up in your brain when you're confronted with a particular problem. On the other hand, maybe you can impress your friends the next time *Jeopardy!* comes on.

The Wonder of Water

Water is the most miraculous substance in the world — maybe in the entire universe. It's no wonder that nearly anyone can sit in blissful meditation next to a body of water — from the thundering waves of a Pacific beach to a mossy trickle in a desert oasis — contemplating the sight and sound of water. Water is, or is responsible for, everything of beauty on earth, but what the heck is it? This section explains this very special substance.

Why it matters

Matter is the stuff that the universe is made out of. You can find lots of different kinds of stuff (called *elements*), and even more combinations of that stuff (called *compounds*). Water is a compound of oxygen and hydrogen — commonly represented by the designation H_2O. Elements like oxygen and hydrogen are made up of smaller stuff called *atoms*. Atoms are made up of even smaller stuff: *Protons* (with positive electrical charges) and *neutrons*

(with neutral charges) bunch together in the center, or *nucleus,* of the atom. *Electrons,* with a negative charge, can be found zinging around the nucleus at certain distances or *shells.* The attraction between positive and negative charges holds the whole atom together. Depending on what kind of element it is, there may be more than one layer of electrons zinging around at different distances from the nucleus.

Each *atomic shell* (the orbital distance from the nucleus of the electrons) will accommodate only so many electrons. When the outer-most atomic shell (the one that's farthest from the nucleus) has all of the electrons that it can handle, that element is said to be *stable* and it won't readily combine with other elements. When it's not full, it is *reactive* and eager to find a partner and form a compound. Different elements have different inclinations to form compounds. Some are snobbish and will only form compounds with a few other elements. Some are so social that they are only found in compounds and are difficult to isolate.

Oxygen and hydrogen, the elements that make up water, are very social elements. They especially like each other. Each oxygen atom is made up of a nucleus of eight protons and eight neutrons, surrounded by eight electrons zooming around in two orbital shells, one inside the other. Hydrogen is the first element in the periodic table of elements because it has the simplest composition possible for an atom: one proton and one electron in one orbital shell. What could be simpler? (See Figure 6-1.) Hydrogen is one of those elements than can't be found in a free state on earth but is present in lots of different compounds. It's even friendlier than oxygen and forms compounds with all kinds of elements, but its favorites are oxygen and carbon.

Meet your density

Water is a lot denser than air. *Density* is the measure of how much stuff is crammed into a given unit of space. In water, even though the stuff is slipping and sliding around, it's pretty well packed together. Compared to air, for example, there's about 770 times more stuff crammed into a given space. That's why water absorbs heat better than air and why it conducts heat better.

Hot stuff

Water is a good conductor of heat, more than 20 times better than air. That's one reason why an air temperature of 75° is quite comfortable for a person, while the same person can become chilled submerged in 75° water — water conducts your body heat away very effectively. Air is a poor conductor of heat and acts as an effective insulator.

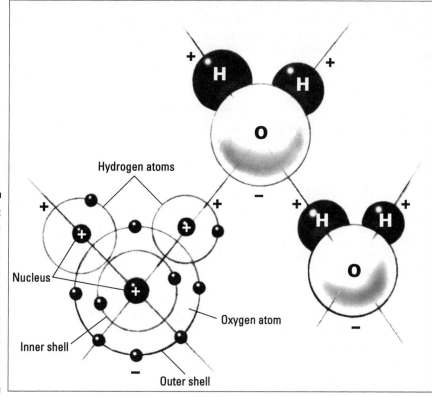

Hydrogen atoms

Nucleus

Oxygen atom

Inner shell

Outer shell

Conduction is one way that heat moves around. When you can't find a potholder and you sear your hand on the handle of a whistling teakettle, you've experienced heat transfer through conduction, uh, well . . . first-hand. The excited molecules in the boiling water and the kettle transfer their excitement to their neighboring molecules and the excitement travels through the handle, and finally to your hand.

Convection — another way that heat moves around — only works in fluids (both liquids and gases) where the molecules are free to move around. When a fluid is heated, it becomes less dense and rises. Cooler fluids rush in to replace the warmer fluids that have vacated the scene. Underwater, the water that is next to your skin is heated by your body and rises. It is replaced by cooler surrounding water. This process, in combination with conduction, is a very effective cooling mechanism, but can make you feel chilled even when the water temperature is in the 80s.

By the way, *radiation* is the third way heat is transmitted. This is the transfer of energy over space by electromagnetic waves. Radiation doesn't really figure into snorkeling or diving much, except after you get out of the water and stretch out on the sun deck.

What you see ain't always what you get

You are already familiar with the way light behaves as it travels through air, if not in theory, by experience. But light behaves differently as it travels through the much denser medium of water.

Wavelengths

Visible light travels through space in waves. Within the spectrum of visible light, different wavelengths are perceived as different colors. Longer wavelengths have less energy, and are perceived as reds. More energetic waves are seen as oranges; even more energetic waves look yellow, green, blue, and so on.

When light strikes an object, some wavelengths are absorbed and some are reflected. An object appears to be a particular color because wavelengths of light are being reflected back to the eye. When something absorbs all the wavelengths, it looks black to you. When it reflects them all, it looks white. Air isn't very dense, so light travels through it easily.

As light passes through the much denser molecules of water, however, it is more quickly absorbed. The lowest-energy waves, reds, are the first to disappear. Oranges disappear next, followed by yellow, and so on. Objects that are red or orange on the surface appear black or gray underwater because the wavelengths of light responsible for those colors are no longer present. Blue wavelengths penetrate clear water better than any others. That's why everything gets bluer and dimmer, the deeper underwater you go.

When the water isn't clear — when it has a lot of particles suspended in it — the light is absorbed even faster. Even in clear water, only 20 percent of sunlight reaches a depth of 30 feet. In really muddy water, it may be as little as 6 feet. The best penetration in turbid water happens in the yellow-green part of the spectrum. That's why murky water looks green.

It's all in the details

Underwater color perception also diminishes underwater because of your physiological responses to the lower levels of light. In low light, the pupil opens completely to admit as much light as possible and you begin involuntarily switching from the color-sensitive day vision to light-sensitive night vision, in which you are less able to distinguish color and detail.

Detail is lost because of the decrease in contrast underwater. If you hold up a thin white cloth on a sunny day, you notice that sharply drawn shadows are softened and not as dark. This is called *diffusion*. Even really clear water diffuses the light traveling through it. The more water it has to travel through, the more diffuse it becomes. That's why shadows look softer and fuzzier the deeper underwater you go, and there is less contrast to help distinguish details.

Refraction

Refraction has a dramatic effect on the way divers see underwater. When light moves from air to water, the light rays are bent, or *refracted,* because light and water have two different densities. The human eye is designed to see in the medium of air — it doesn't work as well in water. That's why divers wear a mask. The mask creates an airspace in front of the eyes, but in order to get to the eye, light must travel through the air, then through the water, and then through the air again. The result is that things look closer underwater by a ratio of about 4-to-3 — when you're four feet away from something underwater, it looks like you're only three feet away (see Figure 6-2). That's why beginning divers always miss the ladder when they reach for it at the end of the dive. Dramatic as this visual distortion is, divers learn to adapt to it quickly.

Refraction also causes that rippling pattern you see on a sandy bottom, or the bottom of a pool. The crests of the surface waves act just like a convex lens focusing light waves into bright spots. The troughs fan the lightwaves out.

Reflection

Reflection is also a lot more dramatic with water than it is with air. Because water so is much denser than air, much more light is reflected off the surface, especially when it strikes at a shallow angle. If you've ever been out on a boat all day and come home with a sunburn under your chin, this doesn't come as a surprise. In the early morning and late afternoon, light strikes the surface of the sea at the greatest angle. That's when the most light is reflected off the surface.

Sound advice

Sound, like light, is also a wave phenomenon, and it also behaves differently traveling through water than it does traveling through air.

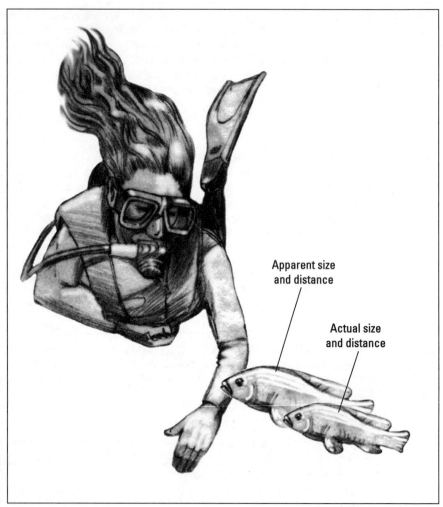

Apparent size
and distance

Actual size
and distance

Figure 6-2:
Because
of the
refraction of
light, things
look closer
underwater.

Sound travels best in a dense environment, like water, because the molecules are all packed together, making it easier for the energy of a sound wave to transfer from one to the next. (By comparison, air conducts sound pretty poorly. Sound travels about four times faster in water than in air.) You can hear very well underwater and over greater distances than you can above water. The trouble is that, because sound travels so much faster, it seems to be all around you, so you can't tell what direction the sound is coming from.

For all that sound wave efficiency, you'd think communication underwater would be pretty easy, but it doesn't work that way. Human vocal chords create sound by vibrating in a stream of exhaled air. That's fine as long as you're in air, but there is very little transfer of sound waves between air and water. That's why you can't hear the people up on the boat talking about how they want to get back to the resort bar and what a big pain-in-the-rear you are, and why they can't hear the grunts and squeaks of that pod of dolphins that showed up just after they decided to abort the dive due to lack of excitement.

So, if a tree falls in the forest, and nobody is around to hear it, does it make any noise? The answer is no. The tree generates sound, because it sends out waves through the medium of air. It doesn't make any noise though, because noise is the experience of perceiving sound waves. What does that have to do with diving? Nothing, but it might be fun to get into a discussion with somebody about it at a party.

It's a Gas

Diving is about dealing with fluids, mostly water and gases.

- Water and other liquids are fluids because they flow; but gases (like air) are fluids also.

- All matter can be compressed with enough pressure, but under the kinds of pressure encountered by divers, liquids are considered incompressible.

- Air is a different kind of fluid than water because it compresses readily under pressure. If it didn't, you wouldn't be able to stay submerged very long on a single tank of air, but because it does, you can.

This compression of air is what brings all of the complications of breathing air under pressure. This section helps clear the air.

What is air?

Earth's atmosphere consists of a mixture of gases, called air. *Gases* are stuff, just as liquids and solids. As such, they have substance and weight — lot less than liquids or solids, but some. The molecules that make up solids are all locked together. The molecules of liquids are close together, but able to slide around. The molecules of gases are farther apart than those of liquids or solids, and they're flying all over the place. That's why gases mix together so easily, and why you don't usually find pure gases in nature.

Air is a mixture of lots of gases, but mostly nitrogen and oxygen — 78 percent of air is nitrogen, 21 percent oxygen and the remaining 1 percent is made up of argon, carbon dioxide, carbon monoxide, helium, hydrogen, krypton (no relation to the stuff that's bad for Superman), neon, radon, xenon, and a few others. For all practical purposes in recreational diving, most of the trace gases can be ignored — only nitrogen, oxygen, and carbon dioxide are important, and carbon dioxide is important only because it is the principal byproduct of human metabolism. Air can, basically, be regarded as simply nitrogen and oxygen (see Figure 6-3).

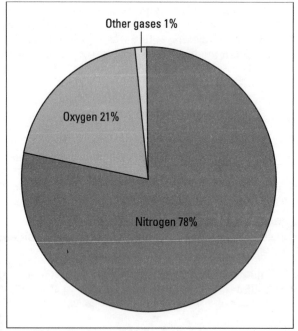

Figure 6-3:
The
composition
of air.

All I need is the air that I breathe

The human respiratory system is designed to exchange gases — it doesn't work in liquids. When liquids get into the lungs, they interfere with the exchange of gases, and this can lead to death in air-breathing creatures. Scuba diving is possible because you continue the vital exchange of gases by taking air with you underwater. Simple enough. But what complicates the picture is the increased pressure, at depth, created by the much heavier water. Increased pressure greatly affects the way the gas exchange takes place.

Although the largest percentage of air is nitrogen, it plays no part in your body functions. Your body absorbs nitrogen, but at surface pressure it neither harms nor helps you — it's an inert gas. There are, however, significant complications to breathing nitrogen under pressure — I address those in Chapter 7.

The cells in your body use the oxygen that's in the air to convert the chemicals derived from food into energy to sustain your life. Some kinds of cells can do without oxygen for a while; others need a constant supply. Brain and nerve cells are the most demanding — without oxygen they begin dying almost immediately — which is why a continuous supply of oxygen is so critical, and why human beings can't survive very long without oxygen. One of the by-products of this consumption of oxygen, called *metabolism,* is carbon dioxide. And just as important to the cells as the consumption of oxygen is the elimination of carbon dioxide — if the cells can't eliminate carbon dioxide, it quickly builds up to toxic levels. Blood transfers oxygen to the cells and carries away carbon dioxide; it is the job of the respiratory system to exchange oxygen for carbon dioxide in the blood.

Oxygen-rich blood leaving the lungs travels to the left side of the heart and from there is carried by the circulatory system throughout the body. Blood vessels branch throughout the body tissues becoming smaller and more numerous until they form millions of tiny capillaries. In these capillaries, gas exchange takes place as it does in the lungs, except that here it is reversed — oxygen is taken up by the cells and carbon dioxide is delivered to the blood to be transported to the lungs for elimination.

After the gas exchange with the cells is complete, the oxygen-poor blood travels — by way of larger and larger veins — to the right side of the heart, which pumps it to the lungs where the reverse gas exchange can take place, and the cycle is completed.

Laying down the law

A number of laws have been formulated to predict the behavior of gases under pressure. Water is incompressible as far as divers are concerned and because the body is made up almost entirely of water, you don't have to concern yourself about it. Most of the human body can withstand tremendous pressures, the only places that create problems are those spaces in the body filled with gas — sort of like on land.

Equality among gases

If you confine a volume of gas, the molecules flying around strike each other and the sides of the container. The impact depends on how fast they're going, and how heavy they are — that impact is the pressure of the gas. Heat excites the molecules and makes them move faster, and when they're moving faster, they're hitting the sides of the container more often increasing the pressure. Not all gas molecules have the same weight. Hydrogen molecules, for example, are very light, while oxygen molecules are relatively heavy. Because it's a lot heavier, an oxygen molecule doesn't have to be flying around as fast to exert the same pressure as a hydrogen molecule, but when the same heat energy is applied to both gases, the hydrogen molecules get flying around a lot faster than the oxygen molecules so they both apply equal pressure to the container, even though the molecules are going at different speeds. This equally among gases is known as the kinetic gas theory.

Because there's a lot of space between the molecules of gases, you can squeeze a lot of it into a smaller space than it normally occupies. When you do, the molecules are a lot closer together, so they're hitting the sides of the container more often, which equals a corresponding higher pressure.

At any given temperature and pressure, within a certain volume of space you always have the same number of gas molecules, no matter what kind of gas it is. All of this egalitarian behavior among gases is known as the General Gas Law, and any gas that breaks it is prosecuted to the fullest extent thereof.

Boyle's Law

In spite of its name, Boyle's Law doesn't have anything to do with cooking pasta or making coffee. Sir Robert Boyle was an Irish scientist working back in the seventeenth century and he was interested in the effects of pressure changes. In one now-famous experiment, he placed a snake in a glass jar that he depressurized and observed a bubble form in the snake's eye — the first recorded observation of the effects of decompression sickness. Boyle is most famous though, for formulating Boyle's Law.

Boyle wanted to know how a given volume of air reacts to a change in pressure, and he came up with this explanation:

If the temperature remains constant, the volume of a gas is inversely proportionate to the absolute pressure.

Boyle's Law can be demonstrated by submerging an open-ended container of air to a depth of 33 feet. That's known as *two atmospheres of pressure* because at 33 feet underwater, the pressure is equal to what it would be at the surface if the atmosphere were twice as thick as it is. At 33 feet, there is twice as much pressure, so the volume of air in the open-ended container is reduced by half. If you submerge the container to 66 feet (three atmospheres), the volume of air is reduced to one-third the original volume. At four atmospheres, the volume is reduced to one-fourth, and so on. See Figure 6-4.

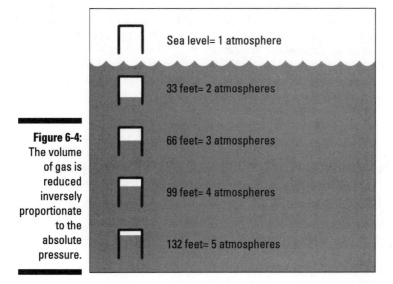

Figure 6-4:
The volume of gas is reduced inversely proportionate to the absolute pressure.

In diving, this means that a breath of air at 33 feet uses twice as much air from your tank as it does at the surface, and a single tank lasts only half as long, at 66 feet it only lasts one-third as long, and at 99 feet only one-quarter as long, and so on.

Charles's Law

Charles's Law also predicts the relationship between a volume of gas and the surrounding pressure, but it adds in another important factor in determining that relationship — temperature. Jacques Charles was a French physicist working in the late eighteenth and early nineteenth centuries. Charles discovered that if a volume of a gas remains constant, the pressure increases as the temperature rises. Or, if the pressure remains the same, the volume increases when the temperature rises.

Suppose you take your scuba tank down to the local dive operator on a really hot day and have it filled to 3,000 pounds per square inch (psi). Then, before you go to use it, a real cold snap hits. So you head down to the beach and set up your regulator and your pressure gauge is way below 3,000. Your tank hasn't been leaking, it's simply been subject to Charles's Law.

Dalton's Law

Because gases mix together so readily, they're almost never found in a pure state in nature. Air, for example, is 78 percent nitrogen, 21 percent oxygen and 1 percent other gases. In mixed gases (such as air), the component gases blend evenly in the mixture, and, each component gas behaves as if it alone occupied the total volume. John Dalton, an English scientist working about the same time as Jacques Charles, formulated this theory now known as *Dalton's Law.* In his spare time, he was the first to describe the atomic structure of matter. In my spare time I was going to clean out the garage, but I fell asleep on the couch watching TV. When I woke up, however, I was able to describe the effects of gravity on drool.

Dalton's Law states:

The total pressure exerted by a mixture of gases is equal to the sum of the pressures that would be exerted by each of the gases if it alone were present and occupied the total volume.

Or, more simply:

The pressure of a gas mixture (such as air) is equal to the sum of the pressures exerted by all the individual gases.

The individual pressure exerted by a particular gas in a mixture is called the *partial pressure.* If you fill a scuba tank with compressed air, the overall pressure increases, but the percentage of each component gas remains the same. So, as the air pressure increases or decreases, the partial pressure of a particular gas increases or decreases along with it. Underwater, the partial pressure of the component gases in air increases; at high altitude, the partial pressure of the same gases decreases.

In essence, you can compare the effects of a gas breathed at higher partial pressure with a greater percentage of that gas breathed at a lower partial pressure. Suppose a very small percentage of carbon monoxide or some other bad stuff is inadvertently mixed into your scuba tank. That's not a good thing, but at surface partial pressure, you won't really notice it. Now you dive to 130 feet and all of a sudden you don't feel very good — the increased partial pressure is the equivalent of breathing a much stronger dose of this toxic gas at the surface.

Henry's Law

Matter is either solid, liquid, or gas. In a solid, the individual molecules are locked together; in a gas, the molecules are relatively distant and flying around like crazy; and in a liquid, they're kind of sliding around next to each other. There's plenty of room in these sliding-around spaces for the occasional molecule, and those of both solids and gases can wander off into these spaces — people call it *dissolving*. That's what happens when you stir a teaspoon full of sugar into your lemonade. Sugar molecules start leaving home to bond with their new friends, the water molecules, and pretty soon they're spread out all over the glass, tucked into those spaces between the liquid water molecules. Gases do the same thing. Carbon dioxide dissolves in water to make soda water. Dissolve a little sugar into that, add some coloring and a little flavoring and you have the basis of a financial empire — better living through chemistry.

William Henry, another English scientist and a close associate of John Dalton, was the first to investigate this phenomenon and formulate a law about it.

Henry's Law states:

The amount of any gas that will dissolve in a liquid at a given temperature is a function of the partial pressure of the gas in contact with the liquid, and the solubility coefficient of the liquid.

In other words, how much gas can be dissolved into a liquid depends on how easily the molecules of liquid bond with the molecules of the gas, along with the temperature and pressure.

Even in solution, gas molecules still behave like gas molecules — they exert the same partial pressure even dissolved in liquid. This is called the *gas tension*. When a gas comes in contact with a liquid, it permeates the liquid until the gas tension equals the pressure of the gas.

When you dive, the temperature differential is insignificant, and so temperature has little effect on the amount of gases that are dissolved into your body, which is mostly liquid. The pressure difference, however, plays a large role. Some body tissues absorb gases easily; other tissues don't. Many other complex factors come into play as well when calculating the amount of gas actually dissolved in the body under pressure, but Henry's Law is the basis of it all.

Murphy's Law

Murphy's Law states:

Anything that can go wrong, will go wrong.

Of course, if that were really true you never would have gotten this far, but it does serve as a reminder that the safest diver is the one who anticipates things going wrong, and is prepared to deal with them.

The first corollary to Murphy's Law

The first corollary is sort of like a restatement of the second law of thermodynamics:

If left to themselves, things tend to go wrong.

Maybe; maybe not. But it doesn't hurt to check all your equipment yourself and always use your own judgment to make the call — you don't want to get into trouble because you were too intimidated, ill-informed, or too lazy to look out for yourself.

The second corollary to Murphy's Law

That Murphy was a really observant fellow. His second corollary states:

Things tend to go wrong all at once.

One complication frequently leads to another, that's what back-up systems are for, but it doesn't help to have backup if you don't know how, or are unprepared, to use it. Periodically, practice using your back-up systems.

O'Toole's Commentary

Murphy was an optimist.

Ignatius J. O'Toole lived a long and obscure life, secluded in his basement apartment. In spite of fanatic precautions, he died anyway. At the end of his life, his greatest fear was said to be that he wouldn't know the difference between death and the life he had led.

Chapter 7

Feelin' All Right

• •

In This Chapter

▶ Staying away from seasickness and problems caused by the sun

▶ Keeping your sinuses and ears healthy

▶ Avoiding barotrauma

▶ Understanding nitrogen absorption and elimination

▶ Being alert for hypothermia and drowning

▶ Brushing up on emergency procedures

• •

Statistically, the greatest hazard to a diver underwater isn't from sharks, malfunctioning equipment, or malicious citizens of the drowned city of Atlantis — it is from the diver's own poor judgment. But traveling and diving do present you with a number of unique — and sometimes stressful — conditions. If you don't take steps to deal with them, you may find your expensive dive trip cut short, spent on your back in your hotel bed or worse yet, in a hospital room. Fortunately, most of the things that can strike you down can be avoided with a little forethought.

Seasickness

The tendency to develop motion sickness varies a great deal from person to person. Some people are at the wheel of the porcelain bus if they make the mistake of sitting in an office chair; others can wolf down sardines and peanut butter sailing around the Horn in a full-on gale. Most people fall somewhere in between. Seasickness is one misery that I've never been visited with, but it sure doesn't look like much fun. Maybe it's because when I was a little kid, I used to think it was fun to play records and spin around until I was so dizzy that I couldn't stand up — don't ask me why. On the other hand, maybe it's because I've lived in California most of my life, where even the ground doesn't stay still very long. Whatever the reason, I don't get seasick easily; maybe you don't either, but if you do, you want to take preventative measures before the rockin' and rollin' starts.

Seasickness is generally less of a problem on a larger boat than on a smaller one, and less on a calm sea than on a rolling one. If it's a problem for you, consider diving from a larger liveaboard vessel over a smaller one, or stay at a land-based resort and dive only in calm waters, or only on days when the sea is flat.

If these options are too confining for you, you can just say "Yes!" to the pharmacological approach. You can find a number of medications that prevent seasickness — Dramamine, Bonine, Scopolamine, and others. They can be taken as a pill and some can be administered *transdermally* (through a patch on the skin). Drugs are effective, but can also cause minor side effects in some people — drowsiness, dry mouth, and so on. Most seasickness medications are over-the-counter products, but check with your doctor to determine which one may be most effective for you.

Some folks swear by *Sea-Bands,* an elastic band developed by the British Navy that you wear around your wrist over an accupressure point that relieves nausea. It seems to work for some people and not for others. The catch is, of course, there's only one way to find out which kind you are. Ginger may also work in controlling nausea, providing you can hold it down. Try it as a tea or in capsules.

Preventative measures are great, but they won't help you much after you're chumming Technicolor gravy over the lee rail. The idea is to take the preventative measures before you go on board. Start the day before if you can, but an hour ahead at the very least. Try to avoid all the conditions that make it worse and make you more susceptible, such as the following:

- ✔ Eating greasy and otherwise hard-to-digest foods
- ✔ Exposing yourself to too much sun
- ✔ Drinking too much alcohol
- ✔ Not getting enough rest
- ✔ Becoming dehydrated

After you're sick, though, there isn't a whole lot you can do. One thing that may provide some relief is to get in the water. Snorkeling or swimming stops the rocking motion, at least for a while. Of course, if the boat is already under way, you have to forego this option and tough it out. In any case, the seasickness shouldn't last more than a day or two. Eventually, you'll adapt to the pitching of the boat, and then you can go through the whole process again, in reverse, when you get back on land!

Problems from Heat and Sun

Lots of great diving takes place in hot, tropical places, and lots of people fantasize about the balmy climate and beautiful beaches. All that stuff is great, but there is a downside too, and it can really spoil your fun if you don't take precautions.

Sunburn

These days the warnings are everywhere: Stay out of the sun, wear sunblock, solar radiation may be hazardous to your health — still, you see people lying on the beach frying their hides like a strip of bacon. If you've just stepped off the plane from some icy northern climate onto a warm, white, sandy beach, it's mighty tempting to stretch out and soak up the sun like a lizard on a flat rock. You should resist the temptation. If you're not used to it (and sometimes even if you are), a fierce tropical sun can really raise heck with your largest organ — your skin.

Be aware that the sunlight bouncing off the surface of the sea, combined with direct rays, will give you that all-over, oven-roasted look and feel. Snorkelers are often lulled into a false sense of security with cool water sloshing across their naked backs and legs and spend hours puttering around the lagoon on their first day at a tropical resort, and then spend the night feeling like they're lying on a barbecue grill. Start with an SPF 45 (or higher) sunblock on your first day in the tropics. After a few days you may be able to step down to a 15, and later on maybe an 8.

Dehydration

Dehydration, an abnormal depletion of body fluids, can strike you surprisingly quickly in a hot climate, especially someplace like Baja or the Red Sea (see Chapter 15) where the air is dry and your perspiration evaporates quickly — you may be sweating like a race horse and not even realize it. Symptoms of dehydration include feeling flushed and experiencing dizziness, headache, and fatigue. In warm climates, dehydration can lead to heat exhaustion or heatstroke (see the following section). Dehydration also makes you more vulnerable to decompression sickness (see the "Nitrogen Absorption and Elimination" section, later in this chapter) because it lowers the quantity of blood available for gas exchange and the elimination of nitrogen from your tissues.

The best way monitor your fluid intake is by the color of your urine — it should be pale yellow. If it gets dark, you're not drinking enough water. Immediately begin drinking lots of nonalcoholic, noncaffeinated liquids. Alcohol and caffeine increase your vulnerability to dehydration: Caffeine is a

---

Cramping your style

Muscle cramps are an involuntary contraction of the muscle, usually the result of overexertion, fatigue, cold, dehydration, or weirdness in your blood salts. Sudden and persistent contraction of the muscle is normally accompanied by severe pain, and for divers, most frequently strikes in the calf muscle. You can relieve this kind of cramp by grabbing the tip of your fin and pulling it back toward your body to stretch the cramped muscle. After you're rid of the cramp, rest the muscle and massage it if you can.

---

diuretic (an agent that increases the volume of urine excreted), and alcohol uses lots of water in the process of being metabolized. I keep a bottle of water with me all the time and drink from it compulsively. Finally, compulsive behavior comes in handy.

Heat exhaustion and heat stroke

Because even relatively warm water cools the body, you're not likely to become overheated when diving, but it can happen. Strenuous exercise, along with wearing a heavy wetsuit in warm tropical waters can get uncomfortable. Normally, when your body gets overheated, it dilates the capillaries in the skin allowing your blood to radiate heat at the surface. At the same time, you perspire, and the evaporation of sweat cools the skin and the blood close to it. A wetsuit, however, prevents this cooling through evaporation. If your body is unable to get your temperature down where it should be, you develop *heat exhaustion.*

You can also become overheated before or after the dive. The symptoms of heat exhaustion are as follows:

- Shallow, rapid breathing
- Rapid pulse
- Weakness
- Cool, clammy skin
- Nausea (sometimes)

These are all signs that your body is straining to get your temperature down, the same way that shivering is an attempt to get your temperature up. Because water conducts heat away from your body so well, submersion in cool water is the most effective way to get your temperature down. Cool compresses, lots of circulating air (such as you get from a fan), and drinking fluid — all of these cool you off through evaporation.

If you can't get your temperature down, you lapse into *heatstroke*. A victim of heatstroke has a strong, rapid pulse. He looks flushed, the skin feels hot, but he's not sweating. Heatstroke is a very serious condition and a medical emergency. Without immediate treatment, heatstroke can result in convulsions, brain damage, and even death.

Sinus and Ear Problems

Any condition that blocks airflow in the sinuses and ears is going to cause problems equalizing air spaces, and may make diving impossible. Most of the conditions affecting sinuses and ears aren't serious, but they can become serious if they're ignored.

Complications from colds, allergies, and sinusitis

There are all kinds of treatments for colds — the good ones will clear it up in about a week, the bad ones in about seven days. In short, you can't do much if you contract a cold. I probably don't have to tell you this, but one thing you shouldn't do is dive. Your breathing isn't up to snuff and a cold will make it difficult, if not impossible, to equalize your ears and sinuses. So, wait a week. You'll feel better. You'll go diving. You'll have a lot more fun.

Allergies can create the same blockage problems, but the congestion is due to an irritant such as pollen or dust rather than a virus. With allergies, you can try a nondrowsy, antihistamine formula, but be careful not to use anything that makes you drowsy — you need to be fully alert while you're diving. And if you can't clear the blockage, you shouldn't dive.

The symptoms of a sinus infection are similar to, but more severe than, a cold or an allergic reaction. An infection in the sinus is usually accompanied by tenderness around the affected area, pain, thick-colored discharge, and sometimes a headache or fever. These are all indications of a more serious condition that usually requires medical treatment with antibiotics before it becomes acute or chronic. You shouldn't attempt to dive if you're suffering from a sinus infection.

Ear infections

Ear infections come in two varieties: inner (or middle) ear and outer ear. They are always a cause for concern and must be treated by a doctor.

Blood in your mask!

Sounds pretty spooky, right? Relax. You have lots of blood vessels very close to the surface, inside your nose, so you don't have to do much to start a nosebleed. Divers sometimes experience nosebleeds due to the pressure changes involved in diving, and they may even accumulate blood in their masks. This looks dramatic, but is generally easy to treat and nothing to get excited about.

✔ Inner ear infections usually start as a complication of a cold or sinusitis, but they can also be the result of water getting into the inner ear through a perforation in the eardrum, which can be a result of not equalizing your ears properly (see Chapter 1). An inner ear infection can be a very serious matter that can result in deafness. Any inner ear infection should get immediate medical attention.

✔ Outer ear infections are either a localized boil or a diffuse bacterial or fungal infection. Boils on the outer ear are like boils anywhere else except that the skin of the ear is attached to the underlying cartilage and there isn't a lot of soft tissue to allow for swelling, making a boil on the ear really painful. You probably won't need any prompting to get to the doctor and have it treated.

Bacterial infections can be treated with antibiotics, but fungal infections generally don't respond well to antibiotics. Fungal infections are more common in the tropics than in temperate climates. A diffuse outer ear infection is really a skin condition and it usually starts in the ear canal and spreads to the rest of the outer ear. If the protective coating in the ear canal gets washed away by too much submersion or by too scrupulous a cleaning, you may be vulnerable to diffuse outer ear infections. Conversely, too much gunk in your ears can interfere with water draining and also make you susceptible to ear infections. So keep your ears clean, but not too clean.

Don't use those cotton swabs to clean your ear canals, even with alcohol. They can push a budding infection deeper into the ear canal and turn a minor problem into a major one.

Exostosis

Exostosis is a bony growth that affects the inner half of the outer ear canal. It develops slowly over a period of years as a response to repeated and prolonged exposure to cold water in the ear canal. It is not an infection and isn't caused by infection, but it can make you susceptible to infection by interfering with water draining from your ears. Exostosis isn't a problem for tropical, warm-water divers, and a hood normally offers sufficient protection for cold-water divers.

Exotosis is more commonly found in surfers than in divers, but it can certainly affect divers who neglect to take precautions and protect their ear canal against exposure. Really bad exostosis can completely block the ear canal and even result in deafness, although the condition can be reversed with surgery.

Respiratory Problems

Being a certified diver won't protect you from developing respiratory problems that may prevent you from diving — temporarily or long-term. It should be obvious that you want to protect your respiratory health, but you may be afflicted in spite of your best efforts. Meanwhile, you see people every day willfully destroying their precious lung function. Go figure.

Complications from smoking

It is truly amazing how many divers smoke cigarettes, cigars, pipes, and other devices designed to smother their lungs. After going through certification training, you'd expect people to have a little more respect for their own miraculous gas exchange organ. But I'm sure you've heard it all before. If you're still sucking those things, I'm not going to beat you up some more here — there are plenty of people around to do that. However, you should seriously consider the risks of combining smoking and diving.

Carbon monoxide (CO) is a tasteless, odorless gas produced by cigarettes, burning petroleum, and other foul stuff like that. Carbon monoxide combines with blood much more readily than oxygen. That's why it doesn't take a lot to kill you. A smoker generally doesn't suck up enough CO to kill him immediately, but smoking raises the level of carbon monoxide in the blood and decreases the level of oxygen. That's why the diving smoker is already *hypoxic* (low on oxygen) when he or she enters the water, and more at risk for hypoxia-related health problems, such as heart attack.

Cigarette smoking is also a well-documented culprit in pulmonary disease such as emphysema and chronic bronchitis. Both of these conditions can result in permanent airway obstruction. When that happens, your diving career is over, for good. Enough said.

Complications from asthma

Asthma is the most controversial health problem among scuba divers and those wishing to become scuba divers. Because it is episodic, and can vary a great deal in severity, opinions about whether or not asthmatics should dive are all over the map. They range from "never under any circumstances," to "not within 48 hours of an attack." It's a murky picture. When you sign up to be certified, you are asked if you've ever had asthma. If you indicate that you have, you will be declined for certification training — even if you only suffered from mild childhood asthma, grew out of it, and have never suffered an attack as an adult. At the same time, there are adults who have developed asthma after having been certified, and continue to dive in spite of it without incident. There are many opinions and very little agreement, except on one thing — nobody wants to get sued, and anybody can find a lawyer eager to prove that you're incapable of taking responsibility for your own life and deserve to be paid millions of dollars because of your lack of judgment.

Pulmonary fibrosis

Pulmonary fibrosis is the medical term for scarring in the lungs. Normally it is the result of one of two diseases — sarcoidosis or pneumoconiosis — but it can also occur without a known cause.

✔ When the cause is unknown, the disease is called *idiopathic pulmonary fibrosis* (IPF). (I hope you're taking notes, there will be a test later.) IPF is quite rare, but anyone suffering with it should *never* dive.

✔ When the cause is *sarcoidosis,* a disease marked by nodules in the lungs and other areas, you may be able to dive. Whether or not you can dive after having contracted sarcoidosis depends on the extent of the disease. The answer will depend on a lung function test, a chest CT scan, and the evaluation of a lung specialist.

✔ When pneumoconiosis – also known as *black lung* or *coal miner's disease* because it's caused by coal dust or silica — is the culprit, whether or not you can dive depends again on a lung function test, chest CT scan, and the evaluation of a lung specialist. The prospects aren't particularly encouraging, so if you want to be a diver you should try to stay out of coal mines altogether. I know it's a sacrifice.

Pneumonoultramicroscopicsilicovolcanoconiosis is the full name of this disease. You can see why it isn't used much, but it does have the distinction of being the longest word in the English language, out-distancing the one fraudulently promoted to you in grammar school: *antidisestablishmentarianism,* by a full 17 letters. (Where else can you get this kind of important information?)

Asthma is a narrowing of the bronchial tubes that results in coughing, wheezing, tightness in the chest and/or shortness of breath. There's no way to tell when an asthmatic is going to have an asthma attack, or how severe it may be. Asthma can obstruct a diver's airflow, and obstructed airflow can lead to barotrauma in the lungs — a potentially deadly problem that's covered in the following section.

Obviously, if you never dive you're safe from these kinds of problems — that's how the most conservative medical view would have it. If you have active asthma requiring frequent medication to control the symptoms, you shouldn't try to dive. On the other hand, if you had childhood asthma and no symptoms as an adult, or if you have otherwise dormant asthma, you may feel unfairly restricted by such recommendations. You may have a point: There is no compelling evidence that diving is significantly more dangerous to divers who admit to having asthma. However, there is an inherent element of risk in diving, and there is an increased risk for asthmatics. How much the risk is increased varies from case to case. What constitutes an acceptable additional risk? Ultimately, it's your responsibility to evaluate the risks and rewards and make that call. If you've ever had asthma, you need to consult with a physician whom you trust to evaluate your condition before you consider getting certified.

Barotrauma

Barotrauma is any injury sustained by an inequality of pressure (see Chapter 6 for more on pressure). Because pressures can vary so radically in diving, barotrauma is always a concern. Barotrauma involves some airspace in the body, most commonly, the lungs, middle ear, or sinuses. It's the result of unequal pressure and either the compression or expansion of one of the body's air spaces. It can result in anything from mild discomfort to death.

Pulmonary barotrauma

Pulmonary barotrauma is injury to the lungs resulting from pressure differences. This kind of injury is most likely to occur as a result of overexpansion of the lungs on ascent.

Scuba is possible because your regulator is able to deliver breathable air at the surrounding ambient pressure. At 33 feet, air is delivered at 2 atmospheres of pressure. A breath of air taken at 33 feet will expand to double its volume at surface pressure, in accordance with Boyle's Law (see Chapter 6). If this expanding air can't be vented from your lungs you are likely to suffer pulmonary barotrauma. That's why the very first law of scuba diving is *never hold your breath*.

Pulmonary barotrauma occurs when the expanding air stretches and then ruptures the little individual air sacs in the lungs where gas exchange takes place — they're called *alveoli*. After the air escapes from the alveoli, it winds up in one of three places, depending on where the rupture takes place:

- **Mediastinal air:** Air gets in the space between the lungs, known as the *mediastinum*. From there it can leak into spaces around the heart, the internal organs, or up into the neck.

- **Pnuemothorax:** Air can escape through the *pleura* (a membrane surrounding the lungs) into the chest cavity resulting in pneumothorax, which can compress or collapse the lung.

- **Air embolism:** Air enters the blood stream as a traveling bubble of air, or an *air embolism*. An air embolism can deprive the brain or heart of blood flow and result in stroke or death.

All of the conditions that result from pulmonary barotrauma are serious, but the most dangerous is an air embolism. All pulmonary barotrauma requires immediate medical attention. Emergency treatment includes administering oxygen and keeping the victim quiet and comfortable as possible

Fortunately, pulmonary barotrauma is rare and it is almost always the result of a diver holding his breath during ascent — a situation that's easily avoided. Still, a small percentage of divers who suffer pulmonary barotrauma don't hold their breath during ascent. These cases are thought to be the result of lung abnormalities that the diver may not even be aware of and that don't cause any problems under normal surface conditions. Although the pressure differences normally encountered in scuba won't damage a normal lung, they may be enough to trigger pulmonary barotrauma in divers with lung abnormalities. If you suspect you may have a problem, it will probably show up in a chest CT scan or an X ray. Check it out before you strap on a tank.

Ear squeeze

Ear squeeze is as common as pulmonary barotrauma is rare. Nearly every diver has experienced ear squeeze at some point. Divers are taught to equalize their ears early and often to avoid this condition. (If you don't know how, check out Chapter 1.)

Ear squeeze is the result of unequalized air space in the middle ear — see Figure 7-1. To equalize the pressure, inhaled compressed air must pass through the *Eustachian tube* — a flexible canal from the middle ear to the back of the mouth. The Eustachian tube acts like a flutter valve — pressurized air passes easily from the middle ear to the throat, which is why divers seldom have problems equalizing on ascent. But air doesn't pass as easily from the throat to the middle ear — that's why when you're descending, you have to perform an air equalizing procedure.

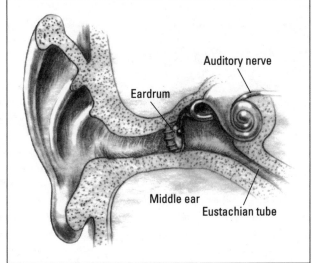

Auditory nerve

Eardrum

Middle ear

Eustachian tube

Figure 7-1:
Ear squeeze
is the
result of
unequalized
pressure in
the middle
ear.

Initially, you experience ear squeeze as a stuffiness in the ears. If you continue to descend without equalizing, you experience sharp pain in your ears as the eardrum is pushed in. If the pressure continues, fluid and blood from the surrounding tissues begin to accumulate in the middle ear — this can lead to middle ear infection. If you descend very quickly, the eardrum may rupture and admit water to the middle ear. This relieves the pain, but cold water in the middle ear generally results in dizziness, and bacteria in the water poses a serious risk of infection, even though the ruptured eardrum may eventually heal.

Sinus squeeze

Colds, allergies, and other upper respiratory conditions can block your sinuses creating an airspace that can't be equalized. *Sinus squeeze* may cause pain in the cheekbones, between the eyes, around the upper teeth, or in the forehead.

As in other unequalized airspaces, hydrostatic pressure draws blood and fluid from the surrounding tissue into the blocked sinus. When you ascend, the expanding air pushes the fluids into the nose, so you may bleed from your nose, as shown in Figure 7-2. If you have blood in your mask or in the back of your throat when you surface, there's a good chance that you've experienced sinus squeeze. Sinus squeeze usually heals by itself and requires no medical treatment, but it can result in infection that may require antibiotics.

Protecting your ears

The following tips can help you protect your ears:

✔ **Equalize:** Equalize your ears continuously as you descend. Don't wait until you feel discomfort.

✔ **Don't descend if you can't equalize:** Never continue a descent if you are unable to clear your ears. Ascend slightly until the discomfort is relieved and try it again. If your ears won't clear, abort the dive.

✔ **Don't dive with a cold:** Colds and allergies can cause tissues to swell, blocking the Eustachian tube. Decongestants may wear off at depth, causing a *reverse block* — pressurized air that's trapped in the middle ear and won't vent when you ascend.

✔ **Never wear earplugs:** Earplugs create a space in the ear canal that can't be equalized. Also, hydrostatic pressure may force the earplugs deep into the ear canal where you cannot remove them easily.

✔ **Get medical attention:** If you experience barotrauma in your ears, or suspect that you may have, consult an otolaryngologist (ear, nose, and throat doctor) immediately.

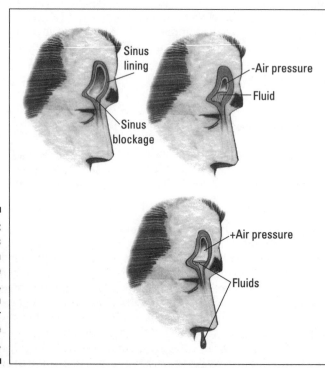

Figure 7-2:
Sinus squeeze can cause nosebleed, most often on ascent or after the dive.

Abdominal squeeze

Everybody knows that certain foods produce intestinal gas. As long as they can be vented, as they normally are, it's not a problem — except maybe socially. Gas that accumulates in your intestines during a dive, however, will expand as you ascend. It can cause discomfort, called *abdominal squeeze,* if it can't be vented fast enough, because the decreased pressure as you ascend increases the volume of gas to be vented. If you experience abdominal gas pains as you ascend, stop your ascent, descend a little if you must, ascend more slowly, and let the gas vent naturally. If you can muster enough of this gas, you may get your own rock 'n' roll talk radio show. If you're satisfied with your day job, avoid gas-producing foods before you dive.

Mask squeeze

Mask squeeze is the result of unequalized airspace between equipment (the mask) and the body (your face) rather than internal airspace, but the mechanics are the same — increased pressure causes the tissues to swell in the unpressurized airspace. The skin keeps blood and fluids from being drawn into the mask. Swelling is usually the most noticeable effect, but sometimes you see bruising around the eyes from the capillaries in the eyes rupturing. It looks bad, but it isn't really serious and generally clears up without complication, usually within a few hours. You may not even be aware of it until you look in the mirror. Actually, you may not even be aware of it then.

Nitrogen Absorption and Elimination

Along with barotrauma, the most significant complication of being under pressure at depth is the absorption of additional nitrogen. Nitrogen is an inert gas — 78 percent of the air you're breathing right now is nitrogen. Nitrogen narcosis is the result of nitrogen absorption, but for the most part, it isn't really the absorption of nitrogen that creates problems — it's the elimination of it after it has been absorbed.

Decompression sickness

Henry's and Dalton's laws (see Chapter 6) predict that additional nitrogen will dissolve in the tissues of your body as you descend underwater. When you come back up again and the pressure decreases, the accumulated nitrogen dissolves out of your tissues and is carried by the blood to the lungs to be exhaled and eliminated. If the pressure is released slowly, as it is when you ascend slowly and make a safety stop, the body can eliminate the excess nitrogen without complication. If the pressure is released too quickly, the nitrogen forms bubbles in the bloodstream — just like a bottle of soda forms

The whole tooth and nothing but the tooth

Occasionally, tooth decay or a poor filling can create an air space in your teeth. It's pretty rare, but it's been known to happen. The result is an unequalized airspace inside the tooth that can result in *dental barotrauma,* or *tooth squeeze.*

If you feel dental pain while diving, discontinue the dive and get yourself to a dentist — you were going to have to go soon anyway.

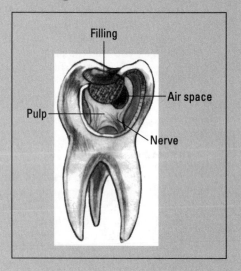

bubbles when you pop off the top. These bubbles cause the symptoms of *decompression sickness* or *DCS.*

The size of the bubbles makes a significant difference in whether or not you suffer from DCS. Divers who suffer no symptoms have been found to have very tiny nitrogen bubbles in their blood after diving. It is the presence of large bubbles, probably created by the combining of lots of smaller bubbles, that manifests the symptoms of DCS.

The bubbles formed in the blood are normally carried away from the tissues by blood traveling from the capillaries back to the heart. If they don't lodge somewhere else first, the bubbles are eventually transported to the very narrow capillaries of the lungs, diffused, and eliminated. If the bubbles are large, they may not get that far. They may lodge in any vein that's too narrow for the bubble to pass and the blockage can create a wide range of symptoms.

Large bubbles of nitrogen in the bloodstream create problems in three ways:

✔ **Blocking circulation:** By lodging in small veins and causing pain. Typically in the joints, usually the shoulders and the elbows first, but it can occur anywhere. This is the origin of the nickname *the bends.*

✔ **Compressing nerves:** Nitrogen dissolves better in fat than in other tissues. Because the nerves are surrounded in a fatty sheath, neurological symptoms are common in DCS — tingling, numbness, and even paralysis.

✔ **Chemical reaction:** The presence of nitrogen bubbles can also set off a chemical inflammatory response that damages blood vessels and affects blood clotting.

Although nitrogen bubbles are believed to be the cause of DCS, they can appear in nearly any part of the body, manifesting dozens of different symptoms. Because there is so much variety in the symptoms, it may be difficult to diagnose DCS, but it does have a few common characteristics. Normally, it doesn't show up right away after the dive. It usually shows up within an hour after the dive, but it can take as long as 36 hours and it generally gets worse over time if left untreated.

DCS is divided into two categories: Type I and Type II.

✔ **Type I DCS:** Symptoms of Type I DCS are less severe than Type II, but still considered serious because it indicates decompression problems, and may very well progress to Type II. Symptoms include:

- Skin bends: This symptom usually manifests as a blotchy, mottled red rash, commonly on the chest and shoulders. It may feel itchy, or tingle.

- Bends: The symptom from which the illness takes its name; that is, pain in the joints and limbs, commonly the shoulders and elbows. Often accompanied by an achy sensation.

✔ **Type II DCS:** The more serious symptoms are classified as Type II DCS. These can be disabling and even life-threatening. Type I symptoms can progress to Type II, which include:

- The chokes or pulmonary DCS: Bubbles that make it to the pulmonary capillaries will normally diffuse into the lungs and be exhaled, but, if they are large and numerous they may back up and block blood flow. This can interfere with gas exchange and reduce oxygen to the tissues, or even cause a shortage of blood to the left side of the heart and circulatory collapse. Symptoms include breathing pain, shortness of breath, and a short cough. The victim feels as if he's not getting enough air (he's not), hence the nickname _the chokes_.

- Neurological DCS: Bubbles forming in nerve tissues can affect movement, sensation, and even functions like heartbeat and breathing. Neurological DCS commonly affects the spinal column causing numbness and paralysis that begins in the extremities and creeps up. Bubbles can also form in the brain causing symptoms similar to air embolism — blurred vision, headache, unconsciousness, and even death.

Recompression

There is only one treatment for any type of DCS: recompression in a hyperbaric chamber. If the treatment is begun quickly, DCS is completely reversible. The victim is recompressed, dissolving the bubbles, and then slowly brought back to normal surface pressure, allowing the excess accumulated nitrogen to be safely eliminated.

A *hyperbaric chamber* is a large, sealed cylinder that can be pressurized to simulate depth. In the chamber, the nitrogen is recompressed, allowing the body to eliminate it slowly and safely. The rate of ascent, determined by the physician who is evaluating the victim, can be controlled from a console. Oxygen is usually administered, and some doctors also use drugs to minimize inflammation and other symptoms.

Hyperbaric chambers are found in most major American cities and in most popular foreign dive destinations, but in some places a hyperbaric chamber may be some distance away and the only practical transport is by air. Increased altitude generally worsens DCS because it lowers the ambient pressure squeezing even more nitrogen from the super-saturated tissues. Even so, the time saved by flying the victim to the nearest available chamber outweighs the risk. The aircraft should fly as low as possible and be pressurized to sea level, if it can be.

Narcosis

Given enough decompression time, nitrogen absorption could be effectively managed to allow recreational divers to go a lot deeper than the 130-foot safe diving limit. DCS isn't what keeps divers from going deeper, however; it's *nitrogen narcosis,* the "rapture of the deep." Nitrogen, dissolved in the brain and nerve tissues at higher pressure, acts as an anesthetic gas, resulting in a state of euphoria that simulates drunkenness — and drunkenness is a really bad idea when you're scuba diving.

Additional nitrogen dissolves in the body tissues (including the tissues of the brain) at higher pressure. The effects are directly related to pressure. At the surface, there is no effect from the nitrogen permeating the body. At two atmospheres there is still no noticeable effect, but at three atmospheres (about 66 feet) mental processes are affected (see Chapter 6). The diver may not notice the difference, but tests have demonstrated a drop in performance at three atmospheres. At four atmospheres of pressure, most divers begin to notice some effects; by four and one half atmospheres, everyone can feel it. Beyond that, it gets real weird down there, and that can mean trouble in a world where the penalty for lapses in judgment can be severe and immediate.

The effects of narcosis vary a lot from one person to the next. Some hardly feel it at all at 130 feet; others start getting goofy at 80 feet. There is one universal constant however: After you start to feel it, it's going to get more pronounced, the deeper you go. Conversely, the effects dissipate immediately on ascending with no apparent side effects.

Any gas under pressure can have a narcotic effect; it isn't restricted to nitrogen. The solubility of the gas in liquid determines its narcotic effect. Nitrogen, for example, is much more soluble than helium (another inert gas) and consequently helium has no significant narcotic effect. That's why a mixture of helium and oxygen, called *heliox,* is used by deep, commercial divers. So, I can hear you asking, why isn't heliox used by recreational divers to avoid narcosis? Well, it's expensive, for one thing, and it has a whole list of its own complications and procedures that divers must observe to avoid problems. For recreational diving, it simply isn't practical. Better you should use air and simply observe the 130-foot limit. That's where all the good stuff is anyway.

The high diver

Reduced air pressure at higher altitudes can precipitate DCS in divers who are experiencing no symptoms at surface pressures. Even though airline cabins are pressurized, they aren't pressurized to the same pressure that you experience at sea level. Usually they are pressurized to an equivalent of between 5,000 and 10,000 feet above sea level. For a diver who still has a lot of nitrogen dissolved in his or her tissues, that may be high enough to trigger the onset of DCS.

Many dive computers advise you as to how long you should wait before you fly after diving, but make it a rule to always wait at least 12 hours. If you're making daily, multiple dives you should wait even longer. Remember, individual physiology being what it is, no recommendation, including that of your computer, can absolutely guarantee that you won't get DCS by flying after diving. The easiest way to handle it is simply not to dive at all on your last day before flying. Dedicate that day to sightseeing, shopping, or lying on the beach.

Diving at high altitude poses a similar problem to flying after diving. The difference, of course, is you begin and end your dive at reduced air pressure, rather than going from sea level to reduced pressure in the cabin of an airliner. You can use the dive planner supplied by your certification agency to plan dives up to 1,000 feet of altitude; beyond that you need special conversion tables and special procedures to dive safely. Some computers compensate for increased altitude all by themselves; other models require you to enter the altitude; still others can't be used at altitude. If you insist on diving at high altitude, take a specialized high altitude diving course.

Oxygen toxicity

Everybody needs oxygen to survive. Healthy people need just as much oxygen as is contained in air (21 percent), and that's all. Kind of nice the way that works. People who are ill and have low blood oxygen are often given supplemental oxygen to boost the amount of oxygen in their blood, but more is not necessarily better. Too much oxygen is not a good thing. It can result in oxygen toxicity — a potentially life-threatening condition.

Normally, you can't inhale enough oxygen to induce oxygen toxicity. Only with supplemental oxygen or an increase in the partial pressure of oxygen can your body absorb enough to be toxic. In recreational diving, oxygen toxicity is not a risk. As long as you stick to your computer or dive tables (see Chapter 3), you won't have a problem. At the maximum recreational dive limit of 130 feet, the partial pressure of oxygen is roughly equivalent to breathing 100 percent oxygen at sea level — it would take at least an hour at this depth to reach toxic levels and recreational dive tables allow only a few minutes at 130 feet. If you increase the percentage of oxygen, however, it's a whole new ballgame.

Enriched air, or *nitrox*, is a specially formulated breathing cocktail with a higher percentage of oxygen than ordinary air. It is becoming increasing popular with recreational divers (see Chapter 12). There are some distinct advantages to breathing nitrox. It is normally 32 or 36 percent oxygen, and substantially lowers the risk for nitrogen narcosis and DCS, but at the same time it raises the risk of oxygen toxicity — particularly on deep dives. Because the first symptoms of oxygen toxicity can be seizures, it poses a threat of drowning.

When enriched air was first introduced, there was a lot of controversy about whether or not nitrox was safe for use by recreational divers. Today, it's regarded as mainstream — most manufacturers make equipment for it and most agencies offer an enriched air specialty. With proper training and use, it's safe, but keep in mind that oxygen toxicity may not offer any second chances if you're reckless.

Hypothermia

You may be perfectly comfortable in 70° air temperature, but become chilled pretty quickly in 70° water. That's because heat is conducted away from your body much more effectively in water. Most divers need some kind of protective exposure suit in water less than 80°. In water 60° or less, an unprotected diver can quickly develop hypothermia.

Hypothermia occurs when your body is no longer able to maintain the core temperature. *Vasoconstriction,* the mechanism that has slowed circulation to your extremities to conserve heat, ceases to function. Immediately, you may feel more comfortable as relatively warm blood rushes to your extremities, but in this condition you lose heat very rapidly as hypothermia sets in.

There are generally three stages of hypothermia: mild, moderate, and severe.

- ✔ **Mild:** Victims of mild hypothermia may be disoriented, have trouble speaking or walking, and may shiver uncontrollably.

- ✔ **Moderate:** Victim's heart rate slows and blood pressure drops. Victim may lose consciousness.

- ✔ **Severe:** Victim is in shock, is unconscious and unresponsive, and has a slow or disturbed heart rate. Death is imminent.

Emergency first aid for hypothermia involves rewarming the body by applying warm blankets and hot water bottles, and (if the victim is conscious) giving hot liquids, although alcohol and caffeinated beverages should be avoided. It isn't sufficient just to wrap the victim up because he's no longer capable of warming himself with his own body heat.

You can protect yourself from hypothermia with some kind of exposure suit. A dive skin is generally sufficient in water over 80°. Down to about 50° or so, a wetsuit should do the job — the colder the water, the thicker the suit, and be sure to include a hood and gloves at the low end. Below 50°, it's time to break out the dry suit. (See Chapter 2 for more about exposure suits).

Individuals respond differently to cold. Fat tissue insulates you from the cold, so overweight divers lose heat more slowly than thin ones. Acclimation also makes a dramatic difference. After a winter of surfing on the California coast, I can dive all day in 80° water without so much as a dive skin and never feel chilled. But after a few weeks in the tropics, I have to resort to using a 2mm wetsuit on every dive.

Drowning

Drowning and near-drowning both involve a victim in the water who's unable to get the required oxygen — the difference is that the drowning victim doesn't survive. Drowning is, as you may expect, the most frequently listed cause of death in fatal scuba diving accidents.

There are two types of drowning and near-drowning:

- ✔ **Dry drowning:** Oddly enough, not all drowning victims inhale water. In about 15 percent of drowning and near-drowning incidents, the larynx of the victim reflexively clamps shut. This is known as *dry drowning*, and these kinds of victims can recover quickly and completely, if you can reestablish their breathing before they suffer damage from lack of oxygen. If you can't, they will essentially suffocate.

✔ **Wet drowning:** When the victim inhales water, called *wet drowning,* the situation is somewhat different. Fluid in the lungs prevents the diffusion of oxygen to the blood, so the victim loses consciousness and dies unless ventilation is restored quickly.

Even if breathing can be restored quickly, the wet drowning victim isn't out of the woods. Water may damage the lungs, causing the lining to swell or leak fluid from the capillaries, sometimes hours or days after the initial incident. This is known as *secondary drowning* and without medical treatment it can be just as fatal.

It isn't always clear what leads to a drowning. Fortunately, for the diver attempting rescue it makes no difference — the treatment is all the same. In fact, it's the same for lung-expansion injuries and decompression sickness as well. See the "CPR (cardiopulmonary resuscitation)" section, later in this chapter, for details.

Emergencies

Scuba diving and snorkeling are sports involving an element of risk, no matter how small it may be. It is always a good idea if you, or at least someone in your party, is familiar with emergency medical procedures such as CPR. The goals of emergency first aid in the field are as follows:

✔ Keep the victim alive

✔ Don't make things worse

✔ Help the victim recover

The ABCs

Get the victim professional medical attention as soon as possible, but in the meantime, you may have to take immediate action to keep the victim alive. Even if you don't have training, remember the emergency ABCs:

A Airway: Check to make sure the airway is clear and free of obstruction. If you think that a foreign body may be blocking the airway, check the back of the tongue with your fingers. If the victim is conscious or semiconscious, be careful that he doesn't reflexively bite you or vomit.

B Breathing: Check that the victim is breathing. If he isn't, you may need to start mouth-to-mouth resuscitation.

C Circulation: Check for a pulse. It's probably easiest to detect at the large artery in the neck next to the windpipe. If there is no pulse, you may have to start CPR, discussed in the following section.

CPR (cardiopulmonary resuscitation)

If the victim has no pulse, you may have to administer emergency CPR. Most local communities give free CPR training, but it is also an integral part of some advanced diver training courses, which have the added benefit of helping your foresee and prevent emergency situations, as well as aid in more common situations, such as assisting a tired diver. Everyone should know CPR. Even if you aren't able to perform it, you may direct someone else. There's no substitute for training, but even theoretical knowledge is better than nothing. Assuming the victim is lying flat on his back, probably unconscious, and that you've done the ABC check and found that the victim isn't breathing and has no pulse, do the following:

1. **Position the head.**

   Gently tilt the head back so that the chin is pointed up. Lift the chin to ensure that the tongue doesn't block the airway.

2. **Breathe into the victim's lungs.**

   Pinch the nose closed and put your mouth completely over the victim's mouth, creating a tight seal. Exhale into the victim's airway. Your exhaled breaths contain 16 percent oxygen — enough to sustain life. Make sure you see the chest rise slightly, indicating that air is entering the victim's lungs.

3. **Check the pulse.**

   Administer two full breaths, and then check for a pulse at the throat. If you feel a pulse and the victim begins breathing on his own, you can discontinue mouth-to-mouth. If you don't find a pulse but the victim still isn't breathing own his own, continue mouth-to-mouth.

4. **Kneel next to the victim's chest.**

   Place the heel of your hand on top of the breastbone, about 1 inch above where the bottom ribs attach. Put your other hand on top of the first hand and straighten your elbows. Push down to compress the chest about two inches in a regular rhythm, 15 times.

5. **Administer two more breaths.**

   Breathe into the victim's lungs as you do in Step 2. Afterward, check for a pulse and to see if the victim is breathing on his own. If not, continue the cycle of two breaths and 15 compressions until medical help arrives.

Emergency situations in the field should be regarded as a worse-case scenario until the situation can be evaluated by a physician. Lung-expansion injuries should be treated as potential air embolism and any symptoms of DCS should be evaluated by a physician, even if the symptoms go away after a while.

Divers Alert Network

The Divers Alert Network (DAN) is a dive safety organization affiliated with the Duke University Medical Center in Durham, North Carolina. Its mission is to promote diver safety and prevent diving accidents; promote research on diver safety and medical treatment; and provide accurate, up-to-date information about diving and diver safety.

DAN's most popular service is its diving emergency hotline, which offers 24-hour emergency consultation and referral worldwide. You don't have to be a member to call, and you can even call collect. The hotline can refer you to the nearest hyperbaric chamber anywhere in North America and the Caribbean, answer your questions, and help you through an emergency.

DAN has a number of other services, including a nonemergency medical information line that provides information on health and diving issues 9 a.m. to 5 p.m. eastern standard time, Monday through Friday. Another of its great services is low-cost insurance that includes medical evacuation anywhere in the world — what a deal. See the Appendix for DAN contact information.

Part III

Under the Sea

In this part . . .

The oceans are dynamic places — all of that water is moving around all over the planet all of the time. Sometimes the motion is barely detectable; sometimes it's absolutely awe-inspiring. If you're going to submerge yourself in the waters of the ocean, you may get more out of the experience by knowing a little about the ways of ocean waters. The ocean has its share of surprises — that's part of the reason why diving is so much fun — but much of the behavior of ocean water conforms to predictable physical laws. This part takes a look at them, and prepares you to deal with the dynamic ocean environment.

What also makes diving so much fun is seeing all of of the weird and wonderful things that live under the sea. From squirming, iridescent, multitentacled reef-creepers to sleek, silver-finned, blue water missiles, the sea is, well, swimming with fantastic species — each a miracle of evolution.

Yeah, this is the part with the stuff about sharks.

Chapter 8

Ocean Reveries

• •

In This Chapter

▶ Fathoming the world oceans

▶ Going with the flow — ocean currents

▶ Dealing with surf and shore currents

▶ Understanding tidal motions

▶ Evaluating conditions

• •

*T*he oceans have inspired poets and painters (and just about everybody else) for as long as humans have stood on their shores or ventured out in boats on their wide and rolling waters. Three-quarters of the globe have sloshed, leaped, and rolled since the first tick of time; even now, the world's oceans are its great repositories of mystery — nestled into the bays of every continent on earth, tucked along the shorelines, tossing like a titan in an uneasy sleep, or fully awakened to pound the trembling rocks with its great blue-knuckled fists. The moods of the mountains are strange to us and the life of the sky unimaginable, but the ocean is both enigmatic and familiar.

Freshwater diving has its own charm — in places like the Great Lakes, it's very popular — but the vast majority of diving is done in the ocean. From the tropics to the poles, oceans provide a variety of environments and a wealth of diversity. Oceans are constantly in motion. Oceanic motions may be gentle or immensely powerful — waves, currents, tides — they all affect diving.

The World Ocean

The fact is, all the world's oceans, seas, gulfs, bays, and straits are connected in a single immense body of water. A picture of earth from the poles makes this a lot more evident, but continental land masses dictate much of the world ocean's movements, and temperature differences between the tropical and polar regions make an effective barrier to many kinds of marine life, so, for divers, it is more useful to think of the oceans and seas as distinct bodies of water.

In the same way that the world's landmasses are divided into continents, its oceans can be divided into four separate basins: the Pacific, the Atlantic, the Indian, and the Arctic. The Pacific is, by far, the largest — more than twice the size of the Atlantic, which is the second largest. The Indian Ocean comes in third, and the Arctic is the smallest.

You've probably heard of the seven seas? Forget it. Actually, there are 12 seas in the world, but somehow "I've sailed the 12 seas," doesn't have much of a ring to it. All 12 seas are extensions of the four oceans.

- Seven of them are attached to the Pacific: the Bering Sea, the Sea of Okhotsk, the Sea of Japan, the Yellow Sea, the East China Sea, South China Sea, and the Sea of Cortez.

- The Atlantic has five seas: the Black Sea (an extension of the Mediterranean Sea), the Mediterranean Sea, the North Sea, the Baltic Sea, and the Caribbean Sea, plus one gulf — the Gulf of Mexico — and one bay — the Hudson Bay (which is larger than some of the seas).

- The Indian Ocean has one sea, the Red Sea, and one gulf, the Persian Gulf.

- The Arctic Ocean doesn't have any seas attached to it.

There are lots of other seas, like the Arafura Sea or the Aegean Sea, and all manner of bays, gulfs, and straits, but those are names for particular areas of a larger body of water like the Pacific or the Mediterranean.

Extending out into the oceans and seas around the continental landmasses is the underwater plateau known as the *continental shelf.* The width of the continental shelf varies a great deal from place to place, from a few miles to a few hundred miles. The continental shelf is important because that's where the majority of the marine life is concentrated, and that's where most diving is done. Beyond the continental shelf lie the abyssal plains of the deep ocean. The abyssal plains have long been assumed to be watery deserts, but little is actually known about them.

Because they are separated by temperature and landmass, and have evolved in different ways, each of the world's oceans and seas has character of its own. Of course, you may see noticeable differences *within* a particular ocean, but in general, the following sections tell you what you can expect in some of the most popular diving waters.

The Pacific

The Pacific, shown in Figure 8-1, is not only the largest body of water in the known universe, it is the one with the greatest diversity and numbers of species. The Pacific accounts for 40 percent of the world's total sea surface. It tends to be deeper in the north than in the south, and in the west than in the east, with the exception of the far Western Pacific (from the Philippines to northern Australia and west to the Indian Ocean). This is the shallowest part of the Pacific with a corresponding abundance of islands.

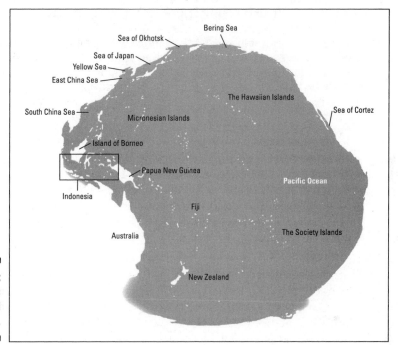

Figure 8-1:
The Pacific
Ocean and
its seas.

The Pacific is also the world's deepest ocean. Average depth is about 14,000 feet. The deepest points are in *ocean trenches* — deep valleys on the underwater plain — near island groups in the western Pacific. There are six ocean trenches in the Pacific: the Mindinao Trench (38,030 feet), the Mariana Trench (36,373 feet), the Tonga Trench (35,911 feet), the Kuril-Kamchatka Trench (34,789 feet), the Philippine Trench (34,640 feet), and the Kermadec Trench (33,155 feet).

The greatest diversity of marine species in the world is found in the Indo-Pacific. About 2,000 different species of fish are known there, and there are probably more yet to be discovered. That number declines as you move east across the Pacific, to only about 300 species along the coasts of the Americas. The far Western Pacific was divided into three separate basins during the last Ice Age. Life evolved independently in each, and when the Ice Age ended and the seas were joined, the diversity of species was tripled. The coral reefs of the Western Pacific support the greatest diversity of marine life in the world, but coral reefs and their inhabitants flourish only in warm, clear tropical waters (see Chapter 9). Corals are sedentary creatures that travel only in the larval state, and only by drifting in the ocean currents. The prevailing east-to-west currents in the tropical Pacific push drifting coral larva to the west, and cold currents in the north and south prevent the coral larva from circulating back to the coasts of the Americas. That's why there isn't much coral growth or diversity of species in the Eastern Pacific.

The west coasts of North and South America with their cool, nutrient-rich upwelling currents (discussed in "A current affair" section, later in this chapter) support large populations of fishes, even though the diversity of species are limited. These waters support one of the world's greatest fisheries. Beyond the continental shelf in the north Pacific, there isn't much to attract the interest of divers until midocean. There you encounter one of the world's most unique island *archipelagos* (group of islands): the Hawaiian Islands.

The Hawaiian Islands are the most isolated chain of islands in the world. Before they were discovered by humans, the Hawaiian Islands were home to more *endemic species* (species found nowhere else) than any other island chain on earth — including the Galapagos Islands in Ecuador (see Chapter 15). Today, Hawaii has the unfortunate distinction of being the island chain with the highest number of extinct and threatened species. Even today, though, nearly a third of Hawaii's fish life is endemic to the islands.

Beyond the Hawaiian Islands, in the tropic of cancer, lie the Marshall Islands. This area of the Pacific is characterized by excellent hard coral growth and lots of open water *pelagics* (species that live in the open ocean, far from land). Farther east are the islands of Micronesia; there you really begin to see the diversity of the Western Pacific. To the north, the islands of Japan offer cold water diving conditions.

The area from the Philippines in the north to Fiji in the east to west to Malaysia in the west, offers the finest diving in the world, in terms of marine life. Many of the world's legendary dive sites are within this triangle. To the south, New Zealand offers fine cold-water diving. Proceeding east across the South Pacific, while people find a noticeable decline in species beyond Fiji, you can still do some excellent diving throughout Polynesia.

The Atlantic

The Atlantic (see Figure 8-2) is the second largest of the world's oceans and is typically divided into the North Atlantic and the South Atlantic. The dividing line is between the far west cape of North Africa and far east cape of Brazil, pinching the Atlantic at the waist.

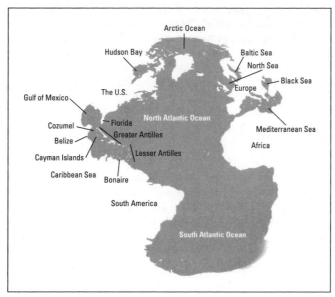

Figure 8-2:
The Atlantic
Ocean.

The average depth of the Atlantic is about 11,880 feet. There are three ocean trenches in the Atlantic — the Puerto Rico Trench (30,426 feet), the South Sandwich Trench (27,270 feet), and the Romansh Trench (25,502 feet). These ocean trenches are the far frontiers of diving. Obviously, they are far beyond the range of scuba diving, and it was once believed that the enormous pressure, dark, and cold of these places would make life here impossible, but in recent years, deep ocean robotic submersibles have brought back evidence of life even in these forbidding places.

In the center of the Atlantic is the mid-Atlantic ridge, where seams between four different tectonic plates are splitting apart.

The tropical waters of the Atlantic have excellent conditions for coral growth, but lack the proliferation found in the Western Pacific and have a relatively low diversity of species. As in the Pacific, a prevailing east-to-west equatorial current, counterclockwise currents in the South Atlantic, and clockwise currents in the North dictate the distribution of corals and the marine life supported by coral reefs. Cool currents travel along the southwestern coast of Africa, preventing coral growth. Coral growth there is also inhibited by the murky freshwater outflow of large rivers like the Congo and the Niger. The western side of the South Atlantic has some coral growth, and diving is becoming increasingly popular in Brazil and other South American nations. But coral growth is inhibited on this coast, to some degree by the enormous outflow of the Amazon River — the greatest of any river on earth — and secondarily by the Orinoco. The best tropical diving in the Atlantic, as you may expect, is in the islands north of the Greater Antilles: the Bahamas and the Turks and Caicos, and along the east coast of the southern United States. As the gulf stream current crosses the North Atlantic, it brings warmer water to Northern Europe and makes diving in Ireland and Scotland more tolerable than you may expect at those high latitudes, but still cold-water diving, to be sure.

The Caribbean

The Caribbean Sea, shown in Figure 8-3, is an extension of the Atlantic Ocean, but separated from it by a long chain of islands called the Greater Antilles — Cuba, Hispaniola, and Puerto Rico — and Lesser Antilles — made up of the Leeward Islands to the north and the Windward Islands to the south. Equatorial currents bring warm water into the Caribbean, making conditions excellent for coral growth. You can find lots of coral, but the diversity is not that of the Western Pacific. About 75 species of coral and 500 species of fish are known in the Caribbean.

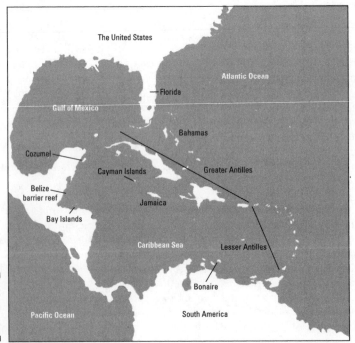

Figure 8-3:
The
Caribbean.

Diving conditions are generally excellent throughout the Caribbean, with the notable exception of Haiti. Haiti's coral reefs have been devastated and the waters badly overfished. In fact, the entire island is nothing short of a complete environmental disaster. The rest of the Greater Antilles have fared better: Both Cuba and Puerto Rico have very good diving, as do all of the Lesser Antilles.

Bonaire, off the northern coast of Venezuela, has instituted all kinds of progressive programs to protect the reefs and thereby attract more dive travelers. Belize, in the Western Caribbean, is home to one of the world's few barrier reefs and diving there is a well-established industry. There aren't any true *atolls* (coral reefs that have grown up around the perimeter of an island, that subsequently sink back into the sea leaving a large coral ring at the surface) in the Caribbean, but Belize has three reefs that have grown on submerged *seamounts* (underwater mountains that almost reach the surface of the sea) in a circular, atoll shape: Glover's Reef, Turneffe Islands, and Lighthouse Reef.

Cozumel, an island off the Mexican mainland, probably shares with Cayman the best established diving industry in the Caribbean — the diving is considered among the very best in the Caribbean. Drift diving (discussed in Chapter 10) is the order of the day in Cozumel, but you can find a more varied menu and an equally well-established industry in the three tiny Cayman Islands, south of Cuba.

Diving in the Gulf of Mexico is inferior to the Caribbean — visibility is not as good, especially near the coastline, and there are very few islands away from the shore.

The average depth of the Caribbean is about 7,500 feet. The deepest point is in the Cayman Trench at 23,430 feet.

The Mediterranean

The Mediterranean is also an extension of the Atlantic, connected to it by the narrow Strait of Gibraltar — see Figure 8-4. The prevailing current in the Mediterranean circulates east along the coast of North Africa, north in the Middle East, and west along the southern shore of Europe.

Figure 8-4: The Mediterranean.

There is no significant coral growth in the Mediterranean and most areas are heavily fished. With the Red Sea so close at hand, there isn't much reason to dive in the Mediterranean, except for the ruins — there are numerous ancient wrecks and even sunken cities in the Mediterranean, particularly in Greece. Unfortunately, the Greek government hasn't been particularly cooperative in allowing divers to view these ancient treasures. Considering the amount of theft of artifacts that's gone on in the past, maybe their position isn't that unreasonable, but hopefully, they'll see the value of dive tourist dollars and allow some limited, well-supervised exploration of these sites in the future.

The average depth of the Mediterranean is 4,560 feet; the deepest point is about 15,990 feet.

The Indian Ocean

Most of the Indian Ocean, shown in Figure 8-5, lies in the southern hemisphere. It is the third largest of earth's oceans and its currents run clockwise in the north and counterclockwise in the south. The Indian Ocean has good coral growth around most of its perimeter, except in the extreme north in the Arabian Sea and the Bay of Bengal. The Andaman Sea, in the east, is a well-established diving area with many of the same Indo-Pacific species that you see in Indonesia and the Western Pacific. Western Australia also has a well-established diving industry — the Ningaloo Reef, near the town of Exmouth of the west coast, is one of the most reliable places in the world to see the world's largest fish, the whale shark. The coast of East Africa also has good coral growth and diving, but the island of Madagascar is another island teetering on the brink of environmental disaster.

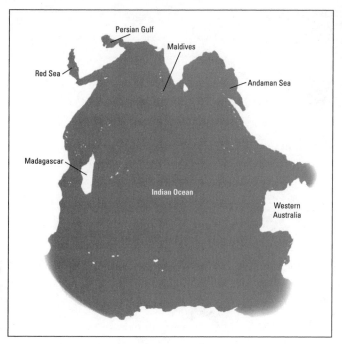

Figure 8-5:
The Indian
Ocean.

Some of the Indian Ocean's best diving is in the Maldives. The Maldives, covered more extensively in Chapter 15, are a chain of 26 atolls extending from just southwest of the tip of India to just beyond the equator. The Republic of the Maldives is a nation of tiny islands — you won't find any mountains or rivers in the Maldives, but there is spectacular diving almost everywhere. The Maldives have an oddly progressive environmental policy — all fishing, including commercial, is done with hook and line. No net fishing is allowed in the islands, and the result is an astonishing abundance of marine life. I have never been on (or heard of) a bad dive in the Maldives.

The average depth of the Indian Ocean is 13,200 feet and the deepest point is in the Amirante Trench, 29,700 feet down.

The Red Sea

The Red Sea is an extension of the Indian Ocean extending in a long, narrow finger to the northwest — take a look at Figure 8-6. In the south, the Red Sea is connected to the Indian Ocean at the narrow strait of Bab El Mandeb. In the north, it is divided by the Sinai peninsula into the Gulf of Aquaba in the east and the Gulf of Suez in the west. In general, currents run north along the eastern shore and south in the west, but currents are modified by the narrow outlet of Bab El Mandeb and aren't normally very strong.

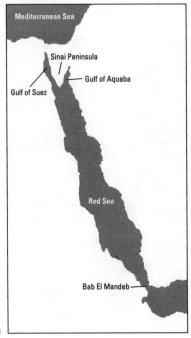

Mediterranean Sea

Sinai Peninsula

Gulf of Aquaba

Gulf of Suez

Red Sea

Bab El Mandeb

Figure 8-6:
The Red
Sea.

The Red Sea has excellent coral growth and many unique, endemic species in the north, particularly in Israel and Egypt. You can find many dive operations well-equipped to help you pay them an underwater visit. The southern half of the Red Sea isn't dived as often and is more pristine. Several liveaboard dive boats schedule regular trips there, and that's probably the best (if not the only) way to dive the area.

Wind on the Water

More than anything else, wind is the engine that moves water. The tides are created by the gravitational effect of the moon and the sun, and have some incidental movement as a result of seismic events, such as earthquakes and volcanos, but wind is the source of most movement in the oceans and seas. Volumes of water on the move in the ocean are called currents and they can be enormous — the Gulf Stream, for example, moving between the tip of Florida and the island of Cuba, can move at up to 4 knots (about 4½ mph) and carry water equivalent to many hundreds of times the volume of the Mississippi River.

A current affair

Water moves within and even between the world's oceans and seas by means of ocean currents. *Ocean currents,* shown in Figure 8-7, are created when persistent, prevailing winds blow on open water and surface water is pushed along by the wind.

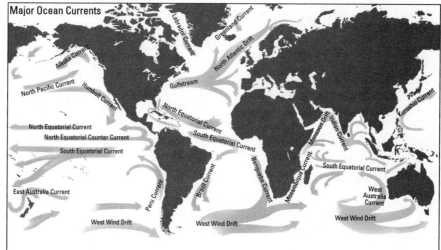

Figure 8-7:
World
oceans
and their
surface
currents.

The prevailing winds in the tropical Pacific, for example, blow from east to west. This creates an equatorial current moving warm surface water from the eastern Pacific off the west coast of central and south America to the western Pacific off southeast Asia. In the middle latitudes, winds blow primarily from the northwest, pushing surface water to the southeast, but fluids (matter capable of flowing, both liquids and gases are fluids) moving north and south are affected by the *Coriolis Effect* — they deflected to the west due to the earth's rotation. Along the west coast of North America, prevailing winds create a current moving to the south. The Coriolis Effect deflects this southerly current to the west — offshore.

As the surface water moves offshore, cool, nutrient-rich waters rise from the depths to replace them. This phenomenon is known as *upwelling* — a second, vertical current from the depths to the surface. Upwelling, along with the nutrients it brings from the depths to the sunlit surface waters, makes the west coast of North America one of the richest marine environments in the world.

Ocean currents ensure the circulation of ocean water, and transport nutrients and marine life from place to place. In general, because of the influence of the Coriolis Effect, ocean currents circulate clockwise in northern hemisphere and counterclockwise in the southern hemisphere. In places where surface currents are free to spread out, such as on the open ocean, the currents usually move quite slowly and are seldom very deep — even a fairly strong surface current may be unnoticeable at a few hundred feet. Where currents are forced into narrow channels between landmasses, they can be very swift and run deep as well — in some places, the Gulf Stream moves water as deep as 2,600 feet.

The nice thing about major ocean currents is that they're well-known and relatively predictable — they don't generally cause problems for divers. In fact ocean currents, like very dependable Gulf Stream current that flows around the island of Cozumel, are a big attraction for divers. Well-nourished marine life in the swift current make Cozumel one of the best drift diving destinations in the world (see Chapter 15).

Waves

While wind creates ocean currents, it is also responsible for the more familiar and visible phenomenon known as *waves* — chop, swell, surge, seas, and surf — they are all the result of wind on the water.

The winds are the result of uneven heating and cooling of the earth's atmosphere and lots of other highly complex dynamics. The winds blow on the water and the friction between the two medium creates waves. A slight puff of wind raises a small ripple in the water that dissipates quickly, but if the wind blows for a long time and over a large area, it raises more significant waves. As the surface of the sea becomes more uneven, the wind has an easier time transferring energy to the sea because it can push directly on the backs of the waves. As the wind continues to blow, the waves become more exaggerated, but there is a limit. When the height of the wave achieves about a 1:7 ratio of the wave length (the distance from crest to crest) the wave breaks and forms what we know as *whitecaps*.

Waves are measured in two ways: the wavelength and the height (see Figure 8-8). Wavelength is the distance from crest to crest; the height is the distance from the bottom of the trough to the top of the crest, vertically. The wavelength and overall size of the waves depends on the strength of the wind, how long it blows, and the size of the area over which it blows (called the *fetch*). Respectable ocean waves can be generated by storms in a fetch of a few hundred miles. The largest wave ever documented was encountered by the U.S.S. Ramapo in the North Pacific after a long period of bad weather — it was estimated to be 112 feet. If just contemplating such a wave makes you run for the

Dramamine, you can take comfort in the fact that such enormous mountains of water are extraordinarily rare. Nearly half of the ocean waves are less than four feet high and 65 percent are less than seven seven feet. The really big stuff, 12 feet and up, only represents 20 percent of the world's ocean waves, and waves over 20 feet represent only 10 percent. When you're out on that liveaboard, hanging on the lee (downwind) rail and offering up your lunch to the snappers, now you know who to blame — the wind!

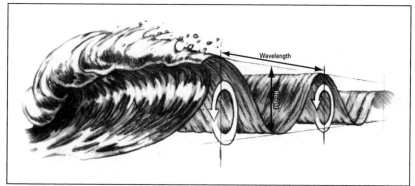

Figure 8-8: Anatomy of a wave.

After waves radiate beyond the area of the fetch, they become less chaotic and consolidated into more regular pulses, with greater wavelength and increasing speed — this is known as *swell*. The direction of the swell is dictated by the direction of the wind that created them. The swell continues until the energy is dissipated, modified, or until the swell encounters a landmass and dissipates its energy by breaking as surf. If the wind blows from the direction opposite the swell, the swell may dissipate completely. If the wind blows again from the same direction, the swell may be enhanced. The wind doesn't have to be blowing at that particular moment to create breaking surf. Even on a calm clear day, large surf, generated far out to sea, can make shore dive entries tricky (see Chapter 5 for more on shore dives).

A wave advancing toward you appears as a moving wall of water — it's not — only the energy of the wave is moving, the water itself moves very little. Next time you're tucked in for the night and you've got the covers pulled up nice and cozy around your chin and you're wondering, like you do every night before you shuffle off to dreamland, "How the heck do waves move through water?" — a simple illustration is at hand. Snap the edge of the sheet and you can watch a ripple of energy pass along the sheet from the point of origin, toward your feet. The wave of energy you create travels through the sheet in the same way a wave at sea travels through the water. Now, at last, you can get a good night's sleep.

The water does move a little as the wave passes. A single particle suspended in the water travels in a circular orbit — drawn toward the advancing wave, up into it and forward as it passes, and finally settling very close to its original position. The orbits are smaller the deeper you go — the energy of the wave is concentrated near the surface. That's why, even when the surface of the sea is very choppy, the water can be quite still just below. *Surge* — a sudden, powerful, but limited motion of water — is most often associated with the orbital circulation caused by passing waves. In shallow water, the surge of a wave passing overhead can shove you around dramatically, but it won't push you far, or for very long. The deeper you go, the less surge you'll experience.

On the surface, ocean waves are the most noticeable way (particularly on a boat) that waters of the ocean move around. Choppy sea conditions can make boat entries and exits tricky. In theory, waves are a very simple phenomenon, but in nature they are tremendously complex. Additional winds may add or dissipate energy, or change the direction of the swell. Two or more wave patterns generated in separate fetch areas may cross or combine to form irregular waves that are larger or smaller. When the peak of a wave combines with the trough of another there is a dampening of the original wave. If two peaks combine, the resulting wave can be much larger than either of the original waves. So-called *rogue waves* are the legendary products of these kinds of coincidental combinations. There are a few horror stories of enormous waves that sweep over the bow of a ship at sea and flood the bridge, 90 feet above the waterline, or simply sweep away the entire superstructure — but you're not likely to encounter any of these mythic giants on a dive boat.

Wave judgment, predicting what a choppy sea is going to do and when it's going to do it, and timing your own actions to coincide (particularly during boat entries and exits) is a subtle skill that takes a lot of practice to develop — don't get discouraged.

Surf

When deep water swells move into shallow places near the shore, the wave energy begins to interact with the bottom. Waves slow down in shallow water, and the wavelength shortens — the following waves catch up — the wave becomes steeper and higher and finally it breaks as *surf*. If the waves are breaking, divers wading out from the shore must cross this area of breaking surf known as the *impact zone*. There's an easy way and a hard way.

To make it easy, you should understand the forces at work in a breaking wave. Waves break when the their height is about one-seventh of the wavelength — an angle of 120 degrees. They reach this critical ratio when the depth of the bottom is about the height of the wave, plus one-third — a three-foot wave breaks in four feet of water. As the wave moves forward into shallower water, there isn't enough water in front of the wave to complete the orbital motion inside it and the wave collapses forward in what we know as surf. The character of the breaking surf depends on the shape of the bottom.

In general there are three types of breaking waves:

- **Surging waves:** Surging waves happen where the shore drops off very steeply into deep water. This type of wave appears quite close to shore and leaps up the beach, sometimes without even breaking. This type of wave has a very narrow impact zone, if any at all, and at first glance it appears to be an attractive entry point for shore diving. When the waves are quite small, it is a good sight, but surging waves hit the beach with their full force undiminished. The surge of even a moderate-sized one can jerk you around like a rodeo cowboy. Handle with care.

- **Spilling waves:** Spilling waves happen where the bottom slopes gradually — these waves release their energy very slowly. Spilling waves peak up slowly and the crest crumbles down the face of the wave. A gradual bottom slope most often means an comparatively wide impact zone. If you're shore diving, it usually means a long way out to the deep water, but the waves you encounter on the trip are relatively gentle and the surge is mild.

- **Plunging waves:** Plunging waves are the kind beloved by surfers the world over. This wave happens when open ocean swell abruptly hits a shallow bottom, as it does along the edge of most reefs. The shoreward rushing swell very suddenly doesn't have enough water ahead of it to complete its orbital circulation and the crest pitches out, creating a hollow wave face and a roaring cascade. The impact zone in this kind of break is normally fairly narrow, but these waves break with tremendous power and are to be avoided by divers unless they're only knee high. If they're bigger, go surfing instead. Fortunately, because all that shoreward rushing water has to get back out again, there are usually rip currents (see the following section) or reef passes that a diver can take advantage of to get beyond the reach of the breakers. The problem then, of course, is getting back in — it's a large mistake to swim out in a rip current, in big surf, without a plan to get back to shore.

Rip currents

Not all of the energy in a wave is dissipated just because it has broken as surf. All of that water piling up on the beach has to go somewhere, and that somewhere is back out to sea. As it does it creates powerful shore currents called *rip currents* (shown in Figure 8-9). Rip currents, or *rip tides* as they are sometimes known, form in between or next to areas of breaking surf. Relatively straight beaches, where waves approach directly on shore, typically develop sand bars on which the waves break. In between the sand bars, channels develop where the rip currents carry water away from the beach and back out to sea.

Where the waves approach from the side, the moving water may form a current moving parallel to the shore, opposite the direction of the approaching waves — this called a *longshore current* (see Figure 8-9). It generally continues parallel to the beach until it meets an obstruction, such as a point or headland, that directs it out to sea as a rip current.

Figure 8-9:
Rip currents
and
longshore
currents.

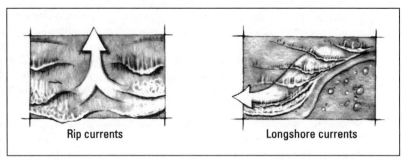

Rip currents   Longshore currents

Both rip currents and longshore currents can be very powerful and alarming to divers caught in them. Longshore currents obviously don't pose as much of a threat as rip currents. Even though they may carry you down the beach, you can still swim directly back to shore. Rip currents are probably responsible for more drowning deaths than any other sea condition. If your're caught in a rip current your first impulse is to swim back to the safety of shore, but swimming back to the beach against a rip current can be an exhausting exercise in futility. Don't try to swim against a rip current. If the current is carrying you out to sea, swim across it, parallel to the beach, until you are clear of it, and then swim back in. Rip currents are seldom very wide, and their force normally dissipates quickly beyond the surf zone, so if you can keep your head, it shouldn't be a problem.

Normally you can spot a rip current as a murky stream of choppy, disturbed water between areas of breaking surf. The strong outflow usually disturbs the regular pattern of the approaching waves. If you have any doubts, toss a small piece of seaweed or driftwood from the beach on the surface: If a rip current is present, it will quickly be carried out to sea. (Don't try this with litter, though.)

Tides

Wind isn't the only force that moves water in the seas, of course. The gravitational pull of the moon, and to a lesser degree the sun, both create the largest waves known, at least in terms of their wavelength. We know these global waves as the *tides*.

Tidal waves

The gravitational pull of the moon draws the waters of the ocean toward it, causing a tidal bulge on the hemisphere facing the moon. As the earth rotates, these *global bulges,* or *true tidal waves,* travel around the world — high tide is the crest of the wave; low tide is the trough. What most people call tidal waves are actually *tsunamis* — waves generated by seismic activity — and have nothing to do with the tides (see the "Tsunamis" sidebar for more information).

If the moon were stationary, these tidal waves (high tides) would pass a particular point on the surface of the earth every 12 hours. However, because the moon orbits the earth in the same direction of the earth's rotation, the period between high tides is a little longer — about 12 hours and 25 minutes.

The sun also influences tidal waves, but because it is so far away, its influence is a lot less dramatic than that of the moon. When the sun, moon, and earth are all aligned — during the full moon or the new moon — the sun augments the tidal effect of the moon creating very low and very high tides. When the sun, moon, and earth are at right angles, the influence of the sun modifies the pull of the moon, creating more moderate tides.

Rising and falling tides are responsible for powerful, localized currents. More extreme tides move more water, but even moderate tides can create powerful shore currents, especially in reef passes, at the narrow mouth of a bay. These currents can make great drift dives, or a very unpleasant surprise, in water that may have been calm only a few hours before. Always inquire locally about the effects and times of tidal changes.

Tidal currents

Large bodies of water connected to the ocean by narrow channels, such as bays or lagoons, can generate enormously powerful currents — as the tidal wave piles up along the outside, water pours through the channel to equalize the sea level inside. When the tidal wave passes, the situation is reversed and water flows out. The larger the body of water and the smaller the channel, the more powerful the current. The presence of islands, or anything else that squeezes the flow of water into a smaller space, increases the force of a tidal current. In places where the tidal flow of a large bay or lagoon passes through a relatively narrow channel, such as in San Francisco Bay, on the California coast, an extreme tide can make a current that roars like a whitewater river.

Tsunamis

Tsunami waves are generated by seismic events, such as earthquakes and volcanic eruptions. The wavelength of such waves can be very long — over 100 miles — while the crest of the wave may be no more than a foot or two. In deep ocean, a wave like that is almost impossible to detect, but when it approaches shallow water, the results can be catastrophic.

Tsunamis move quite fast, up to 500 mph. When the tsunami wave hits a shallow bottom, the front of this very long wave slows, the wave piles up, and then breaks in an enormous wall of water. Tsunami waves are frequently preceded by the surrounding bays and

shoreline dropping precipitously as the water in the trough preceding the wave and rushes out to complete the orbital cycle — hence the name "tidal wave."

Tsunamis can create destruction on a spectacular scale. The violent eruption of Krakatoa volcano in 1883 produced a tsunami that ranged between 60 and 120 feet high. Tens of thousands of people were killed and a full-sized naval gunboat anchored off Sumatra was carried two miles inland. But as spectacular as they are, tsunamis are relatively rare, even in the Pacific basin, where there is lots of seismic activity and they are most common.

Probably the most dramatic of these tidal changes is the phenomenon known as the *tidal bore*. In spite of the name, a tidal bore is a phenomenon entirely unrelated to cocktail parties. It is, essentially, a tide change so sudden that it arrives as a cresting wave. A tidal bore requires very specific circumstances and conditions. It occurs in rivers and narrow, funnel-shaped bays (the Bay of Fundy in Nova Scotia is famous for its tidal bores), with a shallow bottom, during extreme tidal changes. The incoming tide is slowed by friction against the shallow bottom until the outgoing current is moving faster than the incoming tide. The incoming tide can build into a large turbulent tidal wave that moves up the channel with great force. The Seine River, in France, is subject to periodic tidal bores (called the *mascaret*). It has been known to arrive in Paris as a 20-foot wall of water traveling 15 mph. Such a tidal bore was responsible for the death of Victor Hugo's newly married daughter and her husband, whose misfortune it was to be sailing on the river in front of the author's home when the tidal bore arrived.

True tidal waves, such as tidal bores, are entirely predictable and avoidable, and the kind of tragedy visited on Hugo is rare today. The tidal exchange of water is important to the marine life in the lagoon or bay and it can be important to divers, too. Runoff from rivers and sediments and pollution generally make the visibility poor on out-going, or *ebb tides*. Incoming, or *flood tides*, bring clear ocean waters into the lagoon, improving visibility dramatically. The increased visibility and the strong channel current makes them popular places to drift dive (see Chapter 10 for more about drift diving). During these tidal changes, many marine animals congregate in the channels to take advantage of nutrients and plankton being carried in the current. Large filter feeders, such as mantas, are often seen in channel currents during the tidal changes.

Recipe for Blue Water

As important as the movement of ocean water, is the condition of the water itself. Divers are generally concerned with only a few of seawater's many characteristics — visibility and temperature being most important. But in an environment as complex and embracing as the ocean, its traits are often interwoven in subtle and surprising ways, many of which divers have yet to understand.

Hydrologic cycle

The bulk of the world's water is in its oceans and seas, but it is constantly in the process of being cycled through the atmosphere in what is known as the *hydrologic cycle,* shown in Figure 8-10. Water in the ocean is evaporated (turned to water vapor) by the sun. In the atmosphere, it condenses into clouds and falls as precipitation on the sea or on the land. Water that falls on the land runs off as streams and rivers and eventually returns to the sea, or it sinks into the ground and flows slowly back to the sea as groundwater.

In the process of returning to sea, ground and surface water leach minerals from the soil and carry sediments and organic compounds to the sea. Traces of every naturally occurring substance can be found in the oceans, and recently, traces of synthetic compounds have begun to accumulate as well — in addition to other pollutants, those compounds that are resistant to natural degradation such as PCBs, DDT, and chlorine-based compounds are of the most concern. They gradually build up in the ocean environment and they are highly toxic to marine life.

Vegetation on land and in shoreline swamps filters out a lot of the sediments and pollutants (pollution of these areas is another problem), but in areas where forests have been cut and swamps filled in, all of this runoff flows directly out to sea, smothering and poisoning the reef.

Most of what is dissolved in seawater is, to no one's surprise — salt. Salinity is measured in parts-per-thousand (ppt). Average seawater has a salinity of 35 ppt. It varies somewhat depending on local conditions — evaporation and freshwater runoff. In the Red Sea, for example, where rainfall is low and evaporation is high, the salinity averages closer to 40 ppt; in the outflow of a river, salinity is much lower. Don't drink it, just take my word for it.

Corals don't do well among the sedimentation and decreased salinity that exists where rivers flow out to sea. That's why you often find a reef pass opposite the mouth of a river.

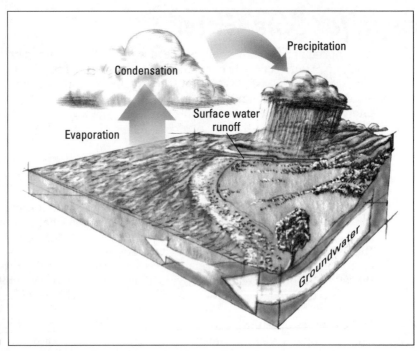

Condensation

Precipitation

Evaporation

Surface water runoff

Groundwater

Figure 8-10:
The hydro-
logic cycle.

Visibility

Visibility is how far you can see horizontally underwater. Visibility can range from a few inches to about 200 feet. There are all kinds of mythic tales about astonishing visibility, but as a practical matter it doesn't much exceed 200 feet — perhaps the only exception is the water under the polar icecaps.

Visibility is affected by a large number of factors. It can vary season to season, day to day, and even hour to hour — currents, weather, plankton, and bottom composition all have a dramatic effect on visibility. Muddy rainwater running off the land can affect visibility close to coastal areas. Plankton blooms, the rapid multiplication of drifting, and microscopic marine organisms can compromise visibility, as can nutrients and particles upwelling from deeper waters, or more locally, a diver's kick or prop wash of a boat.

Human beings are very visually oriented and diving is a predominantly visual activity — obviously, good visibility is preferable to poor visibility. When visibility is poor it's more difficult to keep track of your buddy, you see less of the surrounding marine life, and what you do see may not look as clear or colorful. When visibility is really bad, you may get disoriented in the weightless underwater environment. It may sound absurd, but more than one diver has lost track of up and down when the visibility is really bad. If visibility is that poor you shouldn't dive unless you have special training.

Oddly enough, extremely good visibility can cause problems as well. Because of the magnifying effect caused by the refraction of light underwater, the bottom often looks closer than it really is and divers may fail to monitor their actual depth. *Vertigo* — disorientation and dizziness — bothers some divers ascending or descending in very clear water.

Temperature

The temperature of the ocean has a more profound effect than simply determining what kind of exposure suit you're going to wear. Water temperature in the oceans varies from Fahrenheit degrees in the high 20s in the polar regions to the middle 80s in the tropics. Ocean currents move both warm and cold water around horizontally, influencing marine life locally. But even though the world's oceans are interconnected, they are effectively separated by the combination continental landmasses and temperature.

Temperature and landmass can form an impenetrable barrier to some species. The sea snake, for example, is a species that evolved in the Indo-Pacific region, most likely for terrestrial ancestors on the continent of Australia. Sea snakes are very sensitive to extremes in temperature — they can't tolerate temperatures lower than 68°. They have migrated across the tropical Pacific to the coast of the Americas and across the Indian Ocean to the coast of Africa, but no sea snakes are found in the Atlantic Ocean — they can't tolerate the water temperatures encountered around the cape of South Africa, or the horn of South America, and they don't pass through the Panama Canal because Gatun Lake, on the eastern end of the canal, is freshwater.

Most of the ocean's species, like the sea snake, are cold-blooded — their body temperature is the same as the surrounding environment. With the exception of a few large species like tuna, cold-blooded marine species are unable to regulate their body temperature and therefore exist in a very narrow band of temperature differential. Temperatures vary seasonally, of course, but normally less than 20°.

Thermoclines

Water temperature also varies according to depth. In general, the deeper you go, the colder it gets — bottom water doesn't receive as much solar radiation and it doesn't circulate as quickly as surface water. Sometimes the transition between warm surface waters and cooler deep waters can be very abrupt, particularly when conditions prevent water from circulating freely. These abrupt transitions are called *thermoclines*. Thermoclines are found in both salt and freshwater, at any depth. Sometimes you may even notice a wavy visual distortion at the transition between the two layers. This type of distortion is also sometimes seen between layers of freshwater and saltwater. This kind of stratification is known as a *halocline*.

Chapter 9

What's Down There?

In This Chapter

▶ Understanding the coral reef

▶ Getting to know the reef ecosystem

▶ Avoiding dangerous marine creatures

▶ Discovering other unique underwater environments

Most divers don't dive just for the sensation of being under the water — they dive to see all the extraordinary life that thrives in the water, which is the largest and least-known environment on earth. This chapter shows you what you're in store for.

The Coral Reef

Coral reefs are collective underwater structures. The architects and builders of these fantastic — and sometimes immense — structures are tiny gelatinous creatures called *coral polyps.* All coral polyps, shown in Figure 9-1, have a central mouth surrounded by tentacles, but beyond that they vary considerably in size, shape, and in the form of their constructions. Reefs are constructed by limestone secretion that some coral polyps use to construct their own skeletons. Reefs can grow into enormous structures — the largest on earth and in some cases dwarfing anything ever made by humans. The Great Barrier Reef off the coast of Queensland, Australia, is the largest structure on earth. It's so large (about 1,200 miles long) that it's visible from space. All of this mind-boggling construction from a creature that is, in most cases, no bigger than your fingernail. The greatest number and diversity of marine animals live in and around coral reefs — that's why coral reefs are such a favorite with divers. Corals are divided into two basic groups: *hermatypes* (those that build reefs) and *ahermatypes* (those that do not).

Figure 9-1:
Coral
polyps, like
these, have
a central
mouth sur-
rounded by
tentacles.

Hermatype (HUR-ma-type) coral polyps build reefs by means of a unique partnership with microscopic plants that live within their tissues, called *zooxanthellae*. The polyp supplies the zooxanthellae with carbon dioxide, and the zooxanthellae use sunlight to convert this and seawater into oxygen and carbohydrates. The polyp takes up the excess carbohydrates and makes calcium carbonate (limestone), building the skeleton in which it lives, and producing the fantastic shapes of a hard coral reef. Hermatype corals grow only in clear, shallow seas because, without sunlight, the zooxanthellae produce no food and the coral cannot survive. Most of the hermatype coral's food comes from the zooxanthellae, but they also feed on passing plankton gathered from the current. See Figure 9-2 for an example of hermatype coral polyps. Ahermatype (A-hur-ma-type), or soft corals, contain no zooxanthellae and feed exclusively on drifting plankton. These corals are also found on the reef, but instead of sunlight, they require strong currents that bring plentiful supplies of plankton. These corals tend to inhabit deeper, cooler waters, often in caves or under overhangs where reef-building corals can't survive. (Figure 9-2 shows an example of ahermatype corals — see the color photo section of this book for additional photos of corals.)

Figure 9-2:
Branching corals like this elegant elkhorn (left) are her-matype (or hard) corals. They grow in the calm waters of the back reef. Ahermatype (or soft) corals like these (right), grow where strong currents can bring them food.

The astonishing variety of forms that corals can take depends on a number of complex factors, including *where* on the reef they grow. On the turbulent open-ocean side of the reef, corals tend to take on compact shapes — round or flattened. On the protected lagoon side, they tend to take on the more delicate branching shapes that couldn't withstand the wave impact on the ocean side. In deeper water, they tend to spread out in large plates to collect as much sunlight as possible.

Corals aren't the only creatures that contribute to the building of a reef — calcareous algae, sponges, seaweeds, and a variety of mollusks all chip in, too. A reef is kind of marine version of the rainforest. Like the rainforest, coral reefs teem with life — as much as one-fourth of all marine species in the sea live on the reef at some point in their life cycle. Both reefs and rainforests provide homes for a diverse range of species — many found no where else in the world. The destruction of either of these ecosystems would be an incalculable loss — even from a strictly pragmatic point of view, because they are repositories for the next generation of pharmaceutical drugs and may represent the world's best hope against a host of diseases.

Coral reefs prosper only in a narrow band of water, 30 degrees north and south of the equator (see Figure 9-3). There, you find three basic reef forms:

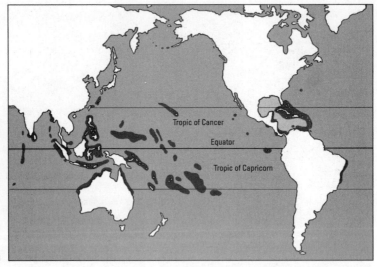

Figure 9-3:
Coral reefs (shown in the darkest areas) thrive in a narrow band around the equator.

- **Fringing reefs:** *Fringing reefs* are shelflike extensions of adjacent shores, usually an island. The theory holds that all coral reefs start out as fringing reefs, because coral polyps colonize the shallow waters around a tropical island. Most of the islands in the Caribbean have fringing reefs.

- **Atoll reefs:** *Atoll reefs* are formed by a chain of tiny islands that fully encircle a lagoon. Over time, a fringing reef collects debris and coral sand in places, forming a chain of tiny *islets* (sandbars that stay above the water line even at high tide) off of the main island — in the Caribbean these are known as *cays* (pronounced "keez") and in the South Pacific, they're called *motus* (MOE-toos). Eventually, coconut palms (and perhaps a few other plants whose seeds have been carried by wind or dropped by birds) take root on these islets, which become the classic, storybook desert islands. Eventually, the original island may sink back into the sea, leaving this chain of islets and reef that circle a lagoon — an atoll reef. Rangiroa in French Polynesia is a good example of a coral atoll.

- **Barrier reefs.** *Barrier reefs* are wall-like coral formations that generally lie further off shore. Barrier reefs are formed on the edges of a *continental shelf* (a shelf that extends underwater, away from shore) or where large islands have become submerged. Barrier reefs can extend for many miles, and are usually separated from the mainland or island by a wide, deep lagoon. The Great Barrier Reef, off the northeast coast of Australia, is the best known barrier reef, as well as the world's largest — it represents 3 percent of the world's coral reefs all by itself.

Encounters with large pelagic animals, like this manta ray, accentuate the feeling of being a visitor in an alien world.

Coral Reefs and a Few of Their Residents

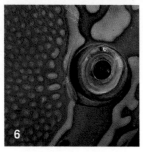

1 You don't have to travel to another planet to find another world populated with weird aliens—the coral reef has it all. **2** The stony skeleton of the coral polyps builds the reef in a remarkable variety of shapes and sizes (depending on the kind of corals), light conditions, and other factors.
3 Anemones are close relatives of coral polyps. In the western Pacific, anemones are almost always found with anemone fish taking

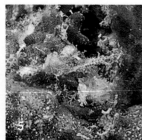

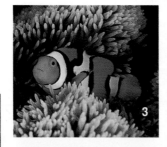

advantage of the stinging tentacles, to which they are immune, for defense. **4** Corals serve other reef creatures both as defense and cover. This pose, by a pair of longnose hawkfish, belies their nature. Although small, they are aggressive predators. **5** Look closely: Some reef creatures, like this scorpionfish, are experts in camouflage. **6** While some species are well concealed, others are wildly evident, dressed out in fantastic, shimmering colors and flamboyant patterns, like this parrotfish. **7** Or, virtually transparent, like this jellyfish.

The coral reef, like this one in the Red Sea, is the most popular place to dive, and for good reason—it is second only to the tropical rainforest in diversity and numbers of animal species.

8 The function of colors in many reef creatures is not well understood, but in some, like this nudibranch, it serves to advertise their presence to potential predators. Most nudibranches have foul-tasting or toxic chemicals in their flesh; their colors serve as a warning.

9 Even though they are sessile (attached to the bottom), soft corals are animals, as are nearly all of the creatures on the reef. The reef has few plants on it.

8

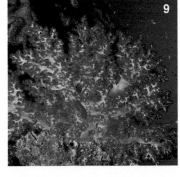

9

The World's Largest Fish
The whale shark can grow up to 50 feet in length and weigh over 25 tons. Like most of the oceans largest animals, whale sharks are plankton feeders and are not aggressive. Encounters with whale sharks are highly prized among divers and snorkelers. (See Chapter 14 for more on taking whale shark trips.)

A lot of what's most interesting in the world's oceans live in the warm, sunlit waters near the surface, and can be seen by using just a mask, fins, and snorkel. Resist the temptation to handle marine organisms—it can be bad for both of you.

Your first taste of scuba diving will be in a pool or some other confined water, under the close supervision of a qualified instructor from an accredited certification agency. After you master the simple

techniques of diving safely and responsibly in a confined-water environment, you're ready to try it in open water. All of the certifying agencies are flexible with their instruction programs and can schedule lessons to fit your schedule. (See Chapter 3 for more on obtaining certification.)

1

1 Manatees are one of the world's most gentle and sweet-tempered animals, but they have become almost permanent residents on the endangered species list. Encounters with them are among the most memorable underwater experiences, but for how much longer?
2 Whale sharks are not yet endangered, but they are elusive, solitary marine animals.
3 Scuba takes you to the deeper parts of the reef, beyond the limits of what you can see with a snorkel.

3

1 A pristine beach backed by palms; warm, clear lagoon waters; and healthy coral growth. A snorkeler's paradise, this one is in the Marshall Islands. 2 With a little training, you can investigate the endless mysteries of the underwater world like these two divers. Just remember that to dive with scuba, you need to be certified (see Chapter 3). 3 Stingrays, like many residents of the underwater world, have a bad (and mostly undeserved) reputaion with humans. While they are capable of inflicting serious injury, they only do so in self-defense, usually when they are stepped on by some unwary wader.

As a beginning diver, you should stay out of overhead environments like caverns and caves. After you gain some experience, you may want to pursue a specialty in cave diving, wreck diving, or any of the many specialties offered by certification agencies.

Sharks, sharks, sharks

What most people know about sharks comes from sensational—and often completely inaccurate—accounts in movies and on television. Sharks, like many other creatures in the sea and on land, can be dangerous under some circumstances, but they don't deserve the kind of exaggerated reputation that they are saddled with. (See Chapter 6 for more on sharks and Chapter 11 for information on shark dives.)

Dolphins are highly intelligent and social, and have captivated the imagination of their distant terrestrial cousins since the first humans went to sea. Dolphin-human interactions are the stuff of legends. Some dolphins, like these wild Atlantic spotted dolphins on the Little Bahama Bank, have become habituated to humans and actually seem to seek out and enjoy our company.

Liveaboard dive boats allow you to sleep right on top of dive sites and experience adventure at sea with other, like-minded passengers.

Building coral reefs is a slow and cumulative venture — wave action, predation, and chemical and mechanical breakdown by other organisms, all slow down the growth of the reef. Depending on the type of coral and the environment, annual growth rates range from a half-inch to about 4 inches. The building of a single reef can take centuries. Parts of the Great Barrier Reef are estimated to be 1,000 years old.

Because they are beautiful and fascinating, coral reefs are important to divers, but they are important to the rest of mankind as well, even if people are largely unaware of it. As natural breakwaters, reefs absorb wave impact and protect low-lying coastal plains and islands from the erosive action of open ocean. As the reef builds (a healthy reef is always a work in progress), the corals provide homes for a colorful and diverse variety of fish, sponges, mollusks, crustaceans, and other less-visible marine organisms. Larger animals that feed on smaller animals, such as crab, lobster, grouper, and parrot fish, are an important source of food for local economies.

The reef community

A healthy reef is a crowded place — it teems with life from the microscopic to the gigantic. The reef supports this enormous community of animals through diversity and interdependence — it is one of the most complex and closely woven ecosystems on the planet.

The world's reefs in danger

The progress of civilization has taken a terrible toll on the world's coral reefs — over 35 million acres of living coral reef have been destroyed in the last few decades. At that pace, 70 percent of the world's reefs will disappear in your lifetime. Sedimentation, overfishing, runoff, dredging, and water pollution all contribute to the destruction of the world's reefs, but the picture is not entirely without hope.

Many countries have begun to appreciate the value of their reefs and are taking steps to preserve and protect them. Native island cultures have effectively managed reef fisheries for centuries, and with new-found appreciation of cultural traditions, the old ways are being given a new look. Development is possible without threatening the world's reef, but long-term, sustainable development must take precedence over short-term gains and short-sighted development. Any of the many not-for-profit organizations working to protect the world's coral reef's welcome your support — see the Appendix for the names of a few of them.

Fish are the most obvious and numerous inhabitants — you can see many varieties of colorful tropicals darting in and out of the coral formations (see the color photo section of this book for some beautiful examples). If you're lucky, you may see larger open water species, such as sharks and rays, which are occasional visitors to the reef.

Don't overlook the other fascinating creatures that live here. Echinoderms, such as stars, feather stars, sea cucumbers, and urchins are relatively large, making them fairly easy to spot. They can be recognized by their characteristic radial pattern. Crustaceans — lobsters, crabs, shrimps, and their kin—are astonishing in their color and variation. Mollusks, sponges, marine worms — the coral reef is second only to the tropical rainforest in it's diversity of species.

The richest reefs with the greatest diversity of marine life are found in the in the western Pacific. There are several reasons for this. During the last Ice Age relatively shallow waters there are thought to have receded into three separate basins, each evolving its own distinct species. Conditions for the growth of reefs become less favorable as you move east across the Pacific and there is a corresponding decline in marine species. About 2,000 different species of fish are known in the western Pacific and there are probably more to be discovered. This number drops to about 600 in the Hawaiian Islands and to only 300 in the relatively deeper, cooler waters of the eastern Pacific.

The tropical waters of the Atlantic and the Caribbean have excellent conditions for coral growth, but also have a relatively low diversity of species, about 75 species of coral and 500 species of fish. From an evolutionary standpoint, the Atlantic and the Caribbean have a way to go to catch up with the western Pacific.

The reef stands between the open ocean and the shore, and develops a number of distinctively different features and habitats — see Figure 9-4. All of them are interesting in their own way, but some are preferred over others as dive sites. Here are a few of the features of a typical fringing-type reef:

✔ **The fore reef:** On the ocean side, where the growth is subjected to breaking waves and currents, the reef exhibits its greatest richness and diversity thanks to clear water, optimum light conditions, and a good supply of oxygen and nutrients from the waves and currents. This area is known as the fore reef — the feature of the reef most highly prized by divers. It usually drops off steeply on the ocean side, creating an impressive wall that sometimes develops spur and groove formations (big coral buttresses with narrow canyons in between). As you move down the wall, the coral community is increasingly dominated by species that are tolerant of low-light conditions. The same strong currents and wave surge that benefit corals can make diving challenging, but this is almost always the most rewarding part of the reef to visit.

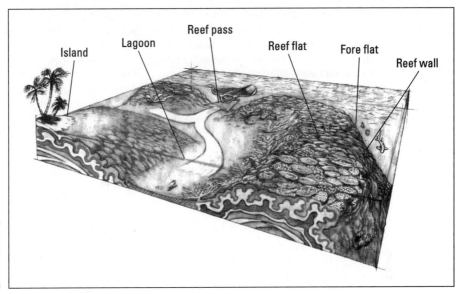

✔ **The reef pass:** Deep-water channels that cut through the reef are known as *reef passes*. They frequently form opposite the mouths of rivers where fresh water outflow and sediment discourage the growth of coral. Reef passes are important because they allow rejuvenating ocean waters to flow in and out of the lagoon. Because a large volume of moving water is often confined to a narrow channel in a reef pass, currents can be very swift. For divers, this is not necessarily a bad thing. A swift incoming tide in a narrow reef pass can provide a thrilling drift dive (see Chapter 10 for more information). Divers enter the water from a boat on the ocean side and glide through the pass, barely flipping a fin. Another great thing about reef passes is that they are a good place to spot large marine life, such as mantas (see the color photo section of this book for an example), feeding in the plankton-rich current.

✔ **The lagoon:** The body of water inside the reef is the lagoon. Lagoons come in a wide variety of widths and depths — see the color photo section of this book for an example. Normally, they have calm waters, a sandy floor, and gentle tidal circulation and are dotted with patches of coral. Delicate, branching corals thrive there, as do many species of marine plants and animals, because they're sheltered from the wave impact of the open ocean. Deeper lagoons may support a secondary reef growth called a back reef. Lagoons sometimes contain another important habitat — seagrass beds. Seagrass is a flat-bladed grass about 6 to 8 inches long that roots in shallow, sandy areas. It is one of the few true plants that grows in the sea and it provides both food and shelter to many marine species, including the juveniles of many that will later take up residence on the reef.

✔ **The reef flat:** The *reef flat* is the area on top of the reef between the open ocean and the lagoon (or the beach, if there is no lagoon). Waters here are very shallow — sometimes only a few inches deep. Portions of the reef flat are occasionally exposed to the air at low tides. Only the most rugged varieties of coral can survive here, and because they can grow only horizontally, large areas of the reef flat are dead and covered with sand, coral rocks, seaweed, and debris. When enough of this material has collected on a reef flat to stabilize, it forms the tiny islets known as a cays or motus (covered in "The Coral Reef" section, earlier in this chapter).

✔ **The mangrove swamp:** Along the shoreline, inside the lagoon, is another habitat vital to the health of the reef — the *mangrove swamp* — thickets of the saltwater-tolerant mangrove trees. They fringe the coastline along estuaries, mudflats, and places where there is plenty of freshwater runoff from the land. Mangrove trees filter sediment from runoff water and their tangle of roots serve as nursery for many species of reef life, providing safety from the larger predators on the reef. The reef life nurtured in mangrove swamps fills the tropical oceans. Some species of juvenile reef fish are 20 times more abundant on reefs associated with mangrove swamps.

Mangrove swamps form the basis of an important reef-associated food chain. Decomposing mangrove leaves feed fungi that are the staple for numerous insects which, in turn, are fed on by shrimp. Shrimp are preyed upon by larger marine animals and harvested by local people. The destruction of habitats such as mangrove swamps have profound consequences for the reef. Both mangrove trees and seagrass filter silt and sediment from the runoff water, guaranteeing corals the clear waters that they need to thrive. They provide habitat for juveniles of the many species and nutrients in the form of dead plants and animals. The reef, in turn, protects the mangrove swamp and seagrass beds from erosion and provides sand and sediment for the roots. Unfortunately, mangrove swamps are often viewed by some people as nothing more than dreary, mosquito-infested wastelands and are the first victims of coastal development.

Flip to the color photo section near the middle of this book for examples of the reef community.

Divers and the reef

The damage that divers do to reefs is minimal in comparison to threats from pollution, boat anchors, and coastal development; however, in sites that are heavily visited, the damage can be significant. Reefs are fragile and corals are easily damaged by a careless hand or a thoughtless kick. Whenever you touch a coral or a sponge, you can damage the protective layer of mucous that covers it, exposing the animal to infection. Like us, corals can usually recover from small wounds of this kind, but human intrusion on a large scale has, in some places, overwhelmed their ability to recover. When that happens, the reef begins to die. When you touch coral, you may be interfering with decades, or even centuries, of growth.

Most damage is done when divers accidentally kick a coral, sit or stand on it, hold onto it to steady themselves, or stir up sediment from the bottom — the sediment settles on the corals, smothering them. These problems are worse wherever divers crowd together to see something extraordinary. Novices tend to do more of this kind of damage than more-experienced divers. The signs are easy to see — patches of dead, algae-covered coral on otherwise thriving coral heads, broken sponges, and piles of coral rubble. It doesn't have to be that way. Thoughtful divers can still enjoy the reef without leaving this kind of devastation in their wake.

The prevailing attitude among responsible divers today is simply not to touch anything on the reef. In general, this is the policy you should observe, but there are some reef creatures who won't suffer any harm from careful handling, and this kind of interactive experience can cement a lifelong affinity with the reef, especially in children enjoying their first snorkeling experiences. This should be done only on tours under the supervision of an experienced guide, or when you have gained enough experience yourself to be completely confident that you won't do any harm, and not be harmed yourself. Many reef creatures are armed with spines, teeth, or venom. Some of them can be deadly, although none is aggressive if left alone. When in doubt, don't touch!

Litter and trash in the water can also create deadly problems for marine organisms. Many divers and snorkelers carry fish food in clear plastic sandwich bags, but these bags create one of the most insidious forms of litter in the ocean. Floating near the surface, plastic bags resemble jellyfish — an important element in the diet of marine species like sea turtles. Ingesting plastic bags can create an intestinal blockage that leads to a horrible, lingering death. *Never* leave plastic bags floating in the water. Keep the reef waters clean for others and for the animals that live there. Never leave any kind of litter or trash in the water or on the beach.

Other kinds of pollution can be rather subtle. Studies have revealed that the pH of the water has actually been changed enough to affect delicate marine organisms by large numbers of divers, in heavily used areas, who urinate in the water!

Consider adding your voice to the growing chorus of those trying to make effective political changes that will protect and preserve our precious natural heritage. In the Appendix, you can find a list of organizations working to that end. I encourage you to support them and help ensure that divers always have healthy thriving reefs to dive on.

The Reef Ecosystem

One of the great attractions of a coral reef is the amazing diversity and abundance of life that it protects. Although tropical rainforests, with their mind-boggling diversity of insect species, surpass tropical reefs in numbers of species, no known habitat on land or sea can match the tropical reefs for species with backbones *(vertebrates)*, and no other habitat has as many different classifications of animal species.

All of these diverse and numerous species live together on the reef by employing a wide variety of survival strategies and behaviors. Some reef creatures are highly territorial and may occupy a few square feet of reef for their entire lives; others are constantly on the move. Some are active during the day; others only at night. Every species on the reef exploits a particular niche.

Aquatic plants

You can find surprisingly few noticeable aquatic plants on a coral reef. The great majority of living things you see as a diver are animals. Even though aquatic plants aren't as evident on the reef as the animal life, they are present — sometimes in large numbers — and an important part of the ecosystem. They include phytoplanktons, algae, and flowering plants.

Phytoplanktons

Phytoplankton (FIE-toe-plank-tun) is made up of microscopic plants floating free in the sea. Like all true plants, phytoplanktons make their own food from sunlight; consequently, they are found near the surface of the sea where there is plenty of light. Zooplankton are microscopic animals floating in the sea — they make up the remainder of the plankton. Plankton is probably most famous as the diet of the ocean's largest creatures — the filter-feeding whales — and only noticeable when it clouds the water and ruins the visibility. Two kinds of aquatic plants can be found in plankton: diatoms and dinoflagellates.

Diatoms are single-cell microscopic critters who possess a cell wall of silica. *Diatomaceous earth,* a white powder used as a filter and an abrasive, is the accumulation of their remains. *Dinoflagellates* are organisms that smudge the dividing line between plants and animals. They contain photosynthetic pigments and can make their own food from sunlight (like plants can), but they propel themselves through the water by means of a whip-like tail (the way animals do).

Algae

Algae (AL-gee) represent a large percentage of aquatic plants. Algae come in a wide variety of sizes and shapes from simple, single-cell organisms to the largest aquatic plant of them all — giant kelp. Algae come in four different varieties:

- **Blue-green algae:** Blue-green algae are more common in freshwater than in the sea, but they can be found in slimy mats at the waters edge.

- **Green algae:** Green is the most diverse of the algae — there are about 7,000 different species. Like blue-green algae, most species are found in freshwater, but about 900 species are found in the sea. They are common in mats, or in slimy filaments in shallow water.

- **Brown algae:** Nearly all the brown algae are marine plants. Browns come in an amazing variety of sizes and shapes, from sea palms to giant kelp. Because of their size and variety, brown algae are probably the best known aquatic plants. They are found close to shore.

- **Red algae:** Like brown algae, almost all the 4,000 species of red algae are marine plants. Red algae are able to absorb the long wavelengths of light that penetrate the furthest into the water, and are found at greater depth than other aquatic plants. Some red algae form a hard external skeleton — either flat or in an upright, branching form — that protects the plant from grazing fish.

Flowering plants

Only two groups of flowering plants have successfully colonized the marine environment — seagrasses and mangroves.

- **Seagrasses:** You can find three different kinds of seagrasses — turtlegrass, eelgrass, and surfgrass. _Turtlegrass_ is common in the tropics in shallow, quiet water on a sandy bottom. _Eelgrass_ is found in shallow, temperate waters, while _surfgrass_ occupies the same climatic zone in places where pounding surf prevents eelgrass from taking hold.

- **Mangroves:** Mangroves colonize the quiet-water shorelines inside tropical lagoons and estuaries, often in dense, tangled thickets. They create an important habitat for many species of marine creatures and birds. Mangrove seeds germinate on the tree. The seedlings then drop from the tree to drift in the current until they are carried to shallow water where they put down roots.

Invertebrates

One of the really striking things about marine _invertebrates_ (species without backbones) is that so many of them have evolved into creatures that remain attached to a single spot for their entire lives. So many of them are branching and bushy-looking, in fact, that biologists originally classified them as plants. Today, we know them to be true animals and a great demonstration of just how different a world lies beneath the sea. After all, how many terrestrial animals can you name that are attached to one spot all their lives? Okay then, how about one spot that's not in front of a TV?

Zooplanktons

Zooplanktons, like all plankton, drift in the ocean currents. These tiny creatures, along with their eggs and larvae, make up the majority of the drifting plankton — there are tens of thousands of species of the single-celled variety (called *protozoans*) alone. Most zooplankton feed on other forms of life, although a few of the protozoans are able to absorb nutrients directly from the water. Most zooplankton graze on phytoplankton, or prey upon other kinds of zooplankton.

Sponges

Sponges are simple organisms. They are a collection of cells organized in a system of canals and chambers through which they filter seawater for food and oxygen. Sponges are among the most conspicuous animals on the reef. They can be seen attached to the sea bottom, most often on the seaward side of the reef. Sponges come in many shapes and sizes, but generally they are either bowl-shaped or flat. Some sponges are preyed upon by fish, turtles, and mollusks, but many contain toxins that make them unpalatable. Some of these toxins show great promise in the field of cancer research.

Corals, anemones, hydroids, and jellyfish

Corals, the architects of the reef, along with hydroids, anemones, and jellyfish make up the *cnidaria* — one of the most important classes of animals in the reef ecosystem. All cnidarians (nid-DAIR-ee-ans) have a mouth, a gut, and a radial form made up of tentacles with stinging cells. Cnidarians come in two basic varieties: polyps and the free swimming medusa form.

Corals and *sea anemones* (a-NEM-oh-nees) are both polyps, and have a similar lifestyle and body design — a central mouth and gut, surrounded by tentacles. In general, anemones are somewhat bigger and are often found individually; corals are colonial animals that form a skeletal structure of calcium carbonate that's strained from seawater.

Hydroids are very similar to corals and anemones, but they can be found in both polyp and *medusa form* — as individual polyps or as colonial jellyfish. Some hydroids such as fire coral, are capable of building their own skeletons, the way true corals do. Others, like the Portuguese man-of-war, adopt the medusa (jellyfish) body form — they look like jellyfish, but are actually a colony of specialized individuals. The individuals responsible for stinging do their job extremely well, by the way — the Portuguese man-of-war is among the most dangerous of all the cnidarians.

Many species of true jellyfish are also renowned for their stinging cells. Jellyfish and other medusa forms also possess a central mouth and gut, but the arrangement is inverted — they are generally bell-shaped, with the mouth and gut on the bottom. The stinging cells, called *nematocysts,* are found in the trailing tentacles. For swimmers and divers, encountering them in the water is never a pleasant experience. Jellyfish travel on the currents, near the surface, where they prey on small fish. They are the largest form of plankton in the sea.

In addition, there are about 80 different species of jellyfishlike creatures know as comb jellies. These are not cnidarians, but members of the class ctenophora (tee-no-FOR-ah). They look a lot like jellyfish, but they possess no stinging cells and capture their food with sticky tentacles. They propel themselves through the water by fluttering their *cilia* (SILL-ee-ah), which are numerous hair-like appendages arranged in rows.

Bryozoans

Bryozoans (bri-ZOE-ans) generally go unnoticed by divers. They are usually small, living in colonies made up of thousands or even millions of individual animals that range from less than an inch across to several feet across. Every individual bryozoan has completely developed nervous, digestive, muscular and respiratory systems. Compared to cnidarians, bryozoans are quite sophisticated. Like hydroids, individuals in the colony are adapted to specialized tasks. Characteristic of bryozoans is an organ called the *lophophore* (LOF-ah-for) — a featherlike projection that filters food from the water.

Worms

Marine worms are represented by three separate classes of critters: platy-helminthes (flatworms), nemertea (ribbon worms), and annelida (clamworms, bristleworms, and tubeworms).

- **Flatworms:** Flatworms include parasitic worms and flukes, as well as thousands of other species, some of which may be seen by divers. A few of the tropical species are brilliantly colored and quite large (up to 6 inches). Flatworms are simple creatures with a rudimentary digestive tract and nervous system — respiration is accomplished through the skin. Flatworms are fairly easy to identify — if it's a worm and it's flat, it's probably a flatworm. Makes sense.

- **Ribbon worms:** Ribbon worms live on the bottom of the sea and are most often found in shallow coastal waters. Ribbon worms are predators that stalk their prey. They normally grow between 5 and 10 feet in length, although one species is reported to reach up to 60 feet. In spite of their respectable size, ribbon worms are not often observed by divers and don't represent any danger. Like flatworms, ribbon worms are *unsegmented* (a smooth, continuous body rather than one divided into sections like an earthworm); unlike flatworms, they have a complete digestive tract.

- **Clamworms, bristleworms, and tubeworms:** These three types of worms are the most commonly observed of all the marine worms. They can be seen crawling over the reef or waving their feathery arms in the current from the end of tubes that they construct on the reef. All of the worms in this class are segmented, like earthworms, and possess complete nervous, respiratory, digestive, and circulatory systems. These worms can be divided into two subgroups: those that live attached to the bottom and those that don't. The ones that attach generally live in a protective tube and have some kind of organ that filters food from the water. These are the Christmas tree worms and tube worms — the two best known of the marine worms. Their filtering organs are often brightly colored and beautifully patterned (see Figure 9-5). Those that don't attach to the reef crawl around on it, seeking their needs.

Figure 9-5:
Christmas tree worms are often brightly colored and patterned.

Crustaceans

Crustaceans are the most abundant form of the class of animal known as Arthropoda found in the sea. You're probably aware of crab, shrimp, and lobster — you may even have included a few of them in your diet from time to time. Because of their popularity as a food source, populations of these larger members of the crustacean family have begun to dwindle in recent years, but most crustaceans are tiny organisms that are very numerous and make up a large part of the oceanic plankton. Although these tiny creatures may not be apparent to divers, they are extremely important as a source of food for larger animals — they are the mainstay in the diet of the world's largest living creatures, the baleen whales.

Crustaceans have made a home for themselves in every corner of the marine environment, from barnacles attached to pilings and boats to crabs in the ocean trenches to sand fleas on the beach. They are one of the most widespread and prolific life forms in the sea.

Mollusks

Mollusks are an enormously diverse group of animals that are, nonetheless, very closely related. All mollusks have a muscular foot and a soft, fleshy body. Some species have a shell; some don't — they have devised a remarkable

Underwater etiquette

Every diver has an investment in preserving the world's reefs. Today, human beings are the dominant life form on earth. As such, the stewardship of its life is a sacred trust. You may not be able to do anything about others who fail to respect the sanctity of life, but you can do what's right, feel good about yourself, and join in solidarity with all those that love the earth and the miracle of life. Here are some tips (Chapter 16 has more):

✔ **Don't touch anything.** Many aquatic organisms, such as corals, are covered with a mucus that protects them from infection. Touching aquatic creatures can wipe away their protective coating and leave them open to disease. While you may have difficulty avoiding accidental contact with marine organisms (especially when you're just beginning), it's a goal worth striving for.

✔ **Practice buoyancy control.** The most common reason divers touch corals and other marine organisms is poor buoyancy control (see Chapter 5).

✔ **Be realistic about your abilities.** Don't try to dive on delicate sites if you don't feel that your buoyancy control is up to it. If you're in doubt, consult with the dive master, explain to him or her your concerns — he or she is going to have a lot more respect for you than if you get down there and start grabbing hold of everything.

✔ **Don't chase or harass marine animals.** Just the presence of divers in the water is enough to alter the behavior of some creatures. Don't make it worse by purposely harassing them. Remember that you're a visitor to their world. Don't start racking up a lot of bad underwater karma. (Read the "Dangerous Marine Creatures" section, later in this chapter, if you need more incentive.)

variety of survival strategies. Bottom dwellers, such as limpets, abalone, and snails, have a shell to protect themselves from predators. Nudibrachs, although lacking a shell, have little to fear as they crawl across the reef — they rely on noxious secretions to ward off predators. Their bright colors and decorative patterns announce their toxicity. Clams, oysters, and scallops not only have a shell, but they spend most of their lives burrowed into the mud or sand.

Perhaps the most interesting of the mollusk family are the cephalopods (SEF-a-la-pods): squid, octopus, cuttlefish, and chambered nautilus (see Figure 9-6). Each of these creatures is a specialized and well-adapted predator. Squid are streamlined, open-water hunters and the stuff of legends. Who doesn't remember Captain Nemo hacking his way from the nasty, sinuous embrace of the giant squid in Jules Verne's *20,000 Leagues Under the Sea?*

Figure 9-6:
The
chambered
nautilus is a
cephalopod
closely
related to
the octopus
and squid.

Both octopus and cuttlefish are found on the reef, and both have demonstrated complex behavior and intelligence that have been compared with mammals. Both species can change color instantaneously, thanks to special pigment cells called *Chromatphores* (crow-MAT-a-fors). These color changes serve as camouflage and as a means of communicating. Cephalopods are sophisticated predators with well-developed sensory organs, including excellent eyesight. They are generally quite timid — although there are some pretty aggressive species of squid — and normally attempt to flee or take refuge in crevices in the reef when threatened. They propel themselves through the water by forcing water from the mantel through a special funnel-like organ. They sometimes try to camouflage their getaway by releasing clouds of ink into the water.

Echinoderms

Echinoderms (eh-KINE-o-derms) can be found on the bottom of the sea and they're usually fairly easy to spot, given their distinctive radial form and relatively large size. If you've seen a starfish (see Figure 9-7), you've seen an echinoderm. All of the sea stars are members of the echinoderm family, but so are animals as diverse as sea lilies, feather dusters, sea urchins, sand dollars, and sea cucumbers — you can tell they're echinoderms because the adult specimens display some kind of five-ray radial symmetry and are spiny ("echinoderm" means "spiny skin"). Sometimes, though, the spiny skin can be extraordinarily subtle. Echinoderms live both attached to the sea bottom and crawling slowly across the reef. Although it may be hard to imagine from looking at them, echinoderms are close living relatives of marine vertebrates.

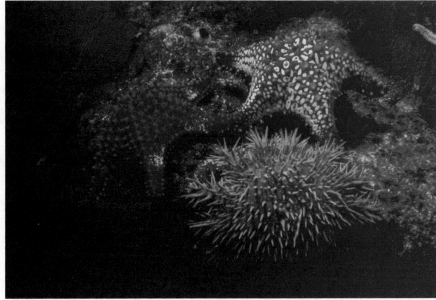

Figure 9-7:
All echino-
derms, like
these
starfish,
have a
distinctive
radial
shape. The
creature at
the bottom
right is the
poisonous
crown-of-
thorns.

Tunicates

Also known as sea squirts, tunicates (TOO-ne-kates) represent the link
between invertebrate and vertebrate species. The larval stage of these animals resembles a tadpole and possesses a sort of rudimentary backbonelike
organ known as a *notochord.* Eventually, the larval stage attaches itself to the
reef and undergoes a radical metamorphosis. The adult tunicate is asymmet-
rical and is often mistaken for sponges, which are far less sophisticated.

Fish

For most people, fish are the most recognizable and immediately evident creatures on the reef, and the reef supports them in a mind-boggling variety of
sizes, shapes, and colors — from tiny gobies less than a centimeter long to the
enormous 40-foot whale shark. There are almost as many species of fish as
there are species of mammals, reptiles, amphibians, and birds combined —
and that includes your brother-in-law, who, I'm perfectly willing to concede,
may only marginally be a form of animal life at all. Whether cruising the deep
waters outside the reef, the turbulent fore reef, or the calm sandy-bottom
lagoon, fish have made a home for themselves in every conceivable kind of
marine habitat. Many tropical reef fish are among the most brightly colored
and boldly patterned animals on earth. Others fish are so well-camouflaged
that you have trouble seeing them even when you know where they are.

Figure 9-8:
Fish take on
an amazing
variety of
forms.

Fish are so diverse in their adaptations that they defy an ironclad definition —
you can safely say that they are cold-blooded, live in water, and conduct their
respiration (at least part time) by way of gills. Of course, now that I've stuck
my neck out I'll get letters from zealous fish gurus, feverishly huddled over
their word processors in the most recondite corners of academia, contradict-
ing every point. I rest my case.

Fish, a variety of which are shown in Figure 9-8, are nearly as diverse in their
behavior as they are in their forms. Some occupy a territory that they defend
against all intruders. Others wander constantly in schools. Fish can be dangerous predators or timid grazers. They can manufacture their own light,
electricity, and fearsome venom. In short, they are everywhere in the sea, are
amazing in their diversity, and are one of the most important reasons people
enjoy diving.

Check out the color photo section of this book for additional photos of fish.

Reptiles

Turtles, sea snakes, one kind of lizard, and a crocodile make up the marine reptiles. By far, the most commonly encountered by divers are the marine turtles, although six of the seven species of marine turtles in the world today are threatened or endangered — entirely due to the activities of humankind.

Sea turtles

Marine turtles are well-adapted to life in the sea compared to their terrestrial relations — their shells, or *carapace* (CARE-a-pace), are flattened and stream-lined, and their legs have evolved into flippers and paddles. In spite of their adaptations, they must still return to the surface to breathe and to land to lay eggs. Destruction of their breeding habitat is one of the principal reasons that turtle populations are threatened worldwide. All species of sea turtles are protected under international treaty, and all six of the sea turtles that occur in United States territorial waters are protected under the Endangered Species Act, but their recovery is slow and still very much in doubt.

The seven species, shown in Figure 9-9, are as follows:

Figure 9-9:
There are seven species of sea turtles worldwide, including two species of ridleys — Kemp's ridley and Olive ridley — represented here in their relative sizes. All species of sea turtles are threatened and pro-tected worldwide.

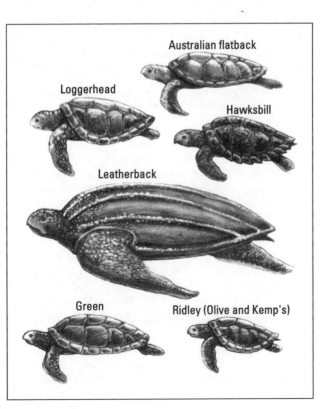

Australian flatback

Loggerhead

Hawksbill

Leatherback

Green

Ridley (Olive and Kemp's)

The question of fish feeding

Snorkelers and divers want to see fish, and the easiest way to bring in a crowd of colorful tropicals is to feed them. But fish feeding is a controversial practice and the long-term consequences on fish populations are not well understood. Sure, feeding will increase the numbers of fish you may see on a given dive, but it may create a dependence on handouts and artificially distort reef populations.

People tend to feed fish whatever they happen to have on hand, usually remains of their own picnic lunch: bread, potato chips, cookies, or cheese. (There is a persistent myth that frozen peas are a good fish food, but you seldom see tropical fish cultivating crops of legumes in a natural setting.) Snacks designed for humans are of little nutritional value to reef fish and the long-term effects of this kind of diet are unknown. In Hawaii's Hanauma Bay, one of the most congested snorkeling spots in the world,

visitors are only allowed to feed fish specially formulated pellets or standard aquarium fish food. If you insist on feeding the fish, this seems a fair compromise. You can pick up a fish food formulated for marine fish at most pet stores. It's inexpensive and nutritionally balanced for the health of the fish.

Another undesirable consequence of feeding fish is that they can become quite aggressive competing for handouts. This may seem insignificant with small reef fish, but it can be a problem with species like moray eels, barracuda, and sharks, who may also be attracted by the feeding frenzy. The best idea is to resist the temptation to feed the fish. One of the great joys of diving is to quietly observe the complex natural behavior of the reef inhabitants — that's an option you don't have when you're mugged by aggressive mobs of fish habituated to handouts.

✔ **Green:** Green sea turtles are 3 to 4 feet in length, and between 200 and 300 pounds. Their carapace is oval-shaped with mottled gray, brown, and cream-colored markings. Greens are probably the most commonly sighted by divers. They frequent shallow coastal waters where they feed mostly on algae and seagrasses.

✔ **Hawksbill:** Hawksbills are a little smaller than greens — about 3 feet long and generally between 100 and 200 pounds. Hawksbills have a beautiful, mottled carapace for which they were, and still are, hunted. Hawksbills can be recognized by their distinctive hooked beak and the jagged edge on the tail-end of their carapace. They are often sighted on the reef feeding on sponges, tunicates, and shrimp.

✔ **Loggerhead:** Adult loggerhead turtles are normally 3 to 4 feet in length and weigh between 200 and 400 pounds. Their carapace is oval and often has a reddish-brown tint. Loggerheads are commonly encountered in the coastal waters of the southeastern United States and in the

Caribbean. They can be identified by their large heads and powerful jaws, which are designed for crushing and grinding the crustaceans and mollusks on which they feed.

✔ **Kemp's ridley:** Kemp's ridley is the smallest and most endangered of all the sea turtles. They are seldom larger than 30 inches, and usually between 80 and 100 pounds. This species has a rounded carapace that is normally olive-gray. They are found only in the coastal waters and bays of the northern Gulf of Mexico, where they forage for crabs. At a single nesting site in Mexico, 40,000 female Kemp's ridleys came ashore to nest in 1947. Today, less than 500 nest on the same beach. They are very rare and a diver is unlikely to see one.

✔ **Olive ridley:** The olive ridley is similar to Kemp's ridley, except that their carapace is more highly domed and has more variation, and some other differences that no one but an expert can detect. Olive ridley's are also very rare and it is unlikely you will see one in the wild, at least for the foreseeable future, although recovery programs are in progress.

✔ **Leatherback:** These are the giants of the sea turtle clan. Specimens of leatherbacks have reached 6 feet in length and weigh as much as 1,400 pounds. Unlike other species, the leatherback does not have a hard carapace, but a smooth, dark leathery hide with seven longitudinal ridges. Leatherbacks are a highly migratory species and are often seen in open water. They feed primarily on jellyfish.

✔ **Flatback:** The flatback turtle is found primarily in the coastal waters of northern Australia — they are sometimes seen as far north as Indonesia and Papua New Guinea, but all of their known nesting sites are in northern Australia. The flatback's carapace is olive-gray and oval-shaped with a flattened dome from which they take their name. Flatbacks average about 3 feet in length and weigh 200 to 300 pounds. They are normally found in shallow coastal waters between the Great Barrier Reef and the Queensland shore, out hunting for sea cucumbers, soft corals, jellyfish, and other soft-bodied marine species.

Sea snakes

Sea snakes are air-breathers. There are about 80 species, all of which live in the tropical Pacific and Indian oceans. Sea snakes are believed to have descended from Australia terrestrial species, but although they breath air, they are completely adapted to the marine environment. Occasionally, a terrestrial species of snake is encountered in the sea, but true sea snakes can be identified by their flattened, eel-like tail. They can be distinguished from eels by their lack of gills — see Figure 9-10.

Figure 9-10:
Sea snakes
are air
breathing
and have a
flattened tail
to aid
swimming.

You can find two types of sea snakes underwater — coastal types that are restricted to relatively shallow coastal waters, and those that are *pelagic,* or open-ocean species. Some coastal types breed and lay eggs onshore and are capable of remaining out of the water for long periods. The pelagic types are highly sensitive to extremes in temperature and can't survive long out of the water. These species are often found in congregations of many animals, far out to sea. They give birth to live young, at sea, who are fully equipped to survive from birth.

Encounters with sea snakes are not common, even in the south Pacific and Indian oceans, but they do happen from time to time. Generally, they are not a problem. Sea snakes are highly venomous, but are seldom aggressive — treated with deference and the utmost respect, they usually go about their business. Because they are sensitive to temperature changes, no sea snakes are found in the Atlantic.

Marine iguana

There is only one species of marine lizard — the marine iguana of the Galapagos Islands. This species, like many of the animals in the Galapagos, exhibits little fear of humanity. They are easily approached on the rocky shoreline, where they sun themselves in large social groups between plunges into the sea to feed on seaweed. Marine iguanas are usually dark-colored and grow up to 5 feet long. Because they stay in the shallow water close to shore, in surf and strong surge, they are seldom seen by divers underwater.

TREAD LIGHTLY

The ethical collector

It isn't surprising that collecting and keeping tropical reef fish in an aquarium is one of the most popular hobbies in North America — the aquarium trade is a more than $2-million-per-year industry. I used to collect, and I understand the attraction. Keeping tropical fish allows you to satisfy the nurturing instinct that most people have, while having something beautiful and fascinating right there in your living room. Nothing wrong with that, but there may be something wrong with the way that some — but not all — of these fish are collected for sale.

Wild tropical fish are collected in one of two ways: hand-netted or stunned with cyanide (or some other toxic substance). If you've ever dived on a coral reef, it's easy to imagine how difficult and time-consuming it might be to catch healthy fish in a hand net; hence the lure of cyanide fishing in desperately poor Pacific island nations. Cyanide fishing is illegal, but the law is difficult to enforce.

The cyanide solution is normally carried in a plastic squeeze bottle and injected into the crevices of the reef where the fish hide. The fish aren't killed, but they are stunned and rendered easy to capture. They generally recover from their initial exposure to the cyanide, but frequently sustain damage to their internal organs. This, coupled with the stress of capture and transport, kills more than half of these fish before they ever reach the pet store — most of the rest die within a few weeks of being introduced to the home aquarium.

Not all of the fish exposed to cyanide in this way die, but mortality among the delicate coral polyps that are exposed is 100 percent. Combined with dynamite fishing, siltation, pollution, overfishing, and other factors, vast tracts of southeast Asian reefs have been decimated. In Indonesia, less than 10 percent of the reefs are still pristine; in the Philippines, less than 5 percent. That's one of the reasons the Philippines, in spite of prime location, a large percentage of the population that speaks and understands English, and good tourist infrastructure, is not more popular as a dive destination.

The only effective way to stop the practice of cyanide fishing is to eliminate the motivation, and the motivation comes from the tropical fish hobbyist in North America. If you're a fish hobbyist or considering becoming one, make sure you buy only fish that are certified.

Certified means that the provider is in compliance with U.S. Fish and Wildlife Service laws, the U.S. Endangered Species Act, and the Convention on International Trade in Endangered Species (C.I.T.I.E.S.). Certified fish are also hand-netted or are raised specifically for the aquarium trade in fish farms. (Fish farms help protect wild species by lowering the cost of these species and discouraging the collection of wild specimens.) Buying only certified fish not only helps preserve the reef, it helps you protect your own investment.

Saltwater crocodile

Saltwater, or *estuarine* (es-CHOO-air-in), crocodiles are the largest of the crocodile family. They can grow to 26 feet in length and weigh in excess of a ton. Like sea snakes, they are found only in the Indo-Pacific. Because they prefer to ambush their prey at the water's edge and need to bear their young on land, the distribution of saltwater crocodiles is more restricted than that of sea snakes; nevertheless, crocodiles have been spotted more than 800 miles out to sea. They are most common in and around Australia, but they range as far north as Palau.

Crocodiles are seldom encountered by divers and because they usually only attack near the shore, it's difficult to determine how much of a threat they represent to divers in the water. It has proved very difficult to find subjects willing to do this kind of research.

Mammals

Marine mammals are the descendants of terrestrial animals that returned to their ancestral home in the sea. In spite of the fact that they are very well-adapted to the marine environment, they have retained certain characteristics that identify them as mammals — they bear live young that they suckle, are warm-blooded, and have hair at some time in their lives (or at least a toupee).

Whales and dolphins are believed to have been among the first terrestrial species to return to the sea and they show the most complete adaptation to an aquatic life. Sea otters are thought to be the most recent to return to the sea, and they retain many terrestrial traits.

Marine mammals never learned to breathe underwater, and, as far as we know, they never invented scuba equipment. Instead, their physiology adapted, allowing them to hold their breath underwater for extended periods (a sperm whale can hold its breath for an hour and a half). To keep warm, they evolved an insulating layer of fat, called *blubber,* or thick fur (or both). To facilitate movement through the relatively dense medium of water, they became sleek and streamlined.

Sea otters

Sea otters make up their own distinct family. Unlike their distant relations, the true seals, they have no flippers, which is the defining characteristic of all pinnipeds (see the following section). Otters are thought to be the most recent mammals to have returned to the sea. In fact, they don't venture far from the shore — they live in relatively shallow water, in the kelp beds that thrive off the west coast of North America. They are 3 to 4 feet long, and usually dark brown with the head and back somewhat lighter — the head of older males can be nearly white. Otters have a short, thick tail and webbed feet. They have no insulating blubber and rely on their dense fur to insulate them from the cold water of the eastern Pacific. They were hunted so heavily for their luxurious fur that the southern sea otter was nearly extinct by the beginning of the twentieth century. They have begun to make a recovery — today they can be seen in a few places off the coast of central California.

Pinnipeds

Pinniped (PIN-eh-ped) means "winged-foot," a reference to the paddle-shaped limbs that are common to all of these creatures. Pinnipeds are divided into the following three families, shown in Figure 9-11:

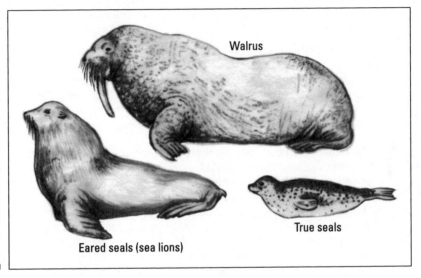

Figure 9-11:
True seals have no external ear, eared seals can turn their hind flippers forward, walruses have traits of both.

Walrus

Eared seals (sea lions)

True seals

✔ **True seals:** There are 19 species of true seals worldwide. It is believed that seals and sea otters evolved from the same ancestral creatures, but seals began their return to the sea long before otters. Sea lions and walrus look similar, but developed along a separate line. True seals can be distinguished from *eared seals,* as they are known, by their lack of external ears, relatively small fore-flippers, and large hind-flippers — their main propulsion in the water. True seals can't turn their hind-flippers forward, so they can't walk on land as the eared seals can. Most seals are found in cool, temperate or polar waters. Only the three species of monk seal — the Hawaiian, Mediterranean, and Caribbean — are found in the tropics. The Caribbean monk seal is no longer found at all, as it is now believed to be extinct. The other two species are severely endangered. Harbor seals are the true seals that are most commonly seen by divers in the temperate regions of the Pacific and Atlantic.

✔ **Eared seals:** Eared seals are believed to have descended from an ancient bear-like ancestor. They have many similarities to true seals, but they can be distinguished by their external ears, large fore-flippers, relatively small hind-flippers, and their ability to turn their hind-flippers forward and "walk" on land. Like true seals, eared seals are mainly found in cool waters that support rich marine life, the notable exception being the fur seals of the Galapagos Islands.

✔ **Walrus:** Walrus are believed to have descended from the same ancestor as the eared seals, but they have characteristics of both eared and true seals. Walruses, like true seals, have no external ear, yet they are able to turn their hind-flippers forward and walk the way eared seals do — they are in a family by themselves. Walruses are found only in the most northern latitudes.

Sirenians

Sirenians (sy-REEN-eh-ans) include the manatees and dugongs (DOO-gongs). All of these animals live in the tropics, but only a little more than 250 years ago, the largest of the sirenians, known as *Steller's sea cow* was discovered in the Bering Sea. Steller's sea cow grew up to 25 feet and weighed almost 2 tons. Like all sirenians, Steller's sea cow was placid and relatively slow moving — within 30 years it had been hunted to extinction.

The name *sirenian* comes from the Greek word for sirens — mythical temptresses. Legend has it that early sailors mistook these ponderous 1,000-pounders for mermaids. I hope I'm never at sea for that long.

Manatees, shown in Figure 9-12, are generally 8 to 14 feet in length and weigh between 500 and 1,000 pounds. Their skin is a fairly uniform gray with a pebbled texture, frequently covered with algae and too often scarred by powerboat propellers. Manatees are sensitive to cold. Every winter manatees gather around the warm springs of Florida that maintain a constant temperature of 72°. This is where they are most often encountered by divers (see Chapter 13). In summer, they disperse throughout the Caribbean and Atlantic to feed. (Check out the color photo section of this book for a photo of a manatee with some divers.)

Manatees and dugongs are herbivores — the descendants of an ancient hoofed animal that also was the ancestor of modern horses, cattle, and elephants. Elephants, in fact, are the closest living relatives of the sirenians. Manatees and dugongs feed on sea grasses and other aquatic plants, and they consume enormous quantities. Manatees have a broad flat tail; the dugong's tail is more flukelike, similar to a dolphin's. You aren't likely to confuse the two — manatees are found in the Caribbean, and dugongs only in the Indo-Pacific.

Cetaceans

Whales and dolphins make up the family of marine mammals collectively known as *cetaceans* (set-TAY-shuns), shown in Figure 9-13. Most people regard dolphins as distinct from whales, but the only real distinction among cetaceans is whether they are toothed whales or baleen whales. Dolphins are actually small-toothed whales.

Figure 9-12:
The gentle West Indian Manatee has been on the endangered species list since it was begun and remains there today.

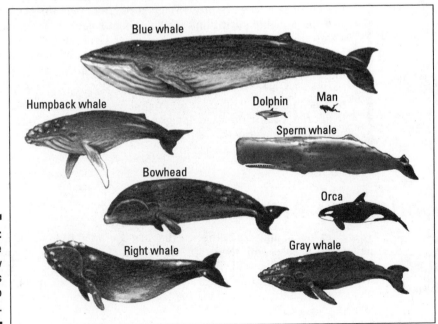

Figure 9-13:
Relative size of a few cetaceans compared to humans.

✔ **Toothed whales:** The most obvious distinction lends its name to this family of cetaceans — toothed whales have rows of cone-shaped teeth that they use to capture and hold their prey. Generally, toothed whales are smaller than baleen whales, but there are exceptions. Toothed whales are also noted for *ecolocation* — a kind of natural sonar they use in hunting. Toothed whales range in size from the smallest species of dolphins, at less than 6 feet, to the sperm whale, where the males approach 60 feet. Sperm whales are probably best known from Herman Melville's literary classic, *Moby Dick*. Not nearly as much is known about sperm whales as is known about dolphins, but it's clear that real sperm whales are no more malicious than dolphins are angelic. Research on the dolphins shows them to be highly social and intelligent creatures, but dolphins also exhibit what, in human society, would be considered rape, kidnapping, and devious political maneuvering. However, dolphin society is too alien to be judged on human terms. You can go on an excursions that specialize in dolphin encounters (see Chapter 13 and the color photo section of this book) — I rank it among the most unforgettable experiences in the underwater world.

✔ **Baleen whales:** The baleen whales are filter feeders. They strain plankton from the water with fibers growing from plates attached to their upper jaws. Baleen whales include the largest of the cetaceans, and the largest of the baleen whales — the blue whale — is the largest creature ever to live on earth. At over 100 feet long and 120 tons, the blue whale is an impressive sight, but one rarely glimpsed by divers. You can find dive excursions that specialize in encounters with some species of the baleen whales (see Chapter 13), most often the humpbacks because of their predictable migrations and their gentle nature. Humpbacks demonstrate an awareness of divers in the water. Generally they are somewhat wary, but at times they seem curious and allow divers within inches.

Right whales are so named because they were the "right" whales to kill for the early whalers — they are seldom seen by divers. They migrate between polar feeding areas and temperate calving grounds, but even in temperate waters their calving grounds are generally a long way. This is also true of the gray whale. The bowhead is the only baleen whale to live exclusively in the polar regions.

Dangerous Marine Creatures

There are lots of animals in the sea that are equipped to hunt for food or defend themselves with teeth, spines, or venom that can cause you harm, but that's true on land as well. This isn't a list of every marine creature that can hurt you — there are thousands. Instead, these are the most common troublemakers, and the most commonly feared. The ocean is not the native environment of humans, so it makes sense that we should feel more vulnerable there, but most marine creatures view us with caution and try to avoid intimate encounters with humans — the best way to avoid unpleasant aquatic encounters is to let them avoid you. In general, the fear these creatures inspire is way out of proportion to the actual threat they represent. But caution is an important survival tool. Information and your own judgment are all you have to make the call.

Things that sting

Stinging things possess stinging cells called *nematocysts* (neh-MAT-o-sists) that adhere to or penetrate the skin, and inject venom. If they can't reach your skin, they can't do their work — that's why wearing a wetsuit or a dive skin is a good idea, even if you're not cold, although that won't protect your head and hands. Some divers wear gloves to protect their hands. My feeling is that wearing gloves encourages divers to manhandle the marine life — better not to touch anything at all.

You can find three kinds of stinging creatures in the sea: those that are sedentary (attached to the sea floor), those that are free swimming, and those that are really sarcastic back on the dive boat.

Sedentary stingers

Because they are attached to the sea floor, this kind of creature is easily avoided. If you see one, or think you see one — steer clear. It's that simple. Still, accidents happen. You may reach out to steady yourself, or to hold your position in a current, and find yourself reaching out to a less-than-sympathetic life form.

- ✔ **Fire corals:** Fire corals aren't really corals at all, but colonial hydroids capable of building their own calcareous skeleton similar to true corals. They are usually yellow-green and brown in color, covered with many tiny pores. Of course, you may have difficulty detecting the color underwater. Fire corals grow in many different sizes and shapes. The effect of their sting ranges from a mild prickling to intense burning. Most commonly, it's a burning itch with redness and pinpoint lesions.

- ✔ **Fire sponges:** Sponges don't have stinging cells, but there are at least three species that can cause you problems. They aren't easy to identify, so just don't touch the sponges. The source of the problem is a little mysterious: It's either the silica spicules in the body of the sponge or a toxin that it produces — it isn't very well understood. It may take up to 24 hours between contact and any kind of symptoms — severe itching and burning, along with swelling and stiffness. Usually the victim develops a rash and sometimes blisters, but oddly, the affected area can also look perfectly normal. Don't pick up sponges washed up on the beach either — they can zap you long after they're dead.

- ✔ **Stinging hydroids:** These guys are hydroids, like fire corals, but they don't build a calcareous skeleton the way that fire corals do. Stinging hydroids look something like a fern and are often mistaken for some kind of seaweed. They are usually the same yellow-green and brownish color as fire corals — although their coloration can vary quite a bit. The effects of the sting are similar to fire coral, but are usually somewhat more severe.

- ✔ **Anemones:** Because of the many species of anemone, their stings can range from unnoticeable to very severe. They are often beautifully colored and look like flowering plants with a radial pattern and tentacles waving in the current. In the Indo-Pacific, anemones frequently serve as home to anemone fish that swim unharmed among the stinging tentacles. Unless you're an anemone fish planning to take up residence, keep out.

Free-swimming stingers

Encounters with free-swimming stingers are usually accidental as well. Typically, a diver swims into the trailing tentacles of a jellyfish without even knowing the animal is there. Most of these kinds of encounters can be avoided by simply being aware of your surroundings. Sometimes the tentacles and stinging cells of these creatures break off and float free in the water. A diver may come in contact with them without ever seeing anything at all. This kind of encounter is hard to avoid, but very rare.

Most species of jellyfish have nematocysts in their trailing tentacles and should be given a wide berth. One species that lives in isolated saltwater lakes in the western Pacific is entirely harmless, and snorkeling among these guys is one of the great snorkeling adventures (see Chapter 13). Intimate contact with jellyfish, however, is normally an adventure that you don't want to have. Most jellyfish are slow swimming and easily avoided, but they may be difficult to avoid if they occur in huge congregations, as they sometimes do. These kinds of gatherings are generally localized and seasonal, and can be avoided with a little prior research.

- ✔ **Portuguese man-of-war:** These are not really jellyfish, but a colonial hydroid that has adopted a jellyfish lifestyle. They are found in tropical and subtropical waters, especially during the warm summer months. The Portuguese man-of-war can be identified by its gas-filled bladder that allows it to float on the surface with its tentacles trailing in the water. The bladder is usually transparent, with a blue tint. Because they drift in the wind, Portuguese man-of-war are often found washed up on a beach. Don't touch them under any circumstances — they can sting you even after they're dead. Most victims of their sting survive, but enough deaths have been attributed to the Portuguese man-of-war to afford them the most serious respect.

✔ **Box jellyfish:** Also known as sea wasps, these are the real bad boys of the jellyfish clan. Their venom is among the most toxic of any marine animal, although most victims survive. They are found only in the warm tropical waters of the Indo-Pacific, especially around northern Australia. Box jellyfish begin life as egg and polyp stages in mangrove swamps and coastal estuaries. Warm summer months bring rains that wash the mature jellies into the coastal seas. They are usually small at the beginning of the summer months, and become bigger, and more dangerous, as the summer progresses. The body of the box jelly is up to 8 inches, trailing stinging tentacles up to 10 feet. They are transparent, with a pale blue tint. Box jellyfish are difficult to see in the water, but local people are usually aware of their presence. Do not enter the water if they are present.

Things that are poisonous

Among the many creatures with venomous spines in the seas, nearly all of them use their spines only for self-defense. They aren't aggressive and, unless you are giving them cause to defend themselves, they are no danger to you.

The following are the poisonous spines:

✔ **Bristleworms:** These are segmented worms; each segment has a pair of poisonous bristles. You can find them in tropical and subtropical waters of the Indian Ocean, Pacific, Atlantic, the Caribbean — just about everywhere it's fun to dive. Just as the name implies, they look like bristly worms (see Figure 9-14). They grow up to 8 inches in length and come in a whole rainbow of colors — some are quite beautiful. Look, but don't touch. If you get nailed by a bristleworm, you can expect intense burning and itching that lasts up to a week, along with swelling and possibly blistering. Some of these things also bite and, you guessed it, the bite is toxic and produces similar symptoms.

✔ **Sea urchins:** Sea urchins are a ball of bristling spines, often with a venom gland at the tip of each one. You can find them in all oceans, but the most venomous ones are in the tropics. The basic spiny shape of the urchin is unmistakable, although they vary in size and color. Urchins' spines are brittle and tend to break off in the puncture wound after they penetrate — embedded spines can lead to further complications beyond the original wound. Not too many people feel compelled to play with urchins, but they are often found in shallow water and may be stepped on accidentally.

Figure 9-14:
Look, but
don't touch.
A bristle-
worm in the
hand is
worth a
week of
misery.

✔ **Crown-of-thorns:** The crown-of-thorns starfish is found throughout the
tropics on coral reefs. They are famous for their periodic population
explosions that destroy huge tracts of reef. Some experts feel these are
natural periodic events; others think that they are the result of an imbal-
ance in the natural ecosystem due to the activities of humankind.
Whatever the cause, they can really devastate a reef and can mess with
you personally, as well. Crown-of-thorns grow up to about 2 feet across,
usually have 13 to 16 starfishlike arms, and their entire top side is covered with short, sharp spines. They don't have venom glands, but the
spines are covered with a kind of toxic mucus. The victims usually survive, but the misery can last for weeks.

✔ **Cone shells:** Of the more than 400 species of venomous cone shells, only
a few species are considered dangerous. The dangerous ones are mostly
in the Indian Ocean and the Pacific, but at least one species is found in
the Red Sea, tropical Atlantic, and the Caribbean. Because of their beautiful colors and patterns, cone shells are very popular with shell
collectors. If you're a shell collector, be very careful with cone shells.
You find them in shallow water on reefs, in lagoons, and in tidal ponds.
Cone shells can extend a long harpoonlike organ from the narrow end of
the shell that's armed with a small, poisonous dart or harpoon. It
doesn't help to pick it up at the wide end, because the harpoon can
reach everywhere around the shell. About one-quarter of the people
tagged by a cone shell don't live to tell the tale. They are especially dangerous to children. If you're a shell collector, collect only shells that are
empty. Never collect, or attempt to collect, live cone shells.

✔ **Stingrays:** Stingrays are bottom dwellers of all tropical and temperate seas. You typically see them on a sandy bottom, partially buried, and when you get too close, they rise in a billowing cloud of sand and glide away on their graceful wings. Stingrays are not aggressive. One of the really exciting and popular snorkeling adventures is swimming among the wild rays that have been hand-fed and habituated to snorkelers at Stingray City, in Grand Cayman (see Chapter 13). Thousands of people swim with these rays every year without harm. Even so, stingrays are capable of inflicting serious injury. Almost always, injuries are the result of a wader stepping on a ray at rest in the shallows. The stingray's tail is tipped with a barbed spine. If it is stepped on, the stingray swings its tail upward driving the spine into the offending limb or body, or effecting a slashing wound. Venom flows along grooves in the spine into the wound. Stingray spines can penetrate most clothing.

The best protection against stingrays is to shuffle your feet as you wade in the shallows, giving the ray plenty of time to flee. Also, never harass a ray that's resting on the bottom.

✔ **Catfish:** Saltwater catfish are found in tropical and subtropical seas. They are usually about 8 or 9 inches long with distinctive black and white longitudinal stripes, and typically travel in large schools. They aren't aggressive, but are capable of defending themselves. Barbed spines protrude along the dorsal fin (the one on their backs) and the pectoral fins (the ones just behind their gills) — each one has a venom gland at the base. Catfish venom is broken down by the application of heat.

✔ **Scorpionfish** and **stonefish:** There are hundreds of different species of these fish, and they count among their fraternity the most venomous fish in the sea. They typically have a snaggled, grotesque appearance, ranging in color from flamboyant to mud plain. Most hunt by ambush and they tend to adopt the same coloration as their surroundings. These fish possess a row of spines along the dorsal fin, sometimes the pectoral and *anal fins* (the ones right before the tail), too. The spines are erected if the fish is threatened — each spine is grooved, or hollow, to pass venom into the wound from a gland at the base of each spine. The severity of the reaction depends on how big you are, where the fish nails you, how many spines nail you, and how deep they go.

The lionfish, shown in Figure 9-15, is the species most commonly encountered by divers. They are often seen on reef walls or on wrecks in tropical waters, singly or in pairs. They are brightly colored with vertical red and white stripes, and have large, lacey fins. They aren't aggressive, but always display the kind of regal confidence that powerful venom provides. They aren't dangerous if treated with respect.

Figure 9-15:
The flamboyant lionfish—beautiful and well-equipped for self-defense.

Stonefish lie quietly in the shallows of the tropical seas of the Pacific and Indian oceans, waiting to ambush passing fish. They are so well-camouflaged that they can be nearly impossible to detect. You really don't want to step on one of these guys — even if you survive, you're in for the worst experience of your life. Stonefish venom is considered the most toxic of any fish. Wear thick-soled reef shoes in suspected areas. If you don't know whether it's a suspected area, ask the locals.

The following creatures have poisonous bites:

✔ **Sea snakes:** Sea snakes live only in the Indo-Pacific. You may encounter them on reefs or in open water. They can be banded, striped, or unpatterned, but they can always be identified by their flattened tail — a feature absent in terrestrial snakes (refer to Figure 9-10). Sea snake venom is similar to cobra venom, but 20 times as powerful. A sea snake typically injects far less venom than a cobra, however. In fact, they sometimes inject no venom — only about 25 percent of people bitten by sea snakes exhibit symptoms of poisoning. No matter what the odds, this is one lottery you want to avoid — a single dose of sea snake venom can kill you three times. Fortunately sea snakes are not aggressive unless handled — they do have the disconcerting habit of being highly inquisitive, however. There are many reports of sea snakes investigating divers underwater, even slithering around their bodies — a very alarming experience for some people. If this should happen to you, do your best to remain calm, keep still, and let the snake investigate. It will swim away eventually.

✔ **Blue-ringed octopus:** These are among the smallest of the octopus clan, but by far the most dangerous. They live in the Indo-Pacific, most commonly around Australia, but also in Papua New Guinea, New Zealand, Fiji, even as far as Japan. Blue-ringed octopuses derive their name from numerous ringed markings on their tentacles that become vivid blue when the animals are disturbed — overall they are a yellow-brown color. They are between 1 and 8 inches long, but don't let their size fool you — their toxic saliva can cause death within minutes. Blue-ringed octopuses are colorful and attractive and often found in tide pools, but they should never be handled.

Things that bite

Not all marine animals are venomous, of course. Some simply possess formidable jaws and teeth that are capable of producing some pretty serious trauma. These animals, particularly sharks, are probably the most feared by inexperienced divers. They have received a lot of sensational press, but their reputation is wildly out of proportion to the actual threat they represent. Perhaps one reason these animals are so feared is that, unlike nearly all the other dangerous marine animals, they can be aggressive at times. Understanding their behavior, and modifying your own can go a long way toward minimizing — or even eliminating — the danger.

✔ **Sea lice:** Not everything that bites causes massive trauma. The term sea lice is often used to refer to any sting or bite from an unseen source in the water — often these incidents are the result of free floating nematocysts that have broken off of a jellyfish or some similar animal — but more accurately it applies to tiny burrowing crustaceans that occur in seasonal, localized outbreaks. These little stinkers have powerful little jaws, and their bites result in nasty little welts. The outbreaks usually occur in the hot months. Some people seem more sensitive to their bites than others. Get out of the water if it's full of sea lice.

✔ **Octopus** and **squid:** Both octopus and squid are cephalopods — there are many different species and they occur in all the world's oceans. Under ordinary circumstances, octopuses are not dangerous. Octopuses are commonly handled by experienced divers without incident — typically, they prefer flight to confrontation. An octopus can and does bite when cornered or mishandled. All octopuses have a parrotlike beak and venomous saliva — not nearly as dangerous as the Blue-ringed octopus, but nothing you want to be on the wrong end of. An octopus bite can result in inflammation, swelling, and sometimes numbness, in addition to the trauma of the wound itself.

Squid also have a powerful parrotlike beak. They have been known to easily splinter a wooden pole that's almost 2 inches in diameter, but squid normally flee from divers in the water. The Humboldt squid (*Dorsidcus gigas*) grows up to 12 feet and is ferociously aggressive when feeding. Squid fishermen claim a Humboldt feeding frenzy makes a shark frenzy look like an ice cream social. Fortunately, this species only occurs in the eastern Pacific, off the coast of Peru, and they only feed at night.

✔ **Eels:** Eels look a lot more ferocious than they are — hovering at the mouth of their hidy-holes in the reef, with their gaping jaws exposing rows of sharp teeth, weaving back and forth like a cobra, looking for an opening to sink their fangs into you (see Figure 9-16). The fact is eels have their mouths open to pump water over their gills so they can breath. Eels are fairly easily tamed by divers — many dive sites have a resident eel completely habituated to handouts. These eels can become a nuisance. They may become overly aggressive if there is competition from other fish for the free lunch. Occasionally, they may confuse the divers fingers or other appendages with the proffered food — always wear trunks.

✔ **Barracuda:** Barracuda live in all the tropic and subtropic waters of the world. They often travel in schools, although you often see large barracuda, 4 to 6 feet long, traveling alone. They are armed with long, sharp teeth in both jaws, but like sharks, the barracuda's reputation is somewhat exaggerated. Barracudas don't normally attack divers. Most experts believe the attacks are a case of mistaken identity — the barracuda are attracted to bright colors and reflective jewelry, possibly mistaking the flashing reflections for fish, especially in turbid water. Leave your jewelry on the boat.

✔ **Saltwater crocodile:** Saltwater crocodiles live in northern Australia and the western Pacific. Crocodiles are ambush predators and are most dangerous along river and estuary shorelines, particularly at night, in the early morning, and during evening hours. Crocs are sometimes encountered many hundreds of miles out to sea, but there is no record of a crocodile attack on a diver in open water.

✔ **Sharks:** Sharks are probably more feared than any other marine animal. For the most part, their reputation as ferocious man-eaters is highly exaggerated. They can be aggressive under certain circumstances, and some do attack without warning. Attacks can, for the most part, be avoided, and understanding the shark's needs and behavior can help keep you from becoming the victim of a shark attack.

Figure 9-16:
Eels look
scary and
are capable
of inflicting
a serious
bite, but
they only
bite divers
in self-
defense.

Of approximately 350 different species of sharks (you can see several examples in the color photo section of this book), only a handful are considered dangerous to divers. The whale shark, the largest fish in the world, is a docile plankton feeder and many divers travel to special destinations to encounter this spectacular fish in its natural environment (see Chapter 13 and the color photo section of this book). In fact, many divers arrange to encounter one of the really dangerous sharks, the great white, in its natural environment, but usually from the safety of a shark cage.

Statistically, shark attacks are rare. You're twice as likely to be struck by lightning and 3,000 times more likely to die in your car on the way to the shore. Most of the sharks encountered by divers represent no danger, as long as they aren't chased or harassed. Most divers, after they become familiar with seeing sharks in the wild, delight in watching these graceful, magnificent animals.

Sharks have a lot more to fear from you than you do from them. In the past five years, the world has seen an enormous explosion in the popularity of shark products — and a corresponding rise in the worldwide shark catch. Shark fins, for shark-fin soup, command as much as $250 per pound. A bowl of it in Hong Kong sells for as much as $90! Of the 125 countries involved in the trade of shark products, only 4 have any kind of management plan for the fishery. Because of their long life and relatively low reproductive rate, sharks are very vulnerable to fishing pressures. A number of environmental organizations (see the Appendix) have mounted campaigns to try to save sharks before it's too late.

Shark attacks on human beings do occur. The damage that a shark does in an attack varies tremendously and depends on the type of attack, the species of shark, and other factors, but less than a third of shark attacks result in a fatality. Most commonly, a shark attack is a single bite that results in slashing wounds and profuse bleeding. Shock and loss of blood are the most immediate dangers. Ninety percent of all shark attacks happen at or near the surface, and close to shore. Survival chances are good if the victim gets immediate medical attention. Of the 350 species of sharks, about 12 are known to have attacked humans. Of those, the following four species are considered the most dangerous (see Figure 9-17).

- **Bull shark:** Bull sharks are common reef sharks in all tropical and subtropical seas. They are powerful-looking, stocky sharks with a short, square snout and small eyes. Normally, bull sharks will avoid divers, but they are easily attracted to bait. Shark dives that purposely attract sharks with *chum* — parts, blood, and other kinds of bait — occasionally attract bull sharks. They can become quite aggressive in the presence of bait and may be stimulated to attack.

- **Oceanic whitetip:** Some experienced mariners regard the oceanic whitetip as the most dangerous of all sharks. Oceanic whitetips live in tropical and subtropical waters worldwide and prefer a deep ocean environment. Around the Hawaiian Islands, they are frequently reported following pods of pilot whales. They are usually about 10 feet long, a grayish-bronze color on top and light-colored underneath. They have a distinctive, rounded dorsal fin that's tipped with white. The behavior of oceanic whitetips is unpredictable. They can be sluggish and indifferent, or aggressive and very dangerous. There have been attacks on divers, but oceanic whitetips are most often encountered in deep ocean and very rarely on reefs.

- **Tiger shark:** Tigers live in all tropical and subtropical seas, on the reef, and in open water. Tigers grow up to 18 feet long and as much as 3,000 pounds, with a broad, square snout and a thick, heavy body that tapers to a slender tail. They take their name from the dark vertical stripes on their backs, but the stripes tend to fade with age and are not a reliable means of identifying tigers. Tiger sharks are opportunistic feeders. Young tigers (under 6 feet) tend to feed near the bottom on fish. Larger tigers move up in the water column, consuming whatever they find in midwater. The biggest tigers (over 9 feet) occupy the surface waters and eat whatever they can find there — and I mean anything! All of the stories of exotic rubbish found in the stomachs of sharks are usually about tigers. Their indiscriminate eating habits are well-documented and undoubtedly why human beings wind up on the menu from time to time. Tiger sharks often appear sluggish and lethargic in the water, but after they adopt feeding behavior, they are very persistent in their attacks. This accounts for the higher rate of fatalities among tiger shark victims.

- **The great white:** Most people consider the great white the most dangerous of the sharks, maybe even the most dangerous animal in the world. It isn't hard to see why — the powerful gaping jaws of an enormous white shark, lined with rows of razor-sharp teeth. The media, of course, has seized on this terrifying image, exaggerated it, and exploited it for every nickel it would yield, but after all is said and done, there is still an element of truth in the menace of white sharks. They are spectacularly powerful and impressive animals—diving with white sharks, from the protection of a shark cage, is a popular and profitable venture in South Australia and in South Africa.

  Great white sharks grow to 18 feet and can weight over a ton. They live in open waters in all temperate and tropical seas, but are rare in the tropics and seem to prefer temperate waters, especially where they can find their favorite prey — seals and sea lions. Because they feed primarily on pinnipeds, great whites employ a

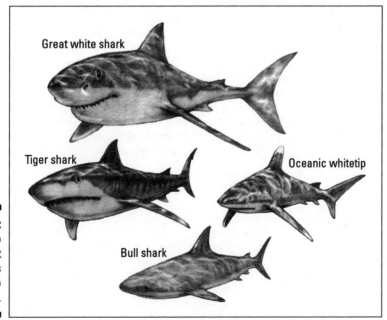

Figure 9-17:
The top four most dangerous sharks to divers.

Great white shark

Tiger shark

Oceanic whitetip

Bull shark

different feeding behavior than most sharks, relying on stealth and surprise attack. Divers, swimmers, and surfers on the surface may resemble the profile of a pinniped; even worse, a pinniped in trouble. Many shark experts feel that white shark attacks on humans are simply a case of mistaken identity.

Don't dive unprotected in waters where white sharks are known to hunt. Avoid the haul-out spots of seals and sea lions, especially on open coast. If you're not sure where these places might be, consult the locals.

Special Underwater Environments

Coral reefs aren't the only places to dive. There are many spectacular places to dive where there are no reef-building corals. Some of them require specialty certifications and extra precautions (see Chapters 10 and 12), but others can be enjoyed with nothing more than an open-water certification, and a few are accessible to free diving and snorkeling.

Kelp forest

Kelp are large seaweed that thrive in underwater forests in cool, temperate waters. They are extensive along the coast of California, in New Zealand, and along Canada's east coast. Gliding through these towering giants, in a cathedral-like atmosphere with long shafts of light flickering through the long and sinuous leaves, or *fronds,* is an experience you never forget. The Monterey area, in northern California, and the Channel Islands in Southern California, are some of the best places to dive in a kelp forest. The California kelp forest benefits from an upwelling current that brings nutrient-rich, cool bottom waters to nourish the rich marine life. Water temperate in the kelp forest usually hovers in the 60s in summer, dropping into the 50s in winter. A heavy wetsuit or a dry suit is required. Winter can bring rough water and heavy surf, but sometimes better visibility. Average visibility is about 60 feet, but it can be much less.

Wrecks

Wrecks have their own undeniable fascination. There is something compelling about swimming over or through the sunken endeavors of other human beings. War wrecks are probably the most compelling of all, and the western Pacific has an abundance of them. Chuuk lagoon, where United States air forces caught the combined Japanese fleet in Operation Hailstorm (1944) is probably the most famous wreck-diving destination in the world (see Chapter 15). More than 60 wrecks litter the bottom of Chuuk lagoon.

War wrecks aren't the only kind of wrecks you can explore — even the most mundane old freighter takes on an air of mystery and romance encrusted with marine life, hung with soft corals, and swarming with fish. If you're interested, underwater archaeology is a specialty that you can get involved in (see Chapter 12). You must get special training to do marine archaeology or wreck penetration, but some divers find wreck diving more appealing than any other kind of diving.

Artificial reefs

Artificial reefs are a relatively new idea. Essentially, they are sunken wrecks — obsolete ships or planes — purposely sunken to attract marine life and divers. The southeast coast of Florida has a number of these sunken artifacts. A number of ships have been scuttled off British Columbia, along with one in the Cayman Islands, and more are planned. A wreck on a barren sea floor quickly attracts fish and other forms of marine life. Proponents of the practice claim that everybody wins because divers enjoy them, but there is some disagreement from those who claim the sea bed is being turned into a junkyard, with the true, long-term consequences on the environment unknown.

Cenotes

On the Yucatan peninsula, as in many low-lying tropical areas, the bedrock is limestone, the remains of ancient coral reefs. This limestone is often riddled with caves, and the caves are frequently flooded with groundwater. In places, there are vertical shafts that extend to the surface; in other areas, the ceilings of these subterranean caverns may collapse to form _cenotes_ (see-NO-tays). These sunken ponds are often connected to enormous labyrinths of submarine caves filled with lots of spooky and wonderful formations such as stalactites, stalagmites, and flowstone.

- _Stalactites_ are rock formations that look like icicles hanging from the ceiling. They form when the cave is above water and water drips from the ceiling, depositing limestone until it builds up in a large, tapering shaft.

- A _stalagmite_ builds up, in the same way, on the floor of the cave where the dripping water lands. It resembles an inverted stalactite, more or less, and often the two grow until they meet in the middle to form a column.

- _Flowstone_ builds up in the same way where water flows across the floor of the cave rather than drips.

Visibility in some of these cenotes can be more than 200 feet. As long as you avoid an overhead environment, you can dive in a cenote with an ordinary open-water certification. To explore the caves and caverns, however, you must have a cave diver specialty.

Freshwater

Cenotes aren't the only kind of freshwater environment where you can dive. Lots of divers explore lakes, sunken quarries, rivers, and other freshwater environments — there are undoubtedly those who have never dived in ocean water at all. A cubic foot of freshwater weighs a little more than 62 pounds, while the same amount of seawater weighs 64 pounds due to all the dissolved salts. What it means is you won't need quite as much weight when diving in freshwater as you do in saltwater.

Part IV
The Wet Set

The 5th Wave   By Rich Tennant

Doug shows the vacation video he shot diving among the pool toys

Watch how close I'm able to get to the noodles.

In this part . . .

The planet that you live on is covered with great places to go diving and snorkeling. In this part, I show you the options for land-based and *liveaboard* (living aboard a boat) dive vacations, in both warm and cold water destinations. I also take you on a quick trip around the world from a diver's perspective, to see what each potential dive destination has to offer. Finally, I show you how to keep up your diving skills between vacations, and I take a look at some of the specialties that you can pursue.

Chapter 10

The Dive Traveler

In This Chapter

▶ Choosing the right place
▶ Sizing up a liveaboard
▶ Evaluating a resort
▶ The varieties of dive experience

So, you have a few dives under your weight belt and you're thinking that you want to see something a little more interesting than that old abandoned cistern up the road — but where to go and how to get the most for your diving dollars?

Where you go depends on what kind of diving you want to do and, of course, how much money you have to spend. But there are other, more subtle considerations you should not ignore. Choosing the right dive destination is the product of making a series of choices: The more honest you are with yourself, the more likely you'll come back with great stories, wonderful memories, and more feverish plans for the next trip. This chapter shows you how.

Running Hot and Cold

The world of dive travel can be divided into two broad categories: warm water and cold water destinations. Warm-water destinations are found in the tropics — within 30° of the equator and in areas where a strong ocean current moves large masses of warm water from the tropics into a temperate zone. Anything over 75° can be probably be considered warm water, anything under, cold, but that's a completely arbitrary distinction. Nearly all of the temperate zones are cold water diving. If you're a devotee of cold water, the west coast of North America has some of the best cold water diving anywhere in the world from Baja to southern Canada (actually the tip of the Baja peninsula just pokes into the northern boundary of the Tropic of Cancer, and the water is often quite warm there). Diving even goes on under the polar ice! Brrrr!

Most people feel that warm-water destinations are more diver-friendly, but cold water is really more of a psychological barrier than a physical one — beginning divers do their first open water dives in cold water every day. Not sure what to base your choice on? The following two sections detail a typical dive in both destinations.

Hot stuff

Your warm-water dive adventure may happen something like this:

You spend the day reading paperbacks and peeking through the twisting clouds at expanses of the bluest ocean below the plane window. In late afternoon, the pilot announces your descent to the little tropical island, and when she banks for the final approach, you can see the dazzling stretch of beach and the fingers of reef under the white crests of breaking waves, reaching up from dark water. By the time your bags are transferred to the resort and you're settled in, you have just enough time for an evening stroll on the beach under a flaming sunset, wading ankle-deep in the bath-warm lagoon.

After breakfast the next morning, you tote your gear bag down to the dive shop along a manicured path that winds through coconut palms and big-leafed, tropical plants. Birds squabble in the treetops and a tropical breeze as soft as their wingbeats fans your face. After you sign in at the dive shop, they provide you tanks and weights and direct you to the dive boat tied up at the jetty.

On the water, the dive boat cuts across the flat lagoon and you watch giant coral heads pass under the keel in the shimmering blue. On the way to the site, you get your gear set up and go over the dive plan with your buddy. The boat motors through the reef pass. Outside the reef, small seas add a bit of a roll to the motion of the boat. At the dive site, the guide briefs you about the dive: Swim east along the coral wall, look for an overhang ornamented with dense growth of lavender and pink soft corals at 70 feet, and then work your way up along the coral wall.

You suit up, do your buddy check, and on a signal from a crew member, make a giant step into the water. One by one, the other divers step off the boat, until everybody is floating on the surface. With a signal from the guide and confirmation with your buddy, you purge your BC, and the warm, clear waters close over your head.

Visibility is over 150 feet and the top of the wall is 40 feet below. For a few seconds, the startling visibility seizes you with a sensation like vertigo, but you settle into a slow drift to the top of the wall. You float silently before the solid, big-knuckled corals that buttress the top of the wall while swarms of tiny colored tropical fish slash through pools of trembling light. You adjust your buoyancy and send the "okay" to your buddy. Beyond the edge of the wall, you see a pair of spotted eagle rays winging through the blue abyss 100 feet down. You descend the face of the wall to 70 feet and work your way east.

Enormous sea fans reach out from the wall. A huge school of glittering blue fish, striped with yellow, rises around you from the depths. Stately lionfish swim slowly among the soft corals. You come upon a large, green sea turtle gnawing on a sponge — it looks up, and then placidly resumes its breakfast.

You finally reach the overhanging ledge of coral. It is the mouth of an enormous cavern — 30 feet high and 20 feet deep. The ceiling is hung with a dense, inverted forest of soft corals. The delicate, pale colors are barely detectable at this depth, in the gloom of the cavern. When you turn your dive light on them, all of the subtle shades come to life, and some kind of creature that you don't recognize scuttles away into the deeper recesses.

Above the overhang, a big moray peeks out of a crevice in the reef. You try to coax him out and he obliges about half his length before he retreats into the crevice again, hanging at the threshold, working his jaws, and displaying his formidable teeth. When you finally get back to the top of the wall, a pair of whitetip reef sharks appears out of nowhere. You settle into a sandy spot between the coral heads and quiet your breathing so as not to scare them off. Sleek and gray, they circle at a cautious distance, but close enough for you to see their strange silver eyes sizing you up. After one circle, they swim off in the direction from which you've come. Suddenly, you hear the sharp metallic rap of your buddy banging on his tank. His eyes are wide with awe and fixed on something over your head. At the same moment you fall into deep shadow, as if a large dark cloud has blocked out the sun. The pale belly of a giant manta ray is passing directly over your head. You could reach up and touch it, but you check the impulse.

It's a huge animal, 20 feet from wingtip to wingtip; even at its relaxed pace, it's traveling faster than you can swim. Pursuit would be futile. You're content with savoring this intimate view of its graceful flight. It circles to the blue edge of your visibility, and then turns and swims back passing over your head near the surface with slow beats of its broad graceful wings.

Your buddy signals that he's low on air and when you check your computer, you discover you are, too — more than 45 minutes underwater has passed in what seems like only a few minutes. At the safety stop, you exchange excited gestures. Back on the surface, you can see the crew of the dive boat running excitedly back and forth and pointing beyond the stern where the manta's wingtips break the surface. A rare sighting for the boat crew, but for you, just another dive in the beautiful tropical ocean.

Cool stuff

A cool-water dive may go more like this:

Putting on your 7mm wetsuit, complete with hood and gloves is no easy task, but it gives you a few quiet moments to contemplate the glassy swells rising and falling in the offshore kelp, like the breathing of a fantastic giant, sleeping peacefully, snuggled against the rugged California coastline. A squadron of brown pelicans swoops low on the water, wingtips skimming the surface, searching for breakfast. The cold, upwelling waters provide nutrients for thriving marine community.

You and your buddy discuss the dive plan, go through your pre-dive check, and then shuffle down the beach to the shore. Wading out backward, with the small surf breaking on your legs, you feel that familiar sense of excitement return. When the water's deep enough, you switch to your snorkel and swim easily for the edge of the kelp bed 100 yards offshore, and even though you're still bulkier than you're used to, the weight of your equipment has been lifted.

You pass over a bright orange bat star on the sandy bottom, but see few fish. The water is cold on the exposed parts of your face, but after a few minutes you cease to feel it.

Ahead you can see the swaying trunks of giant kelp, rising to the surface in a thick forest from the bottom, 30 feet down. Just inside the kelp forest, you switch to your regulator, signal your buddy, purge your BC, and sink slowly to the bottom at 30 feet. The sand is punctuated with rocky outcroppings. You glide between the kelp trees swaying in the surge and through the cathedral light filtering between the fronds. You spook a large bat ray from its hiding place and a little farther on a slow-moving electric ray. Visibility is about 40 feet and the bottom gets rockier as you follow the slope down to 70 feet. A school of blue rockfish parts to let you pass. Hydrocorals, barnacles, starfish, sponges, enormous anemones, and several kinds of nudibrachs (see Chapter 9 for more on these creatures) crowd each other for space on the rocky bottom. Huddled in a crevice is one of the most wonderfully grotesque creatures you've ever seen — a big monkeyface eel. Your buddy tries to coax the creature from his hiding place without success.

Suddenly, as if it had materialized from thin water, a small, spotted harbor seal is pirouetting through the kelp, swooping in and making dizzy circles through your rising streams of bubbles. He even follows you as you continue through the forest of kelp, but after a few minutes he loses interest and disappears as mysteriously as he arrived. Along the edge of the kelp forest you're surprised to discover a giant Pacific octopus slithering over the bottom. Normally, these shy animals only forage at night — he's wary, but not overly alarmed. After a few minutes, he appears to accept your presence and reaches out a cautious tentacle to explore this visitor from another world. The communion is oddly moving, but brief, and what has driven this bold octopus from his daylight cover will have to remain a mystery — your pressure gauge reminds you that's it's time to start back.

Near and far

If you live in North America and you opt for warm water, your choices fall into two broad categories: quick trips and expeditions.

✔ **Quick trips:** For North Americans living east of the Rockies, the Caribbean and Florida are quick trips — only a few hours flight time, with lots of regularly scheduled flights. From the West Coast, Hawaii is just as close as the Caribbean.

These closer-to-home dive trips, with familiar cultural attributes, usually require little time spent schlepping baggage through airport terminals or wedged into the coach-class iron maiden, while providing exactly the kind of quick break from the corporate pressure-cooker.

✔ **Expeditions:** Unfortunately, Hawaii and the best Caribbean destinations don't compare with the Indo-Pacific. From Fiji west to the Red Sea, you're in diving heaven, but it's a long haul to get there.

Throughout the Indo-Pacific nations, it can be rare to see a North American, and the local cultures and customs can be so foreign that they are entirely mystifying. Of course, that is one of the great attractions of a dive expedition — seeing things far away and exotic and unlike anything, anywhere near anyplace you call home. Such a trip usually takes longer and costs more, but may makes a more lasting impression.

By Land or by Sea

After you target a potential destination — warm water or cool — for your diving vacation, your next decision is whether you want to spend it at a land-based dive resort or on a liveaboard dive boat. Each has its advantages and its drawbacks. Both cover the spectrum from basic accommodations to full-on luxury. Generally, your choices are slightly more restricted with a liveaboard just because there aren't as many.

Liveaboards

Liveaboard dive boats are for those who want to dive and don't want much else from their vacation. The dive boat travels from site to site, usually at night while you snooze, and arrives at the next site by morning ready for an intensive schedule — commonly four or five dives a day. For the dedicated tank-sucker, this is absolute heaven; for anyone else, it can be crushingly boring.

If you're one of those people who's not happy without a regulator between your teeth, the liveaboard happy-face list goes something like this:

✔ **More pristine sites:** Liveaboards travel to the sites beyond the reach of resort day boats and, consequently, those sites show fewer signs of wear and tear than the ones dived daily by resort operations.

- **More potential adventure:** Liveaboards often travel far off the beaten path and give you a glimpse of how the local people really live. Excursions ashore are often included.

- **More flexibility:** If the weather goes bad or conditions change, a live-aboard boat can sometimes take another route or find an alternative place to dive.

- **More new friends:** Close quarters and shared adventures makes friends fast. It's not unusual to make lifelong friends on a dive trip. Of course, if you get stuck with some jerks, you can have the opposite experience (see the frowny-face list that follows this one).

- **More dives, all the time:** Usually four or five per day, and no time-consuming boat ride back and forth to the resort.

- **Less travel time:** Taking less time to get to dive sites means more time to lie around on the sundeck or in your air-conditioned cabin during the times that you're not diving.

- **Less portage:** No need to haul your gear down to the day boat in the morning or back to your room at night, all damp and stinky.

- **Fewer bugs:** When you're camping at sea, you don't have to deal with all the mosquitoes, no-see-ums, sand flies, and numerous other hungry little stinkers that find fleshy humans so delicious and proliferate so vigorously in the tropics. This is a real bonus in places where malaria and other tropical operatives are looking for a body in which to set up shop.

- **Sweet dreams:** On a liveaboard, you drift into dreamland right on top of all those world-class dive sites.

But, of course, it's not all sweet dreams. Even the biggest liveaboard can seem like a pretty small place at sea for a couple of weeks, especially when relationships among the passengers and crew are less than harmonious. On a liveaboard boat in Queensland, Australia, not all that long ago, the paying guests actually mutinied against one particularly unpopular captain — now that must have been a fun cruise! The frowny face list looks like this:

- **Confined space:** A liveaboard can seem uncomfortably small, because of the company or simply because of limited physical space. On a liv-aboard, you're assigned a cabin, which is usually small with limited storage — not the kind of place you can spread your junk all over like you can in a bungalow or hotel room. You may also share a cabin with someone else — you may come away with a new friend or wind up praying for the trip to be over.

- **Rolling and pitching:** If you're prone to seasickness, life aboard ship in a period of bad weather can be a nightmare. You can take preventative medications, to be sure, but some have side effects, and two weeks of gobbling tablets very few hours may be more than you want to deal with. At a resort, you can pick your times and medicate accordingly.

✔ **Limited scenery:** You can get pretty tired of looking at the same couple of cabins and the same deck space every day — and blue ocean in every direction doesn't add much variety. Many liveaboards schedule shore excursions to break things up a little, but some don't — some don't even go anywhere near shore.

✔ **Limited menu:** On most liveaboards, the food is good — sometimes spectacular. Liveaboard operators know that food is important to hungry divers. Still, you normally don't have the kind of choices that you have at a resort, especially when a resort is near a town with restaurants. Of course, there are no guarantees that the food will be good. It can be just plain bad. You may drop a few pounds, but that's not something you necessarily want to do on your hard-earned vacation.

✔ **Limited culture:** If your liveaboard makes shore excursions, you may get a peek into the lives of the locals that other visitors don't normally get, but you probably won't get to see the tourist attractions everybody else sees unless you schedule it yourself as a side trip. Tourist attractions are attractions for a reason.

✔ **No shopping:** If you like to come back with lots of souvenirs of your travels or dicker for the killer values at the local marketplace, you'd better check the boat's itinerary. They don't usually stop to shop, and don't have much storage on board if they do. The options are scheduling your own side trip or buying what you find in the airport.

✔ **No escape:** If you absolutely hate life aboard ship — or just aboard this particular ship — you're still stuck until the boat docks. The rest of the passengers don't want to abort their trip just because you're unhappy. If you've never been on a liveaboard before, you should probably make you're first trip a one- or two-day excursion to see whether you like it.

Resort-based

The alternative to a liveaboard dive trip is a resort-based vacation. If you want to see more of the country's culture and history than you're going to find underwater, or if you're traveling with kids or with a non-diving companion, consider staying at a resort. Resorts can be summer-camp Spartan or Hollywood decadent. They can range from completely dive-dedicated to "I-think-there-may-be-a-dive-shop-in-town."

Be sure to do a little research to ensure a good match, but consider the general advantages of a resort:

✔ **More room:** Spread your junk all over the room. Luxuriate in your own private bathroom — fresh towels, somebody to make up your bed, sometimes even a little fruit basket or mint on the pillow. Turn the kids loose on the beach while you sip a cool drink in the shade. You get the idea.

✔ **Other activities:** Volleyball, waterskiing, wakeboarding, parasailing, and napping on the beach are all fun stuff that you can do in addition to diving. Did I mention the rotating guest population and the possibilities of meeting other people?

✔ **Cultural attractions:** Geologic wonders, historical sites, music, dance, and other unique cultural attractions — you see much more of it at a resort than on a liveaboard, unless the liveaboard schedules excursions. And even if it does, you can expect it to be a limited visit, in the company of the group.

✔ **Restaurants and shopping:** Locals welcome your shopping dollar — sometimes with remarkable deals. If you're a bargain hunter, you won't get as many opportunities on a boat.

✔ **No chumming:** You won't spend any time enjoying that view over the leeward rail that's so common to victims of motion sickness. Of course, you may pick up a land-based bug.

✔ **Flexibility:** If you don't like your resort, hey, you're out of there. Check please! Call me a cab! Check in down the road or zoom off to a new place entirely. It's up to you.

Of course, there's a downside to spending your vacation in a dive resort as well.

✔ **Day-boat crowds:** The number of divers on your liveaboard is constant and fairly predictable. At a resort, you take your chances — it may be one or two; it may be a whole platoon — and it can change day to day. The same beautiful dive that you and your significant other enjoy one day can be magically transformed into an underwater three-ring circus the next, complete with 47 neon-wetsuit clowns!

✔ **Long boat rides:** Sometimes it's a long way between the best site for a resort and the best site for a dive. You may end up in transit for an hour or even longer. That kind of travel time normally means no more than three dives a day: morning, afternoon, and night. Some liveaboards, however, keep this schedule as well.

✔ **More impacted sites:** Sites that are heavily visited start to show signs of wear and tear. Even if the divers never touch anything (which never happens), some of the wildlife begins to avoid the place after a while.

✔ **More bugs:** The eternal summer, luxuriant plant life, and generous rainfall of the tropics create a congenial environment for members of the insect family — and they often make their presence felt even in the most upscale resort.

Most resorts employ day boats to take you to the dive site, but in some places you can also make shore dives. When this is the case, you can seek out a more intimate experience than you'll probably find on a day boat. Consider renting a car and traveling the coastline to make shore dives — another good way to get some privacy and find better-preserved dive terrain.

Choosing a Liveaboard

Liveaboards come in all kinds of shapes and sizes: monohulls, catamarans, and trimarans, from less than 30 feet to over 100. A liveaboard serves as hotel, restaurant, and dive shop all in one — and sometimes even as a photo-processing lab, too. A lot of the most modern boats were designed and built to be liveaboard dive vessels, but you can find plenty of worthy craft out there that have been converted from fishing boats, ferries, private yachts, and so on. Most liveaboards are power boats, although some have motors and are fully rigged for sail, too. You can find exceptions, but in general, bigger boats are more luxurious than smaller ones; smaller boats hold more intimate groups.

Size matters

Big boats have more room — that usually translates into a more varied menu, larger cabins, more room for stowing your junk, more fresh water, and more deck space. Large boats also generally have more people on board and that may mean bigger groups of divers. Some small boats are quite luxurious, but on these, you'll pay the same higher rate that you would on a larger boat. How big is a big boat? Liveaboards come in all kinds of sizes and shapes, which can give them different handling characteristics, but as a rule, any-thing under 65 feet is a small boat; anything over is considered large.

A larger boat is more stable than a small one, with less rolling and pitching on a rough sea. If you're prone to motion sickness, a larger boat is going to be more comfortable than a smaller one, everything all else being equal, but also consider the itinerary when making your plans. On a protected coastline or island chain where you won't encounter rough seas, a small boat may be all you need. If your trip includes open ocean crossings, a bigger boat is probably going to be more comfortable.

Numbers matter

How many divers a boat can comfortably handle isn't simply a function of the size of the boat, although size does make a big difference. How the boat is set up and how the dives are run make a difference, too. Large boats that cram a lot of divers on and dump them all in the water in the same place, at the same time, are referred to as *cattle boats,* and not because they serve steaks.

But just because a boat is large, doesn't mean it's a cattle boat. Some large liveaboards stagger the dive schedule, putting smaller groups in the water at different times; some use smaller boats to take small groups of divers to dif-ferent sites. Make sure you find out how the dives are handled on any liveaboard that you're considering.

Ownership matters

Liveaboard vessels are either privately owned and operated or are part of a fleet. Boats in a fleet operate like other kinds of franchise operations, say the imaginary meat-flavored sandwich restaurant chain that I'll call Burger Boy. One thing we know in advance about Burger Boy: No matter where in the world you go, the dining experience is going to be very similar. The corporate office sets the standard that all the outlets follow. The same thing is true on franchise dive boats — all the boats operate by pretty much the same standardized procedures. Normally, the home office handles all the advertising and booking for the individual boats. This kind of liveaboard is dependable and usually very good about addressing any problems you have, although that may not happen right away. Some divers like the dependable familiarity of this fleet liveaboard approach, but others find it as flavorless and impersonal as a meat-flavored sandwich.

The experience on an individually owned and operated boat varies a great deal in comparison to that of a fleet boat. The success of the individual operation depends largely on the knowledge and experience of the captain and crew — the whole experience tends to take on their personality. On a boat where the captain is also the owner, you can bring any problems to his or her attention right on the spot. Of course, if you don't like the answer, you've exhausted your options, but owner operators are generally very concerned about their reputations: Their business depends on it.

An individual operation seldom has the capital to invest in a huge multi-million dollar boat. Accommodations are basic, but more personalized. Individual operators also can be more flexible and may be willing to change the itinerary to accommodate the customers. Most individual boats are solid, well-run businesses, but there are a few that survive charter to charter. On such a boat, you may run the risk of finding yourself broken down in a faraway foreign country, waiting on repairs that the owner can't afford to make, or even showing up at the dock only to find out that the boat has gone out of business. The probability of getting a refund is pretty low. It's up to you to research any prospective liveaboard.

Liveaboard checklist

The following is a list of things that you want to consider when choosing a liveaboard:

- ✔ **How big is the boat?** A larger boat generally means more space and more room for amenities. Where do you store your dive gear? Ask about the amount of deck space, too.

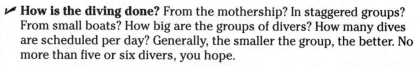

✔ **How is the diving done?** From the mothership? In staggered groups? From small boats? How big are the groups of divers? How many dives are scheduled per day? Generally, the smaller the group, the better. No more than five or six divers, you hope.

✔ **Accommodations:** How big are the cabins? Are they air-conditioned? Will you have a private shower and toilet (called a *head* on-board ship) or share them?

✔ **Crew:** What is the ratio of crew members to paying passengers? How many dive guides does the operation have? As a beginner, you want to take advantage of the guides. Ideally, you and your buddy get your own personal guide for every dive. It probably won't happen that way, but if you request it, it's surprising how often they can oblige — it doesn't hurt to ask. More likely, you'll have one guide for every five or six divers, but that should be the maximum.

Dive guides are often one of the more underutilized resources on the boat. They know the area and they can show you stuff you wouldn't otherwise find.

✔ **Food:** Diving makes you hungry. How often are you fed? Who's the chef? What's the menu like?

✔ **Water:** Does the boat have a desalinization unit or does it rely strictly on storage tanks? Fresh water is always important — and limited — on a boat.

✔ **Financial stability:** How long has the operation been in business? How has it handled past emergencies?

✔ **Photo processing:** Many liveaboards have on-board E6 processing — if you're a photographer, you'll want to know if yours does. Also, does the boat have 24-hour electricity and a place to charge your batteries with 110 volts?

Choosing a Dive Resort

Like liveaboards, resorts come in all shapes and sizes. The key to selecting the right dive resort is to evaluate your own needs. Hey, maybe you don't even want to stay in a dive resort. In some places, Cozumel for example, you can simply rent a hotel room or any other kind of accommodation you can find, and shop around among the bounty of dive shops crowding each other for space along the Malecon.

The accommodations

Your budget is probably of prime importance. Depending on where in the world you're going, a resort can set you back a few dollars a night to more than $700 — and that doesn't include the diving! Essentially, the more you pay, the more amenities you get. No surprises there.

More than likely, you'll dive with the dive shop that's affiliated with your resort. Most dive resorts are on beachfront property, but there are a few that aren't — these resorts generally provide transfers to the dive shop.

At some resorts, diving is just one of many activities offered. Others are completely dive dedicated and if you're not diving, there isn't a lot else to do, except maybe read a book. Some resorts cater to families; others to singles.

Some resorts are all-inclusive and include food and drinks in the package price. Some include food, but not drinks; some include neither. Find out how far your resort is from town. If your food is not included and your only alternative is an overpriced on-site restaurant, the place may not be such a bargain after all.

The diving

Resorts and their affiliated dive shops handle their diving in several different ways. A small resort may deploy a party of four divers in a small boat; a large one might send out two or three large dive boats packed to the *gunwales* (the top edge). A place that loads up a boat with as many divers as can fit and dumps them all in the water in the same place at the same time may be cost-effective for the resort, but it's too crowded for the consumer.

The dive sites can be (and frequently are) a long way from the resort. If the resort has fast, modern powerboats, that may not be a big deal, but if it takes two hours to chug out there in some old boat, on a hard bench, in cramped quarters, you may think twice about it.

Most resort dive shops keep their equipment well-maintained and up to date, but you are, after all, trusting your life to their air, from their tanks. If you feel the need to ask about their equipment, go right ahead. If they have any hesitations about answering your questions, that's not a good sign. If you have doubts about the quality of the air, don't use it. Dive with somebody else or don't dive at all. If you've already paid for the dive, get your money back. If they won't give it to you, your suspicions are confirmed. Spread the word.

Dive resort checklist

Use the following checklist to evaluate your resort options:

- ✔ **What's included in the price?** Food? Drinks? How many restaurants are on the premises? Do they pick you up and drop you off at the airport?

- ✔ **How far is it from town?** You may find better bargains and better quality at restaurants and shops off the premises, but you have to be able to get there.

- ✔ **Does the resort offer other activities?** This is especially important if you're traveling with children under 12 or other nondivers. Maybe *you* have other interests, too.

- ✔ **Does the resort have a dive shop?** Is there a dive shop on the premises or does it contract out with a local, independent company? One isn't necessarily better than the other, but if they contract with a local shop, find out how far away it is. How the transfers are handled? How the tanks are filled? How are you taken to the dive sites?

- ✔ **The dive schedule:** How many boats do they have and how many divers do they put on each boat? How are the dives scheduled? The optimum number depends partially on the size of the boat and the nature of the dive site, but more than 15 generally starts to look like a crowd.

- ✔ **How many dives per day?** This can vary anywhere from two to five dives per day. If the dive sites are a long way, don't expect more than two. If you want to dive five dives a day, better make sure that's what the resort offers, or check out a liveaboard, instead.

  Find out if they have night dives and shore diving, too. A night dive can be very exciting and allows you to get in one more dive each day. Lots of places offer unlimited shore diving, but it's uncommon to have exciting diving right in front of the resort.

- ✔ **How far is it to the sites and how long is the boat ride?** Just because the sites are a long way from the resort (or a long boat ride away), doesn't mean that they aren't worthy. Far-away sites are often more pristine than those close by. Even if it's not completely pristine, a classic spot like Blue Corner, in Palau (see Chapter 15), is well worth the long trip — but a long boat ride to a ho-hum spot stinks.

What Kind of Diving?

The key to selecting a destination is to honestly evaluate your skills and ask questions. Whether it's a liveaboard or a resort, ask the booking agent or the management exactly what you can expect from the dive. If they don't know, talk to somebody who does. This is one of the advantages to booking with a dive travel specialist who knows the areas and can make sure you're well matched to the destination. You want to ask questions about the following:

✔ **Current:** Strong current is probably the element of diving that gives beginning divers the most trouble. You can't fight strong ocean currents. You have to figure out how to deal with them on their own terms — that takes time and experience. If you're a beginner, you're better off staying in a current-free environment until you're comfortable with the other aspects of diving.

✔ **Depth:** Beginning divers generally use air faster than more experienced divers, and all divers use air faster on a deep dive than they do on a shallow one. As a beginner, it doesn't make much sense to book at a place where all the sites are 100 feet or below. It won't take you long to go through your tank and you won't get much underwater time, leaving you frustrated and unsatisfied.

Other than currents and depths, all diving is simply swimming around underwater and having a look around, but different terrain and different conditions have inspired different names for the kinds of swimming around and having a look around that you do. Some resort areas feature one kind of diving or another; it's a good idea to be acquainted with the varieties so you can make an appropriate choice. If you really don't like drift diving, for example, you can probably find a better place to go than Cozumel.

Reef dives

Reef dives are the backbone of all tropical diving. You normally make *a reef dive* on a gently sloping fore reef or submerged reef flat (see Chapter 9 for a description of a reef). The best marine life is usually between 30 and 70 feet. Corals and tropical fish are the staple sighting on a reef dive, although occasionally, you see something quite unusual like a manta or a whale shark. Reef dives usually have lots of small animals for photographers and (generally) mild conditions excellent for beginners. Until you gain enough experience to feel comfortable in the water, stick with easy reef dives — 60 feet or less, with minimal current.

Drift dives

Drift diving is done where there are strong currents. You get in the water, submerge, and drift along in the current, barely kicking a fin. The pickup boat follows along tracking your bubbles, and then scoops up all the divers when they surface at the end of the dive. A drift dive in a brisk current is one of the most thrilling experiences in diving. It's like flying over the surface of another world. To add to the excitement, strong currents bring in nutrient-rich water that supports more, and bigger, marine life — great clouds of tropical fish rise from their hiding places in the reef to feed in the current. Here you are most likely to see big pelagic animals like mantas, tuna, or whale sharks.

Drift diving isn't difficult, but it can be tricky. That's why it is considered an advanced type of diving. Because currents are generally stronger at the surface than near the bottom (see Chapter 8 for the more on currents), it's important that you're able to equalize your ears quickly and get to the bottom. If you have trouble equalizing and have to hang in the water too long, you may find yourself separated from the group or your buddy.

Water flowing over formations on the reef can create all kinds of local currents, including up and down. You must be prepared for and able to deal with these eventualities. You also have to be able to perform a safety stop, without a line, in moving water, so good buoyancy control is important. Drift diving is most often done where open ocean or tidal currents are forced through a narrow channel, such as in a reef pass, or meet with an underwater obstacle, such as a reef wall. It's a great ride, but you need to be pretty salty before you tackle a drift dive.

Wall dives

The seaward side of a coral reef can range from a gentle downward slope to an absolutely vertical wall. In fact, the seaward side can even be undercut beyond vertical. These vertical dropoffs are the home of many wonderful creatures and a visit to their upended world is known as a *wall dive*. Different marine creatures have evolved to take advantage of conditions at different depths, so you're more likely to encounter a greater diversity of species along a wall than on an ordinary reef dive. Some walls drop off hundreds, or even thousands, of feet and upwelling nutrients can create rich marine environments — they are often thickly populated with sponges, sea fans, and other kinds of filter feeders.

Because walls are ordinarily exposed to the open ocean, currents, and surge, (like drift dives), wall dives are generally considered more advanced dives, but some conditions permit beginners. Make sure you have an experienced buddy if you decide to give it a try.

Night dives

Just like on land, the underwater world is a whole different place at night. *Diurnal* critters (those that are active in daylight hours) are tucked into the reef, sleeping, and the *nocturnal* crew is out foraging for food. Many of the things that you can see on a *night dive* can't be seen during the day. Night diving is an advanced specialty. All the certifying agencies offer training in it, and nearly every resort and liveaboard offer night dives.

Night dives are normally shallow dives, conducted just after sunset, at a beginner dive site. Most divers don't need any additional challenges when dealing with the handicap of darkness.

Kelp dives

Probably the most spectacular cold-water diving is done in those towering thickets of the world's largest aquatic plant, the giant kelp (see Chapter 9). This is known as a *kelp dive.* On the west coast of the United States, there are plenty of places where a beginning diver can go to enjoy the beauty of the kelp forest, but if you're new to kelp diving, buddy with a diver who has experience.

Kelp diving presents its own unique hazards, the chief and most obvious being entanglement. Most entanglement happens at or near the surface, where the kelp is thickest and there are lots of ends to get snarled in. The simplest solution is to avoid surface swimming. To do that, you need good buoyancy control. You may also need to brush up on your compass navigation as well.

Some places in the kelp forest are simply not appropriate for beginning divers. A thick mat of kelp is as much of an overhead environment as a cave. Go with an experienced kelp diver and avoid heavy cover. Make sure to carry a dive knife, too.

Wreck dives

Going on a *wreck dive,* or at least going inside of a wreck, requires special training, but there are lots of wrecks you can dive on as a beginner just as you would a reef, and a few that you can even snorkel to. Wrecks attract fish that take residence there, just as they would on a reef. In some places, ships and other kinds of hardware are intentionally scuttled by dive clubs and local governments to create artificial reefs. This practice is somewhat controversial. While one side points to the increase in marine life around these artificial reefs, others consider the practice nothing more than submarine littering.

Authentic wrecks offer a dash of history and human drama to go along with the usual marine life. Some of the most impressive wrecks are in Chuuk lagoon in the Western Pacific (see Chapter 15). Chuuk lies about an hour's flight time southeast of Guam. The wrecks in Chuuk (formerly called Truk) lagoon are the result of a U.S. Naval air raid on the combined Japanese fleet in 1944. This single naval action, code-named "Operation Hailstorm" sent more than 50 Japanese ships to the bottom — a ghost fleet of huge battle-scarred warships, thickly encrusted with hard and soft corals and swarming with colored tropicals. About 50 different wrecks have been located and around half of them are dived regularly. If you love wreck diving, Chuuk is heaven.

If you don't have specialized training however, you should not attempt to penetrate any underwater wreck. No matter how enticing it may look, don't enter holds, passageways, or any other overhead environment. Don't pick up artifacts around the wreck either, especially around war wrecks like those in Chuuk. Even today, divers still find an occasional live and highly unstable explosive.

Shark dives

Diving for the express purpose of seeing sharks is becoming increasingly popular. Sharks are truly magnificent and ancient animals and worthy of everyone's admiration. *Shark dives* generally fall into two categories: baited and unbaited.

✔ ***Baited shark dives*** are commonly conducted by taking a bucket and a frozen block of fish heads or some other garbage down on the reef. Divers kneel on a sandy spot on the bottom in a circle around the bait and wait for the sharks to show up (mainly bull sharks and other kinds of reef sharks). In most of the areas where these dives are regularly carried out, the sharks have become habituated to the procedure and seldom disappoint. They swoop in like a pack of trained seals to snap up the snacks. Sometimes, the guides hand-feed the sharks, but that practice can be risky, as a guide in the Maldives found out when the shark took the offered fish and his hand, as well. Shark dives like this are practiced all the time without incident, but sharks competing for food are potentially dangerous, and there have been a small number of attacks on divers.

Another common practice is to dump fish parts off the boat and let the current carry them off in a trail that brings in the sharks. This practice is usually carried out to bring in the big marine predators like blue sharks, makos, and great whites. After the sharks show up, the divers enter a sturdy steel cage that's secured to the boat, and burn up rolls of film and a two-year supply of adrenaline while the sharks cruise by within a few feet. Sometimes they even test the bars of the cage with their enormous razor-sharp teeth! Very little is known about these spectacular ocean predators, but a single look at their spectacularly powerful jaws tells you everything you need to know about the business end of a great white shark. There's no reason to exaggerate the danger posed by these beautiful animals, but to underestimate the danger would be a big mistake.

✔ ***Unbaited shark dives,*** in which you seek and dive in places that sharks are known to frequent, are another method, but you take your chances on a sighting. The advantage to this approach is that a calm and patient diver is much more likely to see the shark behaving as it normally would, rather than hustling for a handout.

Chapter 11

Where in the Watery World?

. . . .

In This Chapter

▶ Evaluating the top dive destinations

▶ Getting your shots

▶ Packing like a pro

▶ Diving with disabilities

▶ Traveling with a nondiving companion

. . . .

*A*fter you become a diver, diving becomes the main factor in determining your travel plans. But even the most dedicated diver can't dive all the time, and it's a good idea to take a break every few days to allow your body to completely eliminate any residual nitrogen. So, while you're hanging around off-gassing and planning your next dive, you may want to check out some of the other attractions of your exotic, far-away place — as long as you're already there and all. Topside attractions (or hazards) may even influence where you decide to take your dive vacation — everything else being equal.

Another Topside Attraction

Topside attractions can, broadly speaking, be divided into two categories — geographical and cultural. Just as you decide what kind of diving you want to do, when choosing topside attractions, consider whether you're the kind of person who prefers to stand in awe before a natural wonder or somebody who appreciates the exotic intricacies of a human culture. Perhaps you want to see one kind of wonder of one trip, and another kind the next time — it's your call.

Even when diving is your primary interest and reason for going, reserve some time to see the other sights. After all, if you travel halfway around the world and return without seeing these things, you're really going to feel like an idiot — maybe not right away, but someday.

The majority of the world's dive travel is done in tropical countries with their warm, clear waters and abundance of reef life, and most of the countries in the tropics are far less developed than North America or Western Europe. In fact, a large part of the world considers the things we take for granted to be luxuries. That is not to say luxury accommodations aren't available, but the number of amenities you demand, or are prepared to do without, have a bearing on the price.

As a general rule, geographic and cultural wonders are more exotic the farther away they are. As you leave the beaten path, the situation may change radically. In some of the most adventurous places, you won't find the kind of tourist infrastructure that can offer the luxury accommodations that you may be used to, but hey, that's why it's adventure!

Around the World in 68 Paragraphs

You have many things to consider when selecting a dive destination, so, to make things a little easier, in this section I list the world's most popular dive destinations and their corresponding topside attractions:

The Red Sea

✔ **The diving:** Red Sea diving is first rate, with great diversity of species, especially reef fish with many endemic species and some large *pelagics* (deep water species) like mantas and whale sharks, as well. The Red Sea is famous for its beautiful soft corals, and there's lots of great hard coral too (see Chapter 9 for more information about corals). The northern end of the Red Sea is the most heavily visited and less pristine than the south, but trips to the south are more difficult to arrange.

✔ **The land:** The Red Sea is surrounded on all sides by a narrow band of desert lowland backed by rugged mountains. If you love the desert, it is truly impressive. Many of the arid valleys, known as *wadis,* that run into the mountains shelter fragile oases that support a surprising diversity of wildlife.

✔ **The culture:** The vast majority of people in the area of the Red Sea are Arabs and the dominant culture and religion is Islam. Westerners tend to regard Arabs and Muslims as a homogeneous group, but there are many different ethnic groups among the peoples around the Red Sea. Not all Muslims are fanatic fundamentalists, but it is an essentially modest and conservative culture dominated by the precepts of Islam. The big bonus in the Red Sea region is the wealth of historic Egyptian treasures along the Nile valley — the pyramids, the Sphinx, innumerable artifacts, temples, museums, and ruins.

✔ **The downside:** Cairo is one of the most crowded and polluted cities in the world. There have been well-publicized terrorist activities throughout the Middle East, and although this danger is generally exaggerated, it is something to consider.

East Africa

✔ **The diving:** The coasts of Kenya and Tanzania both offer excellent diving, typical of the Indian Ocean. You can find great diversity in reef fish and corals, and offshore currents offer good possibility of spotting big pelagics like whale sharks and mantas. Pemba Island, off northern Tanzania, is a well-known spot with excellent diving.

✔ **The land:** East Africa is one of the few places in the world where wildlife topside is as diverse and spectacular as it is underwater. Between them, Tanzania and Kenya have over 40 national parks and game reserves and both offer safari tours in the world's most spectacular grasslands and their inhabitants — lion, leopard, rhino, elephant, crocodile, and so on.

✔ **The culture:** East Africa is the home of more than 120 different tribes including the famous Masai, who are found mainly to the west and south of Nairobi, Kenya. Outside of the cities, Africa's people are largely herders and farmers, but many still maintain traditional ceremonies and practice traditional art forms.

✔ **The downside:** Several bad diseases are loose on the African continent, but that shouldn't be a problem if you exercise reasonable caution, and update all your vaccinations before you go (see the "Immunizations" section, later in this chapter, for additional information). There is some street crime in the cities and comparatively wealthy tourists are an obvious target — don't be an obvious tourist. Caution and forethought is called for, but the danger should not be exaggerated.

The Seychelles

✔ **The diving:** Typical of the Indian Ocean, Seychelles diving is excellent. You can find great diversity of species among reef fish and corals and a good chance of seeing big pelagics like whale sharks and manta rays.

✔ **The land:** Topside natural history is the other big attraction in the Seychelles. The islands are sometimes referred to as the "Galapagos of the Indian Ocean" — many of the unusual animal species are endemic to the islands. Bird life is the main attraction, but other unique species like the giant tortoise thrive here, too.

✔ **The culture:** The people of the Seychelles are a mixture of African, Malagasy, and French culture. The Seychelles are believed to have been noticed by Arab traders about 1,000 years ago; since then they have been visited and populated by a broad ethnic mix, making the predominant culture an interesting and exotic mixture. Tourism is a major industry.

✓ **The downside:** If there is a downside to the Seychelles, it's probably the fact that they are so far away — the opposite side of the globe from North America. It's a long flight, but there is an international airport on the main island of Mahe.

The Maldives

✓ **The diving:** By law, all fishing in the islands is done with a hook and line, including commercial fishing. The Maldivians have been vigilant about protecting their marine resources from overexploitation and the result is a thriving ocean. As a result, diving in the Maldives is good almost anywhere you fall off the boat. I've even seen sharks, napoleon wrasse, and mantas while *snorkeling!*

✓ **The land:** The Maldives are a collection of uniform, low-lying coral islands. Aside from coconut palms and some interesting bird life, there aren't any spectacular geographic features topside.

✓ **The culture:** The original settlers are believed to have come from Southern India and Sri Lanka, but many people of Arab and African heritage populate the area. The Republic of the Maldives is a Muslim nation and adheres to the relatively conservative precepts of Islam, but it is a good deal less restrictive than the Arab states of the Middle East. Most westerners won't find much in the way of entertainment in the culture of the Maldives, but Maldivians produce wonderful weaving and lacquer work.

✓ **The downside:** Like the Seychelles, it's a long way to the Maldives from North America, often involving several connecting flights. And if you don't like coral atolls and coconut palms, you better take a book — a long book, or maybe two long books.

Thailand

✓ **The diving:** Thailand also has great Indian Ocean diving, perhaps not quite as good as the Maldives, but still excellent, particularly in the Andaman Sea and the Similan and Surin Islands near Phuket. Diving is also done in the Gulf of Thailand, but visibility is generally better in the Indian Ocean.

✓ **The land:** Thailand is something of a transitional zone for terrestrial wildlife. In the northern half of the country, the species are mostly those typical of southeast Asia; in the south the fauna begins to take on the character of Malaysia, Borneo, and the Sunda Islands. That's a lot of diversity. The area is particularly rich in bird life. In Thailand, you can take an elephant safari, spend the night in a rainforest tree house, and see a whale shark — all on the same trip!

✔ **The culture:** For westerners, Thailand is wonderfully exotic. Thai art, music, dance, and theater all have a long history and rich tradition that is still very much alive. Modern Thai artists are busy blending traditional forms with western influences to create exciting fusions of both. Thai cuisine is world famous for its aromatic, spicy flavors — exploring the cuisine of Thailand could be a whole trip unto itself. If you like to eat, and you like it exotic, Thailand is going to be near the top of your list.

✔ **The downside:** Thailand is not a dangerous country, but there is some crime, particularly in cities like Bangkok. Violent crime is rare compared to the United States, mostly it is credit card fraud, hotel burglary, or some kind of confidence game. Although illegal, drugs — often fraudulent or deadly powerful — are widely available in Thailand. Because sex is a booming industry, the rate of HIV infection and venereal disease is appallingly high.

Malaysia

✔ **The diving:** Malaysia occupies most of the southern end of the Malay Peninsula (West Malaysia) as well as two large provinces (Sarawak and Sabah) on the northern end of the island of Borneo (East Malaysia). The diving here is among the world's best, particularly in the South China and Sulu Seas in East Malaysia. This area of the world boasts the greatest diversity of species anywhere — creatures big and small. The west side of the Malay Peninsula receives the outflow of many large rivers — visibility is not as good as in other areas, so it isn't as popular with divers.

✔ **The land:** Just like below the waterline, Malaysian rainforests are home to an incredible diversity of creatures and have served as a last stand for some of Southeast Asia's increasing rare and endangered species. There is still a lot to see in Malaysia's rainforests, but heavy logging pressures and recent catastrophic fires have devastated huge tracts — the long-term effects still remain to be seen.

✔ **The culture:** Malaysia is a Muslim country, but like the Islam practiced in the Maldives and Indonesia, it's a good deal less strict and conservative than the kind practiced in the Arab countries of the Middle East. There is considerable Hindu influence in Malaysia as well.

✔ **The downside:** Malaysia is a country ambitious to pursue development. It has been very successful, but sometimes at a high price, environmentally. Deforestation through logging and the devastating fires of 1997 and 1998 threaten the reefs with sedimentation from runoff.

Indonesia

- ✔ **The diving:** As in Malaysia and the Philippines, the diving in Indonesia features the greatest diversity anywhere in the world in both large pelagic animals and small reef creatures. Indonesia covers a very large area, however — in some places the reefs are pristine; in others, they have been damaged. Check locally before you go.

- ✔ **The land:** Indonesia is a land of tremendous diversity — low-lying coral atolls and brooding, black-shouldered volcanoes. There's always something to do and see topside in Indonesia. In the east, tigers stalk through the forests of Sumatra and the last of the Javanese rhinos graze in Ujong Kulon nature reserve. In the province of Kalimantan on the island of Borneo, thousands of bird species chatter in the dense rainforest canopy and, prowling in the gloom underneath, miniature deer, sun bears, and the endangered orangutan — the old man of the forest in his shaggy orange coat. In the east, the wildlife resembles Australia, with lots of marsupials, parrots, the resplendent bird-of-paradise, and in many places, you can see rare and fantastic animals found nowhere else on earth, like the famous Komodo dragon. Indonesia is a naturalist's dream.

- ✔ **The culture:** Indonesia is made up of over 300 separate ethnic groups with as many distinct and colorful customs. They come in the whole rainbow of human skin tones and worship every God known to man, although officially, Indonesia is a Muslim country. Many isolated groups still live in primitive conditions while their countrymen send e-mail on the Internet. In places like Bali and Toraja, the culture is itself a world-renowned tourist attraction. Probably no other country on earth offers as many exotic cultural attractions as Indonesia.

- ✔ **The downside:** Modern Indonesia is a country in the midst of political upheaval. Political power in the country is concentrated in the hands of the Javanese, but because there are so many distinct ethnic groups spread throughout a large country of isolated island groups, there is a good deal of smoldering resentment. It's not focused on American tourists, but there is the admittedly remote possibility of getting caught up in a situation while traveling in the country, particularly in a big city like Jakarta.

The Philippines

- ✔ **The diving:** Like Malaysia and Indonesia, the Philippines boasts the greatest diversity of marine life on earth. Philippine reefs, unfortunately, have been damaged and destroyed in many places. There are still lots of great dive sites however — notably on the island of Palawan and on Tubbataha reef in the Sulu Sea, designated as a World Heritage Site by UNESCO (see the Appendix for more information). The Philippine government has made a concentrated effort to protect and restore its natural heritage, but check into local conditions before you book. Maybe it's the bad press, but for some reason the Philippines are somewhat underrated as a dive destination.

✔ **The land:** The Philippines are also somewhat underrated as a topside attraction. You can find many unique natural features ranging from the world's smallest monkey to the world's most extensive rice terraces — the 100-square-mile World Heritage Site in Ifugao.

✔ **The culture:** Philippine culture is exotic, but because of its long-standing association with the West, and particularly the United States, there is also a great deal about the Philippines that is familiar. English is widely spoken, and western customs and preferences are well-known. At the same time, isolated groups of native people still live much as they have for generations.

✔ **The downside:** Overburdened infrastructure, pollution, and all of the other side effects of a large and mostly poor population exist here. The Philippines is making progress, but slowly. Even Tubbataha reef, a World Heritage Site, shows some damage from dynamite and cyanide fishing.

Australia

✔ **The diving:** The Great Barrier Reef (GBR) off the Queensland coast in Eastern Australia is the largest reef in the world — a World Heritage Site — and home to one of the largest and most efficient dive industries operating anywhere. Townsville, Cairns, and Port Douglas all have dive operators and fleets that visit the GBR daily. Not only is Queensland's diving well-organized, it's among the best in the world — all the diversity of the Indo-Pacific on 1,200 miles of barrier reef. There's plenty of diving in western Australia as well, though not on the scale of Queensland, and South Australia is famous for its great white shark dives.

✔ **The land:** The continent of Australia is one of the most ancient and isolated land masses on the planet. Its flora and fauna have evolved in isolation for more than 50 million years and the result is a large number of unique endemic species from kangaroos to cockatoos. Australia also has a wide range of climates from dense tropical rainforest to scorching desert — for a naturalist, it's an endlessly fascinating continent.

✔ **The culture:** North Americans won't find much exotic in Australian culture. Like the United States, Australia was originally settled by convicts and misfits of British society without much regard for the native inhabitants. Australia has not had the waves of immigrants that the U.S. has however, non-Caucasian European immigration to Australia has only been significant since the '40s, so, if anything, the culture is even less varied than the U.S. On the other hand, if you're uncomfortable with strange languages and unfamiliar cultural practices, you're going to be pretty comfortable in Australia.

✔ **The downside:** There's not much downside to diving down under. Australians are well-aware of the value of their natural resources, especially the Great Barrier Reef. It is protected by law and in most places, quite pristine. There are the usual host of stinging and biting sea critters including the famous saltwater crocodile, as well as some pretty bad-news critters on shore.

Papua New Guinea

✔ **The diving:** The diving in Papau New Guinea (PNG) is similar to what you will find on the northern Barrier Reef in Australia, with the addition of thousands of World War II wrecks encrusted with coral and swarming with fish. PNG doesn't have a barrier reef like Queensland, but instead has fringing reefs around the mainland and the many offshore islands, and a few atolls.

✔ **The land:** PNG ranges from steamy tropical lowland to alpine lakes and meadows along the mountainous central range. In between, in the rugged highlands and mountain valleys is where you find most of PNG's wealth of flora and fauna. PNG doesn't have a lot of large mammalian species, but it is heaven for bird lovers, with 38 of the world's 43 species of birds-of-paradise and more kinds of parrots than anywhere in the world.

✔ **The culture:** The culture of the Papuan highlanders is one of the country's great tourist attractions, but there are only a small part of one of the most culturally diverse nations in the world. It is estimated that more than 700 languages are spoken in PNG and more anthropologists per square mile than anywhere else in the world.

✔ **The downside:** Intertribal warfare has a long and violent history in PNG. Although this kind of violence doesn't normally involve visitors, it is a familiar way to settle disputes. PNG has a large problem with violent crime, especially in the cities like Port Moresby. It also has a highly sexist culture — women are considered subservient to men and abuse of women is, unfortunately, pretty common. If all that isn't bad enough, PNG is also expensive.

Micronesia

✔ **The diving:** Palau, in the west, has some of the most famous dive sites in the world, and at least one, Blue Corner, that has to be considered a contender for the title of "World's Best Dive Site" (take a look at Chapter 15). The island of Yap is equally famous for its dependable manta sightings, and Chuuk lagoon harbors the world's most famous and frequently dived ghost fleets (flip to Chapter 15). Micronesia covers a vast tract of the North Pacific from the equator to the Tropic of Cancer, from Palau to the Marshall Islands. The diversity of marine species declines as you travel east from Palau, but it's good everywhere and comparatively pristine in the east.

✔ **The land:** The diversity of species topside also declines as you travel east in Micronesia. Fruit bats, crocodiles, and a wide variety of birds found in Palau disappear by the time you reach the Marshalls, which has little else but seabirds. While the eastern islands are principally low-lying coral atolls, the western islands are generally higher volcanic islands, sometimes capped in limestone. The high islands usually have rainforest, some wildlife, and sometimes truly unique and fascinating features like the Rock Islands in Palau. The atolls have coconut palms and maybe a few tropical pines, and, uh, did I mention coconut palms?

✔ **The culture:** The high islands, with their better soil and more available water, allowed for agriculture and the development of more elaborate societies. In some places, such as on the island of Yap, many of the traditional customs have survived almost intact; other places, like Guam, have been entirely absorbed by modern monoculture. The people of the low, eastern islands have traditionally made their living almost entirely from the sea and routinely travel long distances over open ocean in small canoes. Their navigational prowess is legendary and their customs and language are spread out across the whole of eastern Micronesia. At the end of World War II, Micronesia became a territory of the United States and was managed (and mismanaged) by various bureaucracies until the late '70s, when the islands finally began to assume some autonomy. The Northern Marianas voted for U.S. commonwealth status; Pohnpei, Kosrae, Chuuk and Yap joined to form the Federated States of Micronesia; and the people of the Marshall Islands and Palau voted to become separate, independent republics. In all of the states of Micronesia, the English language is spoken and Americans feel at home, even while in an exotic tropical country.

✔ **The downside:** The U.S. stewardship of Micronesia did a lot more to foster welfare and government works than it did to build a strong, sustainable economy. Unfortunately, after the islanders became habituated to the arrangement, Uncle Sugar pulled the plug. Today, there are a good number of Micronesians hovering in the impoverished economic twilight between their lost heritage and the twenty-first century. There aren't many crimes of violence against tourists, but keep any property that you value on your person or securely locked up.

Fiji

✔ **The diving:** There is a noticeable drop-off in the diversity of marine species from Australia to Fiji, and between Fiji and the Polynesian islands further to the east. Diving in Fiji is excellent, nonetheless, and Fiji is known for its brilliant soft corals, nourished by strong inter-island currents.

- ✔ **The land:** Fiji is made up of both high volcanic and low-lying coral islands. The two largest islands — Viti Levu and Vanua Levu — are of volcanic origin. Topside, the number of species in Fiji declines as you proceed east, just as they do in the rest of the Pacific. Fiji has more species than Polynesia to the east, but fewer than Papua New Guinea and the Solomon islands to the west.

- ✔ **The culture:** Fiji is the land where two waves of Pacific immigration merge — the Melanesians and the Polynesians. The original Fijians were mainly Melanesians with dark complexions, but for many centuries they have traded with the Polynesians, principally Tongans, in the eastern islands. Even today, Fijians in the eastern islands tend to be of lighter complexion than those in the west. Traditional Fijian life is based on village communities and although modern Fiji has officially adopted a capitalist economy, many of the old communal traditions and values survive. Fijian people are generally regarded as some of the warmest and friendliest anywhere in the world. Curiously, ethnic Fijians are a minority in the islands — toward the end of the nineteenth century, British colonial sugar planters brought in thousands of east Indians to work as field laborers, and today, 50 percent of the population of Fiji are ethnic Indians, with their own language and customs.

- ✔ **The downside:** There aren't any serious downsides to traveling in Fiji, aside from the usual list of immunizations you will require (see the "Immunizations" section, later in this chapter). Just remember, Fiji operates on island time. Don't be in a hurry. Chill out.

Polynesia

- ✔ **The diving:** Beyond Fiji, the diversity of marine species drops off. Polynesian reefs are not as spectacular as those farther to the west, but they're good for encounters with pelagic species such as sharks and mantas.

- ✔ **The land:** The islands of Polynesia are made up of both high volcanic islands and low-lying coral atolls. You find less diversity than you do in the islands further to the west, but the sculpted peaks of islands like Bora Bora and Moorea are so beautiful that it almost doesn't matter. It is enough to lie on a white sand beach and contemplate the clouds drifting across their green shoulders. The Society Islands, in particular, are celebrated for their scenic beauty and attract high-rolling tourists from all over the world.

- ✔ **The culture:** Polynesian culture is another of the great attractions of these South Pacific islands. Arts and crafts and the legendary beauty and spectacular dance of Tahitian people make these islands worth the trip, even if you never dive at all.

✔ **The downside:** For the most part, Polynesia is pretty expensive. Nearly everything has to be imported, which, understandably, drives up the price, but even local products have a hefty price tag. On the other hand, it's nice to go somewhere in the world where Americans are well-liked.

Hawaii

✔ **The diving:** The bad news is that the marine diversity in the Hawaiian islands is about a fourth of what it is in the Western Pacific. The good news is that many of the species that you see in the islands are unique, endemic critters. The other good news is that there is plenty of modern infrastructure to facilitate your plans — lots of operators with state-of-the-art equipment and fast boats.

✔ **The land:** The Hawaiian Islands are the most isolated archipelago in the world. There was a time when the islands had more unique endemic species than anywhere else, including the Galapagos. Unfortunately, a tragic number of those species are now extinct, and most of the remainder are endangered. More creatures go extinct in Hawaii than anywhere else in the world, and, as you might expect, Hawaii has more endangered species than anywhere in the world. In addition to all the strange and wonderful creatures you can't see anymore, Hawaii has a dramatic, volcanic landscape — both active and extinct.

✔ **The culture:** If you really aren't at all comfortable in a land where strange people, with their strange ways, are speaking a strange language, you can go to Hawaii where strange people, with their strange ways, are speaking a familiar language. There are still a few places where vestiges of the original Hawaiian culture exist, but for the most part it has been transformed into a hotel stage show and a Saturday luau in an Aloha shirt theme park. Shopping malls, TV, traffic, junk food — all the comforts of home.

✔ **The downside:** See the two previous bullet points.

The Galapagos Islands

✔ **The diving:** Straddling the equator and bathed in the confluence of three different ocean currents, the waters of the Galapagos are a rich environment for an abundance of marine life, especially large schools of fish and pelagic species like hammerhead sharks and rays. Strong currents are common in the Galapagos, though — it is not really the best place for beginning divers.

✔ **The land:** The Galapagos are every bit as fascinating today as they were when a budding, 26-year-old naturalist by the name of Charles Darwin visited them to collect specimens and the information he would use to compile his seminal work, *The Origin of the Species,* 26 years later. Most animals still exhibit no fear toward other animals, including humans, and they can be closely approached. With Galapagos seals, penguins, giant tortoises, and marine iguanas, the islands are still a unique natural treasure. Unfortunately, they have suffered environmental impact since Darwin's time, partly because of their popularity as a tourist destination.

✔ **The culture:** There is little that can be called culture in the Galapagos. Before the islands became a popular tourist destination, they were uninhabited except for the occasional fishermen. Today, more than 14,000 permanent residents from the Ecuadorian mainland occupy the Galapagos for the express purpose of servicing their 50,000 annual visitors. The new islanders have brought along their cats, rats, dogs, goats, burros, and pigs, all of which have wreaked havoc on the native wildlife.

✔ **The downside:** Diving in the Galapagos is not for beginners. There is plenty to do and see for nondivers, but the trip isn't cheap.

Central America

✔ **The diving:** Most of the diving in central America is done on the Caribbean side of the isthmus, but there is some great diving on the Pacific side in Costa Rica. The Bay Islands in Honduras, Belize, and the Yucatan all have well-established dive industries. Belize has one of the world's great barrier reefs and a lot of the southern end remains unexplored by divers. The island of Cozumel, off the Yucatan peninsula, has one of the largest and most active dive industries in the world, as well as some of the best diving in the Caribbean (see Chapter 15).

✔ **The land:** Central America's rainforests shelter incredible biodiversity. Over 850 species of birds have been identified here, more than in North America, Australia, or Europe — from the scarlet macaw to the resplendent quetzal, here you find some of the most gaudy and glittering plumage in the avian world. Even the frogs are colorful. You can find monkeys, jaguars, sloths, anteaters, tapirs, and 10 percent of all the world's butterfly species. From a naturalist's point-of-view, Central America is nothing short of fantastic.

✔ **The culture:** Although the dominant culture of Central America is Spanish-speaking Latino, there are a surprising number of other distinct ethnic and cultural groups — many different groups of native peoples, particularly on the Caribbean coast, where trade and travel have been carried on for centuries. There are numerous fascinating Mayan ruins in Mexico, Belize, and Guatemala.

✔ **The downside:** Central Americans have not always received the best treatment from their neighbors to the north. In some places there is lingering resentment, but for the most part people are friendly and helpful.

Hurricane Mitch tore a wide swath of destruction across most of Honduras in the fall of 1998 and that nation will be a long time recovering. Belize City has a serious problem with street crime. Even in broad daylight it isn't safe to walk the streets. Steer clear of Belize City.

The Caribbean Islands

✔ **The diving:** There is a kind of uniformity to the diving in the Caribbean. The number and distribution of species is pretty much the same from the Belize barrier reef to the Bahamas. The Caribbean has a ways to go to catch up with the Western Pacific as far as diversity goes, but it does have excellent conditions for coral growth and reef building, and the species that are here thrive in the warm, clear waters. The Caribbean also has a well-developed dive industry and its proximity to the United States makes it perfect for a quick getaway.

✔ **The land:** Caribbean Islands range from mountainous to low-lying, but you won't find the classic coral atolls of the South Pacific. The low-lying islands are generally ancient reefs that have been geologically uplifted. The most significant islands in the Caribbean, however, lie along the archipelago of the Greater and Lesser Antilles — from Cuba in the northwest to Grenada in the southeast. Many of these tiny islands are nations unto themselves with a distinct national character and pride, but they hold in common a warm and hospitable character that is common to the Caribbean.

✔ **The culture:** Ever since they were first discovered by Europeans, the Caribbean islands have been a stopover between the old world and the new. They have absorbed every influence and people who have passed through whether they were stealing gold from the native people for the Spanish treasury or on their way to the slave market in New Orleans — fabulous cultural potpourri and a work in progress.

✔ **The downside:** Almost every year, the Caribbean is visited by hurricanes. It's nothing that you want to be caught in, but you normally have plenty of warning. The reefs that lie in their path aren't so lucky. Some of these monster blows can damage reefs so severely they may be many years recovering. If that's not bad enough, some Caribbean nations are an economic disaster, as well. Haiti is so poor that the people have virtually denuded the entire landscape and the surrounding waters — it is a bona fide ecological and economic disaster, and without help, a few other Caribbean nations may be looking at a future nearly as grim.

Cautions

If you're going to travel, you need to be aware that some unpleasant things can happen. That way, you can be prepared to deal with them and minimize the effect they have on your trip. So, what are the pitfalls awaiting travelers? Well, ranked from the most common to the most rare they are as follows:

- ✔ **Lost luggage:** This is the most common problem for travelers abroad. The airline sends your luggage to the wrong place in a trip involving a change of planes. More than 90 percent of the time, the luggage is successfully recovered.

- ✔ **Oversold flights:** Second most common travel complaint is getting bumped. That's right, the airlines are at it again.

- ✔ **Quickstep:** Otherwise known as traveler's diarrhea. Dehydration can be a serious side effect, especially in hot, tropical countries.

- ✔ **Rip-off:** Usually by currency exchange with a street vendor, a taxi driver, or some other shady entrepreneur; less often by a pickpocket in a public place.

- ✔ **Traffic accident:** Taking into account only those in which the traveler is actually injured.

- ✔ **Airplane crash, fire, natural disaster, or terrorist activity:** Pretty unlikely, but it's worth noting that the likelihood is higher, depending on where you go. The highest incidence of terrorist activity is in South America, notably Colombia and Peru.

You can't get there from here

There are countries in which United States citizens are forbidden to travel or spend money. Of course, the political climate in the world is in a state of constant flux and these restrictions are often complicated and ever-changing. For the most up-to-date info, call the Department of State at 202-326-6168.

Immunizations

There are an awful lot of bugs out there looking for a nice cozy home and before you travel abroad, you should take steps to make sure you don't become it. Research shows that 80 percent of adults don't keep up with routine immunizations. If you're planning to travel, you should update your routine immunizations before you go.

- ✔ **Tetanus-diphtheria:** Booster.
- ✔ **Poliomyelitis:** Booster.

- ✔ **Measles:** Not required of anyone born before 1957 when the disease circulated freely through the population — they are considered immune by previous exposure. Everybody else should be vaccinated.

- ✔ **Mumps:** Adults are generally considered immune as the result of previous exposure; children should be vaccinated.

- ✔ **Rubella:** Recommended for women of childbearing age, who are not immune, provided they aren't pregnant. A blood test may be necessary to determine immunity. Vaccinated women should not become pregnant for three months.

- ✔ **Influenza:** Recommended for those at risk for complications.

Children under age seven need the usual childhood immunizations, so you may have to work out the best schedule with your pediatrician.

In addition to your routine immunizations, you need to get any additional inoculations relevant to the area in which you plan to travel. Lots of bad boys thrive in tropical climates — cholera, hepatitis A and B, Japanese encephalitis, typhoid fever, dengue fever, yellow fever, and malaria — so make sure your body is an unfriendly habitat. The International Association for Medical Assistance to Travelers (IAMAT) can provide a chart that advises you of all the immunizations you will need for wherever you go, for a small donation. It also has an international directory of member doctors. Write to IAMAT at 417 Center Street, Lewiston NY, 14092.

Malaria has long been the scourge of the tropics; infection is spread by the bite of the anopheles mosquito. For a long time, chloroquinine has been the drug used as a prophylactic to combat malaria, and in some places it is still effective, but a chloroquinine-resistant strain, *plasmodium falciparum,* is now present in many areas of the world. It is the most dangerous form of malaria and requires a regimen of mefloquinine hydrochloride, also known as Lariam, as a preventative. All malaria preventatives must be started at least a week before you enter an infected area, and continued for up to four weeks after you leave. IAMAT can provide a chart on World Malaria Risk, or you can call the Center for Disease Control at 404-639-1610.

Pack It Up

Now that you are sufficiently terrified of terrible exotic diseases, plane crashes, pickpockets, and revolutions, be advised that millions of Americans travel abroad every year and safely return without so much as a stubbed toe. As a matter of fact, stubbed toe is the most common injury among travelers abroad — so turn on the light before you start stumbling around your hotel room in the middle of the night in search of the bathroom. Now, with your mind at ease, it's time to pack that bag.

Any experienced traveler will tell you that the lighter you can travel, the better. The less stuff you have, the less you have to haul around the airport, get lost or stolen, keep track of in transit, and otherwise fret about. If you can get away with only carry-on luggage, you're way ahead of the game — you don't even have to wait for your luggage at the airport. If you have a dive bag, however, that isn't very likely.

Dress for success

The clothing you take is going to depend on what you plan to do besides dive. The dress on dive boats and around most tropical resorts is vacation casual — t-shirts, shorts, and sandals. On most dive trips, you don't need much else. For men, almost any kind of long pants and shirt with a collar are considered formal wear. In some countries, particularly those that are pre-dominantly Muslim, women should dress more conservatively in public places — your host at the hotel or resort can fill you in on what's appropriate.

Build your own list to suit, but keep it short. Remember, you have all that dive gear to haul and probably camera gear, too. Here's my tropical list as a starting point:

- ✔ **2 tank tops**
- ✔ **2 pair of underwear**
- ✔ **1 polo shirt (formal wear)**
- ✔ **1 pair of sandals**
- ✔ **1 pair of shorts**
- ✔ **1 pair of long pants** with zip-off legs, so it also serves as a second pair of shorts
- ✔ **1 pair of cross trainers and socks for hiking**
- ✔ **1 windbreaker**
- ✔ **1 baseball cap for sun protection**

That's it. If I need anything else, I buy it on the way. Stick to fabrics that are cool — cotton seems to work best. Wear clothes that are loose and allow cooling airflow around your body.

Other stuff

Of course, you also need your dive gear — check out the diver's checklist in the Appendix for that — and a few other miscellaneous items. Again, here's my list to use as a starting point:

✔ **Passport**

✔ **Plane tickets**

✔ **Money:** In traveler's checks.

✔ **Sunscreen:** One really strong, and one slightly less so, for after you become accustomed to the tropical sun.

✔ **Sunglasses**

✔ **Pocket knife**

✔ **Flashlight:** With extra batteries.

✔ **Toilet kit:** Razor blades, toothbrush, and so on.

✔ **First aid kit:** Bandages, antiseptic, diarrhea medicine, motion sickness medicine, mosquito repellent, and so on.

✔ **Notebook and pens**

✔ **Reading material**

✔ **Resealable plastic bags**

✔ **Pocket compass**

✔ **Nutrient bars**

Sometimes, I take more stuff if I'm planning to be camping out or away from resources where I can buy the things I need. For example, it rains a lot in the tropics, but I find it easier to buy a cheap umbrella when I arrive and get rid of it before I leave, but if I'm going to be in a rainforest lodge for a few days, I bring a rain poncho.

Staying Healthy

Traveling upsets all of your daily routines and, unless you're somebody who travels often enough to have travel routines, you're playing it by ear — grabbing a snack here, catching a nap there — not the best conditions for fostering optimum function of your immune system. There are also the ordinary conditions and inconveniences of travel in the tropics that can turn into a problem if you fail to pay them the proper attention.

Eat right

The temptation is to eat whatever is handy and quick. You're on the road, you're in a hurry. Who's got time? This deep-fried butter on a stick will do. My advice: take the time. You're on vacation, remember? Eat a balanced diet, with lots of fruits and vegetables — they abound in the tropics, especially exotic fruits. Wash them well, if you know the water is safe. Peel them if you have any doubts. Southeast Asia, in particular, has a bounty of delicious fruits that you've never heard of — and then there's the durian (see the "Durian don't come easy" sidebar). Try it if you dare, and good luck.

Drink right

It's important to drink lots of fluids in a hot tropical climate. Dehydration can happen very quickly and can lead to heat exhaustion and even heat stroke (see Chapter 7). Beer and similar alcoholic drinks are not the answer. I don't care what Jimmy Buffett says, alcohol dries you out, so you should avoid overindulgence. Of course, tap water in many tropical countries may be suspect and can be the cause of traveler's diarrhea, leading to further dehydration. Fortunately, bottled water is available almost everywhere in the world these days. Keep a bottle with you at all times and sip from it constantly — the best insurance that you'll keep your fluid levels up. The best way to monitor your fluids is to check the color of your urine. It should be pale yellow. If it gets darker, you need to drink more fluids.

Durian don't come easy

One of the most prized items of produce in Southeast Asia is a large, spiky, green, oblate spheroid known as the durian — modestly described as an acquired taste. True, this particular fruit isn't easily appreciated by the western palate. Inside the spiky skin is a soft, white, custardlike flesh that is scooped out and eaten. No problem, but the smell is not something that westerners normally associate with anything you'd purposely put in your mouth. Okay, Americans are gustatory sissies, I'll concede that, but even rugged Europeans, accustomed to gulping down cheeses that would gag a starving turkey vulture, are no match for the aromatic authority of the mighty durian. They don't call it the king of fruits for nothing.

The rumor is that durian tastes like onions and caramel, which sounds repulsive all by itself, but durian devotees swear it is incomparable. Personally, I've never met a Westerner who could get one down and I have never gotten a sufficient description of the flavor from an Asian friend. All I can go by is the smell, or rather, stench.

There really is no description that can capture the essence of the olfactory durian experience: decayed corpses, boiled in putrid, backed-up, septic tank effluvium, strained through the filthy sweatsocks of 40,000 sufferers of terminal trench foot, and steeped in the toxic bog of an industrial chemicals plant? No, something's missing.

But don't take my word for it. I couldn't pass muster, but I'm a culinary xenophobe. If you can conquer the king of fruits, I'm anxious to hear the tale.

Take cover

The sun is much stronger in the tropical latitudes than it is in North America or Europe. Use a strong sun block early and often. Your skin is your body's largest organ and a bad sunburn can make you really sick and uncomfortable, and even ruin your entire vacation. Take it seriously. Use a strong sunblock when you first arrive — SPF 45 or stronger. After you're accustomed to the sun, you can cut back to a SPF 15 or so. You should also have a hat or a cap to give your head a little extra protection.

Don't get bugged

The same warm, humid conditions that make the tropics so attractive to humans is generous to members of the insect kingdom — many of whom make their living off any hapless fleshoid who strolls into range. Most people are familiar with mosquitoes, of course, and there are plenty of them in the tropics. In some places (not everywhere) there are species that carry malaria, so it is wise to maintain a regimen of preventive drugs if you're traveling in those areas (see the "Immunizations" section, earlier in this chapter). It's also useful to have an effective mosquito repellent, and even sleep under mosquito netting, if necessary.

Mosquitoes aren't the only biters, of course. *Sand flies,* also called *no-see-ums,* are the next most common and those little stinkers can really tear you up. I remember seeing a German tourist on the cays in Belize, who looked like he contracted a ferocious case of the measles — the work of sand flies. By the time I left I didn't look much better. These vicious little swine are so small you can't even see them, but the bites itch like a horrible case of poison ivy. They seem to favor some people over others — you'll probably find that it's you over everybody else. Mosquito repellent doesn't work on these guys, but Avon Skin-So-Soft seems to help. Other kinds of biting bugs are less numerous and usually a localized phenomenon.

Disabled Divers

Physical disabilities often limit participation in outdoor activities, but diving is one in which a large number of disabled people can participate. For many, the weightless world underwater provides a kind of freedom you don't normally experience under the tyranny of gravity.

The problems for disabled divers are more often encountered at resorts and dive boats that aren't handicapped accessible than in the water, but more and more resorts are becoming aware of the needs of a rapidly growing disabled diver market. For now, disabled divers are most often accommodated in really popular destinations like Cozumel and the Cayman Islands — not in the most exotic places, not yet anyway. Most of this is possible thanks to the work of the Handicapped Scuba Association (HSA), a nonprofit that has been helping disabled people get in the water since 1975. It organizes trips, helps handicapped people get certified and do everything else that needs doing in order to allow the handicapped to realize their diving potential. If you're handicapped or know someone who is, you may contact HSA via phone at 212-498-6128 or by e-mail at Suehsany@aol.com. Flip to the Appendix for more contact information for HSA.

Traveling with Nondivers

Not everyone is going to share your enthusiasm for the underwater world. Some of those nonbelievers may even be members of your own family. Maybe they're still too young to strap on a scuba tank. But, whatever the case, if you take your scuba vacation with nondivers, you can't expect them to put their lives on hold while you go explore the reef. The situation calls for compromise, and as long as you're not a member of the House Judiciary Committee, you should be able to find lots of creative ways to do just that.

Maybe you have to cut your diving down to one dive a day or even less. That can be enough, if it's the right dive. Talk to the local dive operator to get the inside information about the local sites. Explain your situation and have them help you plan your dives to maximize your underwater time. Don't be afraid to use them as a resource; you're paying for it.

If there is some activity that you're not particularly keen on, that your companions enjoy — say, shopping — perhaps you can arrange your diving, while your partners pursue their hobbies, and then meet up later. Everybody's happy.

If you're traveling with prescuba-aged children, your partner may be willing to look after them while you dive, but a better idea is to put your scuba diving agenda on the back burner and take them to the beach together. Introduce them to the wonder of the watery world by taking them snorkeling. If you don't, you may some day kick yourself for missing this, especially if you have the chance to do it in a warm, clear tropical lagoon. The magic of the reef will still be there on your next dive, but that other magic doesn't come around too many times, or stay very long.

Chapter 12

Keeping Up

● ●

In This Chapter

▶ Diving locally

▶ Expanding your underwater horizons

▶ Moving beyond recreational diving

▶ Protecting your reefs

● ●

*I*f you haven't been diving for a while, your skills get rusty. It's not like riding a bike — something you only need to learn once and never review. Skills such as buoyancy control (see Chapter 5) are subtle things and require fine tuning to maintain. If you can only take one vacation a year, and that's the only time you ever go diving, don't expect to be the same diver you were when you went home last time. You need to keep diving to keep your skills sharp. Even if you can't get away more often, there are still ways to polish your skills on the weekend — or whenever you can — even if you're not lucky enough to live on some hospitable coastal area.

Without Luggage

Of course a weekend getaway to a diving spot is fine if you live close enough to one of those places to swing it, but if you don't, you can usually find a freshwater lake, a flooded quarry, a river, or a spring. There aren't too many places that don't have some body of water somewhere. Naturally, you want to make sure it isn't hazardous in some way. If you usually dive only in saltwater, remember that your buoyancy is reduced in freshwater, so do a test to determine the proper weight (see Chapter 4). Don't overlook the local pool if you can't find anything else — it may not be the most interesting place to dive, but it can help you keep your skills sharp.

The best way to find out about all these great local places (and to find a dive buddy, if you don't have one) is through your local dive club. These guys will know everything there is to know about the local submarine scene — count on it. Plus, you have new friends (providing that *you're* not too objectionable) and somebody to talk about diving with — what a deal. You can locate one of these clubs through your local dive shop.

Gettin' up there

If you do find a nice, clear, local lake with friendly conditions, make sure you take the altitude into account. Dive tables and computers calculate your nitrogen uptake and elimination based on a dive ending at sea level. At altitude, you're under less atmospheric pressure than at sea level, making you more vulnerable to decompression sickness (see Chapter 7). Your dive table is good up to 1,000 feet, but beyond that, you need special conversion tables and procedures to dive safely.

If you have a dive computer, it may compensate for the increased altitude. Some models do it automatically; with others you have to enter the altitude; still others won't do it at all. If you're really interested in high altitude diving or if that's all there is in your neighborhood, you can take an altitude diver specialty course.

Refreshments

If you simply can't find the time to get out there once in a while and keep those skills finely honed, you don't have to give up on diving. That's what refresher courses are for. All of the certifying agencies offer them. You do a short review with a CD-ROM, workbook, or video; review the stuff with an instructor; and make a confined water dive to buff up your skills. You can usually do it all on a weekend before you jump on the plane and head off on your dream vacation. When you get there, you'll be zooming all over the reef with complete confidence.

Shape up

Diving isn't the Iron Man competition, and you don't have to be an Olympic athlete to do it, but it can sometimes be demanding and it's not a good idea to let yourself become a maggotlike couch creature, either. Diving is statistically very safe, but most of those who die while diving do so as a result of a heart attack precipitated by unfamiliar vigorous exercise. It doesn't take that much to be in shape for diving, and it will improve the rest of your life as well. Try running, walking, or any kind of aerobic exercise, three times a week. Stay at it until you work up a little bit of a sweat.

Eat a balanced diet, too. Nag, nag, nag. You've heard this about four million times by now, right? Okay, I'm not going to waste ink hammering you about it again. You know you need to do it, so make it happen.

Ever Onward

Some people are perfectly happy making dive after dive, year after year, without even keeping score in their logbook. Others want that official stamp on their accomplishments. Some are just as happy with a wreck as a reef, while others get fixated on some particular aspect of the sport, like photography or cave diving, and they don't want to do anything else. You can find lots of specialties and sidetracks in the world of diving, after you've mastered the basics.

Obviously, you can climb the scuba hierarchy as far as you care to go. You can also pursue some of the other diving specialties. (See the "Professional and technical diving" section, later in this chapter, for descriptions of some dive specialties.)

Photography and video

This is probably the most popular specialty in the world of diving. Beginning divers (and lots of old-timers, too) are so blown away by the amazing world they see underwater, they want to bring back pictures of it to share with their friends — maybe to sell to one of those dive magazines. Why not? They pick up one of those little waterproof, throw-away cameras, burn a roll, and are somewhat disappointed with the results. One thing leads to another and before long they're into it for $25,000 and hauling four or five giant trunks full of gear with them on every trip — a full-on, dive-photo nerd.

But before you start going into hock for a lot of camera gear, you should ask yourself what you hope to accomplish with it?

- **Six-foot photos:** Those little throw-away cameras are okay down to about six feet. They may be fine for snorkeling, but for anything below six feet, they simply don't do the job.

- **Amateur photos:** If you want souvenirs from your dive — and nothing more — you still need to shell out money for a camera, possibly a housing, and lights, if you expect to come back with anything worth looking at. Lights are important because of the way light travels in water (see Chapter 6). Even this basic gear is a respectable investment.

✔ **Amateur videos:** As far as souvenirs go, I think video is more effective than still pictures — it gives you a better feel for the underwater terrain, the way the divers move through it, and the way the fish and other marine creatures move. You can spend anywhere from a few hundred to many tens of thousands of dollars on video equipment. To some degree the results you get will depend on the equipment, but it also depends on your knowledge of the underwater world — anticipating what will happen, getting in position to get the shot, and so on. So, having a lot of top-of-the-line gear doesn't necessarily mean that you'll come back with killer tape. Obviously, the better diver you are, the easier it is for you to get all of the creative shots you can imagine.

✔ **Professional photos:** Divers who take up this hobby almost always want to have their work published in dive magazines, sooner or later. Some even imagine a career as a glamorous dive photographer, jetting to all the world's best dive sites and coming back with the stunning images that blow that cantankerous and jaded editor over at *Sport Diver* magazine right out of his overstuffed chair! Well, maybe so, but in the words of the sage: Don't quit your day job.

Dive magazines don't pay very much — they don't have to with all those amateurs out there flooding their offices with pictures. Even the long-time professional dive photographers usually have some other work going to pay the bills — they sell their images through a stockhouse, they lead photo safaris, and so on. Besides, that editor's chair isn't as overstuffed as you may imagine. Magazine publishing is a lean, mean, and highly competitive business.

Still, if this is your all-consuming passion, go for it. You may be the great, unheralded artistic genius of underwater photography and I don't want to be responsible for discouraging you!

Enriched air

Air is mostly nitrogen, some oxygen (about 21 percent) and traces of some other gases (see Chapter 6 for more). Oxygen is the only gas in the mix that's important to your metabolism. You don't use the nitrogen, but you absorb some of it into your tissues. Under pressure, you absorb more of it, and it can create problems for you when the pressure is relieved (see Chapter 7). So if the oxygen is all that you need and the nitrogen causes problems, why not get rid of the nitrogen and just breathe oxygen underwater? Because some oxygen is good, but too much is toxic.

Displacing some of the nitrogen in air with oxygen has its advantages, as long as you can avoid oxygen toxicity — less nitrogen means less risk of decompression sickness and narcosis. Enriched air, or *nitrox* as it is sometimes known, is air that has been tinkered with to contain a higher percentage of oxygen — usually between 32 and 36 percent — enough to reduce your uptake of nitrogen, but not enough to induce oxygen toxicity with proper use.

Exotic mixed gases

Nitrox isn't the only fancy breathing mixture concocted for diving. *Heliox* is made by substituting helium for the nitrogen. Heliox is used by commercial and military divers for very deep diving, usually more than 200 feet, not because it doesn't create decompression problems (it requires just as much decompression time as compressed air — sometimes more), but it doesn't cause narcosis, the big problem for very deep divers (see Chapter 7). Helium does, however, conduct heat much better than nitrogen, so divers using heliox get colder, faster. Below 300 feet, heliox can cause high pressure nervous syndrome, an uncontrolled shaking. Divers

venturing into this range generally switch over to trimix.

Trimix is heliox with some of the nitrogen put back in (usually about 15 percent) to slow down nerve conduction and lessen the risk of high pressure nervous syndrome. This is the stuff used by the deepest technical divers (see the "Deep diving" section, later in this chapter). Mixtures that include hydrogen, argon, and neon have all been used for various experimental applications, but none of these mixtures, including heliox and trimix, have any use in recreational diving.

You don't have much danger of oxygen toxicity when breathing regular compressed air. Even at the maximum safe recreational diving limit of 130 feet, you'd have to stay there for at least 12 hours before you got into significant risk. Not many people can make a tank of air last 12 hours. With enriched air, however, the situation is different. It is possible for a diver breathing enriched air to be at risk for oxygen toxicity — but when used responsibly, with proper training, it is safe.

Divers, particularly older divers, who use enriched air often report feeling warmer, less fatigued, more alert, with less dry mouth — generally better — after a day of diving than they do on compressed air. That, of course, is anecdotal evidence, but enriched air diving is becoming increasingly popular with recreational divers. Conceivably, it may even replace compressed air in recreational diving some day. For now, it's a specialty and requires special training. If you're interested in diving with enriched air, take the specialty certification course before you attempt it. See the Appendix for a list of certifying agencies.

Professional and technical diving

Recreational divers, like lots of people who become involved in a hobby they really like, often dream of turning pro or at least taking it to pro levels — professional and technical diving.

By far, the majority of divers who turn pro do so by becoming dive instructors for one of the major certifying agencies, but military, police, oil exploration, salvage divers, scientific, and archaeological divers are all professionals, as well. In essence, anybody who makes money for diving is a *professional diver*. Many of these divers require specialized training and equipment to perform their underwater jobs, because they often have to dive deeper and stay longer than is permitted by the restrictions of recreational diving.

A *technical diver* is someone who is diving outside the limits of recreational diving, but isn't doing it for profit. So what are the limits that separate the technical diver from the recreational diver? Traditionally, recreational diving:

- ✔ Uses only compressed air (enriched air has blurred this distinction).
- ✔ Has a depth limit of 130 feet.
- ✔ Is done with a buddy.
- ✔ Has no planned decompression stops (excluding safety stops).

Beyond these limits, you're engaged in technical diving. Undoubtedly, I'll get arguments about the definition from technical divers, who, like nerds of every variety, are obsessive and compulsive about their passion. But that's okay; this is one field where being an obsessive, compulsive nerd is a big advantage, and just may save your life.

The following sections discuss specialties that you can pursue.

Wreck diving

There is a kind of fascination in gliding silently through the sunken remains of human history encrusted and overgrown with the irrepressible vitality of nature, that can't be duplicated in any other form of diving — that's the lure of wreck diving.

Both wreck diving and cave diving can be done on compressed air, within 130 feet of the surface, and with a buddy, but they both require specialized training, and therefore, qualify as technical diving by my definition.

Diving on a wreck is spooky and wonderful, but there are many additional safety considerations to account for including corroding structures, entangling cables and lines, the possibility of unexploded ordinance, overhead environments, and so on. A simple open water certification is sufficient to swim over and around a wreck, but you need more training to explore it further. You should never attempt *wreck penetration* (swimming inside) without special training.

In addition to diving on some of the notable wrecks littering the world's seas, after you're trained as wreck diver, you can get involved in the field of marine archaeology and perhaps make a real contribution to our collective understanding of marine history.

Cavern and cave diving

If you're always wondering what may be lurking in those dark hidden recesses of the reef, consider pursuing a specialty in cavern diving. Cavern diving, shown in the color section of this book, is within 130 feet of the surface and no deeper than 70 feet (for example, 70 feet down, 60 feet over) and within sight of the cavern opening. Never attempt cavern diving without specialized training.

Cave diving has claimed the lives of a lot of divers, but there are still those who love pitting themselves against the odds and tackling the spooky, high-risk environment of caves. These divers are sometimes rewarded with stunning other-worldly sights and water so clear that they seem to be suspended in space. Cave diving is technical diving though, and the procedures and safety limits are rigorous — you don't get many second chances in a pitch-black underwater cave. Specialized training and equipment is absolutely essential if you're interested in cave diving, as is strict adherence to the limits and procedures — under no circumstances should you attempt cave diving without extensive training and preparation.

Deep diving

Some people just get a kick out of going deep, for no other reason; other deep divers go deep to visit wrecks or even to explore caves. Deep diving may be complicated by the specific characteristics of exotic breathing mixtures such as heliox and trimix (see the "Exotic mixed gases" sidebar in this chapter), by the protracted bottom times, and by long decompression stops at different depths, sometimes switching to different gas. It's complicated and requires lots of knowledge, planning, and experience.

Deep diving is well beyond the limits of recreational diving and often involves several kinds of specialized training and many years diving of experience — and it can still be quite dangerous. This is usually the kind of interest that attracts you gradually, over a period of years as you build experience.

Eco-Diving

There was a time when the ocean was a vast and mysterious realm that seemed as limitless as the infinite reaches of space — both as a resource to exploit and a place to dump our trash. The ocean is still mysterious, but it has become alarmingly clear that it is not inexhaustible as a resource or a garbage dump.

The world population continues to grow exponentially, particularly in the certain parts of the world, and two-thirds of the current world population lives in coastal areas. In 50 years, it is estimated that over 7 billion people will be crowding the world's coastlines. The pressures from that burgeoning population on fisheries and coastal development, and the destruction and pollution that inevitably follows in its wake, threaten the world's delicate coral reefs and by extension, every living thing in the sea. If life disappears in the sea, life on land won't be far behind — most of the breathable oxygen in the atmosphere is the result of planktonic life in the oceans.

As a diver, the evidence is more apparent to you than nondivers who haven't taken advantage of the privilege to visit this wild and wonderful world. Year after year, you can see the degradation of the priceless underwater heritage. Inexperienced divers are sometimes responsible for some minor damage to the reefs, and every diver should strive to leave the reef as pristine as he found it, but on the whole, diver damage is trivial compared to the wholesale destruction wrought by coastal development, sedimentation resulting from the loss of rainforests, pollution from the increasing use of toxic chemicals, dredging of channels, destruction of mangrove swamps, and a whole host of other human activities.

It is the duty of every diver to bring to the attention of the nondiving public the importance and condition of the oceans. Flip to Chapter 16 for more ideas on how you can help. Consult the Appendix for a list of organizations working to protect the world's oceans—they are all deserving of your support.

Part V
The Part of Tens

The 5th Wave   By Rich Tennant

TINY LAGOON DIVE TOURS

Dive among our many man-made reefs

"Did you want to take the Schwinn bicycle dive, the Weber gas grill dive, or the Craftsman riding lawn mower dive?"

In this part . . .

This is the part where I get to talk about my favorite places to snorkel and dive. Of course, by doing that, word will get out, more people will visit these destinations, and the areas may be more vulnerable to damage by careless divers. Hmm.

But I know that I don't have to worry about you, because you're a responsible diver and plan to follow the environmental guidelines that I outline in this part. You're also a safe diver, so you're going to observe the ten rules of safe diving that are in here.

So, I can relax — in fact, I'm going diving! See you out there.

Chapter 13

Ten Great Snorkeling Adventures

● ●

In This Chapter

▶ Snorkeling with big marine creatures

▶ Discovering exotic snorkeling destinations

● ●

You don't have to use scuba gear to have some of the greatest diving adventures in the world. In fact, most of the locations in this chapter are best experienced by snorkeling.

Many of these destinations are special because you can view weird and wonderful ocean creatures that you've never seen before; others are magical places all by themselves; a few are both. You'll undoubtedly come up with your own list of ten great snorkeling locations; in the meantime, you won't be disappointed by starting with any of these.

Spotted Dolphins — Little Bahama Banks

Nearly everyone who has ever seen the wild Atlantic spotted dolphins that inhabit the Little Bahama Bank (see Figure 13-1) raves about the experience. Several different groups (called *pods*) make their home there and over time, they've become entirely comfortable in presence of snorkelers in the water — sometimes they even seem to welcome the interactions.

The encounters began when the dolphins came to investigate the treasure divers who were searching the shallow, white-sand bank for wrecks. Eventually, the word spread to the larger diving community; before long, divers were coming from everywhere to swim with these remarkable creatures. Today, dolphin trips on liveaboard vessels are something of a mini-industry. A whole fleet of boats prowl the bank during the summer searching out the pods — most of them based in Florida ports.

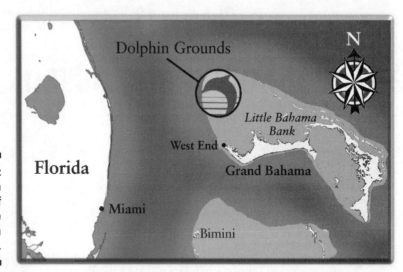

Figure 13-1:
Dolphin
grounds of
the Little
Bahama
Banks.

You can find dolphin charters advertised in all of the diving magazines. For most tours, the itinerary goes something like this: depart a Florida port in the evening, and overnight to West End, Grand Bahama, while you snooze peacefully in your cabin. In the morning, you clear Bahamian customs and head out to the bank. With a little luck, you could spot your first pod before sunset.

Dolphins are attracted to the bow wake of the boats and never seem to tire of riding the pressure wave in front of the bow. After your boat has collected a few dolphins under the bow, everybody gets into their snorkeling gear. The pilot cuts the engines, and the divers slip as quietly as possible into the water. You hear them before you see them — squeaking, whistling, and clicking that seems to come from everywhere at once. Then suddenly, they circle and pirouette around you with unbelievable grace and speed. (See the color photo section of this book for some amazing photos of dolphins and snorkelers.)

Dolphins are highly intelligent and live in complex social groups. Individual animals in a particular pod demonstrate different personalities, and overall temperament differs from pod to pod. Atlantic spotted dolphins grow darker and more spotted — and less playful — as they age. The calves are a nearly uniform light gray and the older animals look almost black and speckled with white spots.

A few snorkelers swimming on the surface aren't a lot of entertainment for an active young dolphin. They quickly become bored and disappear. If you want them to hang around a little longer you'll have to do something to hold their interest: diving, swimming in spirals, loops, or anything else that you can think of. I had good luck on one trip using a Dacor's Seasprint — a small hand-held underwater scooter. Dolphins flocked to me as soon as I entered the water with it — they seemed to be attracted to the noise it made, and it held their interest. No mechanical device, however, can keep up with a dolphin after it decides that it has had enough.

Recommended operators:

- ✔ **Liveaboard:** Ocean Explorer, 14 South Via Lucinda, Stuart, FL 34996-6410; phone: 561-288-4262 or 1-800-338-9383; fax: 561-288-0183; e-mail: oceaexp@aol.com

- ✔ **Liveaboard:** Sea Fever, P.O. Box 398276, Miami Beach, FL 33239-0276; phone: 1-800-443-3837, or 954-202-5608; fax: 954-385-7175; e-mail: seafever.com; Web site: www.seafever.com

Manatees — Crystal River, Florida

There's only one word to describe a manatee, anthropomorphic as it may be — they are, well, sweet. So sweet, in fact, they should be at the head of the line if the meek really do inherit the earth. The manatee's gentle disposition and trusting nature, however, have led to a head-on collision with the juggernaut of human civilization, so the real question is whether they'll be around much longer, much less inherit anything.

For the time being, you can see them gathered around warm-water springs of central and southern Florida every winter. Manatees are unable to tolerate water that's colder than 68° for very long. As water temperatures in the Caribbean sink (between November and March), manatees congregate around Florida's springs, which maintain a constant temperature of 72°.

Manatees are almost always found in shallow rivers and estuaries, usually munching some aquatic plant. An adult is normally between 8 and 14 feet in length and can weigh up to 800 pounds. They appear in the green gloom like an enormous sausage with a flat tail, a pair of odd-looking flippers, and a sort-of walruslike face. But manatees are more closely related to elephants than they are to the cranky walrus — they are gentle, slow-moving, and some seem to enjoy having their rough pebbly-gray hide stroked. Manatees are one of the few marine creatures that it's okay to touch, but only if they'll let you. Don't chase or harass them, but if they come to you, you can pet them. If they don't completely charm you, you better hit the yellow-brick road with your brother the Tin Man and see if you can find a heart somewhere. Because manatees are so docile and gentle, they make the perfect big animal encounter for children and first-time snorkelers, and an unforgettable experience for anyone.

Crystal River, the best place to see manatees, is on the central west coast of Florida on highway 19, north of Tampa and southwest of Ocala (see Figure 13-2). If you and your buddy are the type who prefer to blaze your own trail, you can rent a kayak at the Paradise Park Marina and paddle over to King Spring where the manatees gather. Please obey the restrictions, though: Don't chase or harass the animals, and don't follow them if they enter the roped-off area immediately around the island — it's a manatee sanctuary.

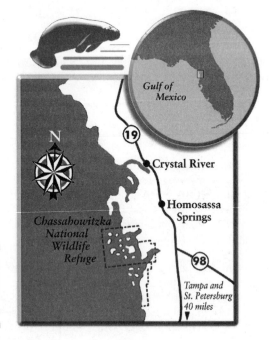

Figure 13-2:
Crystal
River,
Florida.

For a few extra bucks, you can go with a small group on a pontoon boat, which makes a great snorkeling platform complete with side curtains against the possibility of brisk winter winds. You also get a thermos of hot cocoa when you're ready to get out.

Recommended operators:

- **Land-based:** American Pro Dive, 821 SE Hwy 19, Crystal River, FL 34429; phone: 800-291-3483

- **Land-based:** Bird's Underwater, 8585 Pine Needle Terrace, Crystal River, FL 34428; phone: 904-563-2763

Stingray City — Grand Cayman

Stingray City is the most famous — and most photographed — site in the Cayman Islands. A white sand bottom, clear-blue waters, and hordes of hungry, but nonaggressive, southern stingrays make it popular among snorkelers and scuba divers alike (see the color insert for an example of diving at Stingray City).

Stingray City, shown in Figure 13-3, is in North Sound, on Grand Cayman Island, just inside another popular dive site — Tarpon Alley. The only drawback is that it gets pretty crowded. Everybody wants a piece of the action, and there's plenty of it. The rays here are completely comfortable with humans and to being hand-fed by divers. The rays gather here on a large sand flat in 12 to 15 feet of water and they don't wait to be invited. If you have food, they mob you immediately — gliding all around you, even bumping you and rubbing up against you. Even if they can't see the food, they can smell it. Don't worry, though, there're harmless enough, but if you insist on feeding the rays, keep the food out of sight until you're ready to offer it. When you do feed the rays, hold the food out in an open palm. Look out for the gangs of yellowtail snapper and blue tangs — tropical fish that get large and tend to get somewhat rambunctious in the feeding frenzy and don't always take the time to discriminate between fingers and fish sticks.

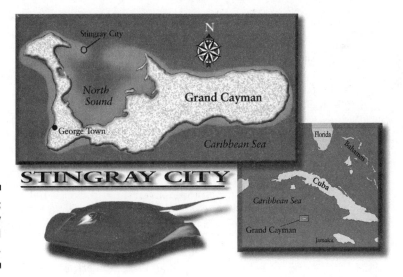

Figure 13-3:
Stingray
City, Grand
Cayman.

Southern stingrays are a fairly uniform gray or black on top, with white underneath. They grow to a maximum of 5 feet across, although the ones you see at Stingray City are generally a lot smaller. The females are larger than the males and both genders have a long thin tail that is tipped with a venomous barb, used for self-defense — most often when the animal is resting on the bottom.

Even though the rays at Stingray City are comfortable with divers, you should keep in mind they are still wild animals. Don't attempt to grab at them — you may find out more about their self-defense mechanism than you want to know. Allow them to come to you. They will, believe me. Don't pet them either, as tempting as that may be. All fish wear a protective coating of mucous — petting them rubs it off and makes them vulnerable to infection.

Recommended operators:

✔ There are so many dive operators on Grand Cayman, and so much competition for your tourist dollars, it's really tough to make a recommendation, so I won't. It's pretty hard to go wrong, but it's not impossible — ask around and compare.

Molokini — Maui, Hawaii

Little Molokini Island, an arid, crescent-shaped sliver of land that's just 2 ¾ miles off Maui's Makena coast, is Hawaii's most spectacular marine reserve (see Figure 13-4). Molokini isn't renowned for any large marine species — although with some luck you may spot mantas, whale sharks, or (at the right time of year) humpback whales — it's just a really neat place to dive and snorkel. In fact, the only thing wrong with Molokini is that so many people agree with me. It gets really crowded, but it's still worth the trip.

Leave as early in the day as you can. Lots of day boats leave from Makena Beach; book passage with the earliest one. Call around for departure times and prices, and book the night before. Usually the boat provides coffee and a continental breakfast, all of your gear, and lunch afterward for around $50 per person — somewhat less for children. Even the trip over is delightful, lying in the protected waters of the Alalakeiki Channel, surrounded by Maui, Kahoolawe, and Lanai. The seas are nearly always calm, and in the winter there's a good chance that you can spot humpbacks on the way.

After the day-boat fleet arrives, you may have some trouble finding a place to enjoy Molokini without a couple dozen pairs of fins churning the water like a Mississippi paddlewheeler everywhere you look. That's the time to get out and take a little lunch break. The majority of snorkelers who visit stay in the

Figure 13-4:
Molokini
Island, off
the Makena
coast of
Maui.

water less than half an hour. If you're patient, take a long lunch break, and find a captain who's willing to cooperate, you can get back in the water again when the frenzy starts to tail off.

Within its encircling arms, Molokini shelters an interior bay that's relatively shallow, sloping down to about 120 feet at the open end. The bottom is sand, coral reef, coral rubble, and sand channels. Because of its distance from the larger island, the visibility is almost always good — sometimes spectacular. Molokini's clear, clean water is ideal for coral formation, and healthy corals provide habitat for other kinds of marine life. Nearly all of Hawaii's marine species are represented here, many of them *endemic* (found nowhere else). And the island attracts plenty of open ocean visitors as well — humpbacks, whale sharks, mantas, turtles, dolphins, and even monk seals. With a little luck, patience, and good timing, you may encounter one of these species and take home your own magical Molokini memories.

Molokini is also a great dive site for scuba if you're a certified diver.

Recommended operator:

✔ **Land-based:** Mike Severns Diving, P.O. Box 627, Kihei, Hawaii 96753; phone: 808- 879-6596; fax: 808-874-6428

Humpback Whales — SilverBank and Tonga

You may see humpback whales in Maui, but you won't be able to get anywhere near them in the water. Hawaiian whales are vigorously protected by United States law — coming too close to them in the water is considered harassment and can subject you to a serious fine or jail time. That isn't the case everywhere in the world, however. If you want a more intimate view of humpys, your best options at present are the waters of the Silver Bank, in the tropical Atlantic, northeast of the Dominican Republic, and in the waters around the island of Tonga in the South Pacific. (See Figure 13-5 for maps of both areas.)

Both of these whale populations have become somewhat comfortable in the presence of snorkelers, and the laws of these countries allow for limited encounters with the whales. For their part, the whales don't seem to mind the presence of a few snorkelers. They tend to regard their distant terrestrial cousins with anything from indifference to mild curiosity. Obviously, if you

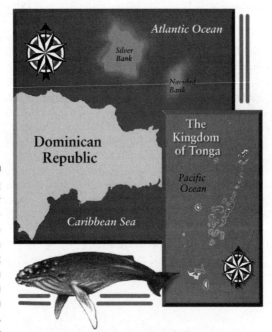

Figure 13-5:
The Silver Bank, northeast of the Dominican Republic; the Kingdom of Tonga in the South Pacific.

have the rare privilege of getting in the water with these remarkable animals, you should behave as a polite guest. Don't chase or harass them in any way — it's not really smart to get a 40-foot, 30-ton animal mad at you.

Fortunately, humpbacks appear to be amazingly tolerant and gentle creatures, and even though you may have seen them in all kinds of films and photos, you're never really properly awe-stricken until you look into the ancient and mysterious eyes of one of these immense, powerful mammals — no film or poster can prepare you for that.

Snorkeling with humpbacks is real adventure, but you should wait until you've gained a good deal of snorkeling experience and feel very comfortable in the water before you attempt it — not so much because of the whales, but because these encounters take place in deep-blue water, some distance from shore, often in currents or choppy seas. These are strictly liveaboard trips, so you have to be comfortable living in a boat, as well.

Recommended operator:

 ↙ **Liveaboard:** Predators, Mammals and Us, 2000 Broadway, Suite 1204, San Francisco, CA 94115; phone: 415-923-9865; fax: 415-776-8489.

Bunaken Island — Indonesia

Tiny Bunaken Island is one of a cluster of small islands in Manado Bay, off the northern tip of the larger Sulawesi Island, that make up the Bunaken-Manado Tua National Marine Park in Indonesia (see Figure 13-6). These islands are uniquely positioned on the edge of the rather deep waters of the Sulawesi Sea, and nutrients from these deep waters well up to nourish the most diverse community of marine life in the world.

Bunaken is a small, crescent-shaped island, surrounded by a flourishing coral reef that drops off in a steep wall. The island forms a bay on the south coast and the protected reef flats there provide the best snorkeling. The adventure starts as soon as you hit the water — if you're working on a list of the unusual for your log, you'll be able to write in a few, normally deep-water gorgonian corals that can be found along the edge of the wall, very close to the surface.

Bunaken isn't spectacular because of a particular species; it's spectacular because there are so many species in such abundance. Both soft and hard corals crowd the reef, swarming with huge schools of butterflyfish, triggerfish, and anthias. Along the edge of the wall, divers often see barracuda, rays, sharks, eels, turtles, and other relatively large marine animals.

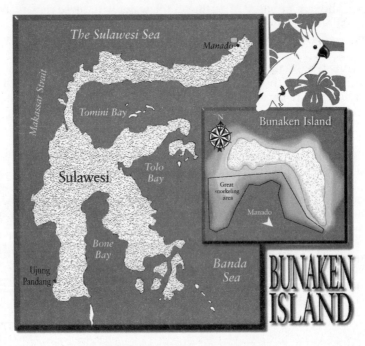

Figure 13-6:
Bunaken and the islands of Manado Tua-Bunaken Marine Park.

Not only is Bunaken gorgeous below the waterline, it's lovely topside, as well. Bunaken Island itself is a low coral island with beautiful, white-sand beaches, dotted with coconut palms. In the distance, the towering volcanic cone of dormant Manado Tua adds a dramatic touch. Day trips can be arranged from the city of Manado, where you can find an abundance of accommodations and restaurants. Manado itself is one of the most picturesque cities in Indonesia and because it has more in common with the cities of the Philippines than it does to Jakarta, it's an Indonesian city where Westerners usually feel relatively comfortable.

Recommended operators:

- **Land-based:** Nusantara Diving Center, Molas Beach. P.O. Box 1015, Manado, Indonesia 95242; phone: 63988; fax: 60368 or 63688
- **Land-based:** Murex, P.O. Box 236, Manado, Indonesia 95123; phone: 66280; fax: 52116

Sperm Whales — the Azores

Snorkeling with the pods of sperm whales that gather near the Azores, a group of islands in the North Atlantic, about 600 miles off the coast of Portugal (see Figure 13-7), is another opportunity to swim with some of the ocean's largest and most impressive creatures. It's also one of those trips where you should have some experience in the water before you attempt it. As with the humpbacks, these encounters take place in deep water, often in choppy seas.

The whales you see on these trips are normally pods of females and their calves. They're a lot smaller than the mature males who average 50 feet in length and weigh in at a svelte 40 tons, but they're still plenty impressive. Sperm whales are impressive in a lot of other ways, too: They're the largest of the toothed whales and the deepest diving mammal known (depths of 7,400 feet have been recorded). Don't worry, you won't have to go down there looking for them. The females and their calves, or *nursery pods* as they're called, spend most of their time lounging on the surface. Even when the females dive to feed, they leave at least one adult on the surface to baby-sit the calves.

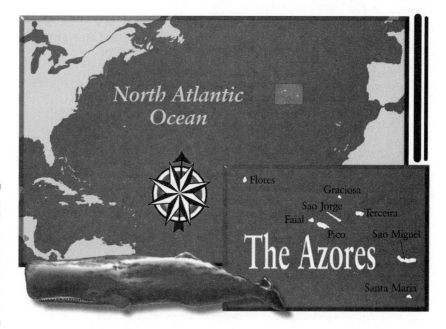

Figure 13-7:
Pods of sperm whales in the Azores offer real adventure to snorkelers.

Sperm whales have a reputation for being ferocious and evil-tempered, but the reputation is mostly a holdover from whaling days, and is largely unwarranted. A sperm whale may try to defend its life when chased and harpooned, but not many people consider that evil anymore. In fact, nursery pods seem to regard their old nemesis, man, with benign indifference, at least when you're in the water on snorkel gear — a more forgiving attitude than some species I can think of.

Sperm whales have a complex social structure that's organized much the same as that of elephants. The nursery pods are made up of mature females, their calves, and immature whales of both sexes. These groups share matrilineal heritage and generally stay in warm equatorial waters where ocean upwelling provides good food sources. When the males of these groups get to be about six years old, they head to the temperate and polar regions in bachelor pods. For the next 10 to 15 years, they hang together eating, playing, and growing. They are sexually mature in their teens but can't really compete with the mature males for breeding rights until they reach their mid-20s. It's somewhat less likely that you'll see a male sperm whale, but in the Azores they show up every year between January and July when the females are ready to mate. If you do see a male, you'll know it — the males are a lot bigger than the females.

Always exercise caution in the water with sperm whales. Even if the animal doesn't have any malicious intentions, a creature that large and powerful can wreak serious injury and death quite by accident. Be safe.

Recommended operator:

✔ **Liveaboard:** Predators, Mammals and Us, 2000 Broadway, Suite 1204, San Francisco, CA 94115. Phone: 415-923-9865; Fax: 415-776-8489.

Jellyfish Lake — Palau

Palau is one of the most unique and beautiful places in the world. It is world famous as a scuba diving destination, but if there ever were a place custom-tailored as a snorkelers paradise, it would look a lot like Palau. Palau is an elongated archipelago of islands encircled by a huge reef (see Figure 13-8). Among the many islands, in the calm waters of the lagoon, you can splash down almost anywhere and witness one of the most diverse marine environments in the world, but Palau ups the ante by providing one of the most unique topside environments in the world as well — the Rock Islands.

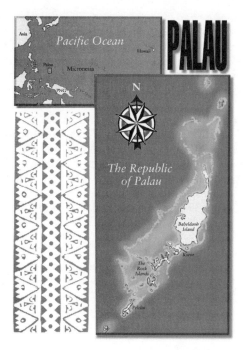

Figure 13-8:
The
Republic of
Palau.

The Rock Islands are the remains of ancient coral reefs that were raised by volcanic uplifting millions of years ago. Since then, they have been sculpted and undercut by erosion into fantastic shapes — some are huge and thick with impenetrable jungle; others are barely big enough for a single, scrawny coconut tree. Most of the islands are uninhabited and in the maze of twisting waterways between them, they conceal caves, passages, and perfect, secluded white-sand beaches overhung with dense rainforest that teems with cockatoos, parrots, and giant fruit bats. That alone makes for a pretty fantastic day's snorkeling — kayaking and snorkel trips through the islands are becoming increasingly popular. But secluded among the islands is another of Palau's mysterious secrets and one of the most unusual snorkeling adventures anywhere in the world — the jellyfish lakes.

Millions of years ago, when geologic forces uplifted the Rock Islands, small saltwater lakes were isolated in the deeper depressions. A few species were trapped in these lakes as well, but without much food, not many survived. One of the few that did are jellyfish of the genus Mastigias, and they managed it by making some radical adaptations. Over time, they developed a symbiotic relationship with an algae living within their tissues. The algae capture sunlight and provide nutrients for the jellyfish through photosynthesis. In return, the jellyfish swim near the surface of the lake during the day and move the algae around so they can get optimum sunlight. In the absence of predators and the need to capture food, the jellyfish have lost their stinging tentacles. Snorkeling in one of Palau's jellyfish lakes, surrounded tens of thousands of these harmless, pulsating little golden blobs, bumping into you and sliding across the back of your neck and along your arms and legs, is one of the most bizarre and unforgettable experiences you may ever have in snorkeling gear.

You need a guide to find one of these lakes, and after you get to an island containing one, you still face something of a challenge getting to it. They all require a hike through dense jungle on a wet, slippery trail lined with wicked limestone daggers, sculpted from the base rock by erosion. If that isn't bad enough, one species of rainforest tree oozes a poisonous black sap that raises a fiery rash and blisters like super poison oak. Be careful where you put your hands.

After you make it to the lake, you may have to swim around some before you find the jellyfish — they migrate across the surface during daylight hours to stay in optimum sunlight. After you do, you're in for an amazing experience. Keep in mind that Mastigias are a delicate species. Swim with care so as not to damage them. I recommend that you wear just one fin in the lake. This will prevent you from accidentally scissoring the jellies.

Recommended operator:

✔ **Land-based:** Sam's Dive Tours, P.O. Box 428, Koror, Republic of Palau 96940; phone: 680-488-1062; fax: 680-488-5003; e-mail: samstour@palaunet.com

Whale Sharks — Western Australia

The whale shark is world's biggest fish — up to 50 feet long and weighing as much as 50,000 pounds. Impressive numbers, but they don't even begin to capture the thrill of swimming alongside one of these monsters. It is one of the greatest and most sought-after experiences in the world of diving. Whale sharks are found in all the world's tropical and temperate oceans, except the Mediterranean, most often near reefs, and often as solitary individuals. It's difficult to predict where and when you may find a whale shark, but the coral spawn on Ningaloo reef in Western Australia, following the March full moon, draws large numbers in to feed, making it the most dependable spot in the world for spotting the big sharks.

Western Australia's whale shark adventure begins in the town of Exmouth, a remote, arid, windswept, red-earth outpost on Northwest Cape (see Figure 13-9). The reef runs very close to shore here, and the whale sharks come in to feed between February and May, peaking during the coral spawn in March. In spite of their size, whale sharks are hard to spot from the water or from a boat. Most of the operators use spotter planes to help with the search. When the plane locates a shark, its position is radioed back to the boat; the boat then circles around in front of the shark and the divers enter the water. As the shark approaches, the divers swim along, keeping up as best they can. (See the color section of this book for an example.) Even though a whale shark appears to be cruising along at a leisurely rate, it's usually faster than divers can maintain for very long. The boat picks up the stragglers, and then circles ahead of the shark again. This game of leap frog continues as long as the shark allows it to. This is an adventure for the more-experienced snorkeler. Keeping up with a whale shark can be a demanding job and the seas are often choppy.

Your first view of a whale shark can be a stunning event — looming up out of the blue gloom surrounded by schools of smaller fish and covered with clinging fish called *remoras* (also known as sharks suckers) like a whole reef on the move — a reef with a enormous gaping mouth that can be almost 10 feet

Figure 13-9:
Ningaloo reef in Western Australia is the most dependable place in the world to sight whale sharks.

wide and lined with thousands teeth! Wow! Before you panic and exit the water like a Polaris missile, you should know that whale sharks, like most of the oceans biggest residents, feed exclusively on the oceans smallest critters — plankton, and very small schooling fish. They aren't the least bit interested in having any terrestrial primates on the menu, and you can't even see their teeth — the biggest ones are only about a 10th of an inch long.

Like lots of other aquatic creatures, whale sharks are distinctly *countershaded* — light-colored on the bottom and dark on the top. The head is the broadest part of the body, tapering to a tall *semi-lunate* (crescent moon-shaped) tail. The body has a number of distinct longitudinal ridges, and the dark-colored back is speckled with pale yellow and white spots.

Whale sharks vary widely in temperament. Some are wary and hard to get close to; some seem completely indifferent to divers and allow them to approach quite closely. You may have even seen pictures of divers hitching a ride by clinging to the shark's dorsal fin. Don't do this. Even if the shark tolerates it, it's not a good idea. Apart from being against the local laws and adding stress to the shark, when you do release your grip, as you must eventually, or if the shark decides to bolt, you're in a pretty good position to get yourself slapped silly by its enormously powerful tail.

Recommended operator:

✔ **Land-based:** Exmouth Diving Centre, Payne St., Exmouth, Western Aus. 6707; phone: 011-61-08-9949-1201; fax: 011-61-08-9949-1680. e-mail: bookings@exmouthdiving.com.au

Lizard Island — Queensland, Australia

Any list of great snorkeling spots has to include the Great Barrier Reef (GBR), but at 1,200 miles long, the GBR gives you plenty of options to choose from. Shuttling divers and snorkelers out to the barrier reef is a major industry in towns like Cairns, Townsville, and Port Douglas in Northern Queensland, and any one of them would make a good choice for a dive or snorkel holiday. If you want something really spectacular and just a little different, though, consider Lizard Island, shown in Figure 13-10.

Lizard is further north than any of the other resort islands on the barrier reef, and closer to the barrier reef than any of the other continental islands. It's not cheap, and you're not paying for luxury either — the resort (the only one

Figure 13-10:
Lizard Island, the premier far north Queensland resort, has great snorkeling and is only minutes from some of the best sites on the Great Barrier Reef.

on the island) is nice, but it isn't fancy. What you get is location, location, location — an isolated island paradise just a short hop from some of the best spots on the barrier reef, loaded with perfect beaches and superb snorkeling off every one.

The island has its own airport and that's how most guests arrive. There's no regular ferry service. The flight's an hour from Cairns, and like everything about Lizard, it's not cheap. Most visitors stay at the resort — it's the only one on the island, but it isn't the only place to stay. You can camp on the island in a small campground at the north end of Watson's Bay, but you need to get a camping permit in Cairns first. The campground has water, but you'll have to bring everything else you need and take your trash with you when you go. Don't expect to be welcomed at the resort. For all of these reasons, not many people opt for the camping option.

If you stay at the resort, you can find great snorkeling right in front, along the northeast shore of tiny Osprey Island. If you prefer complete seclusion, it won't be hard to find either. The resort only has 40 rooms and is a short walk to Sunset, Pebbly, or Hibiscus beaches, a little to the south, all of which will quickly relieve any congestion. If you're feeling particularly antisocial, head over to the other side of the island to Trawler Beach or Coconut Beach. With a dingy or a kayak, you can explore the virtually unlimited possibilities of the north point or the Blue Lagoon to the south. All of the water sports equipment is included in the resort price.

Scuba diving boats cost extra, but you should tag along at least once when the day boat is running divers out to the famous sites, like Cod Hole or the Ribbon Reefs on the Great Barrier Reef. The water is spectacularly clear; the marine diversity and numbers are astonishing. The reef is nearly pristine and if you get a really good day, you'll remember it for the rest of your life. Some of the scuba diving sites on the GBR are good snorkeling sites, as well. Cod Hole, for example, is the home of a gang of giant groupers (up to 6 feet long) that have become completely habituated to handouts from visiting divers. It's a famous dive site, but it's also a great for snorkelers and more-experienced free divers. The dive is only about 30 feet and the groupers, or *potato cod* as they're known Down Under, come nearly to the surface looking for a handout.

If you stay at the resort, you'll go out on to the reef on their day boat, or use one of the dinghies that's included in the price. It's also possible to book day passage to Lizard and the nearby reef out of Cairns.

Recommended operator (the *only* operator!):

✔ **Land-based:** Lizard Island Resort, Private Mail Bag 40, Cairns, Queensland, Australia, 4870; phone: 011-61-070-60-3999; fax: 011-61-070-60-3991

Chapter 14

Ten Rules of Safe Diving

In This Chapter

▶ Getting proper training and using the right equipment

▶ Remembering to *never* hold your breath while scuba diving

▶ Diving with a buddy and a good dive plan

▶ Aborting or canceling a dive when necessary

▶ Diving deepest first, and then ascending slowly

Diving is quite safe — and a lot of fun — when you observe the rules of safe diving. This chapter gives you ten ways that you can minimize the inherent risks of diving.

Get Proper Training

You don't need to have official training to snorkel. Lots of people teach themselves how to snorkel, but most certifying agencies can teach you how, if you prefer.

Don't assume, however, that because you flip through this book or have a cousin who shows you how to use his regulator in the pool, that you're prepared to try open water scuba diving. It's great that you're interested in scuba and want to do it, but your next step should be to sign up with a legitimate certifying agency (see the Appendix for the list).

Certain activities in your daily life increase your level of risk — if you stay in your house all day, your level of risk is somewhat lower than if you take a walk down the street or drive your car to the mall. Scuba diving also elevates your level of risk, but not much — not as much as driving your car to the mall, anyway. Most people find these levels of risks acceptable. Without proper training, however, the risk is unacceptably high.

Use Proper Equipment

Use complete and correct equipment that's well-maintained. Examine and test the equipment before you go diving, particularly if you haven't used it in a while. Have your equipment periodically inspected and serviced by a qualified technician.

Don't loan your equipment to anybody who isn't certified and don't use it for any purpose for which it isn't intended. You don't want your name showing up on that list of Darwin awards — awards given to those who have done the most to improve the human gene pool (by eliminating themselves from it through a particularly ludicrous act of idiocy).

Never Hold Your Breath While Scuba Diving

Your regulator is designed to deliver air at the same pressure as the surrounding water. If you hold your breath and ascend with that air in your lungs, the air is going to expand and very bad things are going to happen. The solution? Don't hold your breath. Simple. Breathe normally and continuously whenever you have a regulator in your mouth — problem solved!

Okay, I hear you saying, "But my cousin Mergatroid (the same guy who loans his equipment to uncertified divers) told me he held his breath when he saw a bunch of hammerheads so the bubbles wouldn't scare them away, and nothing happened to him. He's fine. Well, he kind of drools a lot, but he did that before." Yeah, some divers do hold their breath and live to tell the tale — that doesn't make it a good idea. So, keep it simple — *never hold your breath while using scuba.*

And while we're on the subject, don't hyperventilate excessively when you're free diving — see Chapter 1 for more on hyperventilating properly.

Don't Dive Alone

Always dive with a buddy — hopefully one who knows you and your abilities, and has approximately the same interests and level of experience. There is a growing cult of solo divers, and maybe after a couple of hundred dives you'll start turning into one of these misanthropic cranks yourself. If so, do everybody a favor and keep it to yourself — this kind of pointless adventuring can have unintended consequences.

Dive with a buddy. Solo diving doesn't make you some kind of romantic hero; it makes you a fool.

Plan Your Dive

Underwater, communication is somewhat limited. If you have a plan that both you and your buddy understand, you're a lot less likely to run into trouble.

- ✔ Familiarize yourselves with the diving area.
- ✔ Agree on time and depth limits, and go over emergency procedures before the dive.
- ✔ Review the hand signals (see Chapter 5).

Know your limitations and keep your plan within them. (See Chapter 4 for more information on dive plans.) Remember that time-honored axiom of dive instructors everywhere: "Plan the dive, dive the plan." Often, divers have a great plan, but when things change underwater, they abandon it. This is when problems arise.

Don't Be Afraid to Cancel a Dive

Evaluate your skills and the conditions, honestly and objectively. It's no fun to get underwater and feel stressed during the entire dive, or worse, have the situation get out of control. Diving is full of unknowns, so don't put yourself in a situation where you won't be able to handle an emergency if it should arise.

Don't Be Afraid to Abort a Dive

 If you're uncomfortable or don't feel up to a particular dive for any reason, don't hesitate to abort the dive and return to the boat or shore. There's no good reason to do it if you're not having fun. It's only going to sour the experience for you. The ocean will still be there the next time.

Do the Deepest Part of Your Dive First

The deeper you go and the longer you stay, the more nitrogen you absorb. The more nitrogen you absorb, the more nitrogen you have to eliminate from your tissues to reduce the risk of decompression sickness (see Chapter 7). By doing the deepest part of your dive first, you minimize your nitrogen absorption and facilitate the off-gassing process.

Don't Touch Anything

Lots of marine creatures bite or sting, and many of them are venomous. Even if the creatures won't harm you, the odds are pretty good that you won't be doing them any good by handling them. By keeping your hands to yourself, you won't stress the marine life or put yourself at risk.

Ascend Slowly

Don't wait until you've exhausted your air. Begin your ascent when you and your buddy still have sufficient air remaining in your tanks. Go slowly, no faster than 1 foot per second, and look to the surface for obstacles or boat traffic. Make a safety stop at 15 feet for 3 minutes before you surface. (See Chapter 5 for more on ascending safely.)

Chapter 15

Ten Great Dive Destinations

In This Chapter

▶ Diving the legendary sites

▶ Exploring historical wrecks

▶ Discovering my ten top diving destinations

Anyone who has been diving a while develops his own list of favorite places. You will undoubtedly develop yours, too. As the editor of a dive magazine, I've had the privilege of developing my list from dive destinations all over the world. This chapter lists the places that I like. I chose them because I think they are great overall diving destinations, or because they offer something really unique. I've been to plenty of places that I have no desire to go back to, but I'd be on a plane tomorrow to any of the destinations in the chapter, if I had the chance.

Blue Corner — Palau

Palau has a reputation for being one of the best dive destinations in the world and much of that reputation is the result of just one site — Blue Corner. Blue Corner takes its name from an underwater coral peninsula forming a 90-degree angle that juts out into deep blue water at the top a vertical wall on the southern end of the surrounding reef. The drop-off plunges over a thousand feet to the ocean floor, and the incoming tide pulls upwelling waters from the deep and over the top of the wall. Tiny marine organisms feed in the nutrient-rich current, supporting a whole pyramid of larger and larger predators, topped by sharks — lots and lots of sharks.

Dozens of blacktips, whitetips, and big gray reef sharks stalk silently in the current. And it isn't just sharks. Enormous schools of just about everything in the Western Pacific with fins crowd in on you as you tumble head over teakettle along a dizzying walls that are jammed with giant sea fans and dripping colored soft corals as big as an English oak. People say that you used to be able to see marlin, sailfish, and big schools of tuna, too, but that's become rare since the long-line fishing boats began working the waters. Old-timers like to tell you how much better Blue Corner was ten years ago. That may be true, but even today, anyone who can't get excited about a dive at Blue Corner should check his pulse.

Palau lies in the far Western Pacific, north of the Irian Jaya half of the Papua New Guinea Isle and east of the Philippines (see Figure 15-1). It's the most fertile and diverse area of the world ocean. Typically, dive boats tie up along the wall and the divers follow the mooring line down to the drop-off of the wall. The current is quite strong, so it's important to stay with your buddy. Divers drift along the wall out to the tip of the corner at whatever depth they choose with the wall on the right, the open ocean on the left, and the fish everywhere. The wall is absolutely choked with sea fans and soft corals, and just about everything else that lives in the sea. It doesn't matter what depth you choose to view it, but most divers stay around 70 feet to conserve air.

Figure 15-1:
Blue Corner
and the
dives on the
southern
reef of
Palau.

When you reach the corner, you allow the current to push you over the top, and most divers hang on to the edge of the wall to watch the show until their air gets low. If you want to see a good example of why you shouldn't touch the coral, the top of the Blue Corner wall is it. In fact, the coral is so trashed by thousands of groping human hands, there has been talk of installing a permanent railing for divers to hang onto — kind of an undersea hitching post — a bizarre concept if there ever was one.

In spite of the damage that has been wrought, Blue Corner is still one of the finest dives in the world, and that is exactly the problem — the place is being loved to death. At times, up to 25 dive boats are moored over the site — and all those divers are in the water. Blue Corner may be one of those places that needs to institute some kind of controls to save the area.

The easiest way to get to Palau is to fly directly to Guam, from Honolulu (about 7 ½ hours), overnight in Guam, and then on to Palau (about 2 hours).

Recommended operators:

- ✔ **Land-based:** Sam's Dive Tours, P.O. Box 428, Koror, Republic of Palau, 96940; phone: 011-680-488-1062 or 1-800-794-9767; fax: 011-680-488-5003

- ✔ **Land-based:** Fish 'n' Fins, P.O. Box 142, Koror, Republic of Palau, 96940; phone: 011-680-488-2637; fax: 011-680-488-1070

Chuuk Lagoon — Chuuk

The state of Chuuk (pronounced "chuke"), one of the Federated States of Micronesia, is made up of about a dozen small islands inside of an enormous lagoon, with a few islands that lie outside. Chuuk, like Palau, is part of the Micronesian island chain (see Figure 15-2) — about a thousand miles to the east — but its diversity is nowhere near what you'll find in Palau. Chuuk isn't the kind of place that will overwhelm you with its fascinating topside attractions. Still, it has something that you won't find in Palau, or anywhere else in the world for that matter, and that particular feature has made it one of the world's most popular diving destinations — the ghost fleet of Chuuk lagoon — the largest and most spectacular collection of sunken war wrecks anywhere in the world.

Chuuk's wrecks are largely the result of a single military action in February, 1944. A United States naval bombing raid, code-named Operation Hailstorm, surprised and sank most of the Japanese combined fleet anchored in Chuuk lagoon. By the time it was over, more than 60 Japanese ships lay on the bottom. Today they form an underwater museum and artificial reef teeming with fish and hung with brilliant soft corals where visiting divers can marvel at the triumph of life — and the shattered wreckage of war — at the same

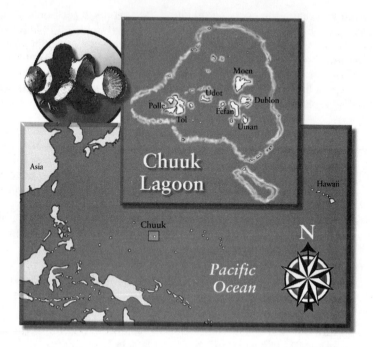

Figure 15-2:
Chuuk
lagoon,
home of the
world's best
wreck
diving.

time. The holds of many ships are still filled with trucks, tanks, boxes of
ammunition, and other materials of war, and in some of the twisted holds and
blasted decks are the more mundane and haunting articles of everyday life —
bicycles, lanterns, dishes in the galleys, and in some of the ships, skeletal
remains.

There are wrecks in the lagoon for every level of experience — some that can
even be visited by snorkelers. The current is not a problem inside the lagoon.
Waters are generally calm and still, but visibility is generally more limited
than in the open ocean waters of the Western Pacific — 60 to 100 feet, as
opposed to 80 to 150. Novice divers can dive some of the wrecks — they
aren't deep and they don't involve penetration of the wreck — while others
shouldn't be attempted by anybody but an expert. Keep in mind there is no
recompression chamber on Chuuk, so you must mind your computer and
dive conservatively. Don't attempt wreck penetration unless you are specially
trained to do so. (See Chapters 10 and 12 for more information on wreck
diving.)

Chuuk is unquestionably the finest wreck diving destination in the world.
Lots of places have started the practice of scuttling obsolete vessels offshore

to create artificial reefs and thereby attract divers, but Chuuk is the real thing. All of the wrecks in Chuuk are part of an historic underwater park, and are protected by law. You must be accompanied by an official guide when you visit the wrecks and no artifacts of any kind may be removed. The sense of authentic drama and history that permeates the remains of these great, creepy, juggernauts of war cannot be duplicated in an underwater junkyard. If you're into wreck diving, you must one day dive in Chuuk. Fly direct to Guam from Honolulu (7 ½ hours), and then to Chuuk (1 ½ hours).

Recommended operators:

- ✔ **Liveaboard:** SS Thorfinn, c/o Seaward Holidays, P.O. Box DX, Moen, Chuuk, FSM, 96942; phone: 011-691-330-4253; fax: 011-691-330-4253

- ✔ **Land-based:** Blue Lagoon Dive Shop, P.O. Box 429, Chuuk, FSM, 96942; phone: 011-691-330-2769

Palancar Reef — Cozumel

Cozumel diving is widely considered the best in the Caribbean — a claim that's difficult to dispute. What makes Cozumel so good is the most famous of all ocean currents — the Gulf Stream. It sweeps around the island from south to north supplying a steady, year-round flow of warm, clear water, nourishing the marine life, and ensuring that nearly all diving in Cozumel is drift diving. If you're not comfortable whizzing along in a brisk current, you can find plenty of tamer dives on the inner reef, but you won't see the best stuff that Cozumel has to offer that way. (Chapter 10 has more on drift dives.)

The best dives take place on the outer reef, along the southwest tip of the island, and the finest of the sites out there is the Palancar Reef (see Figure 15-3). Palancar is three miles of coral canyons, arches, tunnels, and overhangs, festooned with giant sea fans, sea whips, huge colored tube and barrel sponges, and swarming with groupers, lobsters, morays, parrotfish, grunts, porkfish, and all the other familiar Caribbean species you have (or will) come to know and love.

Naturally, all this fine submarine terrain, in conjunction with fantastic package deals and a relatively short flight from the United States (less than two hours from Houston, Texas), makes Cozumel one of the most popular dive destinations in the world. Fortunately, Cozumel's reefs are spacious, and there is enough wide-open underwater range to satisfy even the most lonesome regulator cowboy, but with all those divers lining up for splashdown, it can get crowded, especially during the high season — December to May.

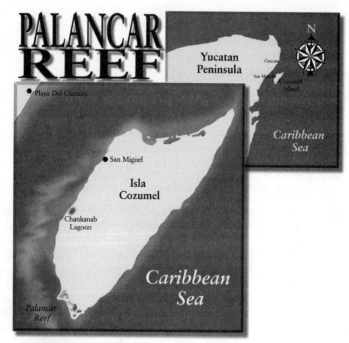

Dive shops have sprouted up in San Miguel (Cozumel's only real city) like mushrooms after a spring rain — but all dive operators are not created equal, an axiom that is especially true in Cozumel. Rumor holds that fly-by-night operators without a clue have been known to follow the dive boats of their more-experienced competitors just to find a decent site — obviously this can add considerably to the congestion at a particular site. Spend a little time shopping for your operator — the good ones see to it that you get what you pay for during your time on the reef. Make some calls (nearly all of them have 800-numbers), and if you don't get the answers you like, try somebody else. Of course, the easiest way to go is to sign on with one of the great package tours. You generally save money and grief — these people know the island and steer clear of the bogus operators.

Recommended operators:

- ✔ **Land-based:** Del Mar Aquatics, P.O. Box 129, Cozumel, Quintana Roo, Mexico, 77600; phone: 800-692-3422 or 011-52-987-21833

- ✔ **Land-based:** Dive Palancar, Diamond Resort, Cozumel, Quintana Roo, Mexico, 77600; phone: 800-433-0885

- ✔ **Land-based:** Dive Paradise, 601 Melgar, Cozumel, Quintana Roo, Mexico, 77600; phone: 011-52-987-21007; fax: 011-52-987-21061; e-mail: applep@cozumel.czm.com.mx; **Web site:** www.dparadise.com

Galapagos Islands — Ecuador

The Galapagos Islands were made famous as the inspiration for Charles Darwin's theory of natural selection, originally presented in his seminal work *The Origin of the Species.* A genius like Darwin may have cooked up his theory in any number of places in the Pacific, but the Galapagos, with a remarkably high count of quirky and specifically adapted species, certainly made it easier. That much, at least, hasn't changed on these unique islands, 600 miles west off the coast of Ecuador, bisected by the equator, and swimming in the confluence of three distinct and fertile ocean currents (see Figure 15-4).

Underwater, these waters provide more nonstop action than a Schwarzenegger film festival, including big schools of the ever-reclusive hammerhead sharks, schools of cownose rays numbering in the hundred, the rare king angelfish, as well as numerous other local oddities like the red-lipped batfish, the sally lightfoot crab, the marine iguana, and the Galapagos's own unique brand of sea lions and penguins.

Figure 15-4:
The Galapagos Islands.

There aren't a lot of beginner dives in the Galapagos. The islands are rugged, they don't have the fringing coral reefs and lagoons typically found in other tropical dive destinations, and they are swept by powerful currents. The currents are not only strong, they're weird and unpredictable — they can go more directions than the wash water in your Lady Kenmore — up, down, side to side — sometimes all in the same dive. You should probably wait to visit the Galapagos until you've gained some diving experience.

The Galapagos are best dived by liveaboard (see Chapter 4 for more on liveaboard diving). The islands are 97 percent national park, and what accommodations there are on land don't necessarily cater to the whims of divers. Furthermore, the northern islands of Wolf and Darwin, where some of the best diving takes place, require a 16-hour crossing from San Christobal and the airport. In spite of the inconveniences, extended travel time, experience required, and other restrictions, the Galapagos will provide some of the most memorable diving of your life.

The Galapagos are reached by way of the international airport in either Quito or Guayaquil, and from there to San Christobal in the Galapagos.

Recommended operators:

✔ Use a liveaboard in the Galapagos. Book it through a good dive travel specialist.

Bunaken Island — Indonesia

North Sulawesi and the islands of the Bunaken-Manado Tua group are blessed with great conditions for diving. Bunaken Island lies about a mile offshore from the city of Manado, on the northern tip of the Indonesian island of Sulawesi (see Figure 15-5). The Sulawesi Sea, to the north, drops off into relatively deep water and the upwelling, nutrient-rich water nourishes the reefs around Bunaken. The place also benefits from being at the heart of the greatest diversity of marine life on the planet. Some estimates put the total number of fish species here at over 3,000 (new ones are still being discovered), and the number of coral species at over 500. By comparison, Palau, only 720 miles to the northeast, has only about 1,300 species of fish — less than half the number found in Bunaken Reserve.

Bunaken island is surrounded by good coral growth all the way around. The crescent-shaped island forms a bay along the south coast and conditions here are great for beginning divers — there is normally very little (if any) current, the water is warm and clear, and the marine life is abundant. The

Figure 15-5:
Bunaken
Island and
National
Marine
Park.

fringing reef forms a steep drop-off, and the surface is a living tapestry of
hard and soft corals, sponges, and every other kind of filter feeder in the sea.
The corals swarm with schools of anthias, pyramid butterflyfish, and black
triggerfish. Morays and sea snakes slither among the crevices and sharks,
barracuda and rays patrol the blue beyond.

You can explore at least seven different dive sites on the south side of
Bunaken, each with its own distinct character and charm. You can find several good sites on the north side as well, but the currents here are stronger
and conditions require a bit more experience.

Dive boats cross the channel daily from Manado to ferry divers to the sites at
Bunaken, and the other four islands that make up the reserve. Manado is best
reached by air from Jakarta or Manila. The easiest route is direct flight to
Manila, and then on to Manado.

Recommended operators:

- ✔ **Land-based:** Nusantara Diving Center, Molas Beach. P.O. Box 1015, Manado, Indonesia 95242. Phone: 63988; Fax: 60368, or 63688.

- ✔ **Land-based:** Murex, P.O. Box 236, Manado, Indonesia 95123. Phone: 66280; Fax: 52116.

Great Barrier Reef — Queensland, Australia

The Great Barrier Reef (GBR) is so big that you simply can't dive the whole thing in a single lifetime. From stem to stern, it's roughly the same length as the entire west coast of the United States. The GBR is the largest living thing in the world, the biggest barrier reef (or reef of any kind) in the known universe, and the only living thing on the planet that can be seen from an orbiting space shuttle. Even if you can't dive the whole thing, you can have a really good time with some localized exploration, picking and choosing your spots.

Even though you can see it from space, you can't usually see it from shore. That's because the reef lies a good 15 miles from shore, even in the far north, near Cooktown, where it comes in close. By the time you get to the southern end, 1,200 miles away, it's almost 180 miles offshore. You have a lot of choices in a place that big, but the most practical, from a diver's point of view, is the far north — from the towns of Cairns and Port Douglas (see Figure 15-6). The reef is close here and there are plenty of fast day boats to take you out to the reef, get in two or three dives, eat a picnic lunch, and get you back by dark.

Cairns is the largest city in the far north and its economy is almost entirely fueled by tourism. Divers make up a substantial percentage of the visitors, and the local diving industry is well-equipped to provide for your needs. Cairns is a modern city with its own international airport, plenty of accommodations, and lots of other fascinating attractions, such as bush walking and whitewater rafting, within striking distance. Port Douglas, on the other hand, is a smaller town, just up the coast. It's not as well-developed as Cairns, but it has its own day fleet running out to the reef, so it accesses sites further north that the boats out of Cairns do. Cairns also has a fine wreck dive accessible by day boat, the SS Yongala.

Generally, you have three options when selecting a day boat out of either city:

- ✔ **The big cats:** Large catamarans that transport 100 to 300 passengers out to the reef. They are very fast and usually moor at a permanent floating platform out on the reef. Many experienced divers turn up their noses at this option because these boats don't cater exclusively to divers. They also include snorkelers, along with people who don't plan to go in the water. Scuba divers are usually transferred to smaller dive boats, and taken to sites away from the crowd. Big catamarans can be a good value, especially if you're traveling with a nondiver.

- ✔ **Dedicated dive boats:** Very fast boats that visit more remote dive sites, further away from the platforms and the crowds. Experienced divers tend to favor this option. These boats cater to the desires of divers and can usually find whatever the day's party of divers wants to see.

- ✔ **Bargain boats:** Well, you get what you pay for. These guys are usually much slower than the other boats, so they don't generally make it to the outer reef, where you find the most spectacular diving. They rarely are able to do more than two dives and they often try to get as many passengers on board as possible, whether they're divers or not.

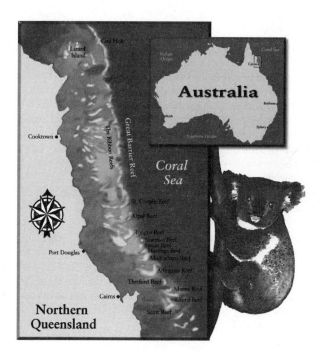

Figure 15-6: Cairns, Port Douglas, and the GBR in the far northern section of Queensland.

If the idea of shuttling back and forth to the reef every day (about 24 miles to the outer reef from Cairns) doesn't appeal to you, you have yet another option — book passage on a liveaboard. Some of these boats venture further out into the clear waters of the coral sea to more remote reefs like Holmes, Osprey, and Bouganville. These outer-reef destinations are more suited to experienced divers, but they also dive the protected, shallower sites of the inner reef, which are perfect for beginners. Before you book, make sure to talk to them about the level of diving that you're comfortable with.

Recommended operators:

- ✔ **Liveaboard:** Undersea Explorer, P.O. Box 5740, Cairns, Queensland, 4870; phone: 011-61-70-514777; fax: 011-61-70-514-888; e-mail: adventures@adventures.com.au; **Web site:** www.adventures.com.au

- ✔ **Land-based:** Quicksilver Diving Services, Marina Mirage, Port Douglas, Queensland; phone: 011-070-995-050; fax: 011-070-994-065

- ✔ **Land-based:** Deep Sea Divers Den, 319 Draper St., Cairns, Queensland; phone: 011-070-510-455

- ✔ **Land-based:** Pro Dive Cairns, Marlin Parade, Cairns, Queensland; phone: 011-070-315-255; fax: 011-070-519-955

Papua New Guinea

The island of Papua New Guinea (PNG) is the second largest island in the world (after Greenland), and is shared by Irain Jaya in the west (part of Indonesia) and the nation of Papua New Guinea in the east (see Figure 15-7). This is the part of the Western Pacific that has the greatest bio-diversity in the world. Expect great diving — you won't be disappointed. PNG is one of the last truly wild places on earth. Even today, the island still has villages that have only the most marginal contact with the outside world. Everything about the place seems to be overflowing with vitality — from the smoking volcanoes to the teeming reefs to the dizzying rainforests and colorful highland sing-sings.

All of that wildness comes with a price, however. PNG doesn't have the kind of tourist infrastructure that is commonplace in the rest of the world, and you may have to suffer some inconveniences. PNG is not the place to wing it, unless you're an expert at that kind of travel. Not only is it primitive, but it can be astonishingly expensive. Use the services of a dive travel specialist, and consider staying on a liveaboards — PNG has several, and this is a good place to try one out, if you haven't yet.

If you want to stay with a land-based operation, Madang, a town on the north central coast, is a pretty good bet, and Madang lagoon is swarming with marine life and a couple of WWII wrecks to boot. Madang is one of the most tourist-friendly towns in the country, but even there you can run into problems, so make sure that you have your stay completely lined-up before you get there. The diving makes whatever inconveniences you may suffer getting there, worth it.

Milne Bay, at the southeastern tip of the island, is also high on the greatest dives list. The strong currents in the China Strait nourish abundant marine life and brings in creatures, but this area is better suited to more advanced divers. Kimbe Bay and Walindi on New Britain Island, along with Kavieng on New Ireland also have great diving, and enough tourist infrastructure to keep you comfortable. Any of them make a good land base for a PNG dive adventure.

Figure 15-7:
Papua New
Guinea.

The reefs of PNG are strikingly similar to those of the northern Great Barrier Reef. This isn't really surprising, because the Torres Strait, separating PNG from Australia's Cape York Peninsula, is only a little more than 100 miles across, and the barrier reef itself extends nearly to the southern coast of Papua. Most ethnologists believe that Australia's aborigines and the Papuans share a common ancestry. The aborigines are believed to have crossed from PNG to the Australian continent at least 40,000 years ago during the last Ice Age. Of course, no such barrier exists for the creatures of the sea.

No visit to PNG would be complete without a visit to the highlands and the rainforests. PNG rainforests don't harbor large, spectacular mammals like tigers or orangutans, but the bird life and insects are among the most diverse and fascinating in the world. The unique culture, customs, and costume of the highland people is one of the country's great tourist attractions, and a must-see for anybody visiting the country. Try to schedule your visit so that you can see one of the highland *sing-sings* — these are big ceremonial get-togethers, during which local people sing and dance in native costume. Set it up beforehand and make sure you have a good guide.

Recommended operators:

  ✔ **Liveaboard:** M.V. Febrina, P.O. Box 4, Kimbe, West New Britain, PNG; phone: 011-675-983-5638; fax: 011-675-983-5441; e-mail: `cheryl.wpdc@r130.aone.net.au`

Finding more tour operators

PADI, the world's largest certifying agency, maintains a Web site and toll-free number that are jam-packed with information about dive tour operators. Although I've listed one or two recommended operators for each destination in this chapter, PADI offers a more comprehensive list — more than 400 PADI resorts in premier dive destinations around the world. Get in touch with them in one of three ways:

  ✔ Give them a call at 800-729-7234, extension 339, (toll free in the US only) or 949-858-7234, extension 339. They're available from 7 a.m. to 5 p.m Monday through Thursday, and 7 a.m. to 4 p.m. on Fridays — all Pacific standard time.

  ✔ Send them an e-mail at `trade@padi.com` with some basic information — desired location, number of divers and nondivers traveling, desired departure and return dates, preferred hotel accommodations (ocean view, budget, and so on). They'll provide you with a list of ideal resorts.

  ✔ Check out the PADI Travel Network Web site at `www.padi.com/PTN/`. There, you can use an online reservation form to request information about your potential dive destination.

✔ **Liveaboard:** M.V. Chertan, c/o Sea New Guinea Pty. Ltd., GPO Box 7002, Sydney, Australia, 2001; phone: 011-02-267-5563; fax: 011-02-267-6118

✔ **Land-based:** Walindi Resort, Febrina, P.O. Box 4, Kimbe, West New Britain, PNG; phone: 011-675-983-5638; fax: 011-675-983-5441; e-mail: cheryl.wpdc@r130.aone.net.au

Great White Wall — Fiji

There are a lot of great places to dive in Fiji — Bega, the Mamanuccas, Kadavu, Quamea, and, Taveuni, probably the best-known island for diving. You won't find such great diversity of species as you do further to the west, but it hardly matters. Fiji, shown in Figure 15-8, is blessed not only as a dive destination, but as precisely the kind of place people imagine when they think South Pacific paradise — beautiful islands surrounded by sparkling blue lagoons, white-sand beaches backed by shady groves of coconut palms, warm and charming native people — it's all here. Fiji also has the distinction of being one of the best places in the world to see soft corals.

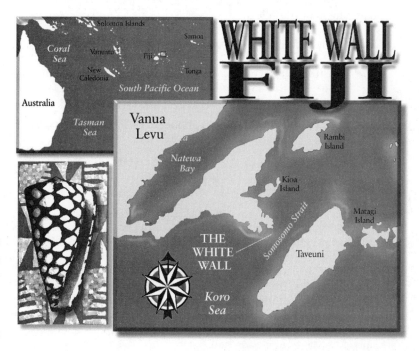

Figure 15-8: Fiji Islands and the Somo Somo Strait.

Soft corals are *filter feeders,* meaning that they thrive in places where strong currents bring them a continuous supply of food. Where there is good soft coral growth, there are generally strong and persistent currents. This is true throughout much of Fiji, so if you're not comfortable in a brisk current, this may not be the place for you. There are plenty of protected sites in Fiji, but you won't see the best diving that the place has to offer.

The best single site Fiji has to offer, in the opinion of many, is the Great White Wall with its soft corals. Between the islands of Taveuni and Vanua Levu, the narrow Somo Somo Strait funnels powerful currents that nourish an incredibly fertile reef. At its narrowest, the passage is a mere two miles — in this part of the reef you find the Great White Wall.

It's called the Great White Wall because the vertical face of the reef is densely covered with luminous, white, soft corals from about 75 feet down to about 220 — it's a breathtaking sight that you can't find anywhere else in the world. Soft corals aren't the only thing you'll find, of course. The wall begins at about 30 feet. Along the top are lots of other varieties of soft colors. Don't forget to bring a dive light (see Chapter 2) so that you can get the full effect — butterflyfish, parrotfish, unicornfish, and clouds of exotic tropicals are all over the top of the wall, including a beautiful species of red, orange, and blue fairy basselet.

Recommended operators:

- ✔ **Liveaboard:** Nai'a Cruises, P.O. Box 332 Pacific Harbour, Fiji Islands; phone: 011-679-450382; fax: 011-679-450566. e-mail: naia@is.com.fj Web site: www.naia.com.fj

- ✔ **Land-based:** Dive Taveuni, phone: 011-679-880-441; fax: 011-679-880-446; e-mail: divetaveuni@is.com.fj

The Maldives

The most striking attraction of diving in the Maldives is that you rarely find a disappointing site — it's good almost anywhere you roll off the boat. Unfortunately, you can't roll off the boat just anywhere. Tourism is tightly controlled, and some islands are forbidden to foreigners. But for North American folks, the big drawback to the Maldives is that they are so darned far away. In fact, they couldn't be any farther away and still be on earth — they are on the exact opposite side of the globe. It makes for a very long flight, but once you're there, the diving makes up for every grueling hour you spend in that coach-class hell.

In case you're still wondering where on earth the Maldives are, they're that chain of atolls extending from the southwestern tip of Indian to just below the equator in the middle of the Indian Ocean (see Figure 15-9). All of the Maldivian islands are of the low-lying coral variety. The Maldives invented the coral atoll — the word comes from the Maldivian word *atolhu*. The Republic of the Maldives is the world's flattest country — the highest peak in the country is no more than 8 feet above sea level. You could make a higher one in your backyard with a shovel. In fact, if global warming increases the sea level, as predicted, the Maldives will be the first country to disappear off the face of the earth — in about 150 years.

But for divers the Maldives aren't about what is, or isn't, above the waterline, they're about what's down below, and there is plenty. You can get your fill of the Maldives' underwater vistas in two ways: at a land-based resort or on a liveaboard. Land-based resorts are mostly clustered on the islands of North Male atoll. There is plenty of great diving to be done around North Male, but if you have a desire to get to the more remote locations, a liveaboard is probably the best way to go. You can stay in resorts on some of the more remote

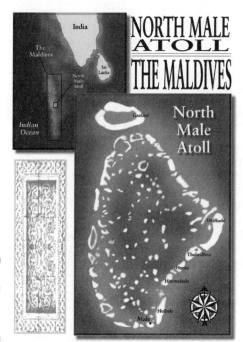

Figure 15-9:
The atolls of the Maldives.

atolls, too, but for most of these, once you're there, you're there for the duration and your selection of sites will be somewhat limited. Another drawback is that most of these remote resorts are quite luxurious and equally expensive. If you're a budget traveler, you're probably better off sticking to the places around North Male.

The Maldives are a long way from North America, but they're not so far from Europe. That's why most of the tourists there are Europeans. English is spoken widely and the people are always friendly and interesting. All of the resorts around North Male have a dive operation, usually run by an organization known as Eurodivers. Fortunately, they're excellent — their operation is first-rate all the way.

More than 100 dive sites are accessible from the resorts around North Male atoll, featuring every kind of underwater topography you can think of — reef passes, overhangs and caves, vertical walls and plunging drop-offs, coral canyons, and coral pinnacles — and inside the lagoon, isolated reefs large and small, known as *thilas,* that rise from the lagoon floor to within a few feet of the surface.

Recommended operator:

✔ **Liveaboard and land-based:** Eurodivers, phone: 011-43-662-442204; fax: 011-43-662-442202; Web site: www.euro-divers.com

The Red Sea — Southern Sinai

The Red Sea and the southern Sinai (shown in Figure 15-10) have probably served more to popularize diving than any other location in the world. Undersea pioneers like Hans Haas and Jacques Cousteau were the first to bring back pictures and tales of this area, and bring the magic of the coral reef to the attention of the public. There have been a lot of divers in the water around the southern Sinai since Haas and Cousteau, and you frequently hear the old-timers talking about how much the area has been degraded since the old days. That may be true, but there's still enough world-class diving here to blow the fez off your cabeza, and it's still one of the best diving areas in the world.

Today, the Red Sea has a well-established diving industry, particularly in the northern reaches — Hurgada, the southern Sinai, and the Gulf of Aqaba. The southern stretches of the Red Sea are more wild and pristine; better explored on a liveaboard.

Figure 15-10:
The Red Sea
and the
Southern
Sinai.

THE
RED SEA

The Red Sea fills an depression in the fault between the African tectonic plate and the Asian and Indian plates. At the southern end, where the Red Sea opens to the Indian Ocean at the strait of Bab El Mandeb, the sea is relatively shallow, restricting tidal flow and, consequently, moderating tides and currents throughout the Red Sea. The restricted tidal flow and high rate of evaporation also result in increased salinity — higher than any other open sea. You may be surprised to find that you need more weight diving here, because the increased salt increases your buoyancy. Even if you're used to diving with a particular weight, do another test before you dive the Red Sea (see Chapters 2 and 4 for help determining the proper amount of weights).

Diving in the southern Sinai is centered around the Egyptian resort town of Sharm El Sheikh and Ras Muhammad National Park. The foundations for Sharm were really laid by the Israelis during their occupation of the Sinai between the 1967 war and the Camp David accords of 1982. When the Israelis moved out, the Egyptians took over with the help of European dive operators, but the place seems less like an Egyptian village than a tourist town on the Sicilian Riviera. The pizza is hot, the nightlife is rocking, and battalions of American and European tourists are shuttled in and out daily. Days are devoted to diving.

Most of the diving is done from day boats, but there are sites that can be accessed from shore as well, and that can be a good way to avoid the crowds if you're experienced and confident enough to mount your own expedition. Most of the operators are modern and well-equipped and there's enough competition to keep the prices reasonable.

The extreme tip of the Southern Sinai is a small peninsula known as Ras Muhammad — one of the most famous dive destinations in the world, and justifiably so. Steep drop-offs dressed out in feathery sea fans and soft coral filigree plunge into the blue depths where jacks, barracuda, and sometimes, sharks circle in the currents. Shark Observatory, Anemone City, and Shark and Jolanda Reefs, are all excellent sites, and you can find plenty of others.

Obviously, Egypt and the Sinai offer other attractions beside diving to fill out your vacation plans. In fact, going to Egypt and not seeing the pyramids, palaces, and antiquities is a little like going to Nepal and not seeing the Himalayas. And after you've made your pilgrimage to the ruins of that ancient civilization of the Nile Valley, make sure you plan to spend at least one night camped under the stars in the powerful silence of a solitary *wadi* in the Sinai desert. You may not come back with any tablets, but you'll get the message.

Recommended operators:

✔ **Land-based:** Camel Dive Club, Na'ma Bay, Sharm El Sheikh, Sinai, Egypt; phone: 011-20-62-600700; fax: 011-20-62-600601

✔ **Land-based:** Sinai Divers, Sharm El Sheikh, Sinai, Egypt; phone: 011-20-62-600697; fax: 011-20-62-600158

Chapter 16

Ten Ways You Can Help Save the Reefs

• •

In This Chapter

▶ Holding dive tours accountable

▶ Keeping your hands to yourself

▶ Controlling your buoyancy

▶ Taking responsibility

• •

*I*t wasn't that long ago that most people regarded coral reefs as inanimate, inexhaustible rock, rather than living organisms. Today, divers know better, so the perception is changing. More and more people have discovered the beauty and endless fascination of coral reefs, but as visits to the world's coral reefs increase, so does the threat to their survival from human activities. Today, nearly 60 percent of the world's coral reefs are threatened. Can they be saved? Yes, but whether divers do their part remains to be seen. In the meantime, when you're snorkeling or scuba diving, this chapter gives you a few tips for leaving the reef at least as healthy as you found it.

Ask Questions

Before you book on a commercial dive boat or with a local operator, ask about their company's environmental policies.

✔ **How do they anchor and discharge waste?** No wastes should be discharged into the environment from the boat — they should all be returned to port for proper disposal. The boat should be tied up at fixed moorings or anchored where it won't damage the living reef.

✔ **How many divers are in a group?** The smaller the better, but more than 15 (depending on the size of the boat) really starts to seem like a zoo — and can stress the marine life.

✔ **What's the policy about touching and feeding?** Don't compromise here.

Let dive tour owners know that preserving the reef is important to you as a customer, and you intend to spend your dollars only with environmentally responsible operators.

Secure Your Equipment

Make sure that your console and octopus, camera, and any other gear isn't dragging across the corals. You can purchase inexpensive plastic clips at your local dive store that help you secure this stuff to your BC and keep it from dangling.

Never Stand on the Reef

No matter how invulnerable they may look, corals are extremely delicate organisms (see Chapter 9). The living polyps on the surface of the coral have retreated into their rocky skeleton, but they are easily damaged by the slightest touch. Snorkelers, in particular, sometimes find it tempting to stand on a coral head in order to adjust their masks or take a look around. Don't. If you have to stand up to make adjustments, find a sandy spot away from the corals.

Control Your Buoyancy

Avoid bumping, accidentally kicking, or hanging on to coral. You may be tempted to hang on to the coral — either to steady yourself or to hold your place in a running current — but even the lightest touch can damage the delicate marine organisms.

Good buoyancy control resolves these problems (see Chapter 5). Make sure that you're properly weighted before you dive on the reef (which really means *near* the reef, but nobody says that). Relax and practice slowing your breathing and controlling your buoyancy. Controlling your buoyancy takes practice, but you'll get it eventually — and be a better diver in the bargain. If you haven't dived for a while, brush up on your buoyancy control with a warm-up dive, far away from sensitive reef areas.

Don't Kick Up Sand

Try not to kick up sand from the bottom when you're treading water in shallow areas or anywhere around living corals. Clouds of sand kicked up by your fins can settle on the delicate corals and smother them.

Don't Touch Marine Creatures

Human beings are an alien species in the underwater world and the innate curiosity of many marine species may overcome their natural caution. If you ever get a chance, take a close-up look, but resist the temptation to touch them, pet them, or hitch rides on them as they pass. Touching animals can stress them, interrupt their natural behavior, or rub off the coating of mucous that protects many marine species from infection. As well-intentioned as your actions may be, you may jeopardize the animal's survival.

Underwater photographers often like to "pose" their subjects for better compositions. Don't. These seemingly innocuous actions can spell doom for marine creatures, especially the kind that attach themselves to the sea floor.

Don't Feed Marine Creatures

Bringing some bread, cheese, or frozen peas into the water with you will attract a swarm of colorful tropical fish, and it may seem harmless enough. However, feeding fish alters the normal behavior of the fish and encourages aggressive behavior. It may also affect the health of the fish by introducing foods that aren't normally part of their diets.

Leave the Area Cleaner Than You Found It

Don't throw litter or garbage in the water or on the beach — some of this waste can be deadly to marine animals. Plastic bags floating in the water are sometimes mistaken for jellyfish by animals, such as sea turtles, that feed on them. Should a turtle ingest one, the result can be fatal intestinal blockages. Take your waste with you.

Also, pick up any litter you find left by people who still haven't developed enough respect for the world to treat it like anything more than a garbage heap. I know it's a pain to pick up after these people as if they were a bunch of careless, self-involved children, but until they grow up, it's your responsibility. To do your part, collect any garbage and litter you find on the reef and take it to a proper disposal or recycling site.

Purchase Only Certified Tropical Fish

If you keep tropical fish, buy only those that are *certified,* which means that they've been collected in a responsible, sustainable way (or bred and raised in captivity). Don't encourage the destruction of the reef by making risky investments in badly stressed or damaged fish caught by unscrupulous collectors. Instead, investigate your sources. Ask your dealer where he gets his fish. Are they certified? How does he know? (See Chapter 9 for more information on how marine life can be damaged by some tropical fish collectors.)

Get Involved

Support and join environmental efforts to protect the world's reefs (see the Appendix for a list of organizations). Join letter-writing campaigns and pressure your government representatives to take action to protect the world's reefs. Make your voice heard. There is still time to save the world's diminishing coral reefs.

Appendix

• •

*I*n this Appendix, you can find lots of organizations, clubs, and publications to support your interest in the sport. There's also a diver's checklist of items to keep on hand, so that you're never caught off-guard.

Diver's Checklist

A blown o-ring or some other minor malfunction can abort your whole dive day. And if you're in some exotic destination that you paid a lot to get to (and aren't coming back to any time soon), you're going to be one unhappy camper. Better to be prepared. This checklist can help:

- ✔ Booties
- ✔ Buoyancy compensator (BC)
- ✔ Camera, strobe, film
- ✔ C-card
- ✔ Computer with spare battery
- ✔ Glow sticks
- ✔ DAN card
- ✔ Decompression tables
- ✔ Dive knife
- ✔ Dive log
- ✔ Dive skin
- ✔ Extra o-rings, Allen wrench, crescent wrench
- ✔ Fins
- ✔ Goody bag
- ✔ Mask defogger
- ✔ Mask(s) with extra mask strap
- ✔ Pressure gauge, depth gauge, compass, dive watch
- ✔ Regulator with second-stage and octopus or alternate air
- ✔ Safety sausage

✔ Snorkel

✔ Towel

✔ Underwater light for night dives (with spare battery or charger)

✔ Weight belt (optional)

✔ Wetsuit

And if you're dive traveling, don't forget to bring the following:

✔ Cotton swabs

✔ Decongestants

✔ Motion-sickness medication

✔ Extra swimsuits

✔ Sunblock (several strengths)

✔ Swim-ear medication

✔ Releasable plastic bags (good for keeping wet things separate and dry things dry)

Additional Tour Operators

In Chapters 13 and 15, I list a few recommended tour operators for my favorite dive destinations. PADI, however, offers a more comprehensive list — more than 400 PADI resorts in premier dive destinations around the world.

PADI, the world's largest certifying agency, maintains a Web site and toll-free number that are both jam-packed with information about additional dive tour operators. Get in touch with them in one of three ways:

✔ Give them a call at 800-729-7234, extension 339, (toll free in the U.S. only) or 949-858-7234, extension 339. They're available from 7 a.m. to 5 p.m. Monday through Thursday, and 7 a.m. to 4 p.m. on Fridays — all Pacific standard time.

✔ Send an e-mail to trade@padi.com with some basic information — desired location, number of divers and nondivers traveling, desired departure and return dates, preferred hotel accommodations (ocean view, budget, and so on). They'll provide you with a list of idea resorts.

✔ Check out the PADI Travel Network Web site at www.padi.com/PTN/. There, you can use an online reservation form to request information about your potential dive destination.

Environmental Organizations

The degradation of the marine environment has become a worldwide problem, but many organizations are working hard to save and restore the precious uunderwater heritage. Here are some of them—they are all deserving of your support.

American Oceans Campaign

Santa Monica, CA 90401

Phone: 310-576-6162; fax: 310-576-6170

or, 600 Pennsylvania Ave. SE, Suite 210

Washington, D.C. 20003

Phone: 202-544-3526; fax: 202-544-5625

Web site: www.americanoceans.org/

Center for Marine Conservation

1725 DeSales Street NW, Suite 600

Washington, D.C. 20036

Phone: 202-429-5609; fax 202-872-0619

Web site: www.cmc-ocean.org

Cetacean Society International

P.O. Box 953

Georgetown, CT 06829

Phone and fax: 203-431-1606

e-mail:
William_Rossiter@compuserve.com,
William Rossiter, CSI President

Web site:
elfnet1a.elfi.com/csihome.html

Channel Islands National Marine Sanctuary

113 Harbor Way, Suite 150

Santa Barbara, CA 93109

Phone: 805-966-7107; fax: 805-568-1582

Web site: www.cinms.nos.noaa.gov/

The Coastal Ecosystems Research Foundation

2648 Tennis Crescent

Vancouver, BC, Canada, V6T 2E1

Phone: 604-224-4729 and toll free for North America: 877-223-2373

e-mail: info@cerf.bc.ca

Web site: www.cerf.bc.ca

CORAL (The Coral Reef Alliance)

64 Shattuck Square, Suite 220

Berkeley, CA 94704

Phone: 510-848-0110; fax: 510-848-3720

e-mail: CORALmail@aol.com

Web site: www.coral.org/Home.html

The Cousteau Society

870 Greenbrier Circle, Suite 402

Chesapeake, VA 23320

Phone: 800-441-4395

Web site: www.cousteau.org/AN/welcomeh.html

D.I.V.E.R.S.

P.O. Box 4241

Fullerton, CA 92834-4241

Phone: 714-832-6087

Web site: www.divers.org

Earthwatch Institute

680 Mt. Auburn St. P.O. Box 9104

Watertown, MA 02471-9104

Phone: 800-776-0188; fax: 617-926-8532

e-mail: info@earthwatch.org

Web site: www.earthwatch.org/

Great Barrier Reef Marine Park Authority

P.O. Box 1379

Townsville, QLD 4810 Australia

Phone: +61-7-4750-0700; fax: +61-7-4772-6093

Web site: www.gbrmpa.gov.au/

Greenpeace USA

1436 U Street, N.W.

Washington, D.C. 20009, USA

Phone: 202-462-1177; fax: 202-462-4507

e-mail: greenpeace.usa@wdc.green-peace.org

Web site: www.greenpeace.org

JASON Foundation for Education (The Jason Project)

395 Totten Pond Road

Waltham, MA 02451

Phone: 781-487-9995; fax: 781-487-9999

e-mail: info@jason.org

Web site: www.jasonproject.org/

Marine Conservation Society

9 Gloucester Road

Ross-on-Wye

Herefordshire HR9 5BU

Phone: 01989 566017; fax: 01989 567815

e-mail: mcsuk@mcmail.com

Web site: www.mcsuk.mcmail.com/

National Ocean Service

1305 East-West Highway

Silver Spring, MD 20910

Phone: 301-713-3074

Web site: www.nos.noaa.gov/

The National Oceanic and Atmospheric Administration

14th Street & Constitution Ave., NW, Room 6013

Washington, D.C. 20230

Phone: 202-482-6090; fax: 202-482-3154

Web site: www.noaa.gov/

Oceanwatch

2101 Wilson Blvd., Suite 900

Arlington, VA 22201

Phone: 703-351-7444; fax: 703-351-7472

e-mail: Oceanwatch@aol.com

Web site: www.enviroweb.org/ocean-watch/

Project Aware Foundation

30151 Tomas St.

Rancho Santa Margarita, CA 92688-2125

Web site: www.padi.com

Reef Relief

P.O. Box 430

Key West, FL 33041

Phone: 305-294-3100; fax: 305-293-9515

e-mail: reef@bellsouth.net

Web site: www.reefrelief.org

UNESCO

UNESCO publishes a list of places considered to be of extraordinary value as a cultural or natural attraction to the people of the world. To see the UNESCO World Heritage list, check out its Web site at: www.unesco.org/whc/heritage.htm

Certification Agencies and Organizations

This section lists some of the certifying organizations around the world.

British Sub Aqua Club (BSAC)

Telford's Quay, Ellesmere Port,

South Wirral, Cheshire L65 4FY

United Kingdom

Phone: 0151 350 6200; fax: 0151 350 6215

From overseas: +44 151 350 62

Email: postmaster@bsac.com

Web site: www.bsac.com

Confédération Mondiale des Activités Subaquatiques (CMAS)

Viale Tiziano, 74 - 00196

Roma, Italy

Phone: + 39 / 6 / 36 85 84 80; fax: + 39 / 6 / 36 85 84 90

e-mail: cmasmond@tin.it/

Web site: www.cmas.org/index.htm

Handicapped Scuba Association (HSA International)

1104 El Prado

San Clemente, CA 92672

Phone and fax: 949-498-6128

e-mail: 103424.3535@compuserve.com

Web site: ourworld.compuserve.com/homepages/hsahdq/

International Association of Nitrox & Technical Divers (IANTD)

World Headquarters

9628 NE 2nd Avenue, Suite D

Miami Shores, FL 33138-2767

Phone: 305-751-4873; fax: 305-751-3958

e-mail: iantdhq@ix.netcom.com

Web site: www.iantd.com/

International Diving Educators Association (IDEA)

P.O. Box 8427

Jacksonville, FL 32239-8427

Phone: 904-744-5554; fax: 904-743-5425

e-mail: ideahq@idea-scubadiving.com

Web site: www.idea-scubadiving.com

International Diving Educators Association (IDEA) — Europe

Via Mulino di Pile 3

67100 L'Aquila, Italy

Tel: 39 0862 318499

Fax: 39 0862 318542

e-mail: HQ@idea-europe.com

Web site: www.idea-europe.com

National Association of Black Scuba Divers

1605 Crittenden St., N.E

Washington, D.C. 20017

Phone: 800-521-NABS; fax: 202-526-2907

e-mail: contactus@nabsdivers.org

Web site: www.nabsdivers.org/

National Association of Scuba Diving Schools, Inc. (NASDS)

999 S. Yates

Memphis, TN 38119

Phone: 901-767-7265; fax: 901-767-2798

e-mail: info@nasds.com

Web site: www.nasds.com

National Association of Underwater Instructors (NAUI) Worldwide

9942 Currie Davis Dr., Suite H

Tampa, FL 33619-2667, USA

Phone: 800-553-6284 or 813-628-6284; fax: 813-628-8253

e-mail: nauihq@nauiww.org

Web site: www.naui.org

Professional Association of Dive Instructors (PADI)

30151 Tomas Street

Rancho Santa Margarita, CA 92688-2125, USA

Phone: 800-729-7234

Web site: www.padi.com

Scuba Schools International (SSI)

2619 Canton Court

Fort Collins, CO 80525-4498 USA

Phone: 800-821-4319 or 970-482-0883; fax: 970-482-6157

e-mail: admin@ssiusa.com

Web site: www.ssiusa.com

Women's Scuba Association (WSA)

6966 S. Atlantic Avenue

New Smyrna Beach, FL 32169

Phone: 904-426-5757; fax: 904-426-5744

e-mail: kingfish@ucnsb.net

Web site: www.jscuba.com/wsa

YMCA Scuba

5825-2A Live Oak Parkway

Norcross, GA 30093-1728

Phone: 770-662-5172 or 888-464-9622; fax: 770-242-9059

e-mail: scubaymca@aol.com

Web site: www.ymcascuba.org

Diver's Alert Network (DAN)

Emergency telephone numbers:

USA: 919-684-8111

Australia: 61-8-224-5116

Europe: 39-85-899-0125

Japan: 81-3-3813-6111 ext. 3318

For information:

Web site: www.diversalertnetwork.org

6 West Colony Pl.

Durham, NC 27705

Phone: 919-684-2948; fax: 919-490-6630

Infoline: 800-446-2671

Magazines and Book Publishers

You can find lots of publications to pick up or subscribe to that support your interest in diving. Here are a few:

Alert Diver Magazine
6 West Colony Pl.

Durham, NC 27705

Phone: 919-684-2948

Asian Diver Magazine
Tanglin, P.O. Box 335 912412

Singapore

Phone: 65-733-2551; fax: 65-733-2291

Email: info@asiandiver.com

Web site: www.asian-diver.com

Best Publishing
P.O. Box 30100

Flagstaff, AZ 86003-0100

Phone: 520-527-1055; fax: 520-526-0370

Discover Diving Magazine
P.O. Box 83727

San Diego, CA 92138

Phone: 619-697-0703; fax: 619-697-0123

Web site: www.scubatimes.com

Dive Training Magazine
201 Main St.

Parkville, MO 64152-3737

Phone: 407-731-4321; fax: 407-369-5882

Web site: www.divetrainingmag.com

Florida Scuba News
5395 Lenox Ave.

Jacksonville, FL 32205-7047

Phone: 904-783-1610; fax: 904-693-0474

Web site: www.scubanews.com

Passport Books
4255 West Touhy Ave.

Lincolnwood, IL 60646-1975

Phone: 800-323-4900

Periplus Editions/Fielding Worldwide, Inc.
4455 Torrence Blvd., Suite 827

Torrence, CA 90503

Phone: 310-372-4474; fax: 310-376-8064

email: fielding@fieldingtravel.com

Web site: www.fieldingtravel.com

Pisces Books/Lonely Planet
150 Linden St.

Oakland, CA 94607

Phone: 800-275-8555

Web site:
www.lonelyplanet.com.au/prop/ptemp/pisces.htm

Rodale's Scuba Diving Magazine
6600 Abercorn St., Suite 208

Savannah, GA 31405

Phone: 912-351-0855; fax: 912-351-0735

email: rsdmgzn@aol.com

Web site: www.scubadiving.com

Scuba Times Magazine
33 Music Square West, Suite 104A

Nashville, TN 37204-0702

Phone: 615-726-4832; fax: 615-255-7238

email: scubatimes@scubatimes.com

Web site: www.scubatimes.com

Skin Diver Magazine
6420 Wilshire Blvd.

Los Angeles, CA 90048-5515

Phone: 323-782-2960; fax 323-782-2121

Web site: www.scubatimes.com

Sport Diver Magazine
330 W. Canton Ave.

Winter Park, FL 32789

Phone: 407-628-4802; fax: 407-628-7061

email: sportdvr@gate.net

Index

• A •

ABCs for emergencies, 140
abdominal squeeze, 133
aborting a dive, 279
absorption of gases in liquids, 119–120
academic training, 61
accessory rings on BCs, 49
adjustable fins, 12–13, 15, 34. *See also* fins
adjustable mouthpiece for snorkels, 33
Advanced Open Water Diver certification, 63
aerobic exercise, 26, 250
ahermatype (soft) corals, 167, 168, 295–296
air. *See also* nitrogen
  Boyle's Law, 116–117
  Charles' Law, 118
  composition of, 113–114
  consumption of, 94, 96
  Dalton's Law, 118–119
  enriched (nitrox), 138, 252–253
  General Gas Law, 116
  heliox, 253
  Henry's Law, 119–120
  human respiratory system and, 115
  oxygen toxicity, 138
  trimix, 253
air bladder of BC, 48
air embolism, 130
airplanes. *See* flying
alcohol, 246
algae, 176–177
allergies, diving cautions for, 24, 125
alone, diving, 278–279
alternate air and inflator hose, 46, 47
alternate air sources
  buddy breathing, 68–69
  emergency procedures, 67–68
  types of, 47
altitude, diving at, 137
ambient pressure, 45
Andaman Sea, 152
anemones, 178, 196
anxieties and fears, 87–88
aquarium fish, 189, 304
aquatic plants, 176–177
Arabian Sea, 152

archipelagos, 148
artificial reefs, 207
ascending
  abdominal squeeze during, 133
  basic technique for, 66–67, 101–102, 280
  breath during, 64, 67, 129, 130
  buoyancy control, 93, 94
  emergency procedures, 68
  safety stop, 67, 101–102, 280
ascent bottles, 47
asthma, 128–129
Atlantic Ocean
  Azores, 269–270
  Little Bahama Banks, 259–261
  overview, 148–150
  seas attached to, 146
  Silver Bank, 266–267
atolls, 151, 170
Australia, 235–236, 272–276
Australian flatback turtles, 187
Azores, 269–270

• B •

Bab El Mandeb, 153
back roll entry, 90–91
bags, dive, 55
Bahamas, 150, 259–261
baited shark dives, 227
baleen whales, 194
barotrauma
  abdominal squeeze, 133
  defined, 129
  dental, 134
  ear squeeze, 130–131, 132
  mask squeeze, 11, 30, 133
  pulmonary, 129–130
  sinus squeeze, 131–132
barracuda, 202
barrier reefs
  Belize, 151
  Great Barrier Reef, 235, 274–276, 290–292
  overview, 170
Bay of Bengal, 152
Bay of Fundy, 162
BCDs or BCs. *See* buoyancy control devices
  (BCDs)

Belize, 151
bends, the. *See* decompression sickness (DCS)
bezel of compass, 51, 97
biting creatures, 201–206
black lung, 128
blade of fins, 13
blood in your mask, 126
Blue Corner (Palau), 281–283
blue whales, 193, 194
blue-green algae, 177
blue-ringed octopus, 201
boat diving. *See also* destinations (diving);
    destinations (snorkeling); scuba diving
  chartering boats versus booking local
    operators, 77
  disabled diver issues, 247–248
  dive plan, 79
  entering the water, 89–91
  exiting the water, 102–103
  final review, 86
  liveaboards, 215–217, 219–221
  marking your gear, 78
  nautical terms, 78
  overview, 77–79
  resort-based, 217–218, 221–223
  safety tips, 77, 79
  seasickness, 78, 121–122
  shore diving versus, 75–76
  warm-water adventure example, 212–213
Bonaire, 151
book publishers, 311–312
booties, 34, 42, 43
bore length and diameter for snorkels, 31
bow of boat, 78
box jellyfish, 197
Boyle, Robert, 116
Boyle's Law, 116–117
Brazil, 149
breathing
  buddy breathing, 68–69
  CPR (cardiopulmonary resuscitation), 141
  decompression sickness (DCS) or the bends,
    70–71, 87, 98, 133–136
  during ascent, 64, 67, 129
  emergency ABCs, 140
  fear of drowning, 87
  holding your breath, 64, 67, 129, 130, 278
  nitrogen narcosis, 69–70, 136–137
  tracking nitrogen accumulation, 71–72
bridge of boat, 78
bristleworms, 179–180, 197
brown algae, 177

bryozoans, 179
buddy breathing, 68–69
buddy system, 65, 278–279
bugs (insects), 247
bull sharks, 204, 205
bullet weights, 85
Bunaken Island (Indonesia), 267–268,
    288–290
buoyancy compensators (BCs). *See* buoyancy
    control devices (BCDs)
buoyancy control devices (BCDs)
  alternate air source with, 47
  attaching inflator hose, 83–84
  draining and rinsing, 105
  importance for protecting reefs, 302
  optional features, 49
  putting on, 85
  securing tanks on, 81–82
  standard features, 48–49
  using, 93–94, 101

• C •

Caicos, 150
calf cramps, 124
canceling a dive, 279
carbon monoxide and smoking, 127
cardiopulmonary resuscitation (CPR), 141
care. *See* maintenance and repairs
Caribbean Sea
  Caribbean islands, 241
  Central America, 240–241
  Cozumel, 151, 285–286
  overview, 150–151
  Stingray City, 263–264
catfish, saltwater, 199
cattle boats, 219
cavern and cave diving, 207–208, 255
Cayman Islands, 151, 263–264
cays, 170
C-card. *See* certification card (C-card) training
cenotes, 207–208
Central America, 240–241
cephalopods, 181–182
certification card (C-card) training
  basic training approach, 61–62
  choosing an agency, 60
  need for, 27, 59
  physical prerequisites, 59–60
certified aquarium fish, 189, 304
cetaceans, 192–194

chambered nautilus, 181–182
channels on fins, 35
Charles, Jacques, 118
Charles' Law, 118
checklists
    for divers, 305–306
    for liveaboards, 220–221
    other travel items, 245
    for resorts, 223
    travel clothes, 244
children, traveling with, 248
choppy sea conditions, 158
Chuuk Lagoon, 283–285
cigarette smoking, 127
clamworms, 179–180
clearing
    masks, 17–18
    snorkels, 19
clothes for travel, 244
cnidarians, 178
coal miner's disease, 128
coated fabric dry suits, 38
cold water
    adventure example, 213–214
    exostosis from, 126–127
    heat loss in, 108–110
    hypothermia from, 138–139
    temperature barriers to species, 165–166
    thermoclines, 166
    warm-water versus cold-water
        adventures, 211–212
    wetsuits for, 25
colds, diving cautions for, 24, 125, 132
color perception, 110–111
coming up. See ascending
comlink, 56
compass, 51, 96–98
computers, 51–52, 71, 99–100
conduction of heat, 108–109
cone shells, 198
confined water training, 61
console, 50–51
continental shelf, 170
contoured snorkels, 33
convection of heat, 109
coral reefs. See also marine life
    atolls, 151, 170
    barrier reefs, 151, 170
    drift dives, 224–225
    formation of, 167–171
    fringing reefs, 170, 172–174
    habitats, 171–174
    protecting, 171, 174–175, 301–304
    reef dives, 224
    wall dives, 225
corals
    ahermatypes, 167, 168, 295–296
    hermatypes, 167–168
    overview, 178
Coriolis Effect, 155
countershading, 274
Cozumel, 151, 285–286
CPR (cardiopulmonary resuscitation), 141
cramps, muscle, 124
creatures. See coral reefs; marine life
crocodiles, saltwater, 189–190, 202
crown-of-thorns starfish, 198
crushed neoprene dry suits, 38
crustaceans, 180
Crystal River (Florida), 261–262
Cuba, 151
currents
    beginners' dive trips and, 224
    drift dives, 224–225
    longshore currents, 160
    overview, 154, 155–156
    rip currents, 159–160
    tidal currents, 161–163
    upwellings, 155
cuttlefish, 181–182
cyanide fishing, 189

Dalton, John, 118, 119
Dalton's Law, 118–119
DAN (Divers Alert Network), 142
dangerous creatures, 194–206
    avoiding, 195
    biting creatures, 201–206
    crocodiles, 190
    poisonous creatures, 197–201
    sharks, 87, 202–206
    stinging creatures, 195–197
Darwin, Charles, 287
decompression diving, 71
decompression sickness (DCS)
    fear of, 87
    from flying after diving, 137
    nitrogen bubbles in the blood, 134–135
    no-decompression diving, 98
    overview, 70–71, 133–135
    recompression, 71, 136
    symptoms, 70–71
    Types I and II, 135

deep diving, 253, 255
defogging masks, 16, 31
dehydration, 123–124, 246
demand valve, 45
density of water, 108
dental barotrauma, 134
depth for beginners' dive trips, 224
depth gauge, 51
descending, 92–93, 132
destinations (diving). *See also* travel
  Australia, 235–236, 290–292
  Blue Corner (Palau), 281–283
  Bunaken Island (Indonesia), 288–290
  Caribbean islands, 241
  Central America, 240–241
  Chuuk Lagoon, 283–285
  East Africa, 231
  Fiji, 237–238, 295–296
  forbidden countries, 242
  Galapagos Islands, 239–240, 287–288
  Hawaii, 239
  Indonesia, 234
  local dives, 249–250
  Malaysia, 233
  Maldives, 232, 296–298
  Micronesia, 236–237
  Palancar Reef (Cozumel), 285–286
  Papua New Guinea, 236, 292–295
  Philippines, 234–235
  Polynesia, 238–239
  Red Sea, 230–231, 298–300
  Seychelles, 231–232
  Thailand, 232–233
  topside attractions, 229–230
destinations (snorkeling). *See also* travel
  Bunaken Island (Indonesia), 267–268
  dolphins (Little Bahama Banks), 259–261
  humpback whales (Silver Bank and Tonga), 266–267
  jellyfish lakes (Palau), 270–272
  Lizard Island (Australia), 274–276
  manatees (Crystal River, Florida), 261–262
  Molokini island (Hawaii), 264–265
  sperm whales (Azores), 269–270
  Stingray City (Grand Cayman), 263–264
  whale sharks (Western Australia), 272–274
diffusion of light in water, 111
diptheria immunizations, 242
disabled divers, 247–248
dissolving of gases in liquids, 119–120
dive anxiety, 87–88

dive bags, 55
dive computers, 51–52, 71, 99–100
dive console, 50–51
dive knives, 53–54
dive lights, 53
dive plan, 79–80, 81. *See also* planning your dive
dive profile, 98–100
dive skins, 37, 39–40
dive tables, 71, 98–99
dive trips. *See* destinations (diving); destinations (snorkeling); travel
dive watches, 53
Divers Alert Network (DAN), 142
diving form, good, 93
dolphins, 192–194, 259–261
double-skirt masks, 31
drift dives, 224–225
drinking on trips, 246
drop-away snorkels, 32
drowning, 87, 139–140
dry drowning, 139
dry suits, 38–39, 40
drying your gear, 105
dugongs, 192
dump valve of BC, 49
dunk bags, 55
dunk tanks, 105
durian, 246

eared seals, 191
earplugs, 132
ears
  ear squeeze, 130–131, 132
  earplugs, 132
  equalizing, 24, 26, 92, 132
  exostosis, 126–127
  infections, 125–126
  protecting, 132
East Africa, 152, 231
eating
  for fitness, 251
  when traveling, 245–246
echinoderms, 182–183
ecological issues. *See* environmental issues
eels, 202, 203
embarrassment, fear of, 87
embolism, air, 130

emergency procedures
  ABCs, 140
  buddy breathing, 68–69
  for calf cramps, 124
  CPR (cardiopulmonary resuscitation), 141
  diving emergency hotline, 142
  for drowning, 139–140
  emergency ascent, 68
  equipment failure, 67–69
  for heat exhaustion or heat stroke,
      124–125
  for hypothermia, 139
  octopus use, 67–68
  reacting to stress, 100
  recompression for DCS, 71, 136
endemic species, 148, 265
enriched air, 138, 252–253
entering the water, 89–91
environmental issues
  environmental organizations, 307–310
  overview, 255–256
  pollutants, 163–164, 175
  preserving marine life, 41, 42, 66, 181, 280, 303
  protecting coral reefs, 171, 174–175,
      301–304
  for snorkeling adventures, 261, 264, 266, 272,
      274
equalizing your ears, 24, 26, 92, 132
equipment. *See* gear
estuarian crocodiles, 189–190
etiquette, 181
Eustachian tubes, 24, 130
exercise, 26, 250
exiting the water, 102–104
exostosis, 126–127
exposure suits
  booties, 42, 43
  dive skins, 37, 39–40
  dry suits, 38–39, 40
  gloves and mittens, 41–42
  hoods, 40–41
  need for, 25, 36–37
  selecting, 39–40
  suit stink, 105
  suiting up, 85
  wetsuits, 25, 37–38, 40

● *F* ●

fauna. *See* marine life
fears and anxieties, 87–88
feeding marine life, 66, 87, 175, 186, 303

fetch area for waves, 156
Fiji, 237–238, 295–296
fins
  calf cramps from, 124
  design features, 35
  flutter kicking, 20
  full-foot versus adjustable, 12–13, 34
  putting on, 15, 86
  selecting, 10, 12–13, 35–36
  trying out in your room, 13, 15
fire corals, 195
fire sponges, 195–196
first aid. *See* emergency procedures
first-stage regulator. *See* regulators
fish. *See also* dangerous creatures
  aquarium fish, 189, 304
  feeding, 66, 87, 175, 186, 303
  overview, 183–184
  poisonous, 197–201
  sharks, 87
  variety of, 183–184
fitness recommendations, 250–251
flatback turtles, 187
flatworms, 179
flexible tube for snorkels, 33
flora and fauna. *See* marine life
flowering plants, 177
flowstone, 207
fluids, 113
flutter kicking, 20
flying
  after diving, 137
  cautions, 242
  with DCS, 136
fog-free coating for masks, 31
food and drink
  for fitness, 251
  when traveling, 245–246
forbidden countries, 242
fore reef, 172
form, good, 93
free diving
  advanced diving, 26
  aerobic exercise and, 26
  buoyancy challenge, 21
  clearing your mask, 17–18
  clearing your snorkel, 19
  defined, 10
  diving weights for, 25
  equalizing your ears, 24, 26
  hyperventilating, 26, 27
  pike dive, 22–23

free diving *(continued)*
  risks, 9
  slant dive, 21–22
  swimming abilities required, 9
  wet suits for warmth, 25
free-swimming stingers, 196–197
freshwater
  cenotes, 207–208
  diving in, 145, 208, 249–250
  haloclines, 166
fringing reefs, 170, 172–174
full wetsuits, 37
full-foot fins, 12–13, 15, 34. *See also* fins

• *G* •

gadgets, unnecessary, 57
Galapagos Islands, 239–240, 287–288
galley, 78
garbage, 175, 303–304
gases. *See* air
gauges, 50–51, 105
GBR (Great Barrier Reef), 235, 274–276, 290–292
gear. *See also* maintenance and repairs; *specific
      pieces of gear by name*
  alternate air sources, 47, 67–68
  booties, 34, 42, 43
  breaking it down, 104
  buoyancy control devices (BCDs), 48–49,
      81–85, 93–94, 101, 302
  checklist, 305–306
  clothes for travel, 244
  compass, 51, 96–98
  dive computers, 51–52, 71, 99–100
  dive watches, 53
  drying, 105
  equipment failure, 67–69
  exposure suits, 25, 36–40
  fins, 12–13, 15, 34–36, 86
  gauges, 50–51
  gloves, 41–42
  hoods, 40–41
  importance of, 278
  maintenance and repairs, 57
  marking your gear, 78
  masks, 11, 13–18, 30–31, 86
  optional gear, 53–56
  post-dive maintenance, 104–106
  regulators, 45–47, 82–83, 84, 104
  renting versus buying, 42, 56
  rinsing, 105

  setting up, 81–85
  snorkels, 12, 13–15, 19, 32–34
  storing, 106
  suiting up, 85–86
  tanks, 42–45, 81–83, 84
  unnecessary gadgets, 57
  weights, 25, 50, 76–77, 84–86
General Gas Law, 116
getting narked (nitrogen narcosis), 69–70,
      136–137
getting out of the water, 102–104
giant stride entry, 90
global bulges, 161
Glover's Reef, 151
gloves, 41–42
going down, 92–93, 132
good diving form, 93
Grand Cayman, 263–264
Great Barrier Reef, 235, 274–276, 290–292
great white sharks, 205–206
Great White Wall (Fiji), 295–296
Greater Antilles, 150–151
green algae, 177
green sea turtles, 185–187
Gulf of Mexico, 151

• *H* •

Haiti, 151
haloclines, 16
Hawaiian Islands, 148, 239, 264–265
hawksbill turtles, 185, 186
head (boat term), 78
headings on compass, 97
heat. *See* cold water; exposure suits;
      temperature
heat exhaustion and heat stroke, 124–125
heliox, 253
Henry, William, 119
hermatype corals, 167–168
high altitude, diving at, 137
high pressure nervous syndrome, 253
holding your breath, 64, 67, 129, 130, 278
hoods, 40–41
hose retainers on BCs, 49
hotline for diving emergencies, 142
humpback whales, 193, 194, 266–267
hydroids, 178, 196
hydrologic cycle, 163–164
hydrostatic testing of tanks, 44
hyperbaric chamber, 136
hyperventilation, 26, 27, 96
hypothermia, 138–139

• I •

idiopathic pulmonary fibrosis (IPF), 128
iguanas, marine, 188
immunizations, 242–243
impact zone, 158
index markers of compass, 97
Indian Ocean
    East Africa, 152, 231
    Maldives, 153, 232, 296–298
    overview, 152–153
    Red Sea, 153–154, 230–231, 298–300
    Seychelles, 231–232
    Thailand, 232–233
Indonesia, 234, 267–268, 288–290
Indo-Pacific marine life, 147, 148
inflatable snorkeling vests, 25
inflator hose, 47, 48, 83
influenza immunizations, 243
insects, 247
inspecting tanks, 44
instruction. See training
invertebrates, 177–183
IPF (idiopathic pulmonary fibrosis), 128
islets, 170

• J •

jellyfish, 178–179, 196–197, 270–272
jewelry, not wearing, 202

• K •

kelp dives, 226
kelp forests, 206
Kemp's ridley turtles, 185, 187
kicking up sand, 303
Kingdom of Tonga, 266–267
knives, 53–54

• L •

lagoons, 173
leaking masks, adjusting, 17
leatherback turtles, 185, 187
leaving the water, 102–104
leeward, 78
Lesser Antilles, 151

light underwater, 110–112
Lighthouse Reef, 151
lights, 53
lionfish, 200
litter, 175, 303–304
Little Bahama Banks, 259–261
liveaboard dive trips. See also
    destinations (diving); destinations
    (snorkeling)
  advantages and disadvantages, 215–217
  checklist, 220–221
  choosing a liveaboard, 219–221
Lizard Island (Australia), 274–276
local dives, 249–250
logbook, 54–55
loggerhead turtles, 185–186
longshore currents, 160
lophophore, 179
lubber line, 97
lycra dive skins and hoods, 37, 39–40

• M •

Madagascar, 152
magazines and book publishers, 311–312
maintaining skills, 249–250
maintenance and repairs
  dry suits, 39
  general recommendations, 57
  importance of, 64–65
  post-dive maintenance, 104–106
  tanks, 45
Malaysia, 233
Maldives, 153, 232, 296–298
mammals
  cetaceans, 192–194
  overview, 190
  pinnipeds, 191–192
  sea otters, 190
  sirenians, 192, 193
manatees, 192, 193, 261–262
mangrove swamps, 174
mangroves, 177
marine iguanas, 188
marine life. See also dangerous creatures;
    environmental issues; specific types of
    marine life
  aquarium fish, 189, 304
  aquatic plants, 176–177
  coral reefs, 167–175

marine life *(continued)*
  dangerous creatures, 194–206
  etiquette, 181, 280
  feeding, 66, 87, 175, 186, 303
  fish, 183–184
  invertebrates, 177–183
  kelp forests, 206
  mammals, 190–194
  nocturnal creatures, 225
  pollutants and, 163, 175
  preserving, 41, 42, 66, 171, 181, 303
  reptiles, 185–190
  sharks, 87, 203–206, 227, 272–274
  temperature barriers, 165–166
marking your gear, 78
Marshall Islands, 148
mascaret, 162
mask squeeze, 11, 30, 133
masks
  attaching snorkel to, 13–14
  blood in, 126
  cleaning new silicone masks, 14–15
  clearing, 17–18
  defogging, 16, 31
  entering the water with, 89
  leaks, eliminating, 17
  mask squeeze, 11, 30, 133
  mustaches with, 19
  options, 31
  overview, 11, 30
  selecting, 30–31
  skirts, 17, 30, 31
  trying out in your room, 13–15
  wearing on your forehead, 86
Master Diver certification, 63
Maui (Hawaii), 264–265
measles immunizations, 243
mediastinal air, 130
Mediterranean Sea, 151–152
medusa form hydroids, 178
Micronesia, 236–237, 283–285
mittens, 41
Moby Dick, 194
mollusks, 180–182
Molokini Island (Hawaii), 264–265
mosquitoes, 247
motus, 170
multi-level dives, 99
mumps immunizations, 243
Murphy's Law, 120
muscle cramps, 124
mustaches and masks, 19

narcosis, nitrogen, 69–70, 136–137
nautical terms, 78
navigating underwater, 96–98
nematocysts, 195
neoprene
  booties, 34, 42
  crushed, 38
  dry suits, 38
  drying, 105
  gloves and mittens, 41–42
  hoods, 40
  wetsuits, 25, 37
neurological DCS, 135
neutral buoyancy, 93
night dives, 225
Ningaloo Reef, 152
nitrogen
  atmospheric composition, 114
  bubbles in the bloodstream, 134–135
  decompression diving, 71
  decompression sickness (DCS) or the bends,
      70–71, 87, 98, 133–136
  human respiratory system and, 115
  narcosis, 69–70, 136–137
  no-decompression diving, 98
  off-gassing, 70
  overview, 69
  planning your dive, 71
  safety stop for eliminating, 67, 101–102
  tracking accumulation, 71–72
nitrox, 138, 252–253
nocturnal creatures, 225
no-decompression diving, 98
nondivers, traveling with, 248
nosebleeds, 126, 131, 132
no-see-ums, 247

ocean trenches, 147, 149
oceanic whitetip sharks, 204, 205
oceans and seas. *See also* currents; surf; tides;
      waves
  Atlantic Ocean, 148–150
  Caribbean Sea, 150–151
  evaluating conditions, 79, 81, 279
  hydrologic cycle, 163–164
  Indian Ocean, 152–153
  Mediterranean Sea, 151–152

overview, 144–145
Pacific Ocean, 146–148
pollution of, 163–164
Red Sea, 153–154, 230–231, 298–300
seas attached to oceans, 146
temperature variations, 165–166
thermoclines, 166
trenches, 147, 149
octopus (cephalopods), 181–182, 201
octopus (gear)
  emergency procedures, 67–68
  overview, 47
  testing, 67–68
off-gassing, 70
olive ridley turtles, 185, 187
Open Water Diver certification, 62
open water training, 61
open-circuit scuba, 45
optional gear, 53–56
O'Toole's Commentary on Murphy's
    Law, 120
oversold flights, 242
ownership of liveaboards, 220
oxygen, 114, 115
oxygen toxicity, 138

● P ●

Pacific Ocean
  Australia, 235–236, 272–276, 290–292
  Central America, 240–241
  Fiji, 237–238, 295–296
  Galapagos Islands, 239–240, 287–288
  Great Barrier Reef, 235, 274–276, 290–292
  Hawaiian Islands, 148, 239, 264–265
  Indonesia, 234, 267–268, 288–290
  Kingdom of Tonga, 266–267
  Malaysia, 233
  Micronesia, 236–237, 283–285
  overview, 146–148
  Palau, 270–272, 281–283
  Papua New Guinea, 236, 292–295
  Philippines, 234–235
  Polynesia, 238–239
  seas attached to, 146
packing lists, 244–245
PADI, 294, 306
Palancar Reef (Cozumel), 285–286
Palau, 270–272, 281–283
Papua New Guinea, 236, 292–295

pelagics, 148, 188
Philippines, 234–235
photography, underwater, 251–252
phytoplanktons, 176
pike dive, 22–23
pinnipeds, 191–192
planning your dive
  boat diving, 79
  deepest part first, 99, 280
  determining amount of weight you
      need, 76–77
  dive profile, 98–100
  importance of, 66, 279
  nitrogen absorption issues, 71
  renting tanks and weights, 75, 76
  shore diving, 79–81
plants
  aquatic, 176–177
  kelp, 206, 226
plastic bags, 175
plunging waves, 159. *See also* surf
pneumoconiosis, 128
pneumothorax, 130
PNG (Papua New Guinea), 236, 292–295
poisonous creatures, 199–201
poliomyelitis immunizations, 242
pollutants, 163–164, 175
Polynesia, 238–239
polyps. *See* coral reefs; corals
pony bottles, 47
pool training, 61
"popping" your ears, 24, 26, 92, 132
port side of boat, 78
Portuguese man-of-war, 196
post-dive procedures, 102–106
preservation. *See* environmental issues
pressure
  abdominal squeeze, 133
  Boyle's Law, 116–117
  Charles's Law, 117–118
  Dalton's Law, 118–119
  ear squeeze, 130–131, 132
  equalizing your ears, 24, 26, 92, 132
  Henry's Law, 119–120
  high pressure nervous syndrome, 253
  mask squeeze, 11, 30, 133
  pulmonary barotrauma, 129–130
  safety practices, 63–64
  sinus squeeze, 131–132
  tooth squeeze, 134

pressure gauge, 50
pressure release valve of BC, 49
professional and technical diving, 253–255
publications, 311–312
Puerto Rico, 151
pulmonary barotrauma, 129–130
pulmonary fibrosis, 128
purge button, 67–68
purge valve
  masks, 31
  snorkels, 33

• Q •

quick-release straps
  on BCs, 49
  on fins, 34
  on weight belts, 25

• R •

radiation of heat, 110
rapture of the deep, 69–70, 136–137
Ras Muhammad, 300
recompression, 71, 136
red algae, 177
Red Sea, 153–154, 230–231, 298–300
reef dives, 224
reef flat, 174
reef passes, 173
reefs. *See* coral reefs
reflection of light, 111
refraction of light, 111–112
refresher courses, 250
regulators, 45–47
  attaching to tanks, 82–83, 84
  first-stage, 45, 82–83
  octopus, 47
  overview, 45–47
  removing, 104
  second-stage, 46, 84
  selecting, 46–47
  testing, 84
remoras, 273
renting tanks and weights, 75, 76
renting versus buying, 42, 56
repairs. *See* maintenance and repairs

reptiles
  marine iguanas, 188
  saltwater crocodiles, 189–190
  sea snakes, 187–188
  sea turtles, 185–187
Republic of Maldives, 153, 232, 296–298
Rescue Diver certification, 63
resort course in scuba diving, 26–27
resort-based dive trips. *See also*
      destinations (diving); destinations
      (snorkeling)
  accommodations, 222
  advantages and disadvantages, 217–218
  checklist, 223
  disabled diver issues, 247–248
  diving quality, 222
respiratory problems, 127–129
ribbon worms, 179
ribs on fins, 35
ridley turtles, 185, 187
right whales, 193, 194
rinsing your gear, 105
rip currents, 159–160
rising. *See* ascending
risks. *See* safety tips and issues
Rock Islands, 270–272
rogue waves, 158
rubella immunizations, 243

• S •

safety sausage, 54
safety stop, 67, 101–102
safety tips and issues. *See also* dangerous
      creatures
  ABCs for emergencies, 140
  abdominal squeeze, 133
  alternate air sources, 47, 67–68
  anxieties and fears, 87–88
  ascent, basic procedure, 66–67,
    101–102, 280
  ascent, emergency, 68
  barotrauma, 129–133
  basic safety procedures and practices, 63–67
  boat diving, 77, 79
  buddy breathing, 68–69
  buddy system, 65, 278–279
  cavern and cave diving, 255
  colds, allergies, and sinus problems, 24, 125,
    132
  CPR (cardiopulmonary resuscitation), 141

decompression sickness (DCS) or the bends, 70–71, 87, 98, 133–136
dehydration, 123–124, 246
dive computer reliability, 52
diving emergency hotline, 142
drift dives, 225
drowning, 139–140
ear infections, 125–126
ear squeeze, 130–131, 132
emergency procedures, 67–69, 140–142
equipment failure, 67–69
exostosis, 126–127
flying after diving, 137
heat exhaustion and heat stroke, 124–125
hyperventilation risks, 27, 96
hypothermia, 138–139
kelp dives, 226
liveaboards, 220
maintaining your gear, 64–65
night dives, 225
nitrogen issues, 69–72, 133–137
nosebleeds, 126
oxygen toxicity, 138
planning your dive, 66
pulmonary barotrauma, 129–130
resorts, 222
respiratory problems, 127–129
rip currents, 160
risks of diving, 9
rules of safe diving, 277–280
safety sausage, 54
scooter dangers, 56
seasickness, 78, 121–122
shallow-water blackout, 27
shark dives, 227
shore diving, 80, 81
sinus squeeze, 131–132
stress, reacting to, 100
sunburn, 123
tank damage, 45
tooth squeeze, 134
travel cautions, 242–243
wall dives, 225
wearing mask on forehead, 86
weight belt quick-release, 25
wreck dives, 227
saltwater catfish, 199
saltwater crocodiles, 189–190, 202

sand, kicking up, 303
sand flies, 247
sarcoidosis, 128
scooters, 55–56
scorpionfish, 199–200
Scuba Diver certification, 62
scuba diving. *See also* destinations (diving)
    aborting a dive, 279
    air consumption, 94, 96
    anxieties and fears, 87–88
    ascending, 64, 66–67, 68, 93, 94, 101–102, 280
    boat diving, 75–76, 77–79, 90–91
    buoyancy control, 93–94
    canceling a dive, 279
    cavern and cave diving, 207–208, 255
    C-card for, 27, 59, 62
    deep diving, 253, 255
    defined, 10
    descending, 92–93
    determining amount of weight you need, 76–77
    dive profile, 98–100
    diver's checklist, 305–306
    emergency procedures, 67–69
    entering the water, 89–91
    final review, 86
    fitness recommendations, 250–251
    getting out, 102–104
    good diving form, 93
    maintaining skills, 249–250
    navigating underwater, 96–98
    post-dive maintenance, 104–106
    professional and technical diving, 253–255
    progression from snorkeling, 10
    renting tanks and weights, 75, 76
    renting versus buying gear, 42, 56
    resort course in, 26–27
    risks, 9
    safe diving rules, 277–280
    setting up your gear, 81–85
    shore diving, 75–76, 79–81, 91
    sign language, 94, 95
    suiting up, 85–86
    swimming abilities required, 9
    training, 26–27, 39, 59–63
    wreck diving, 226–227, 254–255, 283–285

sea anemones, 178, 196
sea conditions, evaluating, 79, 81, 279
sea lice, 201
sea otters, 190
sea snakes, 187–188, 200
sea squirts, 183
sea turtles, 185–187
sea urchins, 197
Sea-Bands, 122
seagrasses, 177
seals, 191–192
seamounts, 151
seas. *See* oceans and seas
seasickness, 78, 121–122
seated entry, 91
second-stage regulator. *See* regulators
sedentary stingers, 195–196
Seine River, 162
seismic activity, tsunamis from, 161, 162
setting up your gear, 81–85
Seychelles, 231–232
shallow-water blackout, 27
sharks
    attacks, 202–205
    fear of, 87, 202
    most dangerous species, 204–206
    shark dives, 227
    whale sharks, 272–274
shore diving. *See also* scuba diving
    boat diving versus, 75–76
    cold-water adventure example, 213–214
    diving the plan, 81
    entering the water, 89, 91
    evaluating conditions, 80–81, 279
    exiting the water, 104
    final review, 86
    overview, 79–81
    planning the dive, 79–80
    preparations, 80–81
    rip currents, 160–161
    safety tips, 80, 81
shorty wetsuits, 37
sign language, 94, 95
Silver Bank (Dominican Republic), 266–267
sinus problems, 24, 125, 131–132
sirenians, 192, 193
skirt of masks, 17, 30, 31
slant dive, 21–22
slates, 54, 94
smoking, 127
snakes, sea, 187–188, 200

snorkeling. *See also* destinations
        (snorkeling)
    clearing your mask, 17–18
    clearing your snorkel, 19
    defined, 10
    first venture (in pool), 15–17
    first venture (in open water), 20–21
    flutter kicking, 20
    inflatable vests, 25
    progression to scuba diving, 10
    renting versus buying gear, 56
    squatting position, 17
    swimming abilities required, 9
snorkels
    attaching to mask, 13–14
    cleaning new silicone snorkels, 14–15
    clearing, 19
    contoured versus drop-away design, 33
    keeper for, 33
    options, 33–34
    selecting, 12, 32–33
    splash guard, 34
    trying out in your room, 13–15
soft corals (ahermatypes), 167, 168,
        295–296
sound underwater, 111–113
Southern Sinai (Red Sea), 298–300
specialty certification, 63
sperm whales, 193, 194, 269–270
spilling waves, 159. *See also* surf
splash guard for snorkels, 34
sponges, 178, 196–197
square profiles, 99
squid, 181–182, 201–202
stalactites, 207
stalagmites, 207
starboard, 78
starfish, 182–183, 198
stern of boat, 78
stinging creatures, 195–197
Stingray City (Grand Cayman), 263–264
stingrays, 199, 263–264
stonefish, 199–200
storing your gear, 106
stress, reacting to, 100
suit stink, 105
suiting up, 85–86
sun
    dehydration, 123–124, 246
    heat exhaustion and heat stroke, 124–125
    sunburn, 123
    travel cautions, 247

surf
  entering, 91
  exiting, 104
  impact zone, 158
  overview, 158–159
  rip currents, 159–160
  types of, 159
surge, 158
surging waves, 159. *See also* surf
swell, 157
swimming pool, first snorkeling venture in,
    15–17
swimming skills required, 9

● *T* ●

tank mounting on BC, 49
tanks
  alternate air sources, 47
  ascent bottles, 47
  attaching regulators, 82–83, 84
  care and maintenance, 45
  codes, 44
  inspection and testing, 44
  overview, 42–45
  pony bottles, 47
  regulators for, 45–47
  removing regulators, 104
  renting, 75, 76
  renting versus buying, 42, 56
  securing to BC, 81–82
  sizes and shapes, 43–44
  steel versus aluminum, 43
technical divers, 254
temperature. *See also* cold water; exposure
    suits
  dehydration issues, 123–124, 246
  heat exhaustion and heat stroke, 124–125
  heat loss in water, 108–110
  hypothermia, 138–139
  thermoclines, 166
  warm-water versus cold-water adventures,
    211–212
tempered glass for masks, 31
testing tanks, 44
tetanus immunizations, 242
Thailand, 232–233
thermoclines, 166
thilas, 298

tidal bore, 162–163
tidal currents, 161–163
tidal waves, 161
tides, 154, 161–163
tiger sharks, 204–205
Tonga, 266–267
tooth squeeze, 134
toothed whales, 192, 194
touching marine creatures, 41, 42, 66
tour operators, 294, 306. *See also*
    destinations (diving); destinations
    (snorkeling)
training
  advanced courses, 62–63
  C-card (certification card), 27, 59–62
  for dry suits, 39
  importance of, 277
  refresher courses, 250
  resort course, 26–27
trash, 175, 303–304
travel. *See also* destinations (diving); destina-
    tions (snorkeling)
  beginners' considerations, 223–224
  cautions, 242–243
  checklists, 244, 245
  cold-water adventure example, 213–214
  disabled diver considerations, 247–248
  drift dives, 224–225
  drinking right, 246
  eating right, 245–246
  forbidden countries, 242
  immunizations, 242–243
  kelp dives, 226
  liveaboard dive trips, 215–217, 219–221
  night dives, 225
  with nondivers, 248
  packing lists, 243–245
  quick trips versus expeditions, 215
  reef dives, 224
  resort-based dive trips, 217–218, 221–223
  shark dives, 227
  topside attractions, 229–230
  wall dives, 225
  warm-water adventure example, 212–213
  warm-water versus cold-water adventures,
    211–212
  wreck dives, 226–227, 254–255, 283–285
trenches, 147, 149
trimix, 253
trips. *See* destinations (diving); destinations
    (snorkeling); travel

true seals, 191
tsunamis, 161, 162
tubeworms, 179–180
tunicates, 183
Turks, 150
Turneffe Islands, 151
turtles, sea, 185–187
two-piece wetsuits, 38

• U •

unbaited shark dives, 227
upwellings, 155
urinating, underwater, 175

• V •

valves
  on BC, 49
  demand valve, 45
  purge valves, 31, 33
  rinsing, 105
vasoconstriction, 138
vents on fins, 35
vests, inflatable, 25
videography, underwater, 251–252
visibility, 164–165

• W •

waistband of BC, 49
wall dives, 225
walrus, 192
warm-water adventure example, 212–213
watches, 53
water. *See also* oceans and seas
  density, 108
  entering, 89–91
  exiting, 102–104
  exostosis from cold water, 126–127
  heat loss in, 108–110
  hydrologic cycle, 163–164
  hypothermia from cold water, 138–139
  light under, 110–112
  navigating under, 96–98
  physical composition of, 107–108
  pollutants, 163–164, 175
  seasickness, 78, 121–122
  sound travel through, 112–113
  thermoclines, 166
  visibility, 164–165

water pressure. *See* pressure
wave judgment, 158
waves, 156–158, 161, 162. *See also* surf
weather considerations, 66, 79, 80, 279
weights
  bullet weights, 85
  determining your needs, 76–77
  for free diving, 25
  for freshwater diving, 208
  integrated with BCs, 49
  overview, 50
  putting on, 86
  renting, 76
  setting up, 84–85
wet drowning, 140
wetsuits, 25, 37–38, 40
whale sharks, 272–274
whales, 192–194
white sharks, great, 205–206
whitecaps, 156
winds, 155–156
windward, 78
worms, 179–180
wreck diving, 226–227, 254–255, 283–285
wrecks, 206–207

• Z •

zooplanktons, 178
zooxanthellae, 168

Wiley Publishing, Inc.
End-User License Agreement

READ THIS. You should carefully read these terms and conditions before opening the software packet(s) included with this book "Book". This is a license agreement "Agreement" between you and Wiley Publishing, Inc. "WPI". By opening the accompanying software packet(s), you acknowledge that you have read and accept the following terms and conditions. If you do not agree and do not want to be bound by such terms and conditions, promptly return the Book and the unopened software packet(s) to the place you obtained them for a full refund.

1. **License Grant.** WPI grants to you (either an individual or entity) a nonexclusive license to use one copy of the enclosed software program(s) (collectively, the "Software" solely for your own personal or business purposes on a single computer (whether a standard computer or a workstation component of a multi-user network). The Software is in use on a computer when it is loaded into temporary memory (RAM) or installed into permanent memory (hard disk, CD-ROM, or other storage device). WPI reserves all rights not expressly granted herein.

2. **Ownership.** WPI is the owner of all right, title, and interest, including copyright, in and to the compilation of the Software recorded on the disk(s) or CD-ROM "Software Media". Copyright to the individual programs recorded on the Software Media is owned by the author or other authorized copyright owner of each program. Ownership of the Software and all proprietary rights relating thereto remain with WPI and its licensers.

3. **Restrictions On Use and Transfer.**

   (a) You may only (i) make one copy of the Software for backup or archival purposes, or (ii) transfer the Software to a single hard disk, provided that you keep the original for backup or archival purposes. You may not (i) rent or lease the Software, (ii) copy or reproduce the Software through a LAN or other network system or through any computer subscriber system or bulletin- board system, or (iii) modify, adapt, or create derivative works based on the Software.

   (b) You may not reverse engineer, decompile, or disassemble the Software. You may transfer the Software and user documentation on a permanent basis, provided that the transferee agrees to accept the terms and conditions of this Agreement and you retain no copies. If the Software is an update or has been updated, any transfer must include the most recent update and all prior versions.

4. **Restrictions on Use of Individual Programs.** You must follow the individual requirements and restrictions detailed for each individual program included with this Book. These limitations are also contained in the individual license agreements recorded on the Software Media. These limitations may include a requirement that after using the program for a specified period of time, the user must pay a registration fee or discontinue use. By opening the Software packet(s), you will be agreeing to abide by the licenses and restrictions for these individual programs that are detailed in the PADI License Agreement. None of the material on this Software Media or listed in this Book may ever be redistributed, in original or modified form, for commercial purposes.

PADI International, Inc., License Agreement and Limited Warranty

WARNING. Don't attempt to learn to scuba dive except under the direct supervision of a certified instructor; otherwise, you will expose yourself to a risk of serious personal injury or death. This book/CD package, the PADI Open Water Diver Manual, and other PADI educational products are intended to be used to learn to scuba dive only in conjunction with a PADI Open Water Diver Course with a certified PADI Instructor.

READ THIS. By using or incorporating in your computer the software included with this agreement, you accept the terms of this legal agreement between you, the end user, and International PADI, Inc. (PADI). The software, open water diver video, and accompanying items are provided to you only upon the condition that you agree to the terms of this agreement.

LIMITED USE LICENSE: This Program is owned by PADI. This is a license, not a sale, and PADI retains full and complete title to the Program and all copies of the Program regardless of the media or form on which the original disc or other copies may exist, including copies made in violation of the terms of this License. The Program or associated documentation is protected by United States copyright laws and international treaties. PADI grants you the right to use one copy of the Program for your personal use only. All rights, including derivative rights not expressly granted, are reserved by PADI. This Agreement, aside from the law of copyright, is governed by the laws of the State of California.

You agree that the computer Program includes trade secrets belonging to PADI. Possession and use of this program shall be strictly in accordance with this license agreement and receipt or possession does not convey any rights to divulge, reproduce, or allow others to use this computer Program without specific written authorization from PADI.

YOU MAY:

1) Either (a) make one copy of the Program solely for backup or archival purposes provided that you reproduce all information (including copyright notices) that appear on the original disk(s), or (b) transfer the Program to a single hard disk, provided that you keep the original disk(s) solely for backup or archival purposes.

2) You may transfer your rights under this License to another party on a permanent basis, provided you transfer the Program and the accompanying materials, retaining no copies. The transferee's use of the Program constitutes acceptance of the terms of this License.

YOU MAY NOT:

1) Use the Program on more than one computer, computer terminal, or workstation at the same time.

2) Make copies of the program package including the materials accompanying the Program, or make copies of the Program except as provided above.

3) Use the Program in a network or other multi-user arrangement or on an electronic bulletin board system or other remote access arrangement. Violations of this article shall include, but are not limited to, uses on Local Area Networks (LAN), browsers, and Internet Web sites.

4) Rent, lease, license, or otherwise transfer the Program Package without the express written consent of PADI except that you may transfer the complete Program Package on a permanent basis as provided above.

5) Reverse engineer, decompile, disassemble, or create derivative works of the Program.

6) Use the backup disks on another computer or loan, rent, lease, or transfer the disk(s) to another user except as part of the permanent transfer of the entire Program Package.

LIMITED WARRANTY. PADI warrants, to the original buyer only, that the media upon which the Program is recorded shall be free from defects in materials and workmanship under normal use and service for a period of thirty (30) days from the date of purchase. Any implied warranty on any Program is limited to thirty (30) days. Some states do not allow limitations on the duration of an implied warranty, so the above limitation may not apply to you.

EXCLUSIVE REMEDY. PADI's entire liability and your exclusive remedy shall be the repair or replacement of the Program that does not meet PADI's Limited Warranty and which is returned to PADI with a copy of your receipt This Limited Warranty is void if the failure of the media upon which the Program is recorded has resulted from accident, abuse, or misapplication. Any replacement Program will be warranted for the remainder of the original warranty period or thirty (30) days, whichever is longer.

NO OTHER WARRANTIES. With respect to the program, PADI disclaims all warranties, other than the above warranty by PADI, either express or implied, including but not limited to implied warranties of merchantability and fitness for a particular purpose. PADI does not warrant that the program will meet your requirements or that the operation of the program will be uninterrupted or error free. This limited warranty gives you specific legal rights; you may have others, which vary from state to state.

LIMITATIONS ON DAMAGES. In no event shall PADI or its members be liable for any damages whatsoever (including without limitation, damages for loss of profits, business interruption, loss of information, or other pecuniary loss) arising out of the use of or inability to use the program or program package, even if PADI or its members have been advised of the possibility of such damages. In no event will PADI's liability for any reason exceed the actual price paid for the license to use the specific program. Because some states do not allow the exclusion or limitation of liability for consequential or incidental damages, the above limitation may not apply to you.

U.S. GOVERNMENT RESTRICTED RIGHT. The Software and documentation is computer software as defined in DFARS 252.227-7014(a)(1). The Government shall have only those rights specified in this Agreement. The Contractor/Manufacturer is International PADI, Inc., 30151 Tomas Street, Rancho Santa Margarita, CA 92688-2125 USA.

Save this license for future reference.

Installation Instructions

The *Scuba Diving & Snorkeling For Dummies* CD offers free, interactive, multimedia Open Water Diver courseware from the Professional Association of Diving Instructors (PADI) — the world's largest and most popular diver training organization in the world.

PADI has over 4,500 sanctioned dive stores and resorts and more than 90,000 professional instructors and divemasters, offering courses and scuba excursions in 175 countries and territories. Seven of every ten American divers and an estimated 55 percent of all divers around the world are trained by PADI instructors using PADI instructional programs. More than eight million certifications have been issued by PADI since its inception in 1966. Presently, well over three quarters of a million divers receive PADI certifications each year. For more information and a list of dive stores and resorts, call 949-858-7234, extension 339 or visit www.padi.com.

To install this free courseware from the CD to your hard drive, follow these steps.

Windows 95 setup

1. **Insert the CD into your computer's CD-ROM drive.**

2. **Choose Start⇨Settings⇨Control Panel.**

3. **Double-click the Add/Remove Programs icon.**

4. **Under the Install/Uninstall tab, click Install, and then click Next.**

   The Command Line for the installation program shows the drive letter for the CD-ROM, a colon, a backslash, and "SETUPCD.EXE" (for example, E:\SETUPCD.EXE). If the command line doesn't appear as listed, click Browse to find the installation program.

5. **Click Finish.**

   The Open Water Diver CD-ROM installation program begins and the Welcome! dialog box appears.

6. **Follow the installation instructions on the screen and restart the computer when prompted to do so.**

8. **Double-click on Install Adobe Acrobat Reader in the PADI Multimedia group and follow the instructions on the screen.**

   You need Adobe Acrobat to print documents from the program.

Read the Readme file!

To solve problems that you may encounter with this CD, including those related to installation, video, screen display, sound, and printing, double-click on the Readme.wri file that's included on the CD. You can also obtain up-to-date technical support at PADI's Web site: www.padi.com.

---

9. **After you install the programs, you can eject the CD. Carefully place it back in the plastic jacket of the book for safekeeping.**

10. **To run the Open Water Diver CD-ROM program, double-click on the PADI Open Water Diver shortcut icon that appears onscreen.**

    You can drag this icon onto your desktop for quick access to your courseware.

Windows 3.x setup

1. **Insert the CD into your computer's CD-ROM drive.**

2. **Choose Program Manager⇨File⇨Run.**

3. **Under the Command Line for the installation program, type the drive letter for the CD-ROM, a colon, a backslash, and "SETUPCD.EXE" (for example, E:\SETUPCD.EXE).**

4. **Click OK.**

    The Open Water Diver CD-ROM installation program begins.

5. **Follow the installation instructions on the screen and restart the computer when prompted to do so.**

6. **Double-click on Install Adobe Acrobat Reader in the PADI Multimedia group and follow the instructions on the screen.**

    You need Adobe Acrobat to print documents from the program.

7. **After you install the programs, you can eject the CD. Carefully place it back in the plastic jacket of the book for safekeeping.**

8. **To run the Open Water Diver CD-ROM program, double-click on the PADI Open Water Diver shortcut icon that appears onscreen.**

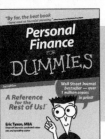

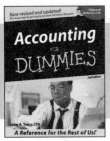

FOR DUMMIES®

A world of resources to help you grow

HOME, GARDEN & HOBBIES

Feng Shui
0-7645-5295-3

Gardening
0-7645-5130-2

Guitar
0-7645-5106-X

Also available:

Auto Repair For Dummies
(0-7645-5089-6)

Chess For Dummies
(0-7645-5003-9)

Home Maintenance For Dummies
(0-7645-5215-5)

Organizing For Dummies
(0-7645-5300-3)

Piano For Dummies
(0-7645-5105-1)

Poker For Dummies
(0-7645-5232-5)

Quilting For Dummies
(0-7645-5118-3)

Rock Guitar For Dummies
(0-7645-5356-9)

Roses For Dummies
(0-7645-5202-3)

Sewing For Dummies
(0-7645-5137-X)

FOOD & WINE

Cooking
0-7645-5250-3

Cookies
0-7645-5390-9

Wine
0-7645-5114-0

Also available:

Bartending For Dummies
(0-7645-5051-9)

Chinese Cooking For Dummies
(0-7645-5247-3)

Christmas Cooking For Dummies
(0-7645-5407-7)

Diabetes Cookbook For Dummies
(0-7645-5230-9)

Grilling For Dummies
(0-7645-5076-4)

Low-Fat Cooking For Dummies
(0-7645-5035-7)

Slow Cookers For Dummies
(0-7645-5240-6)

TRAVEL

Italy
0-7645-5453-0

Hawaii
0-7645-5438-7

Las Vegas
0-7645-5448-4

Also available:

America's National Parks For Dummies
(0-7645-6204-5)

Caribbean For Dummies
(0-7645-5445-X)

Cruise Vacations For Dummies 2003
(0-7645-5459-X)

Europe For Dummies
(0-7645-5456-5)

Ireland For Dummies
(0-7645-6199-5)

France For Dummies
(0-7645-6292-4)

London For Dummies
(0-7645-5416-6)

Mexico's Beach Resorts For Dummies
(0-7645-6262-2)

Paris For Dummies
(0-7645-5494-8)

RV Vacations For Dummies
(0-7645-5443-3)

Walt Disney World & Orlando For Dummies
(0-7645-5444-1)

FOR DUMMIES®

Plain-English solutions for everyday challenges

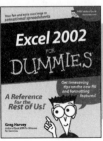

FOR DUMMIES®

The advice and explanations you need to succeed

SELF-HELP, SPIRITUALITY & RELIGION

Sex For Dummies
0-7645-5302-X

Parenting For Dummies
0-7645-5418-2

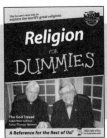

Religion For Dummies
0-7645-5264-3

Also available:

The Bible For Dummies
(0-7645-5296-1)

Buddhism For Dummies
(0-7645-5359-3)

Christian Prayer For Dummies
(0-7645-5500-6)

Dating For Dummies
(0-7645-5072-1)

Judaism For Dummies
(0-7645-5299-6)

Potty Training For Dummies
(0-7645-5417-4)

Pregnancy For Dummies
(0-7645-5074-8)

Rekindling Romance For Dummies
(0-7645-5303-8)

Spirituality For Dummies
(0-7645-5298-8)

Weddings For Dummies
(0-7645-5055-1)

PETS

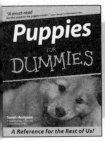

Puppies For Dummies
0-7645-5255-4

Dog Training For Dummies
0-7645-5286-4

Cats For Dummies
0-7645-5275-9

Also available:

Labrador Retrievers For Dummies
(0-7645-5281-3)

Aquariums For Dummies
(0-7645-5156-6)

Birds For Dummies
(0-7645-5139-6)

Dogs For Dummies
(0-7645-5274-0)

Ferrets For Dummies
(0-7645-5259-7)

German Shepherds For Dummies
(0-7645-5280-5)

Golden Retrievers For Dummies
(0-7645-5267-8)

Horses For Dummies
(0-7645-5138-8)

Jack Russell Terriers For Dummies
(0-7645-5268-6)

Puppies Raising & Training Diary For Dummies
(0-7645-0876-8)

EDUCATION & TEST PREPARATION

Spanish For Dummies
0-7645-5194-9

Algebra For Dummies
0-7645-5325-9

The ACT For Dummies
0-7645-5210-4

Also available:

Chemistry For Dummies
(0-7645-5430-1)

English Grammar For Dummies
(0-7645-5322-4)

French For Dummies
(0-7645-5193-0)

The GMAT For Dummies
(0-7645-5251-1)

Inglés Para Dummies
(0-7645-5427-1)

Italian For Dummies
(0-7645-5196-5)

Research Papers For Dummies
(0-7645-5426-3)

The SAT I For Dummies
(0-7645-5472-7)

U.S. History For Dummies
(0-7645-5249-X)

World History For Dummies
(0-7645-5242-2)

Available wherever books are sold. Go to www.dummies.com or call 1-877-762-2974 to order direct.